OFFICE OF THE CARDINAL
1011 FIRST AVENUE
NEW YORK, NY 10022

This remarkable publication by Mr. Thomas G. Young is a deeply appreciated gift to the People of God of the Archdiocese of New York. It tells our story, through the lens of Saint Patrick's Cathedral, up until the time of my appointment as Archbishop and reminds us of the saints and heroes of our Community of Faith over a period of two hundred years.

May *A New World Rising* be a blessing and inspiration for all who have the pleasure of reading it.

Edward Cardinal Egan
Archbishop of New York

Bicentennial Anniversary
Archdiocese of New York
1808-2008

A NEW WORLD RISING

The Story of St. Patrick's Cathedral

A NEW WORLD RISING

THE STORY OF ST. PATRICK'S CATHEDRAL

by Thomas G. Young

SOMETHING MORE PUBLICATIONS
NEW YORK

© Copyright 2006 by St. Patrick's Cathedral

ISBN 0-9622889-5-0

Library of Congress Control Number: 2006940321

Cover: Original artist's drawing of the planned cathedral, commissioned by its architect, James Renwick, Jr.

Layout, design and cover by George McCauley, S.J.

iv

DEDICATION

A.M.D.G.

INTRODUCTION

When I was a boy, my grandmother used to bring me and my two brothers to the Cathedral. We always stopped at the Pieta and the statue of Baby Jesus. She would always remark how my brothers and I resembled the "Child of Earth and Heaven." I don't know how accurate she was, but it always gave us a little shiver of importance. I know that there are countless stories of New Yorkers and people from the whole country who can recall early memories of their visits to this wonderful house of God. Little did I know that many years later I would be called upon to be the Rector of St. Patrick's Cathedral.

The Metropolitan Cathedral of the Archdiocese of New York, the seat of the Archbishop of New York are names that recognize the formality of the place. To the people on the street, however, it is "St. Pat's" — spiritual home to millions. St. Patrick's isn't just a church, it is an icon for the Catholic Faith, beloved and recognized by people throughout the world. Countless visitors come here for spiritual comfort, for inspiration and sometimes just to find a quiet place where they can speak to God. That's the amazing part: in spite of the millions who come through our doors, people can find quiet and peace within the walls of the Cathedral.

The history of the Cathedral is a topic that interests not just historians. It is of value to anyone who sees the connection of this house of worship to the people of the City of New York and to the world at large. This is why, when I first arrived here as the seventh Rector, I asked to see our history. I was amazed that there had been so little written about this history. There were picture books and books about some specific part of our architecture. We were included in texts about the City of New York, the Archdiocese of New York, etc. But a serious study of how the Cathedral came to be and how it has influenced the growth of Midtown Manhattan and, indeed the whole City of New York, was not on the library shelves. We had to reach all the way back to 1908 and the volume of history written by our fourth Archbishop, John Cardinal Farley.

That dearth has been remedied with the present volume. The whole Cathedral family is in debt to Thomas Young for his efforts to bring the history of St. Patrick's to the public. His years of research within the bowels of the Cathedral's record rooms and from the archives of the Archdiocese of New York concentrated at St. Joseph's Seminary in Dunwoodie and from many, many other sources have yielded an interesting, readable account of where we came from and who we are as the premier Catholic Church of the United States. I am very happy to invite you to read this book.

Robert T. Ritchie

Msgr. Robert T. Ritchie

ACKNOWLEDGEMENTS

Publication of this book is due in large part to the generosity and kindness of many people. The eminent historians of the Archdiocese of New York, Monsignor Florence Cohalan (RIP) and Monsignor Thomas Shelley, read drafts of my manuscript and made helpful suggestions. Sister Marguerita Smith, O.P., Archivist of the Archdiocese of New York, donated much of her time and expertise, and offered tireless encouragement. Sueanne Nilsen and Mary Deary gave meticulous attention to the time-consuming task of proofreading. Joseph Zwilling, Roberta Shea, Msgr. Gregory Mustaciuolo, Rev. Edward McMahon, S. J., Msgr. Thomas Nielson, Msgr. Eugene Clark, Msgr. John Ferry, Msgr. Robert Ritchie and Bishop Gerald Walsh were most helpful in a variety of ways. Rev. George McCauley, S.J. made the process of editing and publication easy and rewarding. The leadership of John Cardinal O'Connor (RIP) and Edward Cardinal Egan inspired perseverance. And if I have neglected to name here others who gave their help, I offer my apologies.

My sincere gratitude to all.

TGY

TABLE OF CONTENTS

Introduction   vii

Acknowledgements   viii

Ch. I   Popish Priests and Jesuits: Catholicism in Early New York   1

Ch. II   An Uncertain Welcome   7

Ch. III   A Dream of a Great Cathedral   14

Ch. IV   The Very Stones Would Cry Out: Cardinal John McCloskey   32

Ch. V   Taking Shape: the Years of Archbishop Michael Corrigan   54

Ch. VI   Finishing Touches: the Years of Cardinal John Farley   80

Ch. VII   A Wounded Time: the 'Cardinal of Charity', Patrick Hayes   106

Ch. VIII   A World Re-defined: the Years of Francis Cardinal Spellman   129

Ch. IX   Centennial Diary: the Years of Cardinal Terence Cooke   171

Ch. X   The World Stops By: Cardinal John O'Connor   201

Epilogue   234

Index   237

Glossary   249

Pictorial Meditation after pg. 170

CHAPTER I

Popish Priests and Jesuits: Catholicism In Early New York

In the middle of the nineteenth century when Archbishop John Hughes envisioned a magnificent cathedral for New York to rival the great cathedrals of Europe, the New York City he knew did not yet stretch north on Manhattan Island to where St. Patrick's Cathedral today rises majestically among modern skyscrapers. When he proposed erecting his new building far outside the city limits along the old Middle Road, Fifth Avenue today, his contemporaries mockingly labelled his scheme "Hughes' folly," much as others would later call the proposed purchase of Alaska "Seward's folly," in derision of President Abraham Lincoln's Secretary of State. In 1850, the Fifth Avenue landscape was dotted with farmhouses and occasional shanties inhabited by poor immigrant squatters employed by the City to grade the roads for its northward expansion.[1] Indeed, the site of St. Patrick's Cathedral was at the time an undeveloped lot, a former cemetery with a small church at the Fifth Avenue end and a solitary old mansion at the other end.[2] Yet, the Archbishop recognized that New York would one day resemble other great world cities, and he determined that his structure would be "worthy of our increasing numbers, intelligence and wealth as a religious community, and at all events, worthy as a public architectural monument of the present and prospective crowns of this metropolis of the American Continent."[3] He estimated that there were 200,000 Catholics in the City and that their numbers were increasing rapidly as Catholic immigrants arrived in a steady flow from northern Europe. Fifty years earlier, there had been only one Catholic church, not only in the City, but in all of New York State. The new cathedral, then, was to be a monument heralding the presence of Catholicism in a land where previously the Catholic presence had been negligible.

The story of that presence had begun, not fifty years earlier, but two centuries earlier, when the first priests – members of the Jesuit order – arrived as missionaries to work among the native Americans. One of the first was Father Jean de Brebeuf who worked along the banks of Lake Huron and travelled between that region and Quebec on the St. Lawrence River and the New York border lakes. A priest perhaps better recognized by American Catholics is the missionary saint Father Isaac Jogues (Jean de Brebeuf is also a Catholic saint) whose work among the Hurons in Canada and New York resulted in his martyrdom by the Mohawks, Huron enemies. When Father Jogues passed through New York City, then called New Amsterdam under Dutch rule, to return to his Huron ministry even though he had suffered mutilation at their hands, he found only two Catholics, one Portuguese and one Irish. In 1646, this courageous priest met a cruel death in Auriesville, New York, a death inflicted on him by those to whom he offered only peace and a road to salvation.[4]

New Amsterdam was a Dutch colony until 1664, and since the Dutch were mostly Calvinists, there were few Catholics in New Amsterdam before that date, although Catholic priests and sailors from France periodically stopped there.[5] When the Dutch surrendered the colony to the British in 1664, the English king, Charles II, granted the land to his brother, the Duke of York, a Catholic who would become King James II in 1685 and

Dongan's predecessor as Governor had his head-quarters on the top floor of the building at the right along the Hudson River. The first floor was a popular tavern.

whose title would be used to re-name the colony New York. In 1683, the Duke appointed Thomas Dongan, an Irish Catholic, to be Governor of New York, and in the same year the first Mass recorded in the City was celebrated on the site of the United States Customs House by an English priest. Nonetheless, the English colonists, like the earlier Dutch residents who remained in the colony, were Protestants, and it was unlikely that the number of Catholics increased substantially during Dongan's governorship. And just as King James would be expelled from the throne of England in 1688 because of his Catholicism, so Dongan would lose his office for the same reason. For almost a century afterwards, Catholics were hardly to be found in New York, and when they were, they suffered discrimination, if not persecution. Catholic priests who visited New York to minister to the few Catholic inhabitants did so in disguise and at considerable risk to their own safety, especially after a law was enacted banishing all Catholic clergy — those "Popish priests and Jesuits" — as of the year 1700.[6] On one occasion, an Anglican clergyman thought to be a Catholic priest was hanged as the supposed leader of a plot to destroy the City.[7]

Not until the end of the American Revolution (1774-1783) would Catholics in New York achieve legal acceptance. During the Revolution, British troops occupied New York, and when they left, the first Catholic priest to reside permanently in the City was Jesuit Father Ferdinand Farmer, a German who secretly had worked with Catholics there for many years.[8] During those years, Mass reportedly was celebrated in a loft over a carpenter's shop near Barclay Street in lower Manhattan, and at times in the homes of representatives of the Spanish government who resided in New York. The New York State Legislature repealed the prohibitions against Catholic priests in 1784, and Father Farmer finally walked the streets of the City openly visiting his eighteen congregants. In September of the same year, the Congress of the newly-born American nation moved to New York. The following month, Father Charles Whelan, an Irish Capuchin Franciscan, who had served as a chaplain for the French fleet, reached New York and was asked by the small Catholic community to serve as their permanent chaplain.[9] Thus, he became the first resident priest in New York, although Father Farmer continued his labors as a visitor almost until his death in Philadelphia in 1786.[10] Father Whelan estimated that his flock included about two hundred souls in 1785, the increase probably due in part to the arrival in the new American capital of representatives of governments from Catholic European countries. Still, the largest group were poor Irish immigrants. Only about twenty practiced their faith, so Father Whelan believed it was of paramount importance to provide a permanent church building for worshipping.[11]

Under the chairmanship of the French Consul, Hector St. John de Crevecoeur, the Roman Catholic Church in New York was incorporated, and lots on the corner of today's Church and Barclay Streets were secured for a church building to be called St. Peter's. Crevecoeur had come to America as a young man and purchased a tract of land near New York. He married an American and saw his lands destroyed by both sides during the Revolutionary War. The British imprisoned him in 1780, suspecting him of being a spy for the Americans. When he returned as French Consul General three years later, he found his home burned and learned that his wife had died, although his children had been rescued and were restored to him.[12]

Another of the early Catholics instrumental in building St. Peter's was José Roiz Silva, a Portuguese merchant who was among the wealthiest residents of the City. It was he who advised Father Whelan to purchase the lots for the church on Barclay Street. Another church supporter was Dominick Lynch, a native of Ireland, who had formed a business in Bruges, then part of the Austrian Netherlands, with his partner Thomas Stoughton. Lynch came to New York to manage the American branch and was a zealous activist on behalf of Catholicism in New York. He was one of the fund-raisers for construction of Georgetown Academy, destined to become Georgetown University.[13]

Gathering about him these and other ardent supporters,[14] Father Whelan attended to his people in temporary locations following the

St. Peter's would open the first Catholic school in America. In its present incarnation, the Church — only a stone's throw from a collapsing tower on 9/11 — turned into a staging area for police and fire rescue teams. The rudder from one of the planes actually landed on its roof, making a big hole.

laying of the cornerstone of St. Peter's in October 1785. Despite the gift of $1000 from the Spanish king, lack of funds dictated a slow progress in erection of the church. In the meantime, Father Andrew Nugent, like Father Whelan an Irish Capuchin, arrived to help. Unlike Father Whelan, who spoke Gaelic and French far better than English, Father Nugent was an eloquent preacher who spoke English fluently. But, he had a propensity for controversy and seized upon the congregation's predilection for polished speakers rather than for devoted pastors to ingratiate himself with them, hoping to replace Father Whelan as pastor.

Thus, from the infancy of Catholicism in New York, the seeds of a problem which would plague the Church for the next half-century were planted, namely, attempts of lay trustees to interfere with the appointments of clergy members. Father Whelan had been appointed by Rev. John Carroll, selected by Rome in 1784 to be Prefect Apostolic of the United States with his headquarters in Baltimore. Despite a warning to Father Nugent from Father Carroll, Father Whelan offered to resign to avoid further trouble and Father Carroll had no choice but to have Father Nugent succeed him. On November 4, 1786, Father Nugent celebrated a solemn Mass of dedication for the new St. Peter's assisted by chaplains of the French and Spanish legations, followed by a festive dinner attended by the President of the American Congress, many members of the Congress and the cabinet, and the Governor of New York.

Almost predictably, Father Nugent soon encountered difficulties with St. Peter's trustees and with Father Carroll himself. He was eventually suspended from his duties and was succeeded by Father William O'Brien, an Irish member of the Order of Preachers (Dominicans), who would bring peace to the parish and labor fruitfully for twenty years.[15]

In 1789, the Holy See established the first diocese in the United States and Father Carroll was chosen as its first bishop. The Diocese of Baltimore included all of North America exclusive of French and Spanish territory. In New York, St. Peter's was, for a quarter of a century, the only Catholic parish ministering to a small but growing number of souls. After adoption of the Constitution of the United States, George Washington was inaugurated the country's first president in 1789 in New York, the first capital. He lived in the City for a year until Philadelphia was made the capital while the government awaited the building of Washington, D. C. During that first year as President, Washington's social engagements certainly included dining with distinguished members of St. Peter's parish.[16]

Under the direction of Father O'Brien, St. Peter's parish grew and prospered. In the 1790s, pews were erected in the church and a tower and portico were added with funds donated by Mexican Catholics. Administration of the sacraments and care of parishioners was particularly difficult during these years when a plague of yellow fever afflicted the City. In 1798, three thousand persons died of the malady, nearly one hundred of whom were members of the parish. Helping Father O'Brien was one of the first saintly Catholic laymen of New York, a black slave from Saint Domingue (Haiti today), brought to New York by the family he had served in Saint Domingue. His name was

Toussaint's remains rested in the cemetery of the Old St. Patrick's Cathedral until they were were transferred in 1990 to the present Cathedral. He was the first lay person to be interred in its prestigious crypt.

Pierre Toussaint. His reputation for charity, love of God and zeal for the Church was legendary. Both while a slave and after his manumission until his death in 1853, Pierre Toussaint led an exemplary life devoted to the care of rich and poor alike, donating his resources to anyone in need while working tirelessly for others. His cause for canonization as a saint has been introduced at the Vatican, and numerous New Yorkers pray to him and for the rapid advancement of his cause.[17]

In 1805, Mrs. Elizabeth Bayley Seton, a distinguished Episcopalian socialite, converted to Catholicism at St. Peter's. Spurned by the Protestant community, she suffered great emotional stress but remained steadfast in her newfound faith. She became foundress of the Sisters of Charity in the United States and in 1975 was canonized as the first American-born saint.

As the years passed, Father O'Brien and other priests assisting him administered to a congregation over an ever-widening territory.

Mother Seton writes to a friend in 1817, "Sisters are just now established in New York for the care of orphans. Three branches are gone from our house to sow the little mustard seed — and religion smiles on our poor country in many ways."

The priests visited Catholics living as far north as Albany and many Catholics travelled to St. Peter's from distant points to receive the sacraments whenever they were able to. From about 10,000 people in 1783, the population of the City grew to 24,000 by 1786. Two year later, it was America's second largest city (after Philadelphia), and it continued to grow even after the capital relocated. A free school was opened at St. Peter's in 1800. At the beginning of the new century, Catholics took visible part in the political life of New York. Andrew Morris, one of the trustees of St. Peter's, was an assistant alderman, the first Catholic to hold public office in the City. In 1806, Francis Cooper was elected to the State legislature and, when he refused to take an oath biased against Catholics as required by the State's constitution, the provision was repealed.

If the size of the Catholic population of New York was growing, the problem of serving a huge nationwide Catholic population was formidable. By 1810, there were 100,000 Catholics, seventy priests and eighty churches in the United States, but distribution was scattered and administration of uniform discipline was nearly impossible for a single bishop in Baltimore whose parishes were as far away as Kentucky and a few even farther. Four years earlier Bishop Carroll had proposed the establishment of new dioceses at Bardstown, Kentucky; Boston; New York; and Philadelphia. The division did not take place until 1810, but even then, New York City still contained only one Catholic Church, old St. Peter's.[18]

1. *New Yorker* Magazine, November 8, 1958.
2. Farley, Most Rev. John M, *History of St. Patrick's Cathedral*, Society for the Propagation of the Faith, Archdiocese of New York, New York, 1908, p. 112.

3. *Ibid.*, p. 120.

4. Shea, John Gilmary, *History of the Catholic Church in the United States,* Volume I, Edward O. Jenkins' Sons, New York, 1886, pp. 227-232.

5. Bayley, Rev. J. R., *A Brief Sketch of the Early History of the Catholic Church on the Island of New York,* U. S. Catholic Historical Society, New York, 1973, reprinted from 1870 edition, p. 26.

6. Cohalan, Msgr. Florence D., *A Popular History of the Archdiocese of New York,* U. S Catholic Historical Society, Yonkers, New York, 1983, pp. 4, 5, hereafter cited as Cohalan, *Popular History.*

7. Bennett, William Harper, *Catholic Footsteps in Old New York,* U.S. Catholic Historical Society, New York, 1973, pp. 278-288. John Ury was hanged on August 29, 1741. John Gilmary Shea, commenting on the event, wrote that "the law passed against the Catholic priests was once only enforced, and then to bring to death a Protestant clergyman."

8. Farley, pp. 3, 4.

9. Bennett, p. 368.

10. Bayley, p. 57.

11. Cohalan, *Popular History,* p. 14.

12. Smith, John Talbot, *The Catholic Church in New York, A History of the New York Diocese from Its Establishment in 1808 to the Present Time,* Volume I, Hall and Locke Company, New York, 1905, pp. 29, 30; and Delaney, John J., *Dictionary of American Catholic Biography,* Doubleday and Company, Garden City, New York, 1984, pp. 123, 124. According to Delaney, Crevecoeur's real name was J. Hector St. John and *Crevecoeur* was an addition to the family name. Under the name *Agricola,* he wrote articles published in American newspapers and his *Letters from an American Farmer* described rural life in America.

13. Bennett, pp. 372, 393.

14. One of the trustees of St. Peter's was Cornelius Heeney who served as treasurer and was one of the first Catholics elected to public office in New York. A generous supporter of Catholic charities, he was noted for his work in Brooklyn where he greatly helped in the establishment of St. Paul's Church, still an active parish in the Cobble Hill section. A plaque on the facade of the old building honors his memory. *See* Delaney, p. 248.

15. Cohalan, *Popular History,* pp. 15, 16.

16. Farley, p. 41.

17. Delaney, pp. 565, 566.

18. Smith, pp. 31, 32.

CHAPTER II
An Uncertain Welcome

On April 8, 1808, Pope Pius VII, acting on Bishop Carroll's recommendation, created four new dioceses in America; at the same time, he made Baltimore the first American archdiocese naming Bishop Carroll the first archbishop. Many factors, not the least of which were the wars of Napoleon ravaging the European continent, prevented the news of the Pope's action from reaching America, and it would not be until 1810 that Archbishop Carroll finally was able to consecrate the new bishops, all except the Bishop of New York who was consecrated in Rome. Father Richard Luke Concanen, an Irish Dominican, was the Pope's choice for the New York See. He was esteemed as a scholar and had spent most of his life in Rome. He was born in Kilbegnet, Ireland, on December 27, 1747, and left Ireland in 1764 for Louvain, Belgium to enter the Irish Dominicans. The next year he went to the general headquarters of the Dominican order in Rome and was ordained a priest in the Lateran Basilica on December 22, 1770, having not yet reached his twenty-third birthday. He was to spend almost his entire life in Rome serving as novice master and teacher for the Dominicans, as well as an administrator of his order and as Roman agent of several Irish bishops and Bishop Carroll of Baltimore.

During these years, Napoleon's armies were suppressing religious houses throughout most of Europe, and Father Concanen looked with hope to America as a good location for new Dominican foundations to replace those lost on the continent. Twice he was recommended for a bishopric in Ireland, and both times he declined the honor. But in 1808, at a time when he was so ill that he was not expected to recover, the Pope appointed him Bishop of New York and ordered him to accept. His consecration took place in Rome on April 24,1808 and shortly afterwards he set out for the port of Leghorn (Livorno), Italy hoping to set sail for the United States. Napoleon's embargo on American vessels, however, kept him awaiting embarkation for four months. Realizing the futility of a longer wait, he wrote Archbishop Carroll authorizing him to appoint a vicar general in New York to carry on the work of the Diocese until he could arrange some passage. Archbishop Carroll named Father Anthony Kohlmann, a German Jesuit, to the post. Meanwhile, the Bishop returned to Rome. Finally, in June 1810, more than two years after he was consecrated, he learned that he might be able to arrange passage to New York from Naples. But at the harbor this final attempt at departure was frustrated by police. As he watched his ship set sail without him he prophetically exclaimed: "I may say a farewell to America forever." He died two days later, and his body was interred in the vault of San Domenigo Maggiore Church in Naples. His tomb remained unmarked until 1978 when New York's Cardinal Terence Cooke arranged for a commemorative tablet to be installed in honor of New York's first Bishop who never set foot in his own diocese.[1]

The Jesuit priest, Father Anthony Kohlmann, chosen as Bishop Concanen's vicar general, i.e., first in authority after the Bishop, arrived in the City in October 1808 accompanied by five other Jesuits. The City, whose upper boundaries were south of Canal Street, had a population of approximately 60,000 persons, 14,000 of whom were Catholics. Father Kohlmann found few of them practicing their religion.[2] St. Peter's pastor, Father O'Brien, was in poor health and, until the arrival of the Jesuits, short-handed. But, within a year, Father Kohlmann could report that sermons were being given in three languages each Sunday, that catechism classes were being taught, that religious societies were established, that the church was filled for all services and the confessionals were in heavy use. In fact, it soon became evident that New York's single church could no longer suffice, and Father Kohlmann began to search for a suitable plot for a new building. A Catholic cemetery had been bought by the trustees of St. Peter's Church in 1801 outside the city limits at Mott and Prince Streets, an area of scattered farm dwellings and villas for the wealthy, so rural that "foxes were frequent visitors."[3] Despite criticism of the distant location, the cemetery site was chosen for a church and it was decided that the new building would also serve as the Cathedral for the bishop. At the suggestion of Archbishop Carroll, it was dedicated to St. Patrick. Measuring one-hundred-twenty feet in length, eighty feet in width and over seventy-five feet high, the structure designed by Joseph Mangin, ar-

The years prior to entering the Jesuits in 1803 saw Fr. Kohlmann chaplaining at a hospital in Italy and, before that, ministering so selflessly during a prolonged flu epidemic in Austria that he earned the nickname, 'martyr of charity'. His academic and administrative skills had yet to explode as they would in America and, later, when he spent his remaining days in Rome teaching at the Gregorian University (the future Leo XII was a student) and as consultor to numerous congregations and to the College of Cardinals.

chitect of New York City Hall, was the largest church in New York (*left*). Father Kohlmann blessed the cornerstone at a solemn ceremony attended by three thousand persons on June 8, 1809. This first New York Cathedral was to serve as the center of Catholic life until the present Cathedral opened in 1879.[4]

Although Father Kohlmann's official appointment as vicar general did not come until 1810, as pastor of the only church, he effectively acted with full authority before that time. Because Pope Pius VII was a prisoner of Napoleon, a successor to Bishop Concanen was not appointed until 1814; so it was Father Kohlmann who continued to lay the foundations of the great archdiocese which developed in New York. As a Jesuit whose order held education in high esteem, he early decided to establish a Catholic college in New York. The first faculty of the school located near the new Cathedral consisted of the Jesuits who had accompanied him to New York. By 1810, the need for larger quarters resulted in the purchase of a site four miles from the City near Columbia College's Elgin Botanical Gardens. A large mansion already existed on the site and both boarding and day students attended the school, including the sons of the governor and former governor of the state. No one at the time could have suspected that one day the greatest cathedral in America, the present St. Patrick's, would rise at that location. But in 1813 the Jesuit superior in Maryland ordered the New York Literary Institution, as the college was called, to be closed, since there were too few Jesuits to staff both the New York school and their school in Georgetown. In September 1813, Trappist monks, in exile from France under orders of Napoleon, opened an orphanage in the mansion and remained there until after Napoleon's defeat at Waterloo in 1815. Near the site, a convent for Ursuline nuns, who conducted schools in the neighborhood, was established in 1812. Thus, in his six years in New York — he left in 1814 —Father Kohlmann planted seeds of an expanded Catholic presence both within and outside the City. Perhaps of greater importance was his role in settling the problem of attempts to compel Catholic clergymen to disclose secrets of the confessional. In a case involving a Catholic merchant, Kohlmann successfully argued in the Court of General Session in June 1813 that the seal of the confessional was absolute. The court unanimously agreed that Catholic priests were "protected by the laws and constitution of this country in the full and free exercise of their religion, and this court can never countenance or authorize the application of insult to their faith, or of torture to their consciences."[5] Shortly after Father Kohlmann's departure from New York, the Cathedral was ready to open. Although a new bishop had been named for New York in October 1814, the news of the appointment had not yet reached the City. And so, Bishop John Cheverus of Boston dedicated the building on Ascension Thursday, May 4, 1815.[6]

In Europe, the political, intellectual and religious currents of the times swept away almost a thousand monasteries, priories, abbeys and pious works. The Jesuits weren't spared either. Many monks, nuns and priests sought to serve instead in the New World.

Bishop Concanen's successor, Bishop John Connolly, a Dominican like Bishop Concanen, was born in County Meath, Ireland in 1747 and, like his predecessor, he spent most of his life in Rome. After studies and ordination to the priesthood in Belgium in 1774, he moved to Rome and pursued a career similar to that of the first bishop until his appointment to New York on October 4, 1814. Since he was a British subject and America and Britain were engaged in the War of 1812, he had to stay in the Holy City until the war ended. Although he left Italy in the spring of 1815, he did not arrive in this country until November because he spent time in Belgium and Ireland en route. By that year the increase in population had made New York the largest city in the country with about 20,000 of the 96,000 inhabitants Catholic, most of whom were Irish. Assisting him in his ministry were only four priests stationed in two churches in the City and one church in Albany, one hundred fifty miles north of Manhattan. There was only one school, St. Peter's, and the clergy could rely on no religious sisters for help; nor was there a single charitable institution such as an orphanage.[7] After the fall of Napoleon, both the Ursuline sisters and the Trappist nuns had left, as had the Trappist monks conducting the orphanage north of the City.[8] The Diocese, half the size of Italy, was acutely short of money and clergy and was already plagued by the problem of trusteeism, compounded by division into two camps of trustees and clergy, some supporting the Bishop and some opposing him. While the Bishop remained in the City, where perhaps ten or twelve thousand Catholics lived, the remainder of his flock was scattered as far north as the St. Lawrence River and south through New Jersey,

"We were forty miles from Albany ..."

all then part of the diocese. Dominick Lynch, the merchant who had helped establish St. Peter's Church, had likewise encouraged immigrants to settle on tracts of land he owned in central New York State. The invention of the steamboat facilitated navigation northwards on the Hudson River and Lake Champlain adding to the spread of the population. Moreover, so many Irish Catholics emigrated to New York to find work building De Witt Clinton's barge canal connecting Lake Erie with the Hudson River, the demand for ships surpassed their availability. When construction of the canal was completed in 1825, there were more than 100,000 Catholics in the state, and still there was only a handful of priests stationed in widely scattered churches.[9]

In spite of the enormity of his difficulties, Bishop Connolly's ten years in New York met with some success. He was instrumental in introducing to his Diocese Mother Seton's Sisters of Charity, the order founded in Maryland. Mother Seton's sisters opened an asylum for orphans in the city where she had been born and raised. The Bishop managed to open a free school at St. Patrick's, and in Brooklyn, then a city separate from New York, he built several churches, just as he did in New Jersey and in central and northern New York State. In both 1817 and 1820, disregarding his advanced age and frail health, he made pastoral visitations around his huge territory. In 1825, two of his closest aides died suddenly, the shock undoubtedly contributing to the failure of his own health. He died on February 6th of the same year. Thirty thousand mourners attended his wake at St. Peter's and his remains were laid in the crypt under his Cathedral. The vault containing his body was unmarked and not

The elegant robes mislead. Bishop Dubois would undertake grueling visits to tiny, out-of-the way churches between Buffalo, Montreal, Albany and New York for much of his tenure. The robes also made him an easy target for the incendiarist and rock-throwing Nativists, but apparently did not keep his own church trustees from constantly opposing him.

until 1976 were his episcopal insignia discovered, revealing his burial tomb during a search instigated by Cardinal Cooke.[10]

Three candidates were recommended to succeed Bishop Connollly, one of whom was Rev. John Power, the Vicar General and administrator of the Diocese after the Bishop's death. But, as in the past, authorities in Rome chose a priest from outside New York, Rev. John Dubois, who was appointed in May 1826. Born in Paris in 1764, he was over sixty years of age when he came to New York. Educated at the College of Louis LeGrand, established by King Louis XV as a scholarship school for poor students of intelligence, the precocious John Dubois was enabled to gain a superior education normally denied those outside the noble class.[11] Two of his fellow scholars in the years preceding the French Revolution were destined to be made infamous by that event, Camille Desmoulins and Maximilien Robespierre. John Dubois was ordained in 1787, two years before the Revolution began. By 1791, when the Reign of Terror began to engulf Paris and churchmen were in extreme danger of losing their lives, Father Dubois sought and obtained papers of transit allowing him to leave France. Ironically, it was his former schoolmate, Robespierre, who wrote the papers for him, despite the latter's avowed hatred of clergymen.[12]

The Marquis de Lafayette, admired in America for his support of its earlier revolution, at the urging of his wife issued the priest letters of introduction to prominent Virginians such as Patrick Henry and James Monroe. Arriving in Norfolk in August 1791, the young cleric stayed at the home of Monroe and studied English under Patrick Henry. His thirty-five years in America before the appointment to New York were spent in Maryland where in 1808 he opened a college and preparatory seminary, the same year when he became a member of the Sulpician order. The following year, he welcomed Elizabeth Seton and her sisters, and he was their ecclesiastical superior for many years.[13]

The third Bishop of New York was consecrated in the Cathedral of Baltimore by Archbishop Ambrose Marechal on October 29, 1826. His cross and ring were gifts from Charles Carroll of Carrollton. That a person of so eminent a background and with such high-placed connections should be elevated to the See of New York was not surprising; nor was it surprising that New York Catholics who had expected their own Father John Power to be appointed should express disappointment. But, when Rev. Wiliam Taylor in his consecration sermon, with notable poor taste, referred to the troubles facing a foreign prelate in a congregation composed principally of Irish, and further, that his appointment might have been procured by improper means, consternation was pervasive among the listeners.[14] Unsuitable as the remarks were, they proved to be ominous. Despite his initial polite welcome by the Catholic community and his naturally gentlemanly demeanor (President Andrew Jackson said he was the most complete gentleman he had ever met),[15] he was soon aware of resentment among his people. With only eighteen priests to serve about 175,000 Catholics in the entire diocese, he felt compelled to prove the doomsayers wrong. He travelled during 1828 and 1829 over most of New York and New Jersey and he went to Rome for two years in an attempt to raise funds and find priests to assist him. When he returned, buoyed by a contribution from Roman authorities, he was met by one of the most troublesome problems of his tenure: the outbreak of an anti-Catholic movement in America.

The very fact of increasing Catholic population in America, and certainly in New York, the main port of entry for Catholic immigrants, probably fanned the flames of discrimination spread by its adherents called Nativists. Fears among native Protestants of a Catholic conspiracy orchestrated by "the Pope, the Jesuits, and the Romish priesthood, and the advent of foreigners who yield a blind obedience to the Pope" led to political movements which succeeded in electing local Nativists to powerful government offices such as the mayoralty. Sensationalist publications like *The Awful Disclosures of Maria Monk*, a scurrilous account by a supposed former nun of the evils of life in a Montreal convent, intensified fears and hostility towards Catholics.[16] Printed and verbal attacks exploded into physical violence in the 1830s. Guards had to be stationed around St. Joseph's Church in Greenwich Village in New York and St. Mary's Church was burned in 1831. Bishop Dubois' cherished project, a seminary he had built in 1832 in Nyack, north of the City, was destroyed by fire in 1837, the event surrounded by a strong odor of suspicion. Indeed, the old Cathedral itself was surrounded by Catholics to thwart a threatened attack in 1835. In 1841, the windows of the old Cathedral and the nearby bishop's home were broken by an angry mob. To the end of his life, Bishop Dubois never enjoyed a lessening of bigotry displayed towards himself and his people.

Perhaps more disappointing for him than anti-Catholic violence was the evil voice of trusteeism raised within the Church once again in 1834. When the trustees of his own Cathedral openly interfered with his appointments of clergy, Dubois threatened to interdict the Cathedral, i.e., to forbid the celebration of the sacred liturgy there. The trustees countered by threatening to cut off the bishop's salary; to which attempt he simply replied: "I have seen the horrors of the French Revolution, and could meet them again. I am an old man, I can live in a cellar or a garret; but, gentlemen, whether I come up from my cellar or down from my garret, you must remember that I am still your Bishop."[17]

The trustee problem was not confined to the Cathedral parish; problems spread widely among various congregations as new churches were opened all over the Diocese. The Bishop's age and infirmity caused him to rely on crutches, and antagonism by Nativists and by his own trustees only exacerbated his illness. In 1837 he appealed to Rome for help in administering the Diocese. On November 3rd of that year, the Holy See notified Rev. John Hughes of Philadelphia that he was to be Coadjutor Bishop of New York with the right of succession to Bishop Dubois. The most outstanding American churchman of the nineteenth century was about to introduce to New York his considerable and widely-acknowledged talents.[18]

1. Cohalan, *Popular History,* pp. 21-24; Carthy, Mother Mary Peter, O.S.U., *Old St. Patrick's, New York's First Cathedral,* U. S. Catholic Historical Society, New York, 1947, p. 10, hereafter cited as Carthy, *Old St. Patrick's.*

2. Carthy, *Old St. Patrick's,* p. 5. Anthony Kohlmann was born in Alsace and was ordained in Fribourg, Switzerland. He served as a priest in Austria, Italy, Bavaria, Berlin and Amsterdam before joining the Jesuits in Russia in 1800. After arrival in the United States in 1804, he taught at Georgetown and worked in parishes in Pennsylvania and Maryland before his assignment to New York. *See:* Delaney, p. 305.

3. *Ibid.*

4. Cohalan, *Popular History,* p. 26; Carthy, *Old St. Patrick's,* pp. 7, 8, 23.

5. Carthy, *Old St. Patrick's,* pp. 13-16

6. Smith, p. 52.

7. Cohalan, *Popular History,* pp. 29, 30; Carthy, *Old St. Patrick's,* p. 27.

8. Three Ursuline nuns from Cork, Ireland opened their convent near today's Eighth Avenue and Fiftieth Street. They ministered to twenty-nine pupils in an academy and a "poor school." Their abrupt return to Ireland in 1815 was due to a lack of vocations among their students; their reluctance to assume a debt on their mortgage; their unaddressed need for a special chaplain; and their belief that their students did not measure up to the standards of those they had been accustomed to teach in Ireland. *See "The First Pastor of St. Patrick's"* by Thomas F. Meehan, in *Souvenir of the Centennial Celebration of St. Patrick's [old] Cathedral, New York, 1809-1909,* no publisher.

9. Smith, pp. 61-62.

10. Cohalan, *Popular History,* pp. 34, 36; Smith, p. 64.

11. Cohalan, *Popular History,* pp. 39, 40.

12. Shaw, Rev. Richard, *John Dubois, Founding Father,* U. S. Catholic Historical Society, Yonkers, New York, 1983, pp. 2, 16.

13. Cohalan, *Popular History,* pp. 40, 41.

14. Carthy, *Old St. Patrick's,* p. 53.

15. Bayley, p. 108.

16. Cohalan, *Popular History,* pp. 42-46.

17. Carthy, *Old St. Patrick's,* pp. 62-66.

18. Cohalan, *Popular History,* p. 50.

CHAPTER III
A Dream of a Great Cathedral

John Joseph Hughes was born on June 24, 1797 in County Tyrone in northern Ireland, the son of poor tenant farmers. From his earliest years, he set his goals on the priesthood, while facing discrimination in a part of Ireland where Catholics were few and mostly hated. When he was seventeen, he had to interrupt his education to begin work as a gardener in support of his impoverished family. After three years, he joined members of his family already in the United States where he found work as a laborer and a gardener. The Hughes family home was in Pennsylvania[1] about thirty miles from Emmitsburg, Maryland, where French priests conducted Mt. St. Mary's seminary, a training school for future members of the clergy. Father John Dubois, who, as we saw, later became the third Bishop of New York, was in charge, and when twenty-one-year-old John Hughes approached him several times for permission to enter, he was refused admission to the overcrowded facility. John was employed as a gardener on the grounds of Mother Seton's convent. After he importuned her to intercede on his behalf, Dubois hired him to work on the seminary property while he continued his private studies in preparation for full acceptance to the college. This finally happened in 1820. Six years later, he was ordained a priest for the Diocese of Philadelphia. In that city, his reputation as a preacher and defender of Catholicism against nativist sentiment, then rampant in Philadelphia, grew and quickly spread beyond the borders of his diocese. Much of his fame came because of his writings and his debates against Rev. John Breckinridge, a Presbyterian minister of exceptional talent, and a fierce adversary of Catholicism.

Mathew Brady/NY Public Library

His signature as Bishop was preceded by a cross that seemed to resemble a dagger. He would thus be 'Dagger John' for history's sake — incisive, pointing ever forward, and to be trifled with only at your own risk.

The young priest was several times recommended for the office of coadjutor bishop, i.e., one who assists the ordinary bishop of a diocese, in Philadelphia, Cincinnati and Pittsburgh; ultimately he was appointed to that office in New York.[2]

His episcopal consecration in 1837 was the first ever held in New York, and crowds spilling beyond the doors of the old St. Patrick's Cathedral piled park benches along the outside walls to witness proceedings through open windows. One of the onlookers was James Gordon Bennett, the irascible owner-editor of the *New York Herald* and a Catholic of firm independent bent, who regularly lionized those he favored and excoriated those he loathed. His published report of the occasion expressed his opinion of Irish Catholics when he asserted that the Church displaying the trappings of the Catholic episcopacy for the edification of the average Irish parishioner was the equivalent of pushing "gold rings through pigs' noses." Thus was engaged a combat which would span many years between the new episcopal gladiator and an erudite and unrelenting foe.[3]

Two weeks after the ceremony, Bishop Dubois suffered paralysis, and his assistant was entrusted with almost complete administration of the Diocese. In typical "full speed ahead" fashion, he attacked the trusteeism problem by appealing directly to the Cathedral congregation in a dispute with the trustees, and repudiated them with the overwhelming support of the parishioners. Thus, he firmly established the principle of episcopal authority for the first time in New York's history. In August 1839, Bishop Hughes was made administrator of the Diocese when Dubois' health continued to deteriorate.[4] After the old Bishop died in December 1842 and was buried near the front entrance of his Cathedral, the fourth Bishop of New York embarked on a course to strengthen the position of Catholics or, at least, to remove obstacles which impeded them from fully participating in the civic life of the City. Recalling the mob violence of 1842 when windows of the Cathedral and the episcopal residence were shattered, Hughes, in 1844, filled the Cathedral and the surrounding streets with armed men, successfully dissuading torch-bearing Nativists from a repetition. A happier occasion that year was the ordination of John McCloskey as Coadjutor Bishop of Bishop Hughes.[5]

As the Catholic population grew, Hughes enlisted the help of several religious communities in the work of the ministry, including the Redemptorists, the Christian Brothers, the Fathers of Mercy, the Sacred Heart Sisters, the Jesuits, the Ursulines, the Sisters of Mercy, the Paulists and the Sisters of Charity, all of whom arrived in the diocese before 1850. Orphanages were opened, schools were expanded, colleges were established and the City welcomed its first Catholic hospital. Hughes fulfilled his dream of founding a seminary for New York priests on the site of today's Fordham University, and to serve the enormous influx of immigrants resulting from the Irish famine, he built new churches, especially after 1848. The diocese had grown so rapidly that the Bishop requested that it be divided; this was done in 1847 when the dioceses of Albany and Buffalo were erected.[6]

The architect for the St. John's Seminary and its church was William Rodrigue, whom we shall meet shortly as the main collaborator with James Renwick on the design of St. Patrick's Cathedral. Rodrigue's house can be seen on the left of the seminary building.

Fordham University Archives

Whether he was extolling the contributions of Catholics to American life or defending them against critics like James Gordon Bennett or Bennett's fellow journalist, Horace Greeley of the New York Tribune (although Bennett and Greeley more often contended with each other than with Bishop Hughes),[7] by mid-century Bishop Hughes was recognized as the preeminent religious figure in the United States. His reputation earned him the trust and friendship of national leaders such as Henry Clay and William H. Seward. In the 1840s, he declined an offer from President James K. Polk to lead a diplomatic mission to Mexico. In 1847 he preached in the House of Representatives after receiving an invitation to do so signed by twenty senators and thirty-three representatives. Among them were John C. Calhoun, Stephen A. Douglas and John Quincy Adams.[8] When by 1849 it became evident that, with a Catholic population doubled in size in only ten years, the American Catholic Church required new ecclesiastical provinces, few doubted that John Hughes would become Archbishop of one of those provinces. In July 1850, three provinces were created, and in October Hughes received papal documents designating him the first Archbishop of New York.[9]

On the Sunday after Rome's announcement that New York was a new archdiocese, Archbishop Hughes told the congregation in Old St. Patrick's Cathedral that he intended to travel to Rome for his investiture with the *pallium,* the symbol of an archbishop's authority. During his address he noted the need to make preparations for building a new cathedral suitable for an archdiocese of growing importance.[10] Thus, his dream of a great European-type cathedral, the first of its kind in America, was born when the Holy See recognized the preeminence of New York among American cities. The new ecclesiastical province encompassed all of New York State, all of New England and half of New Jersey, with 200,000 Catholics living in the City alone.[11] Pope Pius IX conferred the *pallium* on the Archbishop in April 1851, but no immediate plans were made for construction of the new cathedral. In February 1852, Hughes told a capacity crowd at the old Cathedral that he was postponing work on his new project until he could first add eight or ten much needed churches to the twenty-two already in the City, in order to accommodate the Catholic immigrants from famine-ridden Ireland who were arriving in record numbers.[12] By the next year the province contained fourteen dioceses besides New York itself, the boundaries of the Archdiocese approximating those of the present day — from Staten Island in the south to the lower end of the Albany Diocese in the north.[13] The tremendous surge in the number of foreigners gave impetus to the Nativist Movement in the 1850s, whose adherents formed the "Know Nothing" political party as a base from which they could rail against Catholics and other "non-desirables." Despite the persecution, Archbishop Hughes was

The Popish invasion envisioned by Thomas Nast. Other cartoons of the day pictured Irish men and women as apes.

~ 16 ~

able to initiate plans for his new cathedral and selected James Renwick, Jr. as his architect. In 1853, he authorized Renwick to begin preparing designs immediately.

James Renwick, Jr. was born in 1818 in Bloomingdale, an area north of the City, today part of the upper west side of Manhattan. His parents were members of wealthy New York families, the maternal Brevoort branch extending back seven generations, the Renwicks four generations. His father, a professor of physics and chemistry at Columbia College, was a man of many talents with interests and competence in astronomy, mineralogy, art and architecture. In addition, he was a respected author, architectural historian and engineer. Two of James Jr.'s brothers were engineers and James Jr. himself pursued the same career at Columbia from which he graduated in 1836. He was awarded his M. A. degree three years later. He worked as an engineer until 1842 and was responsible for supervising the design of the Croton distributing reservoir, an imposing structure located at Fifth Avenue and Forty-second Street on the site of today's equally striking New York Public Library. Without formal training, he mastered the study of architecture, and in 1842 he submitted drawings in a competition for designing New York's Grace Church. He chose the decorated Gothic style then experiencing a revival in Europe. He won the commission and the attention of the international community of architects. From that year until shortly before his death in 1895 his prolific designs were acclaimed both in this country and abroad. He favored the Gothic style, but he frequently used the Romanesque in his drawings of churches, public and commercial buildings and private homes.[14]

Most of Renwick's buildings were in New York, but he also worked in other cities including Washington, D. C. and Chicago. Among his best-known works are the Smithsonian Institution, Vassar College and Washington's Corcoran Gallery. His masterpiece was St. Patrick's Cathedral.

Even though Renwick began his drawings of St. Patrick's in 1853, construction was delayed for several years. In October 1854, before he left to visit Rome, Archbishop Hughes postponed the start of work. The next year, Renwick attended the International Exposition in Paris where he experienced first-hand the Gothic revival in architecture being promoted there. He saw restoration under way in many medieval buildings including the Cathedral of Notre Dame, as well as construction of new Gothic Revival buildings. One of the new churches was Ste. Clotilde, whose design by F. C. Gau very likely exerted an influence on Renwick's plan for St. Patrick's. Since Paris was considered the artistic capital of Europe, its art circles elevated interest in architecture around the globe. It is probable that the intense attention being paid in Paris to the completion of Cologne Cathedral in Germany affected Renwick's plan for St. Patrick's, especially his decision to place twin towers on the west front similar to the symmetrical towers of Cologne. A year after he returned to the United States, he had already completed many designs, and by 1857 he had decided upon a final plan. Excavation began the following year.[15]

To the surprise of many and accompanied by the ridicule of some, the Archbishop chose as a site a plot far from the center of the City in a section considered "as much a wilderness as the site of the old St. Patrick's was in 1808."[16] Hughes resolutely maintained that it would someday be "the heart of the city."[17] The high elevation allowed wide views to the Hudson on the west, to the East River, to City Hall on the south and northward to a region of scattered huts occupied by squatters and an array of wildlife, absent then even the dream of today's Central Park. Columbia College's Elgin Gardens were located where Rockefeller Center is today while the college buildings were near today's Madison Avenue and Forty-eighth Street.[18] One block north of the plot, the Roman Catholic Boys' Orphan Asylum was opened in 1852 by the Sisters of Charity, combining two earlier institutions into one, and caring for about five hundred children.[19]

The plot had a history of failed church ventures dating to early in the century.[20] In 1810, Father Anthony Kohlmann had purchased the site and a mansion from Robert Lylburn who had secured the land from the City of New York in 1799. The price was slightly more than $1,000 and an annual payment of four bushels of wheat.[21] The mansion, located approximately where the high altar of St. Patrick's is today,[22] became the City's first Catholic college, the New York Literary Institution. By 1813 seventy-four students were boarding at the school, but the Jesuit Fathers who conducted it needed teachers at their other college in Georgetown (Washington, D. C.), so the New York college was closed.[23] Dom Augustine was the superior general of Trappist monks who had been exiled from France during the French Revolution. He purchased the property from the Jesuits for use as the international headquarters of his order. He also opened an orphanage in the Lylburn mansion providing care for thirty-three children.[24] But in 1815, after Napoleon's empire collapsed, and because they were unable to raise funds to meet the purchase price asked by the Jesuits, the monks closed the orphanage and returned to France. In 1828, the trustees of old St. Patrick's Cathedral and St. Peter's Church jointly paid $5,500 to use the land as a cemetery, since there was little space available at their downtown burial ground near the old Cathedral. Like the earlier undertakings, this one was doomed to failure because the rocky soil made it almost impossible to excavate for graves[25]. Instead, in 1832, a free vault was erected above ground. There were few interments, however, because another burial ground was found near First Avenue and Eleventh Street which was adequate for interments until the opening of the huge Calvary Cemetery in Queens County in 1848. When Calvary Cemetery opened, remains were transferred from the vault and it was dismantled.[26]

In the 1830s, a chapel in the mansion was used for the celebration of Mass for employees of a home for the deaf located in the neighborhood. In 1840, a small frame church, St. John the Evangelist, was built at the corner of Fifth Avenue and Fiftieth Street with the approval of the trustees of the old Cathedral and the trustees of St. Peter's Church. The mansion became a rectory for the parish.[27] Four years later the priests of the parish shared the mansion with students of a temporary diocesan seminary.[28] That same year, 1844, St. Peter's trustees lost their share of the property to creditors. So hard-pressed for money was St. John's parish that the mortgage on the church was foreclosed in 1846, and for two years the old mansion served as both church and rectory. After the parish managed to scrape together enough cash, the church was repurchased in 1848.[29] Finally, in 1852, because both the trustees of the old Cathedral and the creditors of St. Peter's trustees claimed partial ownership of the land, a suit was brought in Supreme Court to settle claims. The court decided that one-half the property belonged to St. Patrick's trustees. The other half was put on public auction allowing the Cathedral's trustees to secure it with a bid of $59,500 giving them possession of the block from Fifth Avenue to Fourth Avenue (Park Avenue today) between Fiftieth and Fifty-first Streets. (Madison Avenue did not exist until many years later.)

A narrow strip of land, a few feet in width, at one corner of the property had been retained by the City when Lylburn purchased the rest in 1799. Following a custom common at the time, the trustees exchanged with the City a parcel of approximately equal size in a nearby location. And so, by 1852, all the land needed for a site for the Archbishop's grand building was held by the trustees of the old Cathedral.[30] Moreover, Hughes owned

The changing face of farmland, looking south in 1858: A) Columbia College at 49th St.; B) the Boy's Orphanage on 51st. St. and Fifth Ave, behind which the Cathedral spires would one day rise; C) St. Luke's Episcopalian Hospital on 54th St.;D) the Crystal Palace at 42nd St. and Sixth Ave, a replica of the one built in Hyde Park, London, to host the World's Fair. The shanty huts in the foreground were home to many Irish who would be evicted to make room for Central Park.

another large parcel on the block just north of the Cathedral's intended site which he had purchased in 1846. He had intended to locate there all the child-caring institutions of the diocese.[31] As related earlier, the boys' orphan asylum opened there in 1852; in 1857 a division was added for girls on the same plot, both run by the Sisters of Charity. The Archbishop's scheme in 1852, then, seems to have been to make the Cathedral area a center of Catholic life, having at his disposal three times the amount of land which the Cathedral plot encompasses today. The two-thirds not owned today by the Archdiocese of New York was sold off, piece by piece, over many years to meet pressing financial needs.

The name William Rodrigue frequently appears in information about the planning and early construction of St. Patrick's Cathedral, but the extent of his collaboration with Renwick is cloudy. Rodrigue was the Archbishop's brother-in-law, and Hughes engaged him as architect of a new church building when the young priest was pastor of St. John the Evangelist parish in Philadelphia. Rodrigue later married Hughes' sister, Margaret. When the priest was named Coadjutor Bishop of New York in 1838, the Rodrigues moved with him to New York.

Rodrigue's father, a native of France who owned a plantation in Santo Domingo, fled to the United States in 1793 after a slave insurrection, and settled in Philadelphia. William was born there in 1800 and after completing college he studied art for three years in Paris. In 1823 he was employed by the prominent architect William Strickland in the design of the Second Bank of the United States in Philadelphia. Rodrigue's most important work in that city was his design for the Church of St. John the Evangelist. In New York, Bishop Hughes chose him to draw plans for the first building of Fordham University, then called St. John's College. He also designed several churches in the City.[32]

When Bishop Hughes first arrived in New York, he lived near the old Cathedral on Mulberry Street, but in 1852 the trustees purchased a country villa in Manhattanville for an episcopal residence. It was rarely used because Hughes felt, among other reasons, that it was a needless expense to maintain two household staffs. The property was sold in 1856 and a house, still standing at the northwest corner of Madison Avenue and Thirty-sixth Street, was purchased. The location was close to the site of the planned cathedral and Hughes maintained this as his residence until he died.[33] The Rodrigues lived only one block from the Archbishop, and eventually they moved into his residence where they remained until his death.[34] Their close association makes it likely that Rodrigue exerted a major influence on Hughes' decisions concerning the plans for St. Patrick's. Early drawings of the building carry the names of both Renwick and Rodrigue, and the construction specifications document is signed by both men; the contract states that "plans and drawings for said Cathedral [were] made by James Renwick Jr. and William Rodrigue, architects." It is also likely that the *final* product bore the nearly exclusive mark of Renwick alone, since Rodrigue suffered a debilitating illness which confined him indoors for several years after the start of the construction.[35] *The New York Times*, years after work began, reported that the "architect of the building is Mr. James Renwick with whom Mr. William Rodrigue was associated at the commencement of the work as superintendent."[36]

The daunting task of paying for construction of America's first monumental Gothic Revival structure seems not to have deterred the Archbishop's resolve nor to lessen his confidence in the willingness of his people to support it. He prepared for a meeting at the New York Academy of Music to explain his project[37] and ordered the grading of the site in May 1858 even before any money had been subscribed. His plan was to obtain one hundred thousand dollars in donations of $1,000 each from one hundred wealthy New York Catholics to pay for the first year's work. He expected another one hundred thousand dollars in contributions ranging from one hundred dollars to under one thousand dollars during the second year. He believed that after the second year, donations would come from the Catholic churches of the City until the required $750,000 to $1,000,000 he estimated was needed was raised, while allowing for a debt of two or three hundred thousand dollars.

Some funds, he hoped, would come from leasing part of the site east of Madison Avenue for "private dwellings of a choice character ....." His sanguine outlook was based on strong confidence in God's help and his trust that "under the patronage of the most blessed and immaculate Virgin Mother ..." all his dreams would be fulfilled either by himself or by his successors. He asserted: "It is for me to begin the work, and let it be finished by those who can. One thing, however, is certain: that it shall be, as far as possible, worthy of God, worthy of the Catholic religion, and a honor to this great and growing city...."[38]

Some might have considered his optimism simply foolhardiness. Horace Greeley in 1851 estimated that an average weekly budget that year for a family of five was $10.37.[39] Still, Hughes believed that if each adult Catholic contributed one to five dollars each year, his goal would be reached without any hardship for the poor;[40] at the same time he acknowledged that, because of a money crisis at the time, some wealthy people might be hard-pressed to make donations. Despite that, in June he addressed a circular letter to over one hundred leading Catholics and some non-Catholics outlining his hopes:

"The building is to be 312 feet long, 97 feet wide in the clerestory, with a transept 172 feet, and an elevation of 100 feet from the floor to the crown point of the clerestory.... The object only is to ascertain whether there are not in my Diocese, or rather in the city of New York itself [sic], one hundred persons who will subscribe $1,000 each, once for all, to be paid in quarterly installments, if they desire it, during the first year, and to be expressly and exclusively appropriated to carry on the work during the same period .... The success of the second year will depend on that of the first .... I anticipate that, allowing five years for its completion, there should not be a single suspension of the work .... I shall, with the help of God, bless and deposit the cornerstone on the feast of the Assumption of this year, *viz.,*the fifteenth of August, precisely at four o'clock in the afternoon.... I may not have the consolation of seeing it consecrated, but I can not leave for my successor the honor and great privilege of seeing it begun."[41]

Archbishop Hughes paid visits to each of one-hundred-fifty prospective donors and reported that one-hundred-three pledged the requested one thousand dollars. Two of them were non-Catholics. Many others pledged lesser amounts and some more than what was requested; both greater and lesser amounts the Archbishop declined to accept during the initial phase of the campaign.[42] He took personal charge of the finances and informed the trustees that he did not want the Board to be party to any of the contracts. His remembrance of past problems associated with trusteeism may have motivated this directive.[43]

As the day set for the cornerstone blessing ceremony approached, Hughes set into place detailed preparations so carefully that he expected the occasion to "produce a sensation in this new country."[44] The Feast of the Assumption, August 15th, was a fine summer day with temperatures in the seventies, with high cloudiness and light winds.[45] The perimeter of the site was lined by ropes, and at the corner of Fiftieth Street and Fifth Avenue was a two-tiered platform, the lower level accommodating a band, the upper canopied section reserved for the Archbishop and honored prelates invited to attend. St. John the Evangelist Church, which had occupied that very spot, had been removed to the east side of Madison Avenue, a new street which recently cut the property in half, although it was not as yet officially opened. At the spot where the Lylburn mansion had stood (it also was moved east of Madison Avenue and close to Fourth [Park] Avenue), a large wooden cross was erected to mark the place where the high altar was to be built. Flags of the Papacy, the United States and several European countries representing the homelands of New York immigrants were set on the canopy and at points along the periphery of the site.

<Courtesy of the New York Transit Museum>

Five hours before the scheduled 4 p.m. start of the ceremonies, spectators were already assembling. As the hours passed, crowds drifting northward from the City were so large that one news account described New York as a "depleted" city, silent as the sombre streets of Herculaneum, a city buried in ash after the eruption of a volcano on Mt. Vesuvius in Italy. The entire fleet of the City's street cars (*above left*) was ordered to move in one direction only — northward — to provide passage for capacity crowds who found space wherever they could, including on the roofs of the cars; surface railroads on Second, Third, Fourth (*above right, the NY & Harlem line*), Sixth and Eighth Avenues proved inadequate for the numbers attempting to board, the overflow forming an unbroken line of private carriages and pedestrians moving slowly to the upper district. Every street around the dedication area was blocked by vehicles, and the estimated 100,00 spectators occupied every foot of ground from beyond Sixth Avenue on the west sloping down to Fourth Avenue on the east. The dust from the unpaved roads was everywhere, but anticipation of the grandeur of the ceremonies kept the excited crowd orderly and intact all afternoon.

Seven bishops joined Archbishop Hughes and two hundred priests in a long procession from the Lylburn mansion to the dedication platform. One hundred choir boys vested in colorful cassocks and surplices, and one hundred members of the St. Vincent de Paul Society assisted. No religious pageant of equal pomp could have been experienced on this continent before, and the effect on the people was stunning. Cheers were deafening as the crowds swayed to and fro and waved a sea of hats and handkerchiefs. Few of the witnesses could have been within earshot of the Archbishop to hear his address, but those who were learned for the first time that the new edifice was to be named in honor of St. Patrick, continuing the tradition of the first Cathedral. Cheers rose in waves as the news was passed through the heavily Irish crowd. The Archbishop praised the generosity of the first donors noting that some non-Catholics had contributed because they were eager "to see at least one ecclesiastical edifice on Manhattan Island of which their native city will have occasion to be proud." And he declared that "next to Almighty God, the cornerstone of this Cathedral is to be laid under the auspices of the Immaculate Virgin Mary," noting the recent definition in Rome of the dogma of the Immaculate Conception.[46]

~ 22 ~

Following his lengthy remarks, Archbishop Hughes blessed the stone, the first of the building, and set it in the foundation. The stone contained a cavity into which was inserted a parchment on which was recorded in Latin:

> For the greater glory of God, today, the fifteenth day of August, in the year of Our Lord 1858, on the feast of the Assumption of the ever-blessed and immaculate Virgin Mary, Mother of Jesus Christ, Our Lord and God, this first stone of the new Cathedral Church of St. Patrick in New York has been placed with solemn ritual by the Most Reverend John Hughes, fourth bishop and first archbishop of this see; with the assistance of all the bishops of the province and a large number of priests from a variety of places and in the admiring presence of an immense gathering of the faithful.
>
> His Holiness Pope Pius IX as successor of blessed Peter is now happily governing with supreme authority the universal Church of Christ.
>
> James Buchanan is President of these United States; John A. King, Governor of the State of New York; and Daniel F. Tiemann, Mayor of this city.
>
> James Renwick and William Rodrigue are the architects.
>
> P. S. Within a few days of the blessing of this stone there occurred the remarkable placing of an electric cable in the depths of the sea from shore to shore across the Atlantic Ocean; thus has been established the instantaneous transmission of news between America and Europe. While the governments of this country and Britain contributed greatly to the enterprise, the fact that it reached a successful outcome is due mostly to the unsurpassed fortitude of our outstanding citizen, Cyrus W. Field.

Both the parchment and a list of the original donors intended for insertion in the cavity were not immediately sealed within because thousands of onlookers approached the stone to deposit offerings into the cavity after the ceremony. The stone was sealed two years later, on August 15th, 1860, and the walls were built over it so that it "in all probability will never be disturbed by human agency," in the words of Archbishop Hughes. He did not have it marked and visible on the surface of the building apparently intending that it never be opened; he wrote that the names of the donors "though unseen by men... will ever be under the eyes and inspection of God, and may turn up for honor and mercy on the Day of Judgment."[47]

Somewhere in the vast throng witnessing the history-making event was undoubtedly the stone cutter honored with the task of shaping that first stone. Some suggest his name was Cormack McCall, only twenty-two years old at the time, an Irish immigrant who had learned his trade in England. After he left New York he started a new life in Minnesota.[48] And lifted high on the shoulders of his father to see over the heads of those towering over him was two-year-old Michael Lavelle, no more likely than anyone else there to imagine that one day he would assume the rectorship of the building whose beginnings he was observing.[49]

The dimensions Archbishop Hughes revealed in his fund-raising letter of June 1858 were *not* the dimensions he had expected would define his enormous building. Nor were they those of Renwick's original plan. Both men envisioned a far larger structure and one which embodied elements not contained in the design they finally settled upon. The present length of the building, 376 feet on the interior, is closer to the original proposed *exterior* length, greatly differing from the 322 feet exterior length approved at the time of the blessing of the cornerstone. Hughes determined in 1857 that it was necessary to eliminate a chevet of five chapels radiating from the semi-circular apse at the east end and to terminate the Cathedral abruptly behind the main altar. (Two of those chapels may have been intended for use as sacristies.) Renwick's scheme included a separate sacristy extending from the wall of the south aisle near the apse to the property line on Fiftieth Street, but this too was eliminated. He claimed the reason for less ambitious plans was because of the high cost.[50] Others claim it was because space was needed at the east end to construct the Archbishop's residence and the rectory once Madison Avenue was cut through the property.[51] Likely, both considerations contributed to the decision; it is also probable that the decision was for a postponement rather than a cancellation of erecting the chapels and sacristies. In fact, Renwick continued to produce schemes for a Lady Chapel many years after the Cathedral opened, and eventually a Lady Chapel became a reality, although its design was by another architect after Renwick's death.

What were *not* eliminated from Renwick's design, but still were never built, were first: an octagonal tower rising over the crossing of the nave and transept whose gables were broken by eight windows and an octagonal spire over the tower soaring one-hundred-thirty-five feet over the ridge of the roof; and second: twenty-four elaborately decorated flying buttresses extending from the chapel buttresses to the clerestory walls in support of a stone ceiling.[52] The tower, spire, masonry ceiling and concomitant flying buttresses were all eliminated in later years, but there is no evidence to support a conclusion that the decision to remove them was anything more than a postponement of their eventual execution.[53] There is good evidence suggesting that Renwick had experimented with using iron in the ceiling and the spires before he made his final choice for stone. What is certain is that he never intended a plaster ceiling, the unhappy reality of a score of years after he finished his designs, temporary though that reality may have been intended to be.[54] (The temporary ceiling is still in place well into the second century of the Cathedral's life.)

In 1858 the architects sent to the *New York Times* a description of their intended building. They had decided by that time to place two towers on the west front, but *not the twin towers* which were later built. The north tower was described simply as a pointed tower, but the south was to bear a spire with open tracery three-hundred-thirty-three feet high. The buttresses supporting the flying buttresses were described as "immense," much more massive than those finally built, and terminating in the foliated pinnacles along the sides of the building, having no supportive function, as if awaiting completion. The masonry roof was to be "the only one of any size in the United States." No cellar or crypt was planned; the ground was almost solid rock particularly at the Fifth Avenue end. The architects confidently predicted that the foundation would be finished in the autumn after the blessing of the cornerstone and that in three years enough of the structure would be ready to allow for celebration of liturgical services.[55] That would never have happened, since Hughes was determined not to open the church for any services until it was completed, and he did not expect to live to witness that day.[56]

Renwick had examined four types of stone for the Cathedral: glazed or brown free stone; olive free stone; granite; and white marble. Although the cost of marble was estimated to be as much as $50,000 more than the cheapest alternative, and it was the most expensive of the four he was considering, it was the material of choice. The architects wrote: "Our opinion is ... that there is no material which combines the three essentials of durability, beauty, and economy as well as white marble ... our opinion is that the beauty and durability of [white marble] would more than justify this additional expense and our belief is that if constructed of this beautiful material, it will be as worthy of the noble purpose to which it will be dedicated as the work of man's hands can be." They recommended stone called Tuckahoe, Pleasantville or snow flake marble, from the East Chester Quarry which quoted the lowest price of $850,000. The quarry company included in that price, surprisingly low even for a time of economic recession, the entire cost of constructing the building except for the foundations and furnishings. An additional $17,500 was bid for the excavation and foundation work. The total bid of $867,000 guaranteed all the construction material; 3,613,000 cubic feet of marble; and the labor costs for the entire building. Renwick gave three reasons for deciding in favor of the East Chester Company, also known as the Hall and Joyce Company of Westchester County: his own experience working with builders; the character of the builders; and the quality of the marble – "durable, beautiful and almost a precious stone." He predicted that "every year will add to its beauty, and every turn of the setting sun will be reflected by the spires and pinnacles, and thus forming a link with the colors of heaven, will produce the effect of carrying the mind of the beholder to the true object of the building – the worship of the Maker of the universe."[57] Contemplating further economies, Archbishop Hughes requested that the Board of Trustees purchase a quarry. He knew of one for sale for $10,800 containing enough stone to build the entire structure. He reasoned that trustee ownership would "render us independent of the caprices of quarry owners and quarry men."[58]

In a series of meetings extending from December 1858 until March 1859, options were discussed, alterations were accepted and on March 5, 1859 a contract was signed. A final amended contract was agreed upon on March 14th and the commission was granted to James Hall and William Joyce of the East Chester Company despite the "caprices of quarry owners." [59] Provisions specified a fee of $2,500 a year for the architects for eight years. The work was to be completed by January 1,1867, although the Archbishop reserved the right to suspend or discontinue construction at any time.

Curiously, at the end of the contract is the following paragraph: "The parties of the second part [the builders] further covenant and agree that they will not suffer or permit any spiritous liquors to be brought or used on said premises; that they shall instantly discharge any workman who may bring or use the same thereon, and that they will not knowingly employ any workman who shall live or board at any place in which spiritous liquors may be sold, within two blocks east or west, or four blocks north or south, of said premises, under pain of forfeiture of this contract."

In addition to constructing the building proper, the builders were required to construct a terrace wall three-hundred-seventy-six feet in length and the width of the block at Madison Avenue to form a raised terrace except at the Fifth Avenue entrances where a series of steps was to be set. At the four corners of the terrace, granite Gothic posts up to ten feet high were to set off the site. Sidewalks and curbing were required along Fifth Avenue and Fiftieth and Fifty-first Streets. The tracery of the windows was designated in the decorated style similar to those of St. Ouen of Rouen; York Minster and Beverly Minster in England; and St. Gudule in Brussels.[60]

The blocks of marble were to be transported by rail to a lot on the property east of the orphan asylum between Fifty-first and Fifty-second Streets near Madison Avenue. Each stone would be cut by hand in the tradition of the great European Cathedrals and carried to the site by teams of oxen or mules. William Joyce was made superintendent of construction.[61] The foundation stones were huge blocks of Dix Island granite from Knox County, Maine. The Maine quarry, owned by Thomas Dyer of New York City, supplied material in future years for the United States Treasury Building, the Metropolitan Museum of Art and other well-known American structures.[62]

Meanwhile, Archbishop Hughes arranged for a fourth story to be added to the Thirty-sixth Street archiepiscopal residence; this he used to house his considerable library of eight to ten thousand volumes. He usually spent evenings reading in this quiet retreat. Only the family of his sister and architect brother-in-law lived in the house with him; his secretary and other Cathedral clergy resided in the rectory of the old Cathedral downtown.[63] The years were taking their toll on the Archbishop's health, and although in 1857 the Cathedral trustees had increased the yearly stipend for his personal maintenance, his needs were few. He appeared in public less and less frequently. Monsignor William Starrs, his Vicar-general, habitually attended meetings of the Board of Trustees in his place and he corresponded with the trustees through his delegate or by writing to them. [64] Advancing rheumatism made exercise – even movement – painful, often nearly impossible. After a trip to the South early in 1860, he returned home fearing his illness was worse than his physicians were aware of. In May, he collapsed during services for the consecration of a church in Albany; however, he rallied and his recovery was speedy. [65]

His physical problems were exacerbated by the tensions experienced in common with the entire population of the country as civil war approached. Another disappointment was his failure to collect the first portion of the funds pledged for the Cathedral building campaign. Only $73,000 of the $103,000 pledged two years earlier had been paid, and he directed the architects and builders to suspend work as of August 15th, 1860, two years to the day after he had blessed the cornerstone.[66] Discouragement was not despair, however, and he expected full payment of all the pledges by the third week of October when he expected to resume construction of the walls which had reached a height of ten to fourteen feet when work was suspended.[67] But, October came and went without resumption of work. By December, following the election of Abraham Lincoln, South Carolina seceded from the Union and other states followed in rapid succession. War erupted in April 1861 and for the rest of that year the Archbishop focused all his attention on that calamity, as the Cathedral project's relative importance faded by comparison.

Hughes was convinced that death was not far into the future, but when President Lincoln and Secretary of State William Seward, a friend, asked him to undertake an unofficial mission to France in order to try to dissuade the French government from lending support to the South, he departed at once. The journey lasted until the summer of 1862 and included stops in England, Italy and Ireland as well as in France. He returned weaker than ever, so that by the end of the year, he was an invalid.[68] His Cathedral dream was still alive, however, and in December he declared that he had taken measures to resume building in the spring and to expend another hundred thousand dollars on construction. [69] One of the reasons why work had not proceeded earlier, in addition to problems of the war, was a dispute between the two builders, Joyce and Hall, both of whom sought a favorable decision from the courts.[70]

Work did not resume in the spring of 1863 as hoped; it only brought diminishing strength to the Archbishop. After Holy Thursday in April he was no longer able to celebrate Mass.[71] When he attempted to do so in June, he had to be helped to a chair as he appeared about to fall. Later attempts brought similar results. When the New York City draft riots erupted in July, the event could only have further drained his strength and accelerated his death. The riots were the most violent civil disorders in American history. That included a crowd of draft rioters and looters burning down an orphanage (*below*) for black children not six blocks from the cathedral property. Most rioters were Irish who were protesting inequities in the selection process of draftees. Archbishop Hughes invited them to his residence so he could address them from his balcony hoping to convince them to put aside their anger and their weapons. But the five thousand or so who came to hear him speak were probably not those who were taking part in the riots. In fact, there were hundreds of thousands of Irish in the City and the rioters were a small percentage of them.[72]

Too weak to stand, the Archbishop spoke for an hour before the audience left for their homes. It was his last public appearance. By December he was confined to his bed. He died on January 3, 1864 while Bishop McCloskey, his friend and former coadjutor, was reciting prayers for his departing soul. More than 200,000 mourners passed his body resting on a cata-

The New York Historical Society neg. #78726d

falque in the old Cathedral. On the day of the funeral, all the City courts and public schools closed, as did many City departments, including the Mayor's office. Eight bishops and almost two hundred priests participated in a most solemn ceremony after which his remains were laid in a tomb in the crypt under the Cathedral.[73]

1. Rev. Francis J. Hutshe to Cardinal Francis Spellman, Sept. 10, 1955, Archives of St. Patrick's Cathedral, hereafter cited as ASPC. The parents of Archbishop Hughes are buried in Corpus Christi Cemetery in Chambersburg, Pennsylvania.

2. Shaw, Richard, *Dagger John, The Unquiet Life and Times of Archbishop John Hughes of New York,* Paulist Press, New York, 1983, pp. 13-16; 22; 86; 94-l00, hereafter cited as Shaw, *Dagger John*; Cohalan, *Popular History,* pp. 50, 51.

3. *Ibid.,* pp. 126, 127.

4. Cohalan, *Popular History,* pp. 51, 52.

5. Farley, pp. 88, 89.

6. Cohalan, *Popular History,* pp. 57-60.

7. *See:* Fermier, Douglas, *James Gordon Bennett and the New York Herald, A Study of Editorial Opinion in the Civil War Era, 1854-1867,* Royal Historical Society, St. Martin's Press, New York, 1986.

8. W. E. Robinson to *Journal of the Fair,* November 13, 1878, printed in the *Journal* on November 16, 1878, ASPC.

9. Cohalan, *Popular History,* p. 71; Smith, pp. 153, 154; Shaw, *Dagger John,* p. 198.

10. Carthy, *Old St. Patrick's,* p. 85.

11. Hughes, Archbishop John, undated and unpublished paper entitled: *Thoughts and Reflections in Regard to the New Cathedral,* c. 1853, Archives of the Archdiocese of New York, hereafter cited as AANY.

12. Hassard, John R. G., *Life of the Most Reverend John Hughes, D. D., First Archbishop of New York,* D. Appleton and Company, New York, 1866, p. 351.

13. Cohalan, *Popular History,* pp. 71, 72.

14. Rattner, Selma, article re: James Renwick, *Macmillan Encyclopedia of Architects,* Adolph Placzek, ed.-in-chief, Volume 3, Free Press, Collier, Macmillan Publishers, London, 1985. Rattner suggests that Renwick's success was due, in part, to his high social station and to his marriage to Anna Lloyd Aspinwall, daughter of one of the wealthiest men in the country. Her article lists many of his most successful commissions from 1846 to his design of the spires of St. Patrick's Cathedral in 1886-1887. At various times during his career, Renwick had partners, but none of them appears to have worked with him on his designs of St. Patrick's Cathedral.

15. Pierson, William H., Jr., *American Buildings and Their Architects,* Volume 3: *Technology and the Picturesque, the Corporate and the Early Gothic Styles,* Doubleday and Oxford University Press, New York, 1978, pp. 212; 223-224; 226-228; Re: Gau's influence on Renwick's design, *see:* nomination form, National Register of Historic Places, ASPC.

16. Farley, p. 127.

17. *The Cathedral Bulletin,* February, 1956.

18. *New Yorker* magazine, November 8, 1958.

19. Smith, pp. 175, 189.

20. As early as 1878, rumors persisted among New Yorkers that the Cathedral land was a gift to the Church from the City government either totally or in part. *Putnam's Magazine* that year "gave currency" to that belief and for generations after, the story or one similar to it was resurrected and refuted repeatedly. A complete account of the financial transactions from 1799 was first published in the *Journal of the Fair,* a daily newsletter issued during a fund-raising fair shortly before the Cathedral opened. The account was carefully researched on several occasions in subsequent years and brought up-to-date each time a new refutation was issued. *See: Journal of the Fair,* October 24, 1878, ASPC.

21. Quinn, William, V. G., *St. Patrick's Cathedral, A Full Description of the Exterior and Interior of the New Cathedral, The Altars and Windows with Biographical Sketches of His Eminence Cardinal McCloskey and the Most Reverend Archbishop Hughes, D. D.,* New York, 1886, n.p.

22. Corrigan, Most. Rev. Michael, *Register of the Clergy Laboring in the Archdiocese of New York from Early Missionary Times to 1885,* Historical Records and Studies, Volume I, pp. 212-214.

23. Ryan, Leo Raymond, *Old St. Peter's,* monograph series XIV, U. S. Catholic Historical Society, 1935, p. 105

24. Corrigan, pp. 212-214; Ryan, p. 105; Curran, Rev. Francis, S.J., *The Jesuit Colony in New York, 1808-1817,* Historical Records and Studies, 1954. The Trappists first arrived in this country in 1803 and Dom Augustine arrived in New York with four other monks on April 5, 1814. The property had been advertised for sale beginning in March and the Trappists had already moved into the Lylburn mansion by April 11th. One of the Trappists was Rev. Vincent de Paul who had been the superior of the Trappists in Bordeaux, France before the exile. After the orphan asylum was closed, the monks moved north to Nova Scotia where they embarked for a return to France; but Father de Paul remained behind and founded LaTrappe in Tracadie.

Father Vincent de Paul may be Rev. Vincent Merle who had stayed at the orphanage with six brothers to settle business affairs after most of the monks had left. He remained in Nova Scotia until his death in 1853. In his memoirs he referred to the New York property as "the most delightful site of Manhattan Island." He provided many details about life at the monastery-orphanage, recording, for example, that Dom Augustine had founded a community of Trappist nuns who left when the monks did. The Trappists also provided a chaplain for a convent of Ursuline nuns about three or four miles from their monastery. Two of the brothers who stayed behind to settle business matters and who had been ill for a long period died and were buried in an orchard near the mansion. Before the survivors left for Canada, the bodies were transferred to a small nearby cemetery "intended for the poor."

It is interesting that before the fall of Napoleon, Dom Augustine apparently planned to make New York the headquarters of his order. And so, after taking possession of the Lylburn property, he brought all the Trappists in America to that location. Even after he realized that he had insufficient money to meet the price asked by the Jesuits, Dom Augustine continued to attempt to raise the funds, intending to beg if necessary. He did not succeed. For detailed information about the Trappist presence in New York, *see:* Curran, Rev. Francis X, S.J., *The Return of the Jesuits,* Loyola University Press, Chicago, 1966; Rattler, Tarcisius A., O.S.A., *A Little History of Religious Activity on the Site of St. Patrick's Cathedral Up to 1815,* unpublished manuscript, c. 1975, ASPC.

25. Carthy, Margaret, O.S.U., *A Cathedral of Suitable Magnificence,* Michael Glazier, Inc., Wilmington, Delaware, 1984, pp. 28, 29, hereafter cited as Carthy, *Magnificence.*

26. Meehan, Thomas F., compiler, *History and Description, St. Patrick's Cathedral, Fifth Avenue, New York,* Meany Printing Co., New York, 1910, n. p.

27. Kelly, Msgr. George A., *The Parish As Seen From the Church of St. John the Evangelist, New York City, 1840-1873,* St. John's University, New York, 1973, pp. 7, 11, hereafter cited as Kelly, *The Parish.* The trustees allowed the pastor of St. John's, Father Maginnis, four lots about 100 feet square for the little church building.

28. Cathedral Bulletin, September 1946; *New York Times Magazine,* June 4, 1939. According to Msgr. Michael Lavelle, second Rector of St. Patrick's Cathedral, when he attended the blessing of the cornerstone ceremony at the age of two years, the seminary was still there, "an isolated building standing in the midst of fields." He added that "one of its rules was that no young men who were studying there might go into the City. In order that there should be no mistake as to where the City began, Twenty-seventh Street was fixed as its northern boundary."

29. Kelly, *The Parish,* p. 13.

30. Quinn, n.p.

31. Hassard, p. 291; Resolution of the Board of Alderman, March 23, 1897, AANY, Orphan Asylum box, Folder 2, G-43. There were seven acres purchased and these were added to five acres the Archbishop already held. He wrote: "On the twelve acres ... I intend to build all our charitable establishments, as time and circumstances will allow." *See:* Hughes to Rev. Deluol, June 7, 1846 as quoted in Hassard, p. 291.

32. W. Knight Sturges, article in United States Catholic Historian, Winter-Spring 1981. *See also:* Kernick, Francis W., *Architects in America of Catholic Tradition,* Charles E. Tuttle, Rutland, Vermont, 1962; *Metropolitan Journal,* obituary of William Rodrigue, November, 1867.

33. Carthy, *Old St. Patrick's,* pp. 77, 78.

34. Shaw, *Dagger John,* p. 357.

35. *Metropolitan Journal,* November 1867.

36. *New York Times,* April 5, 1868.

37. Hughes, *Thoughts and Reflections in Regard to the New Cathedral,* AANY, n.p.

38. Hughes to Frenaye, May 18, 1858, as quoted in Hassard, pp. 403-405.

39. Garraty, John A., *The American Nation – A History of the United States to 1877,* Volume I, Harper and Row, New York, 1975, pp. 321, 322.

40. Hughes, *Thoughts and Reflections in Regard to the New Cathedral,* AANY, n.p.

41. Farley, pp. 119-121.

42. Hassard, p. 406; Farley, p. 122.

43. Hughes to Trustees, May 29, 1858, AANY

44. Farley, p. 122.

45. Surface Weather Observations, August 1858, United States Department of Commerce, National Oceanic and Atmospheric Administration, Environmental Data Service, National Climatic Center, Asheville, N. C.

46. *New York Times,* August 16, 1858; New York Morning Express, August 16, 1858; Instructions for ceremonies of blessing of cornerstone, ASCP; contract and specifications for construction of St. Patrick's Cathedral, ASPC; Smith, pp. 576, 577.

47. *New York Times,* August 16, 1858; Morning Express, August 16, 1858; Hughes to Fitzgerald, June 14, 1858, AANY; New York Herald, August 16, 1858.

48. Julia Pye to Cardinal Francis Spellman, August 5, 1958, ASPC.

49. *New York Times Magazine,* June 4, 1939.

50. Renwick to Board of Trustees, December 6, 1888, AANY.

51. Quinn, V. Rev. William, V. G., *St. Patrick's Cathedral, New York,* New York Catholic Protectory Society, New York, copyright 1879, n.p. *The Catholic News,* weekly newspaper of the Archdiocese of New York, reported in 1941 that the decision to reduce the size of the Cathedral in order to provide room for residences behind it was made in 1857. *See: Catholic News,* February 15, 1941.

52. Pierson, pp. 237, 265-268; drawings of architect, AANY; contract and specifications for construction of St. Patrick's Cathedral, ASPC.

53. Renwick to Trustees, December 6, 1888.

54. Pierson, pp. 228-232.

55. *New York Times,* August 16, 1858.

56. Hughes to Trustees, May 29, 1858, AANY.

57. Farley, pp. 116-118. *See also:* Sutton Report, November 17, 1941, ASPC.

58. Hughes to Trustees, May 29, 1858, AANY. The Archbishop did not reveal where the quarry was located, but called it a farm of eight or nine acres with a house and a blacksmith shop and enough marble "to build ten Cathedrals." He believed a railway could be built from the quarry to the "lower end of the Asylum lot" to move the stone to the construction site.

59. Farley, pp 116-118.

60. Contract and specifications for construction – St. Patrick's Cathedral, ASPC.

61. Journal of the Fair, October 25, 1878.

62. Shannon, Joseph, *Manual of the Corporation of the City of New York, 1868,* E. Jones and Co., New York, 1869; Lepage to Sturges, July 16, 1980, ASPC.

63. Hassard, pp. 495-499. Archbishop Hughes was accustomed to ride each day to the old Cathedral on Mulberry Street "where he did all his writing, kept his papers, and attended to business." At home, "although he was much attached to Mrs. Rodrigue and her family, he never sat with them in the evenings, and rarely alluded at home to his public actions."

64. Minutes of the Board of Trustees, 1852-1860, Office of the Board of Trustees of St. Patrick's Cathedral, New York.

65. Shaw, *Dagger John,* pp. 337-338; Hassard, p. 382.

66. Hughes to *New York Times,* August 4, 1860. The letter was printed on August 9, 1860; Hughes to Renwick and Rodrigue, undated, AANY; Hughes to Joyce and Hall, undated, AANY.

67. Hughes to Very Rev. Donaghoe, Sept. 27, 1860, AANY.

68. Shaw, *Dagger John,* pp. 345-357.

69. Hughes to Rev. Bernard Smith, December 15, 1862, as quoted in Hassard, p. 493

70. *Ibid.*

71. Hassard, pp. 495-499.

72. Cohalan, *Popular History,* p. 82; Shaw, *Dagger John,* pp. 368-369; *See:* Bernstein, Iver, *The New York City Draft Riots,* Oxford University Press, New York, 1990.

73. Hassard, pp. 502, 503; *Freeman's Journal,* January 16, 1864; *Catholic Register,* January 16, 1864.

CHAPTER IV

The Very Stones Would Cry Out: Cardinal John McCloskey

Bishop John McCloskey of Albany, the former Coadjutor Bishop of New York, expected that he would be named Archbishop Hughes' successor as Archbishop of New York. So did almost everyone else familiar with his credentials and background. He was a friend of Hughes for over a quarter century, and he had been entrusted by Hughes with assignments of great responsibility during that period. Still, he wrote to the Holy See in an attempt to dissuade his superiors from designating him for the post: "I recoil from the very thought of it with shuddering, and I do most humbly trust that such a crushing load will not be placed upon my weak and unworthy shoulders." The Holy Father named him Archbishop of New York on May 6, 1864.[1]

John McCloskey was born in Brooklyn, New York on March 10, 1810, the only son of Irish immigrants who were active members of New York's early Catholic community. As a young boy, he regularly crossed the East River to Manhattan with his parents "in an old and dingy horse boat" to assist at Mass in old St. Peter's Church or at St. Patrick's old Cathedral, since there was no Catholic church in Brooklyn.[2] He studied in private schools in Brooklyn and Manhattan until he was eleven years old, and in 1821 he was enrolled in Mt. St. Mary's College in Emmitsburg, Maryland. Father John Dubois was rector there and John Hughes was a teacher awaiting acceptance to the seminary. Upon completion of his studies, but undecided about his future, he returned home and vacillated between a career in business and in law. In 1827, he suffered a severe accident which resulted in temporary blindness; when he recovered, he announced his decision to become a priest. He finished his studies for ordination at Mt. St. Mary's and in 1834 he became the first New York native to be ordained a priest for the Diocese of New York. Two years of advanced study followed in Rome, after which he was appointed pastor of St. Joseph's Church in Greenwich Village, New York. When St. John's College opened at Fordham in 1841, he became its first president. Finding himself overwhelmed by work, Bishop Hughes urged his superiors in Rome to appoint Father McCloskey to assist him as Coadjutor Bishop in 1843, and he served in that position until Pope Pius IX entrusted him with the new Diocese of Albany in 1847. He was in close contact with Hughes during the next sixteen years just as he had been for years before, and he was at the Archbishop's bedside at the time of his death. In the funeral eulogy he delivered at the old Cathedral, he declared that Archbishop Hughes "had been raised up by God [and] was chosen as His instrument to do an appointed work and was strengthened by His grace and supported by His wisdom for the accomplishment of the work for which he was chosen and appointed...."[3]

Hughes and McCloskey, two giant figures of the nineteenth century American Catholic Church, could not have been more different in temperament. Archbishop McCloskey had sustained the burden of a weak physical constitution all his life, the experience cautioning him to budget his strength by following a highly disciplined regimen. Uncombative, even non-competitive, he avoided all conflict; on the other hand, he carefully, perseveringly and unequivocally faced issues squarely.[4] Few could call him an enemy, he was genuinely loved by most, and he treated all with courtesy and gentleness. Archbishop Hughes had masterfully "welded into one harmonious body the scattered elements" of New York Catholicism, and created an atmosphere of cordiality for the accession of McCloskey. Shortly after the new Archbishop arrived in the City, a grand banquet was arranged in his honor at world-famous Delmonico's Restaurant, attended by citizens of many religious affiliations, a testament to the "new spirit abroad."[5]

Within a year of his appointment, the Civil War came to a close, and the Archbishop renewed the campaign for building the new Cathedral. He began the "delectable" task of begging for funds, which by October had become a decidedly undelectable task; he found it simply "unpleasant work."[6] On St. Patrick's Day, he

sent a circular letter announcing resumption of work as soon as possible, and begging those original subscribers who had not fulfilled their pledges to honor them; and he invited others of substantial means to join the effort. He estimated that there were at least two hundred persons whom God might inspire "with the zeal and generosity" to help him meet his goal by autumn.[7] In September, his success permitted a renegotiation of a contract with William Joyce, now working without James Hall, to supervise the work at a salary of $3000 a year, that amount later reduced to $2800.[8] Construction resumed shortly afterwards. Many responded to the circular request with contributions ranging from $100 to $2000. The trustees contributed to the fund the proceeds of a sale of eight lots on Eleventh and Twelfth Streets, and beginning in 1867, the parishes of the Archdiocese were assessed in amounts of $150 to $5000 each year until 1876. Some churches surpassed their goals, but many fell short, especially in the later years. By 1871, $1,071,035 of the newly-estimated cost had been collected.[9] The amount exemplifies the faith and generosity of many poor Catholics who made personal sacrifices. There were only thirty-eight churches in Manhattan to serve about 350,000 practicing Catholics who were supporting the building both of new parish buildings and the Cathedral. Wages were low and hours were long during that pre-union era of expanding industrialism. In New York, "the trolley drivers and conductors worked fifteen hours a day, seven days a week for $2.50 a day. A factory girl earned four dollars weekly for a ten-hour day" in a six-day work week. Men were paid twice as much.[10] After a fire engulfed the old Cathedral in 1866, and only the stone walls were left in the midst of rubble, apprehension that the rebuilding cost would interrupt construction of the new Cathedral was allayed when insurance claims provided funds.[11]

During the war years, James Renwick had not been idle. His most notable accomplishment between 1861 and 1865 was his design of Vassar College in Poughkeepsie, New

York, and in the same period he completed designs for several other buildings within and outside the City.[12] William Rodrigue was ill for several years and did not join Renwick when he resumed work on the Cathedral after the War. Rodrigue died in November 1867.[13]

Once begun, construction proceeded steadily, if slowly. $100,000 was expended in 1867 and a greater amount was planned for the following year. By 1868, the decision to construct twin spires rather than those of the 1857 design had been made, and the central gable of the west front was completed.[14] It is likely that the decision to eliminate the tower at the crossing was made before 1870, since the columns already built at the crossing are identical in size to the others of the nave and choir; more massive piers would have been required for support were the tower to have been added. Renwick, years later, claimed that those (non-existent) larger central columns "would perhaps have interfered with the beauty of the perspective of the interior."[15] Moreover, the stone used for those columns is Pleasantville marble, identical to that of the lower exterior walls. But, around 1869, the ten-year contract for extracting marble from the Pleasantville quarry expired, and an extension of only a few more years was permitted for removal of stone. In fact, very little was taken from that site after 1870. Instead, the Wild and Manning quarry in Lee, Massachusetts provided the rest of the stone used until the building was finished in 1878. Mr. Wild had been an employee at the Pleasantville quarry when James Hall was president of the company, but the new owner of that quarry was John Mack, and Wild decided to purchase the quarry in Massachusetts. Known as the Lee Marble Works, it had been in existence since pre-Revolutionary War times and provided stone for the United States Capitol Building and the Washington Monument (and in more recent years the Empire State Building). Headstones over the graves of 1,600,000 soldiers were cut from stone from the same quarry. The Lee marble was used at the Cathedral beginning at the height just above the aisle chapels.[16]

Museum of the City of New York

In 1871, over one hundred employees were engaged in work at the quarry and at the construction site. Marble blocks of ten to fifteen tons each were brought to the site on a special branch track of the Harlem Railroad. That year the walls reached the triforium level, fifty-four feet from the foundation; the windows below that level, including all the tracery and mullions, were completed the same year, as were the transepts and the entrances of the west front. Work on the high clerestory was planned for 1872. A reporter who visited the site gives his impressions:

"Inside the walls the picture is a strange one. Much of the ground is grass-grown, and piles of debris, masses of carved blocks of marble, mountains of brick and cement cover the earth here and there. Work is going on

But the stones were there — ready to shout.

but in a lazy, dreamy sort of way. There is no hurrying crowd of workmen (*previous page*); there are no unseemly noises of puffing engines, creaking derricks, and shouting laborers. A single, lonely-looking horse sedately lounges along a path prepared for him, slowly hoisting bricks and mortar to the men at work upon the interior of the walls. A yoke of patient oxen and still more patient driver languidly move big blocks of marble hither and thither on a low sledge. There is no haste; the men work as those who work for all time, and propose to take all the time to do the work in. One has an almost irresistible inclination to lie down and go to sleep somewhere about the place. The loudest noise to awaken him, if he did, would be the chirping of the countless sparrows flitting all about, and his dreams would inevitably be of ghostly ruins in a land of eternal rest and silence."[17]

Although the area was losing its rustic character, only about half the lots north of the Cathedral as far as Central Park were graced by residences. A block east, there were hardly more than one hundred homes from Fiftieth Street to the Harlem River.[18]

In the summer of 1874, Archbishop McCloskey decided that the building was near enough to completion to begin a search for suitable furnishings, especially altars and stained glass. Renwick had been abroad for two years examining "those models which will best suggest what is needed for the glory of the Catholic Cathedrals of America." The Archbishop was in Europe that year visiting outstanding European cathedrals and conferring with artists (and Renwick) about what he wanted for St. Patrick's. He had already decided that the main altar, the episcopal *cathedra,* or throne, the pulpit and the baptismal font would be his personal gifts. His largesse was not the result of a superfluity of personal funds, but came at the expense of personal necessities. For example, after a group of friends presented him with a gift of a carriage and horses in honor of his elevation to cardinal in 1875, he sold both carriage and horses and added the proceeds to his gift for the Cathedral. A single European journey proved inadequate for his search and he repeated his travels in 1878.[19]

On March 15, 1875, John McCloskey received a cable notifying him that he had been created a cardinal priest of the Catholic Church. The stunning news was greeted in the country with overwhelming joy, since he was not only the first *American* cardinal, but the first cardinal in the entire Western Hemisphere. While normal custom required his presence in Rome for the consistory to receive the *galero, the* red hat which is a sign of his office, constrictions of time dictated that ceremonies be held in New York at the old Cathedral. He was to receive the galero at a later date in Rome. When the public ceremony was held in April, "St. Patrick's had never before witnessed a function conducted with such solemnity, pomp and splendor." Seven archbishops, twenty bishops and bishops-elect and several hundred priests processed to the sanctuary in the presence of New York's Mayor William Wickham; Chester Arthur, later President of the United States; August Belmont; and a host of other prominent figures. It was a fitting retirement party for the old Cathedral whose status in a few years was to revert to that of a parish church.[20]

The grandeur of the occasion and the pride of the City at the honor overshadowed a decision which must have been bitterly disappointing for the Cardinal and disheartening for Renwick. In February, just before the happy news arrived, a contract was signed with New York's Power Brothers Company to install a lath and plaster ceiling at the new Cathedral and to abandon the use of stone in the vaulting.[21] According to Renwick, "the great cost of such a ceiling and the delay in completion of the Cathedral, I think were the cause of this alteration."[22] The change was accompanied by a reduction in size of all the buttresses whose function was "to carry the thrust of the ceiling of the center aisles to the buttresses." The architects' specifications had required twenty-four flying buttresses, "fringed and panelled [sic] and coped with moldings."[23] In fact, it was not just the nave ceiling for which stone was intended, but the ceilings of the chapels and aisles as well. The use of plaster in Gothic churches in America was a common practice, and the visual results of substituting plaster for stone were indistinguishable to the viewer inside. It was on the exterior that aesthetics were affected. Renwick tried to lessen the disaster by reducing the height of the outer buttresses by ten feet and by decreasing the depth, but "it was impossible to eliminate altogether the impression of support, and with the flying arches gone, the massive immobility of the buttresses... was dissipated uselessly instead toward an open and every-yielding sky.[24]

Power Brothers had invented a plastering system called the Power patent plastering method using wire netting. So proud were they of their accomplishment that they left for posterity testimony of their work: they prepared a statement, duly notarized and recorded in the County Clerk's Office of New York County and dated September 12, 1876, in which they lauded their skill and the results of their craftsmanship, even listing the names of all the members of their family. They secured the parchment in a glass jar and imbedded it into one of the decorative bosses in the ceiling. It read: "We believe we are warranted in taking the liberty to say to who may find this writing hereafter, that they will say we performed our work in a good and substantial manner and superior to any ever before done on a plastered ceiling in this or any other country, and if any of our children or children's children may be in this land, they may look with pride upon the work done by their fathers." When the jar was inserted, the ceiling was finished.[25] The roof above it was supported by huge wooden beams installed in 1877, a year after the ceiling was finished. The iron slated roof proposed by Renwick was disapproved by Cardinal McCloskey. In the leaders, gutters and valleys of the roof, Renwick directed the placement of pipes pierced with holes and connected to the boilers, his device for melting ice which might form on the masonry thereby causing expansion. The arrangement was his own invention and was completely successful. [26]

Work on the final stages was in progress by the summer of 1876. The towers on the west front were the last parts of the building to be constructed. At the same time, the slow and careful process of installing the glass of the windows began.[27] By the fall of 1878, the building was essentially complete, as complete as the several postponements allowed. As with the flying buttresses, the masonry ceiling, the sacristies and the apsidal chapels, so also, the lanterns and the spires over the towers were left for another generation to build.

As opening day drew nearer, Cardinal McCloskey worried about a shortage of funds. In 1873, the Archbishop's residence was mortgaged by the trustees for $40,000 and the money was applied toward the building expenses. Again in 1874 and 1876, loans were taken for a total of $400,000 and secured by a mortgage on the property.[28] The final drive was a grand fair held in the completed building at the end of 1878. The event opened on October 22nd, and continued daily until November 30th. It was the largest ecclesiastical fair ever held in the United States and "the grandest display of its kind since the great fairs held in the Academy of Music during the [Civil] war years." Mayor Smith Ely of New York delivered an address on the opening night when nearly all the Catholic clergy of the City and its vicinity, as well as many City officials, were present. Fourteen hundred gas jets lighted the inside of the building which was decorated with festive evergreens and flowers arranged around tables, booths and displays. For almost all those who attended, it was their first opportunity to see the interior of the most magnificent, and certainly the largest, church building in America. On the first night, over 25,000 people crowded into the church in stages, and it was reported that it required at least a half-hour to move around the Cathedral due to the huge crowd."

In the following days, while Gilmore's or Garfulla's bands provided entertainment, excited New Yorkers moved about the exhibits displayed under canopies of velvet and gold, and containing objects for sale or for raffle. There were gold, silver, bronze and porcelain items, furniture, paintings, jewelry, glass, Thomas Edison's new invention (the phonograph), mechanized objects, cigars and cigarettes, refreshments and even animals. Here and there were novel attractions such as a seven-hundred-pound bell intended for eventual use in the not-yet-built spires, wax figures of a bride and groom, a weight-guessing concession, a miniature race course, a shooting gallery, billiard tables, a Punch and Judy show, a post office, a glass-blowing demonstration and a display of machines including an electric train, a true marvel in 1878. One attraction was an electric battery which sent shocks through the limbs of men who attempted to appear "full of vigor, writhing under the shock, but too vain to drop the poles until the needle upon the dial ... twitched around to a reputable

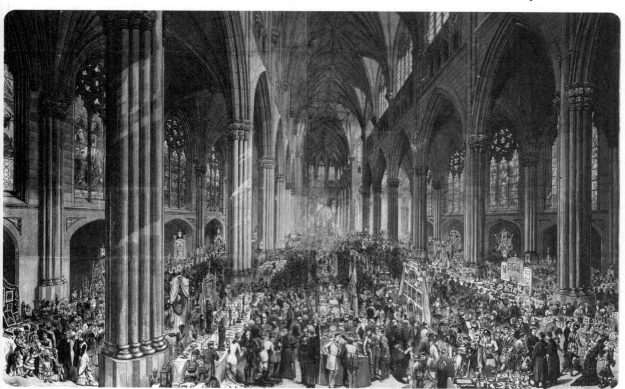

The Fair

figure." The electric train was set on a track course surrounding a castle with seventy guns, all firing at once. The shooting gallery was devised by "Father Farrelly's genius," and earned the Cathedral ten cents for every four shots. The Bohemian glass-blowers fashioned "any article that you name." The Punch and Judy entertainment delighted full-house audiences every evening; undoubtedly the large groups of children, including the orphans of the Catholic orphanage on Fifty-first Street and children from St. Joseph's Institute for the Deaf who attended the fair, comprised a large part of those audiences.

One of the most patronized attractions was the refreshment area which offered stewed oysters, chicken, lobster, roast beef, turkey, corned beef, ham and tongue, sandwiches and salads, ice cream, cakes, the much-in-demand *Charlotte Russe,* and beverages as varied as coffee, wine, beer and ale. Another popular exhibition was a magnificent sword encased in a silver scabbard, ornamented with gold and studded with diamonds. It was to be presented to the American general whose popularity was measured greatest by the votes of those attending the fair. General Daniel Wylie emerged the winner on the final evening from a neck-to-neck race.

Prominent clergymen from near and far, including Cardinal McCloskey who made several visits, led the list of distinguished visitors. On one occasion, Cyrus Field, the creator of the Atlantic cable, accompanied Dean Stanley of Westminster Abbey in London. The famous Episcopal churchman "was full of admiration of all that he saw" and "scarcely could realize that such a grand structure could have been built with small contributions, mainly of the poor." He called the building a "splendid triumph of faith and self-denial." James Renwick was host for a deputation of notable architects from New York, Boston, Cincinnati, Baltimore, Chicago, Newport and Providence. "They were lavish in their praises of the beauty and grandeur of the Cathedral, both in its outward and inward appearance."

Some visitors were not quite so welcome. Pickpockets and thieves found a rogues' paradise at the fair, at least until Sergeant Whitcombe, commanding officer of the police detail, entered upon the scene. Sergeant Whitcombe was of the opinion that some visitors were "some of the well-dressed, expert women shoplifters that infest the down-town retail stores." A local newspaper reported one incident:

"Detectives Ferris and McCormack, of the Police Central Office, while on duty at the Cathedral Fair last night, saw two pickpockets, 'Wes' Allen, an ex-convict, and William Howard. The detectives followed them. Ferris thought he saw Allen attempt to pick the pockets of several ladies without success, and he went closer to him. He then heard Allen say to Howard, 'I have not seen a stone here tonight'. At this time the men were opposite the table of St. Cecilia's Church, and Howard called Allen's attention to a fine gold watch and chain lying under a book on the table. Allen reached for it, and Ferris laid his hand on his shoulder. At the same time McCormack arrested Howard. Allen, when he saw Ferris, slipped away, and darting among the people, ran to a bench on which sat two women, one of whom held a baby. Allen seated himself beside the latter, and picking up the baby, made a show of dandiling [sic] it. But Ferris was positive, and insisted on taking him into custody. Allen then made a great attempt to excite the sympathy of the bystanders by claiming to be innocent, to be the husband of the mother of the baby, and to have been holding it on his lap for some time. He and Howard were taken before Inspector Thorne, in the Central Office. The woman with the child followed them and plead [sic] with the inspector for

Allen, whom she called her husband. Inspector Thorne ordered both prisoners to be locked up."

As the fair drew to a close, authorities feared that the increasing numbers might cause a pedestrian *gridlock*. On November 19th, the crowds were so large that thousands were turned away at the doors. The total raised when the doors were finally closed was $172,625.48.[29]

In the spring of 1879, the altars, pews and other furnishings were ready, and Cardinal McCloskey set the dedication date for May 25th. With an exterior length of three-hundred-thirty-two feet and an interior length of three-hundred-six feet, it was estimated that its 4,674 square yards of space ranked St. Patrick's eleventh in size "among the great cathedrals and churches of the world," immediately after Notre Dame Cathedral in Paris (5,250 square yards). It was slightly less than one-third the size of St. Peter's Basilica in Rome.[30]

The earliest attempts at illuminating the interior, a plan devised by the plumbing contractor, met with gratifying success in producing an effect of both softness and brilliance, "a halo of sunset glory" that overwhelmed those entering after nightfall. About eighteen hundred gas jets were situated about the building, forty-two on each of the nave piers, twenty-five over the side aisle piers where the nave and transepts intersect, sixty jets on the transept window sills, forty on each of the piers near the high altar and the rest dispersed in the chapels, the triforia and the stairs.[31]

The original Fifth Avenue and tower doors, similar to those still in use at the transept, were built of white ash by Smith and Crane of New York. Steam heat produced by boilers was distributed to radiators in the body of the church, and coils released heat under the floor of the sanctuary and in the triforia.[32] Renwick had specified a floor of red and green sandstone, white and blue marble and flagstone laid in Gothic patterns, but this was another casualty of economics;[33] further, the Cardinal worried that the cold produced by a stone floor in winter might necessitate a later installation of a wooden floor above it. So, the floor was made of wood, except in the sanctuary where rich marbles were used. The sanctuary was six steps above the nave floor and the high altar was raised another three steps. Affixed to the floor were four-hundred-eight box pews, eight to eleven feet wide and separated by seven-to-eight-feet-wide aisles. Seating capacity was about 2500 persons. The sanctuary, separated from the transept and nave by a brass altar rail, contained sedelia, or seating stalls, for thirty-eight persons, and was a smaller area than the present sanctuary, beginning one bay closer to the east wall. The wood carving was the work of Paul Guibé of St. Brieuc, France, the same artist who carved the confessionals, the organ front and the reredos of the high altar. The *cathedra,* or Archbishop's throne, was modeled on the work of Adam Kraft who had carved the medieval *cathedra* of Nuremberg Cathedral. Its canopy was supported by Gothic columns crowned by an octagonal lantern with delicate open tracery and statues.[34]

Renwick abandoned his plans for an altar table with a hexagonal baldachino, or canopy, when the east end chapels were postponed. Instead, a massive reredos of Poitier stone, fifty feet high and thirty-three feet wide, was the background for a marble altar table carved in Rome by Carimini. Its niches and panels contained statues and bas-relief carvings of Carrara marble. Paul Guibé's reredos contained statues of Sts. Peter and Paul, various angelic figures and a representation of Our Lord in the central tower. The imposing structure drew immediately to itself, as the center of liturgical rites of the Church, the eyes of those entering at the west. It was Cardinal McCloskey's personal gift, purchased at a cost of $35,000.

On the south side of the high altar, separated from it by a wooden screen, was a temporary sacristy extending forty-eight feet (two bays) from the east wall to a wooden dividing wall across the entire width of the aisle. Set against the wooden wall was an early altar dedicated to St. Joseph. Made of bronze, the altar contained three mosaics on the front panel. Also on the south, located

The high altar circa 1890.

where the present Sacred Heart altar is in the transept, was the original altar of the Sacred Heart. Like the St. Joseph altar, it was bronze with statues and bas-relief sculptures. On each side were Egyptian granite and marble columns supporting bronze statues of Sts. Peter and Paul presented by Pope Pius IX to the Cardinal, who was the donor of this altar also.

In the corresponding location in the north transept was the first Holy Family altar, carved of Caen stone, both white and colored. On the same side of the sanctuary, and awaiting a more permanent solution, was the Lady Chapel, formed by the space of the entire north aisle east of the transept (three bays). The altar reredos, carved in St. Brieuc, was formed out of French walnut. It was filled with figures and crowned with pierced spires. It abutted the east wall; below it was an altar table made of Poitier stone with bas-relief panels.[35]

While this section of the building presented a glorious gathering of rich pieces, the rest of the interior, aside from the masterful architecture, was strikingly empty of decoration. The sixteen niches in the transept walls were devoid of any statuary, and in the spaces for the stations of the cross were still blank panels. None of the aisle chapels contained altars, and no statues were on the narthex walls or at the ground level at the west end. Only a Gothic baptismal font of white marble, covered with a richly carved French walnut spire, and the St. Brieuc confessionals broke the openness of the entire space from Fifth Avenue to the front.[36] But the uniformity of the neutral stone was in dramatic contrast to rainbows of color radiating through the magnificent stained, or painted, glass windows, in an era when no skyscrapers impeded the rays of sunlight on any side of the building.

Thirty-seven lower aisle, transept and apsidal windows held figured glass, while the rest of the windows in the nave clerestory, the rose window and a few near the altars were filled with *cathedral glass,* translucent with geometric forms but with no figures, or with white glass for lighting.[37] The cathedral glass was made by the local firm of Morgan Brothers; all the stained glass windows were made in France by Nicholas Lorin of Chartres or Henry Ely of Nantes. While inspecting one of the windows, Morgan fell to his death from scaffolding. Even though he was not a Catholic (he was a member of the Dutch Reformed Church), the Archbishop of New York gave the "funeral oration," according to family information passed down three generations to the present.[38] Lorin appears to have been entrusted with responsibility of the entire project and he may have awarded a commission for some windows to Ely, but that is not certain. Lorin was born early in the nineteenth century and died three years after St. Patrick's opened. He had exhibited his work at expositions in Paris, Rome, Brussels, Vienna and Philadelphia. It is possible that one or more of St. Patrick's windows were shown by Lorin at the Philadelphia Centenary Exposition in 1876. One author maintains that the St. Henry window was damaged at that time, and that Lorin made the repairs in Philadelphia. The bulk of the windows was made by Lorin, but Ely was the artist for eleven.[39] Only two of the windows identify the artist, the Sacred Heart and the Paschal Lamb windows. The name *Lorin* followed by *Chartres, France,* appears on the face of the step below the figure of Christ in the Sacred Heart window. Lorin had begun studies for the figured windows as early as January 1874, after two meetings in Chartres with Archbishop McCloskey. He planned to visit New York personally, but there are no records confirming that he ever actually came to the City. Lorin's firm is still in existence today. All the windows were donated and they cost more than $100,000, a price Lorin described to Archbishop McCloskey as less than half of what he customarily charged for similar work in France.[40]

The gallery organ was the creation of George Jardine. A native of Dartford, England, where he was born in 1810, he was trained in London and arrived in the United States in 1835. His several establishments were all in New York, the last one located on Thirty-ninth Street where, with his son, he built the two Cathedral organs. He provided other instruments for the cathedrals of Mobile and Pittsburgh and for many other churches. The gallery organ was housed for many years in the Church of St. John the Evangelist, east of the Cathedral site, and built under the direction of the pastor, Father McMahon, but probably it was always intended for the Cathedral. Built at a cost of $30,000, it was forty-five feet high and twenty-six feet wide, with a richly decorated Gothic console case, the work of Paul Guibé; all the pipes were displayed in symmetrical groups. The organ was powered by four pairs of bellows blown by

The organ gallery, with the orignal Jardine organ, in a Cathedral Souvenir Book from 1898. Propriety prevails.

French treadles requiring "four stout men" to work them. There were four manuals, with five octaves of keys on each manual, one of only two such arrangements in the United States. Below, there was a full compass of pedals. Renwick supported the forty-six feet by twenty-eight feet gallery by a wrought iron girder capable of carrying one hundred tons. The gallery could seat one hundred singers. Rich moldings of ash decorated the gallery front and the ceiling underneath.[41]

For three months before the dedication date, William Pecher, the music director of St. Peter's Church and the designated Director of Music of the new Cathedral, had held rehearsals with two choirs of two hundred male and female voices in preparation for the great event. Haydn's *Grand Mass, No. 16, in B flat* was chosen for the liturgy, to be sung by the gallery choir, while the chancel voices prepared Gregorian chants for the processions and common parts of the Mass. James White, an English organist known for his keyboard skills, was engaged for the opening day services. In order to control seating for the large numbers expected to attend, tickets of admission were issued.[42] May 25th, the Sunday following Ascension Thursday, was the Feast of St. Gregory VII. It was a perfect spring day, "of all the days of renown, the gem of days, shining above all," in the words of the choristers. At 10:00 a.m., with an estimated 7000 persons exhausting all the floor space inside, a pageant on a scale never before seen in New York began to unfold, as the long procession of hundreds of priests, twenty-five bishops, six archbishops and America's Cardinal wound its way through the throng in the streets to the west front entrance. A cordon of police who bore themselves with the dignity they deemed appropriate for the occasion added further color, their uniformed ranks separating the multitude from those passing in procession. Their presence proved unnecessary as "the majestic solemnity and beauty of the ceremonies appeared to impress" the crowds, and there were no incidents of irreverence or disorderly behavior. One of the honored guests was James Renwick, whose joy was voiced in his speech following the liturgy. Cardinal McCloskey officiated at the solemn pontifical Mass. A chalice had been presented to him by Pope Leo XIII for the occasion, and the Pope's message was read to the congregation. Bishop Patrick Ryan, coadjutor of St. Louis and a future Archbishop of Philadelphia, who was considered the American hierarchy's outstanding preacher, delivered the sermon. Perhaps moved by the importance of the occasion, he spoke for two hours, later apologizing to the guests at a celebration dinner for his lack of compassion. Nonetheless, his words resounding through the great space were received with joy, as he asserted that "in the multitude and majesty of this temple, the evidence that the spirit of the ages of faith still lives on – that the spirit that planned and erected the vast cathedrals of the Old World survives in... this New World, and here are found heads to conceive, and hands to execute, and hearts to love the glorious monuments that shall until posterity be erected..." was all true. If Renwick's happiness was tempered by his disappointment at the modifications of his grand scheme, the Cardinal's joy was unbridled: he considered the completion of his Cathedral the "crowning achievement of his life."[43]

Not everyone in New York was so enthusiastic about the City's newest monument. Clarence Cook, who wrote about the City's architecture for the Tribune, produced a scathing article in the *Atlantic Monthly* magazine three months before opening day, in which he attacked Renwick's work, not only at St. Patrick's, but even in his designs of Grace Church and the Smithsonian. It was his claim that the work was inferior, especially at St. Patrick's, which, he wrote, was built of limestone. He also stated that the "City was jockeyed out the finest site on the island by the crafty and unscrupulous priest playing upon the political hopes and fears of as base a lot of men as ever got the government of a great city into their power." He maintained that the Archbishop, presumably Archbishop Hughes, had paid only one dollar for the plot. When the facts were laid out for him, he retracted his charges in a subsequent issue of the same periodical. A more studied critique appeared in *The American Architect and Building News* the month of the dedication. The length of the building was criticized as being too short in relation to its height, and aware that it lacked the Lady Chapel, Renwick undoubtedly concurred; the vault was called "unpardonable" and the reversal of plans for the flying buttresses was said to rob the exterior of "all its play of light and shadow." Few could contest the truth of the criticisms; on the other hand, the article lavished praise on the building for its proportions and lines and the nobility of its scale, and on the Church for its courage in undertaking such a monumental project. There was no building on the continent to match its greatness, and nobody disputed that assessment.[44]

To administer the Cathedral, Cardinal McCloskey appointed as Rector, Rev. William Quinn (*left*), who had held the same post in the old Cathedral until the new building opened. He was assisted by several priests, one of whom was Rev. Michael Lavelle, ordained shortly after opening day, and destined to remain until his death sixty years later, and to serve most of those years as the second rector. Father Quinn, who was made a domestic prelate in 1881 with the title *monsignor,* was a stern, abrupt man of acknowledged administrative and financial ability. He was the Cardinal 's closest advisor and his senior vicar general. Born in Donoughmore, County Donegal in Ireland, he came to the United States in 1841, and studied for the priesthood until his ordination in 1845. After four years of parish assignments, he became pastor of St. Peter's Church in 1849, and remained in that assignment for twenty-four years. In 1873, he was transferred to St. Patrick's (old) Cathedral where he served as both Rector and Vicar General of the Archdiocese. The Cardinal depended upon his authoritarian character to carry the many burdens of administering the Archdiocese, and he did so with devotion and skill. An "absolutist in church government," his personality counterbalanced the mildness of McCloskey's; he cared little for conventions or public opinion and was oblivious to ordinary social customs, even those of etiquette. His shortcomings paled, however, when set against his management abilities. Once offered the post as Coadjutor Archbishop of Cincinnati, he declined out of loyalty to Cardinal McCloskey and his duties in New York. He lived with his staff in a rented house at 26 East Fiftieth Street between Madison and Park Avenues until the present parish house was opened in May 1884. One of his assistants was Rev. Charles McDonnell, who became the second Bishop of Brooklyn. Cardinal McCloskey's home was not finished until 1882, so his residence, also rented, was at 32 East 56th Street, shared with his secretary, Father John Farley, who became Cardinal Archbishop of New York in the early years of the twentieth century. The boundaries of the Cathedral parish extended from Forty-second and Forty-fourth Streets north to Fifty-ninth Street and from Seventh Avenue to the East River. The status of cathedral transferred from Mulberry Street to the center of Manhattan, and the old Cathedral reverted to a parish church.[45] The original Cathedral remained dedicated to St. Patrick, but henceforth was called St. Patrick's Old Cathedral.

Regular religious services began at the Cathedral on the Sunday following the dedication. The music program was placed in the hands of William Pecher, who was also the principal organist. The former organist of St. Peter's Church was a native of New York where he received his early education. Subsequently, he attended St. Francis Xavier College in New York, conducted by the Jesuits. At the age of seventeen, he journeyed to Germany to continue his music studies at the Leipzig Conservatory of Music, where he studied under Hauptmann, Richter and Moscheles. When he returned to the United States four years later, he was appointed to the post at St. Peter's, where he served for twenty years until the opening of St. Patrick's. He was a prominent critic of church music and composed several masses. There were two choirs at the Cathedral, the mixed voices adult choir of sixty members directed by Pecher, and the fifty-voice boys' choir under the direction of Rev. Anthony Lammel. The $2800 chancel organ, a two manual and pedal instrument, which was not ready until 1881, was designed by Father Lammel for specific use as a choir organ.[46]

A few days after the opening, an auction was held for rental of pews in the Cathedral. Bids were made for fifty-three pews in amounts ranging from $50 to $2100. Many of the wealthiest Catholics in the City appeared at the auction and pew #1 received its $2100 bid from José F. de Navarro. The second highest pew was acquired through a bid of $750 by Eugene Kelly. De Navarro was recognized as the richest Spaniard in America and was a generous donor to charitable causes. He lived on Forty-sixth Street just west of Fifth Avenue. He was born in San Sebastian, Spain in 1823, and came to the United States as a young man to teach at the Jesuit college in Baltimore. Later he went to Cuba where he began his successful business career. He came to New York in 1855 where he achieved great commercial success. He helped organize the first steam line between the United States and Brazil, was an original director of the Equitable Life Assurance Company and was best known as the builder of the City's Metropolitan Elevated Railway system. His Central Park Apartments were the forerunner of today's apartment houses. Towards the end of his life he established the Portland Cement Company in the United States. W. R. Grace, twice Mayor of New York, replaced Mr. de Navarro as President of the Ingersoll-Rand Company. De Navarro died at age eighty-six in 1909. His daughter-in-law, the actress Mary Anderson, said of him: "He lived an American, but died a Spaniard," since he never became a citizen,

Castle Garden began as a fort some 200 feet from the mainland. It never fired a shot. The fort was ceded to the city which turned it into a public entertainment center. From 1855 to 1890, however, it was the Emigration Landing Depot, receiving 7.7 million immigrants in that period. By now, landfill had connected it to the city, but it still gave some distance to check for diseases among new arrivals and warn them against local entrepreneurs who would be offering them jobs at slave wages or trying to rent them rat-infested apartments or even sell them Manhattan island itself!

considering emancipation from his mother country disloyalty.[47]

The Cathedral parishioners were a mixture of poor immigrants and successful business people. The first altar boy, Thomas Smith, later became Secretary of Tammany Hall. Many parishioners lived in crowded tenements composed of several apartments or flats on each floor, to the east and west of Fifth Avenue. The 1880 census reported 1,206,299 persons living in New York; in 1888, 1,093,701 were living in tenements, defined as homes occupied by three families or more. Many of the tenement residents entered New York as immigrants, the most recent including large numbers from countries other than Ireland. By 1889, more Germans and English than Irish landed at Castle Garden, the place of debarkation (*above*). Following closely after the Irish were Italians, Russians, Poles and Hungarians. Squatters' huts were still in the neighborhood in the 1880s.[48]

A different world was emerging along Fifth Avenue, as fashionable homes of the wealthy were vying one with another to excel in architectural style and embellishment. Cornelius Vanderbilt II's home of brick and white stone in late Gothic and early Renaissance styles opened at Fifty-seventh Street in 1882. At Fifty-first Street, facing Renwick's Catholic Boys Orphan Asylum (*right*), was the triple-home residence of William Henry Vanderbilt; William Kassan Vanderbilt owned the home next to it at Fifty-second Street. Jay Gould's mansion was to the south at 579 Fifth Avenue and Thomas Fortune Ryan's home was at 858 Fifth Avenue. A favorite house of worship for fashionable New Yorkers, St.

Thomas Episcopal Church, opened at Fifty-third Street in 1870. Many magnificent private clubs whose furnishings were often "far superior to anything in England" also graced the neighborhood. On Madison Avenue at Forty-eighth Street was the expanded complex of Columbia College built in the Victorian collegiate Gothic style. The Catholic Girls Orphan Asylum (*right*) was at Fifty-second Street behind the Boys Asylum extending east from Fifth Avenue. On Fiftieth Street between Lexington and Fourth Avenues was the Women's Hospital of the State of New York, and the

The Sisters of Charity of St. Vincent de Paul served both orphan asylums as well as the Boland Trade School which adjoined them in the early 1890s. They also taught in the Cathedral elementary school on 51st St. between Park and Lexington Aves. They made these places possible.

Nursery and Child's Hospital was one block north. Also east of Fourth Avenue in the streets of the lower fifties were commercial buildings including a slaughter house, railroad sheds, the Shaefer Brewery and the Steinway piano factory. The New York and Harlem Railroad separated the elegant homes of the west from the industrial east. Its commuter cars were pulled by steam locomotives along Fourth Avenue, renamed Park Avenue in 1888.[49]

In the spring of 1880, the Trustees of St. Patrick's sold the section of the property bounded by Madison and Fourth Avenues and Fiftieth and Fifty-first Streets. The proceeds, $440,000, were intended for construction of the Archbishop's residence, the rectory and the parish school, but John Stewart, the purchaser, defaulted on provisions of the contract, obliging the Board of Trustees to take a mortgage on the property. Meanwhile, excavation work had already begun in September for a new Archbishop's home. On the following April 16th, Henry Villard and Colonel J. August Page purchased the block, Villard securing the larger parcel which extended from Madison Avenue to a point two hundred feet east of the Avenue, and Page holding the remainder which ran one-hundred-seventy feet to Fourth Avenue. Page later sold his portion to Villard. The Church of St. John the Evangelist, closed on the day the Cathedral opened, was removed, as was the Lylburn mansion which St. John's parish priests had used as a rectory. The Trustees earlier had rejected a bid for more money from a prospective buyer who planned to raise on the site what was called an opera house, but was more likely a music hall. Villard's contract contained a provision that only first-class private homes might be built on the land for a distance of two hundred feet from Madison Avenue. The Archbishop's residence at Madison Avenue and Fiftieth Street was completed in 1882, the same year when construction of the rectory at Fifty-first Street began. Msgr. (Monsignor) Quinn and his staff occupied the new building in 1884. Facing the two residences, Henry Villard's magnificent Italian Renaissance houses, now part of the the New York Palace Hotel, were designed by the firm of McKim, Mead and White and were built between 1882 and 1885.

Excavation of the land for the Cathedral school at Fiftieth Street between Lexington and Fourth Avenues began in 1880. The eighty-feet by one-hundred-five-feet brick building costing $90,000 opened two years later. From its beginning, the school maintained a reputation for excellence. Eleven hundred twenty-five students occupied the desks on opening day, the girls' division staffed by the Sisters of Charity, the boys' section by the Brothers of the Christian Schools.[50]

Cardinal McCloskey had reached his sixty-ninth birthday before the Cathedral opened. As early as six years before, he had considered requesting a coadjutor to assist him; in the spring of 1880, the declining condition of his health and the increasing labor his position required led to his formal request for help. Bishop Michael Corrigan, Bishop of Newark, New Jersey since May 1873, was one of three bishops whose names were suggested for the post. The forty-one-year-old prelate begged that his name be withdrawn, fearing the burden of the enormous responsibilities, since the appointment was for a coadjutor archbishop with the right of succession. This meant that whoever was chosen would become the next Archbishop of New York. When he learned of his appointment four days after the selection was made, he reflected: "One's graces are found in doing the will of God, not one's own will." For the next five years, the Coadjutor would lessen the burden of the aging Cardinal and be afforded the opportunity to become familiar and comfortable with the Archdiocese whose administration would be wholly his in 1885.[51]

The Cardinal's burdens became even lighter as it became apparent that earlier virulently prejudiced treatment of Catholics was declining in the City, perhaps due not so much to admiration of Catholicism as to a pervasive insouciance about religion in general in many quarters. Even the press was more tolerant: "The Sun took the attitude of fairness towards all the sects, and calmly discussed them and their critical moments from the viewpoint of inexorable logic. Catholics patronized it because it treated their religion with fairness, though not always with patience. Horace Greeley in the Tribune adopted a like attitude.... At the last, political leaders found it advantageous to seek out Catholics for certain campaigns.... Catholics had invaded every department of life and had secured eminence and power; in the most exclusive society, in all professions, in every form of business, in politics, in the army and navy, in journalism and letters, in art and education, they had to be reckoned with."[52]

The magnificence of the finest church building on the continent certainly contributed to the admiration, if not the respect, accorded the Church. The use of outstanding designs and materials to decorate the building drew praise. A member of the Kelly family who donated much to beautify the building was satisfied with nothing less than a John LaFarge design for the baptistry gates "in a rich material in keeping with the surroundings."

No less impressive were the many ceremonies conducted with all the splendor the Roman Catholic liturgy possessed, such as the 1881 episcopal consecration of Michael J. O'Farrell, Bishop of Trenton, New Jersey, the first such ceremony held in the building. In 1883, the remains of the founder of St. Patrick's, Archbishop Hughes, were solemnly transferred from the Old Cathedral crypt to the crypt below the high altar of the new building. Before interment, his coffin was placed on a catafalque, allowing the faithful to offer prayers as they streamed past during the night before and until the pontifical requiem Mass on January 30th. Joining the capacity crowd at the service were family members, several bishops, Archbishop Corrigan and Cardinal McCloskey. Later, the coffin was laid in the first of a series of *cubilia* in the crypt wall. Lined with white marble and stone of different colors, the crypt was able to accommodate forty-two coffins.[53]

Cardinal McCloskey's last major celebration was the great Mass on January 12, 1884 in honor of his golden anniversary of ordination to the priesthood. Nine bishops joined Archbishop Corrigan in offering accolades. A statue of the Cardinal was unveiled during the service, and Pope Leo XIII sent a chalice with his personal congratulations. The clergy of the Archdiocese presented the Cardinal with a gift of a new marble pulpit, although it would not be completed until after his death. Draddy Brothers, builders of ecclesiastical furnishings, was the company selected to make the pulpit which James Renwick designed. The Long Island City firm was chosen in April 1886, and commissioned to select white marble from the same quarry which had provided stone for the columns of the portico of the Pantheon in Rome. Other stone included Sienna marble in the columns, Carrara in the pedestal and Mexican onyx in the arch columns. Statuettes of St. Patrick, St. Peter, St. Paul, St. John the Evangelist and St. Andrew were inserted in the wall, and behind was positioned a devise in the shape of a shell to project the voice of the preacher to the congregation. All the carving and finishing was accomplished in Rome and the structure was assembled on a Cathedral pier just outside the altar railing. The symbolic association of St. Patrick's with Michelangelo and Ghiberti traces to the sharing of the materials used by those great artists and the maker of St. Patrick's pulpit. [54]

At the end of the jubilee Mass, the Cardinal, who was known as the "silver-tongued" prelate, reflected on his life's work as if in anticipation of approaching death, which was in fact less than two years away. He presented the congregation with a statistical portrait of the Archdiocese:

What had been one diocese with fifteen churches and about twenty priests at the time of his ordination were in 1884 eight dioceses with nine-hundred-fifty churches served by twelve hundred priests and ministering to over 1,400,000 Catholics. The Archdiocese itself contained about two-hundred-thirty churches and chapels and twenty-nine asylums served by about four hundred priests, including members of more than forty religious orders whose ranks also included 2,300 nuns and religious brothers. The Catholic population had grown to 600,000. Two thousand children were sheltered in orphanages, and five thousand poor children were being trained in industrial schools. Homes for the elderly housed seven hundred people, and there were six hospitals. About one thousand members of the St. Vincent de Paul Society cared for the destitute.[55]

In the following months, as the celebration faded in memory, Cardinal McCloskey's health sank rapidly; perceiving the Cardinal's death to be near, Archbishop Corrigan asked Archbishop Gibbons of Baltimore to agree to preach at the funeral Mass. By the spring of 1885, the Cardinal was able no longer to celebrate Mass, even while seated. Towards the end, indications of Parkinson's disease and a recurrence of malaria caused his weakness to sink into near helplessness.

At his bedside when he died in his residence at 12:45 a.m. on October 16, 1885 were several priests, vicars-general and Archbishop Corrigan.[56] The funeral (*facing page*) for the only Cardinal among sixty-one American bishops and archbishops was surrounded by solemnity. It was said that the "whole world turned out to see the funeral...." After the body was placed on a catafalque in the Cathedral, the Cardinal's red *galero* was set at his feet. For two days before the Mass, throngs passed in prayer. Hundreds of priests and many members of the hierarchy assisted at the requiem liturgy offered by Archbishop Corrigan.

Then, the coffin was carried to the crypt under the high altar and entombed next to that of Archbishop Hughes. Following an ancient tradition of the Church, the red *galero* was suspended from the Cathedral ceiling over the tomb.[57]

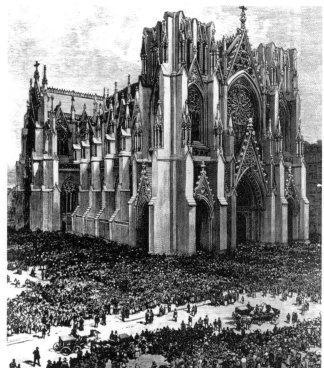

Drawing by Charles Graham

1. Smith, pp. 277-281.

2. *One Hundredth Anniversary – Roman Catholic Diocese of Brooklyn,* Supplement to The Tablet, Newspaper of the Diocese of Brooklyn, New York, October 31, 1953.

3. Cohalan, Msgr. Florence D., *First Prince of the Catholic Church in the United States,* Knights of Columbus Council 4505, New Haven, Ct., 1975, *passim,* pp. 4-44.

4. *Ibid.,* pp. 15, 34.

5. Smith, pp. 283, 284.

6. Farley, *The Life of John Cardinal McCloskey,* New York, 1918, as quoted in Carthy, *A Cathedral of Suitable Magnificence,* footnote 45, Chapter 2. Despite the onerous task, the Archbishop was quite successful in raising large donations. One of his committees secured several large contributions including two over $5000, five of $5000, and forty-two of $1000. He also received financial help from the trustees who sold property, took a mortgage on the property and obtained loans. For specifics, *see:* Carthy, *A Cathedral of Suitable Magnificence,* p. 42.

7. *Circular Letter of Archbishop McCloskey,* Feast of St. Patrick [March 17], 1865, AANY. The Archbishop recognized that some of the original subscribers had found it impossible to fulfill their obligations, that "others have paid in part, and will, doubtless, make good the balance whenever called upon; others, again, may have been awaiting some more favorable opportunity, which, we trust, the resumption of the work will very soon afford them."

8. Pierson, p. 214; *New York Sun,* c. April 1, 1873. According to the great-great grandson of William Joyce, the family lived in New Jersey where they owned quarries. Joyce was buried in Belleville, New Jersey. *See:* Robert Joyce to W. Knight Sturges, undated, but 1973, ASPC. An article published just before the Cathedral opened mentioned some of those associated with William Joyce including Thomas Joyce, the superintendent; "Mr. Dwyer, the foreman stonecutter..."; "Mr. Gibbons, framer; Mr. Oakley Osborne, slater; and the Healy Iron Works of Brooklyn." *See: Journal of the Fair,* October 23, 1878, p. 2.

9. Farley, appendix listing donors; Carthy, *Magnificence,* p. 42 and note 48, Chapter 2; Shannon, p. 464.

10. Cohalan, *First Prince of the Catholic Church in the United States,* hereafter cited as *First Prince,* pp. 48, 49; Cohalan, *Popular History,* p. 89.

11. Carthy, *Old St. Patrick's,* p. 92.

12. Rattner, Macmillan Encyclopedia of Architects, V. 3.

13. Metropolitan Journal, November 1867.

14. *New York Times,* April 5, 1868. It is interesting that the Times article makes mention of a plan to plaster the arches of the nave and aisles rather than to use stone. It is generally recorded, or at least implied, in other records, that the decision to eliminate the stone ceiling came several years later, around 1874. Another difficulty found in this article is the mention of a total of one-hundred-three windows expected to be built in the Cathedral. The Cathedral today has seventy-one windows including the fifteen added when the Cathedral was expanded after the death of Renwick, and one is challenged to consider where one-hundred-three windows would have been placed, even in the original larger plan of Renwick. The Manual of the Corporation of the City of New York for 1868 also reports that "there will be in all one hundred and three windows...." (p. 463.)

15. Renwick to Board of Trustees, Minutes of Board of Trustees, December 1888.

16. *New York Sun,* c. April 1, 1873; *New York Times,* May 5, 1950. The *New York Sun* article charged that there may have been improprieties on the part of the builder, suggesting that the marble used in the upper sections of the Cathedral need not have been used, that there was an ample supply at the original quarry in Westchester County and that the cost of the original quarry marble was lower than that from the (Massachusetts) quarry used later.

17. Bergen County Democrat, February 3, 1871.

18. Farley, p. 151.

19. *Catholic Review,* August 1, 1874; Farley, p. 128; Smith, pp. 286-289. The carriage and the harness of the horses "created a sensation on Madison Avenue" when they were presented to the Cardinal-elect. Among those who were among the presenters and donors were Eugene Kelly and José F. de Navarro, wealthy parishioners about whom further information will be presented later in this volume. Many years later, as Cardinal McCloskey approached the end of his life, the Board of Trustees approved an expenditure of $1200 for another team of horses. *See:* Minutes of the Board of Trustees, December 1883.

20. Cohalan, *Popular History,* p. 96; Carthy, *Old St. Patrick's,* p. 95; Freeman's Journal, March 20, 1875; Smith, pp. 286-289.

21. Pierson, pp. 245-247

22. Renwick to Trustees, Minutes of the Board of Trustees, December 6, 1888.

23. Contract and specifications of the architects, March 5, 1859, ASPC.

24. Pierson, pp. 245-247.

25. *Journal of the Fair,* November 29, 1878; Letter of Power Brothers, copy, ASPC. Some of the ceiling was painted and was executed "in the manner of the fifteenth century." Renwick had specified: "All the ceilings of the chapels, of the side aisles, the center aisle, all the ceilings of the various stories of the towers will be groined arched ceilings vaulted with brick masonry of best hard bricks with paneled [sic] sides, laid in cement mortar of the best description per directions of architects. The principal ribs of ceilings to be 10 x 20 inches, the secondary ribs 12 x 10 inches and the smaller ribs to be bracketed. The filling in of the groins between the ribs will be from 4 to 8 inches thick according to the plans and directions to be given by architects – all the above work to be laid to a close joint in the best cement mortar, grouted in the upper courses and slated, and the centers to be struck when the arches are keyed. Hollow brick, if they can be obtained at

reasonable cost, may be used for the filling in between the ribs.... Flag bond stones will be laid in the main ribs of the center ceiling." (Contract and specifications of the architects, March 5, 1859, ASPC *and Journal of the Fair*, November 29, 1878).

26. *Cathedral Bulletin*, August 1946; Renwick to Trustees, Minutes of Board of Trustees, December 6, 1888. It is possible, even likely, that the date for construction of the roof —1877 — is an error, since Father (later Cardinal) Farley, who was Cardinal McCloskey's secretary, wrote to the Cardinal in August 1876 that the roof was leaking. He wrote: "The roof of the Cathedral withstood the rain better this time than on former occasions thus showing that the repairs are effective...." Still, there was some water seeping around the chancel area. The roofer believed the leakage came, not from poor work, but from cracked slates resulting from tools or blocks of wood thrown by workers to the roofs from the upper windows. The leaking roof, then, was probably the lower roof over the chapels in the chancel area, and the 1877 date may refer to the year when the *entire* roof was completed. *See:* Farley to McCloskey, August 1, 1876, AANY.

27. Farley to McCloskey, July 18, 1876 and August 1, 1876, AANY.

28. Carthy, *Magnificence,* p. 42.

29. *Journal of the Fair*, October 22 to November 30, 1878, *passim;* Frank Leslie's *Illustrated Newspaper*, October 23, November 2, 1878; *New York Times*, November 12, December 1, 1878; Farley, p. 129.

30. Farley, pp. 153-155, 229, 230; *Catholic Review*, May 27, 1879.

31. *Journal of the Fair*, October 28, October 30, November 29, 1878; *Catholic Review,* May 27, 1879; Quinn, n.p. Gas was purchased from the New York Mutual Company.

32. *Journal of the Fair*, November 29, 1878; Quinn, n.p.; *Catholic Review*, May 27, 1879. The heating contractors were "Messrs. Gillis and Geoghegan of 116 and 118 Wooster Street...."

33. Specifications of the architects, ASPC. The tiles were to be not "less than 2 inches in thickness... [and not] less than 2 square feet in superficies," and bedded in cement mortar set in coarse concrete.

34. Renwick to Trustees, Minutes of the Board of Trustees, October 16, December 6, 1888; *Journal of the Fair*, November 29, 1878; *Catholic Review*, May 27, 1879; Drawings of Architect, AANY; New York World, December 15, 1895.

35. Drawings of the Architect, AANY; Farley, pp. 173-175; *The Solemn Blessing and Opening of the New Cathedral of St. Patrick, New York,* Catholic Publication Society, New York, 1879, n.p.; *Journal of the Fair*, November 29, 1878; Quinn, n.p. For the most part, the altars were built in Italy, "but the stones of which they are composed represent many countries on the two continents...." (John Talbot Smith, *Cathedral Bells,* Jenkins Company, New York, 1898.) To clarify the locations of two altars, the altar of the Blessed Mother was against the east wall of the Cathedral where the north aisle ended abruptly. The aisle thus formed a chapel from the east wall to the beginning of the transept. On the south side of the sanctuary, in a corresponding location, was the sacristy, utilizing about half the floor area required for the Blessed Mother (Lady) chapel. The other half, from the end of the sacristy to the beginning of the south transept was a chapel in honor of St. Joseph.

36. Renwick to Trustees, Minutes of the Board of Trustees, December 6, 1888; *Journal of the Fair*, November 29, 1878.

37. *The Solemn Blessing and Opening of the New Cathedral of St. Patrick, New York,* p. 12

38. Stephen B. McNally to Thomas G. Young, August 14, 1989, ASPC.

39. The *American Architect and Building News*, January 19, 1878; Drawings of the Architect, AANY. Ely was the artist for the following windows: *The Life of St. Patrick (called the titular window); Sts. Augustine and Monica; The Sacred Heart; The Three Baptisms; St. Matthew; St.*

Mark; St. Luke; St. John; St. Vincent de Paul; St. Charles Borromeo; Sts. Agnes, James and Thomas.

40. Benezit, E., *Dictionnaire Critique et Documentaire de Peintres, Sculpteurs, Dessinateurs et Graveurs*, Librairie Grund, Paris, 1976; *The Solemn Blessing and Opening of the New Cathedral of St. Patrick, New York*, pp. 20, 21; *Journal of the Fair*, November 7, November 23, 1878; McNally, Augustin, *Historical Guide to St. Patrick's, New York*, Brown-McNally Associates, New York, 1931, n.p.; Drawings of the Architect, AANY; Lorin to McCloskey, January 7, 1874, ASPC. Lorin was planning his visit to New York in May 1874 when he intended to set up a representative in the City, a certain Mr. Dumont-Pallier de Bornoubille [spelling uncertain]. He felt his personal visit was a requirement for achieving success in balancing the proper play of light with his glass. The completed windows may have been installed by "Munstor of Bleecker Street." (*New York Times*, May 18, 1879) The rose window was one of those containing *cathedral glass*.

41. American Art Journal, June 1879, February 1882, August 1886; *The Solemn Blessing and Opening of the New Cathedral of St. Patrick, New York*, p. 21; *New York Times*, May 18, 1879; Renwick to Trustees, Minutes of the Board of Trustees, December 6, 1888; *Journal of the Fair*, November 29, 1878; *Catholic Review*, May 27, 1879.

42. Keokuk Constitution (Keokuk, Iowa), May 21, 1879.

43. Cohalan, *Popular History*, p. 98; *Catholic Review*, May 27, 1879; *New York Times*, May 26, 1879; Smith, p. 291; *Journal of the Fair*, November 29, 1878; Farley, pp. 130-133. Many non-Catholics were in the congregation on opening day. One of the archbishops in the sanctuary was Archbishop Purcell of Cincinnati, a friend of Cardinal McCloskey since the latter's seminary days at St. Mary's in Baltimore where Purcell was President when Cardinal McCloskey was a student. The Archbishop was planning to make an appeal after the celebration dinner to raise $50,000 for his own archdiocese which was "in financial straits." Clerics assisting the Cardinal in the sanctuary included Father John Farley, Father Charles McDonnell, Father William Quinn, and Father Edward McGlynn, all of whom became famous in subsequent years. The ceremonies lasted from 10:00 a.m. until 3:05 p.m., much of the time consumed by the oration of Bishop Ryan, who asserted that the great monument was built chiefly "by the pennies of the poor."

44. The Atlantic Monthly, February 1879; The *American Architect and Building News*, May 31, 1879. Clarence Cook had been assigned to a post at the *Tribune* in 1870 by Whitelaw Reid, who owned the newspaper in the era following Horace Greeley's tenure. Reid later purchased the Villard houses on Madison Avenue opposite the east end of the Cathedral. *See:* Shopsin, William et al., *The Villard Houses*, Viking Press, New York 1980, p. 113.

45. Cohalan, *Popular History*, pp. 98, 99; Smith, pp. 202, 203, 284; , April 17, 1887; *Catholic Review*, May 24, 1879; Carthy, *Magnificence*, p. 50; Minutes of the Board of Trustees, June 1, 1881; interview with Msgr. Florence Cohalan, December 1994 (re: Bishop Charles McDonnell).

46. Carthy, *Magnificence*, pp. 49, 50; *American Art Journal*, August 7, 1886; , February 29, 1904; *Catholic Review*, September 22, 1888; Farley, pp. 224, 225; Minutes of the Board of Trustees, June 2, 1888; *The World*, December 15, 1895. The *American Art Journal* reported that Pecher "regards his facial appearance of no particular interest to mankind, and has sturdily evaded photographic temptations." Referring to reports that he was paid $2000 per year by the Cathedral, Pecher exclaimed: "It's not the public's business," believing people to be unpardonably inquisitive.

47. Eric Beerman to Thomas G. Young, June 5, 1996, ASPC; *New York Times*, February 4, 1909 and May 30, 1879.

48. Riis, Jacob, *How The Other Half Lives – Studies Among the Tenements of New York*,

Dover Publications, Inc., New York, 1971 appendix; Carthy, *Magnificence,* p. 52; Shopsin et al., pp. 23-25; Lavelle to Hayes, June 29, 1931, AANY.

49. Shopsin et al., pp. 23-25; Carthy, *Magnificence,* pp. 50-52; Souvenir of the Centennial Celebration of St. Patrick's, New York, 1809-1909, New York, 1909, n.p.; *Journal of the Fair,* November 7, 9, 16, 1878; *New York Times,* August 30, 1998, Sect. RE, p. 5. There is conflicting information about the dates both the boys and the girls orphanages were built. The authors may refer to different buildings, i.e., it is possible that new buildings replaced the originals, accounting for the discrepancies.

50. Minutes of the Board of Trustees, April 3, June 2, September 1, 1880; 1882 *passim;* Shopsin et al., *passim;* Farley, pp. 114, 150, 151; Carthy, *Magnificence,* pp. 74, 76; Quinn, n.p.; *Stanford White's New York,* exhibition pamphlet of Municipal Arts Society, November 10-December 4, 1992, Urban Center, New York, n.p. Cost of construction of the rectory was estimated at $75,000. The foundations were twelve feet deep and two-and-one-half feet thick. The walls above were Tuckahoe marble. Work began on January 20, 1882 and was finished on July 31, 1883. *See:* Detailed Statement of Specifications for New Buildings, Fire Department of the City of New York, 1883, ASPC.

51. Cohalan, *Popular History,* p. 100; *Memorial of the Most Rev. Michael Augustine Corrigan, D. D.,* The Cathedral Library Association, New York, 1902, pp. 61, 62.

52. Smith, pp. 531, 532.

53. M. A. Kelly to Corrigan, undated, microfilm C-4, AANY; Carthy, *Magnificence,* p. 55; Farley, pp. 134, 174; *Journal of the Fair,* November 29, 1878; The Solemn Blessing and Opening of the New Cathedral of St. Patrick, p. 10. The December 3, 1885 issue of The Art Age stated that Eugene Kelly had donated the gates of the baptistry. The present baptistry is not the original. John La Farge (1835-1910) helped establish the Metropolitan Museum of Art in 1870. He was known for his mural painting and the manufacture and design of stained glass. Some of his work in New York is "unsurpassed in the United States." *See:* Delaney, pp. 309-310.

54. Farley, pp. 135, 176, 177; Cohalan, *Popular History,* p. 101; Minutes of the Board of Trustees, October 7, 1886; various bills for construction of pulpit, box: St. Patrick's Cathedral, folder 6, G-43, AANY; , June 13, 1897. The total cost of the pulpit was about $1600. The railing was made by Travis and Murray, not by Draddy Brothers.

55. Souvenir of the Centennial Celebration of St. Patrick's, New York, 1809-1909, n.p.; Cohalan, *Popular History,* p. 101; Smith, pp. 285, 286; Farley, pp. 136, 137.

56. Carthy, *Magnificence,* p. 57; Cohalan, *Popular History,* p. 103; Catholic Review, October 17, 1885.

57. Carthy, *Magnificence,* pp. 57, 58; Cohalan, *Popular History,* p. 103; *Catholic Review,,* October 17, 24, 1885; Farley, pp. 133-152, *passim.*

CHAPTER V

Taking Shape: The Years of Archbishop Michael Corrigan

In the years after the Civil War, the New York City which Cardinal McCloskey had left behind grew and prospered, much as the Church did. By the 1880s, there was no doubt that New York was perceived almost universally as America's premier city. The City fathers and its wealthy citizens such as J. Pierpont Morgan were quick to take advantage of the most modern conveniences like Thomas Edison's incandescent lamp, while most of the rest of the world depended on gas, or even candles, for illumination. In 1883, when the Brooklyn Bridge opened, the world was awed by the great steel structure with the longest span of any bridge on earth. Two years later, the noble lady of the harbor, the Statue of Liberty, was dedicated, and soon became the most famous statue on earth. Great waves of immigrants, especially Jews from northern and eastern Europe disembarking in lower Manhattan, joined second and third generation German and Irish Americans who found a haven in the City. In the thirty-five years before the 1890s, about seven million aliens stepped off ships at the Battery, so many that the huge Ellis Island immigration center had to be opened. Andrew Carnegie's great music auditorium, Carnegie Hall, made its debut within the boundaries of the Cathedral parish. During this same era, the dream of building the world's largest Gothic cathedral, St. John the Divine, was conceived. Great hotels were opened and businesses were established at dizzying rates of speed. The City, on one hand, flaunted the wealth and social status of its most famous residents while, on the other hand, it often ignored the hardships of the unfortunate majority.[1]

Although skilled workers were sometimes able to amass substantial sums of money, the unskilled often suffered miserably. Early labor leaders such as Terence Powderly maintained that "a deep-rooted feeling of discontent pervades the masses." Still, while poverty was the chief reason for alienation, the perception that a better life was attainable may have increased the bitterness when plans were thwarted or when the speed of attainment was slowed. Indeed, conditions were improving slowly. The eleven-hour day had yielded to ten or fewer hours, and with increasing frequency there was talk in labor circles of an eight-hour day.[2] Regardless of the fact of improvement, the economic reformer, Henry George, gained broad exposure for his belief that an ever-widening gap between the wealthy and the poor would lead civilization itself to destruction. Propagation of the theories of George and other reformers spawned public debate among New Yorkers, and supporters or opponents were found as often among Church officials as among the people at large. Michael Augustine Corrigan, the new Archbishop of New York, was to find that adherents or opponents of George's theories and those of others would mark the prelate's tenure with internal controversy.[3]

Archbishop Corrigan was given the reins of the Archdiocese automatically on the death of Cardinal McCloskey. He was born into a comfortably prosperous family in Newark, New Jersey on August 13, 1839 and, following private education at home, attended school in Wilmington, Delaware; later he entered Mt. St. Mary's College in Emmitsburg, Maryland. He was one of the first students accepted to study for the priesthood at the North

American College in Rome, and after his ordination in 1863 he pursued a doctorate in divinity, the degree awarded to him in June 1864. Never assigned to parish work after his return to America, he taught in the Seton Hall seminary and rapidly stepped up the ranks to the office of president of both college and seminary.

He was named vicar general of the Newark Diocese and, in February 1873, became Bishop of Newark, at age thirty-three the youngest member of the episcopacy in the country. An active and competent administrator, he was no less a zealous shepherd. Cardinal McCloskey, who had consecrated him a bishop, was pleased to learn that Bishop Corrigan was appointed the Cardinal's Coadjutor seven years later.[4]

"There was a sort of child-like innocence, simplicity and lack of self-consciousness which contributed strongly to the impression of permanent youthfulness of nature which was always obtained by those who saw much of the Archbishop." His recreation centered typically on the study of mathematics and astronomy, and he instinctively shied away from public view. He had a "remarkable power of concentration" which accommodated his predilection for academic pursuits. He was fluent in French, Italian and Latin and he read Hebrew, Spanish and Greek proficiently. Once on a stroll along Fifth Avenue, he joined in conversation with a native of France who was a teacher in a private school. As the two continued walking, the discussion in a smooth-flowing French with "only the slightest foreign accent" moved between French classics and late French literature.[5] The Archbishop received the sign of his episcopal office, the *pallium*, in March 1886, during an investiture ceremony attended by the elaborate pageantry which by this time was expected. Three archbishops, twelve bishops and four hundred priests participated in the ceremony attended by an overflow crowd, the most illustrious member of which was the Governor of New Jersey.[6]

Within a year, a disagreement involving Rev. Edward McGlynn, an advocate of Henry George's theories, and Archbishop Corrigan erupted in newspapers and in public forums. McGlynn's refusal to obey directives of the Archbishop resulted in his suspension from his duties. Later, he was excommunicated from the Church by Roman authorities, although several years later he was restored to parish work. During Archbishop Corrigan's seventeen years in his office, this issue — and others of national import — were in the forefront. He was never named a cardinal, as many expected he would be because of both his talent and the importance of his office; the controversies hovering about his administration may have precluded a red hat, perhaps not so much because Rome was displeased with him, but

*Fr. McGlynn (table left) and Henry George (table right) at the 2nd National
Single Tax Conference, in Chicago, 1893.*

because curial officials were reluctant to appear eager to stamp their approval on either side
of the fiery public issues.[7]

Internal disarray did not forestall improvements at the Cathedral. The Girls Orphan
Asylum, as we saw, opened east of the boys division in 1885.[8] From the time the Cathedral
doors opened in 1879, no construction had been undertaken to complete the building,
but the same year when the girls orphanage opened, work began to raise the spires on the
west front facing Fifth Avenue. The marble chosen, Beaver Dam marble, closely resembled
the two varieties used earlier. It came from a quarry in Cockeysville, Maryland, fifteen miles
from Baltimore. The same stone was used for the columns of the United States Capitol
building and the Washington Monument. Peter Hamilton, a master builder, was in charge
of the project, under the direction of the Baltimore-based George Mann Company, which
bid $200,000 for the right to the contract. $120,000 of that amount had been contributed by parishioners. During three years, Renwick's exquisite masonry soared higher and
higher until the finial crosses attached to the peaks by copper rods reached the three-
hundred-thirty-feet mark in October 1888. More than fifty feet had been added in 1887
and the building was seventy feet short of completion by August of 1888. So, in the final
two months, more height was added than during the entire previous year. These tallest
church spires in America were surpassed in height only by Philadelphia's City Hall, which,
by the turn of the century, was itself surpassed only by the Washington Monument. The
new octagonal spires rested upon octagonal lanterns with windows and fine tracery. Pinnacles were set on the eight-corner buttresses. The spires were built in two stories terminating in foliage finials supporting the crosses.[9]

After scaffolding was removed, glass was positioned in the towers in 1889 and a spiral
masonry staircase replaced temporary step ladders in the south tower. Renwick estimated
that by 1888 two million to two-and-one-half million dollars had been expended, and
Archbishop Corrigan announced that the next project would be the addition of some east
end chapels including a Lady Chapel.[10] But Renwick's thoughts were for a permanent
sacristy. Both in 1886 and in 1887 he wrote to Archbishop Corrigan outlining his proposal. He indicated, further, that Msgr. Quinn, the first Rector, had approved his plans.

The sacristy was to be located "under the window of the south side aisle and extending from the south wall of the Cathedral to Fiftieth Street," protruding from where the Archbishop's sacristy is today. To this day, that sacristy has not been built, but sacristies were constructed below ground several years later. Nonetheless, even after the lower rooms were finished, an additional above-ground sacristy remained under consideration.[11]

While the spires were being built, Msgr. Quinn's physicians advised him to make a trip to Europe in the hope that a long rest would improve his failing health. After he was accorded a testimonial dinner at Delmonico's Restaurant, he left for the continent in mid-1886. His health appeared to be improved after he spent several months in France and Ireland, but four days after he left Nice destined for Ireland, from which country he expected to leave for home, he died suddenly in Paris on April 15, 1887. Rev. Michael C. O'Farrell of St. Theresa's Church in New York, his travelling companion, administered the last sacraments to him. He was buried in Calvary Cemetery.[12]

Rev. Michael J. Lavelle (*below*) was temporary administrator of St. Patrick's during Msgr. Quinn's absence and was chosen to succeed him as Rector. Thirteen days after the Cathedral opened in 1879, the newly-ordained Father Lavelle was given his first parish assignment at St. Patrick's; he spent the rest of his life in that assignment. He was the most widely-known of all the rectors, and held many other offices while administering the Cathedral. He was born in New York to a family of comfortable means on May 30, 1856, and he was baptized in Old St. Patrick's Cathedral. His father carried him to the laying of the

Ministering at the Cathedral from 1879 to 1939 — 52 of those years as Rector — his openness and leadership led to an untold number of programs and services.

cornerstone of the new Cathedral when he was two years old. Following elementary school, he attended LaSalle Academy, conducted by the Christian Brothers, and he continued his studies under their guidance at Manhattan College. A year after he was awarded his B. A. degree, he entered St. Joseph's Seminary in Troy, New York, and was ordained in the new Cathedral on June 7, 1879. At age twenty-three, he was much younger than the usual age for ordination. He was thirty years old when he was made temporary administrator, and less than a year later he was named Rector.[13]

From the day he assumed his office, numerous events and activities quickly grew in number under his close supervision. He monitored the completion of the spires, aided by John Coveney, the building engineer who was hired in 1884 after his predecessor fell to his death from the Cathedral roof. Coveney was a loyal worker for fifty years until his own death in 1934.[14] Aware of his administrative ability, Father Lavelle recognized that he was a priest before all else and that his primary work for the people of God was pastoral.

His parish consisted of 12,000 members who filled the pews joined by many visitors each Sunday during six scheduled Masses or vespers services, and at many weddings and other special liturgies. Often there were visiting celebrants or guest preachers augmenting the regular staff of priests who assisted Father Lavelle and rationed their time between the usual demands of parish work and the unusual demands of Catholic America's great religious monument with an international reputation. The staff included Rev. Thomas McCloskey who became President of Fordham University after joining the Society of Jesus (Jesuits). With a mixture of slight embarrassment and mischievous delight, Father McCloskey later told how, as a young altar boy accompanying Archbishop Corrigan during an *asperges* rite (when the celebrant sprinkles the congregation with holy water), he stepped on the bottom of the Archbishop's vestment causing him to stumble and spill out the water over the rest of what he was wearing. Vestments were dampened, but not spirits, as they two became good friends.[15]

In those early days, on a typical working Saturday, the sacristan was accustomed to arrive before the 5:30 a.m. opening, to light the burners in the north aisle Lady Chapel where Mass was offered at 6 o'clock. When the Fifth Avenue doors were opened, a small group of worshippers was waiting under the dim light of the flickering gas lamps on the streets outside. Some came to pray before beginning a day's work, some stopped on their return from a night shift, all depositing their lunch pails unattended just inside the door, unconcerned that a thief might intrude into so sacred a place. By the start of the Mass, the early arrivals were joined by elegantly attired ladies or gentlemen ferried to the doors in expensive carriages, some, perhaps, praying for a safe journey on a steamer to Europe. Father Lavelle frequently offered the first Mass and customarily spent the next half-hour in meditation and silent prayer before hearing confessions of penitents until the end of the 7:30 Mass. Archbishop Corrigan's normal practice was to celebrate one of the morning Masses and to kneel in one of the pews for thanksgiving prayer afterwards. At the 7:30 Mass, more silk, less denim and cotton were evident in the clothes of congregants. No matter the hour or the financial condition, devotion was intense and attendance was faithful. In the following hours until mid-morning, visitors streamed through the aisles in constant flow. "The merchant princes rub elbows with seedy seekers for work to keep body and soul together," one reporter observed. The sacristan, recognized by his flowing dark robes, answered visitors' queries, explained features of the building to them or directed them to the tomb of the Archbishops.

At 10 a.m., one of the curates made his way down the north chapel aisle to the baptistry where he began the rite of baptism for four infants — three foundlings and one child born of privilege — over whose foreheads the same indiscriminating water of salvation flowed. Meanwhile, the sexton, William T. A. Hart, who later in life conducted a funeral business on Madison Avenue, prepared the altar for a festive service presided over by the Archbishop. At ll o'clock, the roar of the grand organ signalled the start of a wedding procession with all its concomitant pomp. A prosperous banker and his bride were united in marriage during a solemn Mass. The episcopal blessing was bestowed on them before the couple processed to Fifth Avenue and a waiting fleet of grand carriages. Within a half-hour, the white altar draperies signifying joy were replaced by the purple of mourning; the pews began to fill with figures in clerical garb of priests, monks and nuns gathered to pray for the soul of a deceased priest whose casket was solemnly carried up the central aisle and set on a catafalque before the altar. Filling the sanctuary were priests attending the Archbishop who ascended his throne to preside over the obsequies. An hour later the scene changed once again when the sanctuary lights were extinguished and the bustling movement of tourists resumed; visitors continued to enter, make rounds of the building and leave throughout the afternoon. At 4 o'clock all the priests of the rectory staff and the Archbishop himself occupied the several confessionals in the chapels to receive penitents patiently awaiting in lines. Confessions were heard until ll p.m. with an hour's interruption for dinner. After the last penitent left, the doors were secured for the night.[16]

The ordinary routine as just illustrated was often interrupted by extraordinary liturgies such as those of the 1886 synod and the annual New Year's Day Mass attended by some six thousand members of the Holy Name Society of the Archdiocese, a group pledged to "diminish profanity in themselves and in others." Under Fr. Lavelle's leadership, the parish sponsored active societies including the Cathedral Literary Society which arranged lectures; the League of the Sacred Heart; and the Cathedral Club. Rev. Joseph McMahon, a priest on the staff, founded the Cathedral Free Circulating Library in 1887, and served as its director until it merged with the New York Public Library in 1904. It was the largest Catholic circulating library in the United States. To support the library, Fr. McMahon organized the Cathedral Library Association. He also helped Fr. Lavelle, who was president, to establish the Catholic Summer School of America. If anyone could rival Fr. Lavelle in ability, Fr. McMahon came the closest. He was at St. Patrick's from 1886 until 1900. He was an excellent public speaker and in the public forum he vigorously defended Catholic interests. An example of his commitment occurred years after he left the Cathedral, when he engaged officials of St. Luke's Hospital in a dispute. They had refused him permission to visit a parishioner who was a patient, because he was a Catholic priest.[17]

In 1888 there was a joyous liturgy in the Cathedral celebrating the Archbishop's silver jubilee of priestly ordination. The same year, Rev. John Kellner succeeded Fr. Lammel as Director of the Boys Choir; he held the post until 1892 when James Ungerer succeeded him. Twelve years later, Ungerer was appointed the second music director of St. Patrick's.[18] Also in 1888, James Renwick wrote a report for the Board of Trustees in which he made recommendations for future projects at the Cathedral. He was especially anxious that plans for a Lady Chapel and a sacristy be revived and that the temporary plaster ceiling be replaced by one of galvanized iron with zinc ornaments on wrought iron frames, rather than the wooden supports in place; surprisingly, he did not suggest a masonry ceiling as had been in his first design. His concern was that wooden frames were dangerous, and he advised that, until such time as replacement was made, regular inspections should occur to guarantee "future stability of the cathedral." Conversely, he was confident that the masonry work was "as good as in any building erected in modern times, and will want very little done" for years to come. Undoubtedly aware of the financial pressures the Trustees faced, he did not recommend that the flying buttresses removed from plans in the 1870s be restored at that time. The danger of fire in the ceiling area greatly concerned him and he proposed that an iron tank be installed in one of the towers. He wanted a pump built to force water from the tank into pipes pierced with holes and set along the ridges of the roof and also between the roof and the ceiling, so that both could be saturated in the event of fire.

Another suggestion was that a system of chimes be erected in the north spire using vulcanized rubber springs to relieve vibration and resultant damage to the masonry. He reminded the Board that it was the expressed wish of Archbishop Hughes that wealthy Catholics provide funds for altars in the nave chapels, still empty nine years after the building opened. [19]

Renwick's dream of a completed cathedral would not be realized in his lifetime. Instead, in the decade beginning in 1890, attention was directed at embellishing the interior, especially adding several altars, statues, a set of bells and stations of the cross. Father Lavelle, on the other hand, did not abandon Renwick's hopes: he was working to secure donations for a Lady Chapel at the Madison Avenue end of the building. In April 1890, he expressed the hope that Eugene Kelly, a successful banker married to a niece of Archbishop Hughes, might contribute the means to build the chapel. One of Kelly's sons, however, informed the Rector that it was improbable that funds would be forthcoming during the elder Kelly's lifetime, but that Mrs. Kelly and her sons planned a memorial after the elder Kelly's death. Eugene Kelly died four years later, but the memorial took several more years to be realized, and the cost was far higher than the $100,000 Fr. Lavelle estimated was needed in 1890. [20]

In the same year, 1890, Daniel Daly, the father of one of the parish priests, Rev. William J. Daly, presented the first of many aisle chapel altars. The chapel was dedicated to St. Veronica, and the altar, designed by James Renwick in a simple Gothic style, had a mosaic on the reredos depicting the impression of the Holy Face which Christ left on St. Veronica's veil during His journey to Calvary. This, the only mosaic in St. Patrick's, was copied from a famous original, and it reproduced the original's oddity: the eyes of Jesus seemed turned upward or downward, or appeared to be closed, depending on where the observer was standing. Archbishop Corrigan consecrated the chapel in February the following year. [21]

To the altar shrines, like this one of St. Anthony (the most popular of all), the faithful bring their prayers — for a child struggling or a parent who cared, for a memory that still hurts or a plan in the works, for lonely friends or nations at war. Keeping the flame of faith alive.

In memory of four of his predecessors named John, the Archbishop personally gave the $5400 cost of the chapel dedicated to St. John the Evangelist. Renwick's firm designed the altar and John Draddy of New York's Draddy Brothers, the company which had built the pulpit, was awarded the contract in August 1892. Draddy went to Siena, Italy to find high quality marble and worked on the altar in Carrara. Archbishop Corrigan reviewed photographs of early models and asked Draddy to modify Renwick's design, sending Draddy his own pen and ink sketch. It was Draddy's idea to station an eagle, the sign of the Evangelist, at the foot of the statue. The chapel was consecrated in May 1894.[22]

Obviously pleased with Draddy's first effort, Cathedral authorities chose him to complete several more chapel altars. The artist was born in 1833 and built his reputation for excellence in sculpture in Cincinnati before he moved to New York. He found another opportunity to prove his skill when he was awarded a contract to produce another altar, this one to replace the original Holy Family altar. Joseph Donohoe of San Francisco, an associate of Eugene Kelly, had donated the original, but in 1891, he contributed an additional amount of $11,100, the cost of a beautiful new work of art in honor of the Holy Family. Once again, Renwick produced the drawings and Draddy did the sculpture in Italy. Except for the high altar, this was the most massive structure in the building and its addition brought a touch of elegance to the north transept. After it was consecrated in 1893, the Trustees expressed thanks to Mr. Donohoe in the form of an illuminated album. The donor graciously expressed his belief that making the donation was an honor in itself.[23]

The newest shrine, and likely to draw many visitors, is that of everyone's friend indeed, St. Jude.

Draddy's next sculpture, again designed by Renwick, was one which, from its creation until the present, has drawn large numbers of devotees, the Altar of St. Anthony. A relief panel in the center of the reredos contained an image of St. Anthony with the Child Jesus. On the left is a statue of St. Monica and St. Ann's statue is on the right. Mrs. Joseph Donohoe, the wife of the Holy Family altar donor, gave this gift to the Cathedral and the Archbishop consecrated it in November 1894.[24]

The same year, Draddy completed work on the St. Augustine altar, donated by Augustine Daly, America's most famous theatrical manager, who opened many theatres including those named after himself in New York and London. He was acclaimed for his inspired direction, and his troupe achieved worldwide renown. John Drew and Ada Rehan headed his company which specialized in Shakespearean comedy. Daly was granted the Laetare Medal for distinguished service to the public the same year he made his donation. Archbishop Corrigan dedicated the altar the following January. Next came an altar in honor of the young Polish Jesuit, St. Stanislaus Kostka. Not one of Draddy's works, it was both designed and built by Peter Theis. The consecration was in June 1896, the twenty-fifth anniversary of the ordination of Rev. P. Rigney, whose sister was the donor.[25]

In 1888, the founder of the religious congregation, the Brothers of the Christian Schools (Christian Brothers), had been beatified, a step on the path to canonization as a saint. To honor the event, the Brothers gave an altar named after their founder, John Baptiste de la

Salle (who was later canonized). The Brothers themselves furnished the drawings and the Borgia Company of New York built it. Archbishop Corrigan consecrated it in November 1900, the last altar dedication ceremony while he was Archbishop.[26] There remained only two vacant aisle chapels. Until the altars were ready, most of the chapels contained confessionals. Now, with most chapels filled, eight confessionals were built between the chapels by the Pottier and Stymus Company, effectively acting as separating walls. [27]

The Cathedral exterior had niches for fifty-one statues, twenty-one on the west front and fifteen each on the north and south sides. None had been filled until the Stoltzenberg Company of Roermond, Holland, was commissioned to sculpture a statue of the Immaculate Conception in 1893. The following March it arrived aboard a steamer from Amsterdam. The nine-feet tall, 1000 pound Savoniere stone sculpture, placed north of the grand portal, was matched by one in honor of St. Joseph south of the portal, also made by Stoltzenberg. Figures of Sts. Peter and Paul, the Apostles and several angels were planned for the other niches on Fifth Avenue, but they were never commissioned. Mrs. C. Finney donated the Virgin statue and the other was a gift of Mr. Stoltzenberg.[28]

Inside, in the north and south transepts, the sixteen niches awaiting statues received the first in 1891. Six were in place four years later. The statues of St. Francis de Sales and St. Ambrose in the upper tier on the south wall arrived in 1891, a gift of Mrs. Joseph Drexel who donated also the statues of St. Gregory the Great and St. Jerome set in the same tier, and those of St. Anselm and St. Bernard below them. The statues of St. Bonaventure and St. Alphonsus Liguori in the lower tier were gifts of the Franciscans and Redemptorists respectively. All the lower statues, portrayed as seated, were the work of Joseph Sibbel, a German artist from Dulman, who studied in Munster before he emigrated to the United States in 1873. He started in Cincinnati, but after he opened a New York studio, he produced a series of *alto relievos* for the Cathedral of Hartford, assuring him of prominent recognition. His reputation for realism and originality of design spread rapidly, assuring him of commissions for statuary from churches throughout the country. His work in St. Patrick's Cathedral is considered outstanding, as are his figures in St. Joseph's Seminary in Yonkers, New York; in St. Paul's Cathedral in Pittsburgh; and in St. Francis Xavier Church in St. Louis. He died in New York in 1907.[29]

On the north wall, the statues of St. Dominic and St. Thomas Aquinas in the upper tier and all the lower tier statues (of St. Athanasius, St. Gregory Nanzianzen, St. Basil the Great and St. John Crysostom) were gifts of Mrs. Joseph Drexel. The likely sculptor was John Draddy.[30] Two niches remained empty until later in this century. A Scottish artist, John Massey Rhind, was selected to carve figures for the lower tier. He came to the United States in 1889 at the age of nineteen, and lived near Gramercy Park in New York. Among his other notable works is the Astor Door at Trinity Church in New York, and decorative work at federal and municipal buildings. His sculpture earned him a gold medal at the St. Louis Exposition of 1904. The statuary in both the north and south transepts represented saints known as Doctors of the Church, Greek ones on the south, Latin on the north.

In 1896, shortly after Renwick's death, his firm collaborated one more time with Draddy Brothers to produce an exceptionally beautiful holy water well costing almost $3000. It was finished two years later and erected where the gift shop is today. Joseph Rutledge, the verger of the Cathedral, donated the pure Carrara marble carving.[31] Similarly, two exquisitely carved marble holy water fonts in the narthex were given in 1890 by the Sanctuary Society members. Another society, the League of the Sacred Heart, presented both funds and some of the precious material for one of the most beautiful of all the Cathedral's treasures, a magnificent ostensorium, or monstrance, for exposition of the Blessed Sacrament. The studios of Armand Calliat in Lyons used diamonds, other precious stones, gold and silver from pieces of jewelry donated by many people to form the vessel — a reminder of their personal sacrifices was evident on the face of their gift. The exquisite piece, which provided a suitable setting for exhibiting the Body of Christ, was ready in 1893.[32]

Of all the treasures brought to St. Patrick's in the 1890s, some consider the finest the fourteen stations of the cross. The devotion of the stations, tracing from medieval times, requires only the placing of wooden crosses at fourteen locations, or stations, around a church, but, traditionally, artistic representations of the events each station recalls have been erected with the crosses. Archbishop Corrigan wanted original creations unlike any in the world, so, in 1891, he engaged a famous Dutch architect, Dr. Peter J. H. Cuypers, to design them. The Stoltzenberg Company of Roermond Holland, which also executed the two statues on the front of the Cathedral, used sketches Renwick had made to set a general tone for what he envisioned. Cuypers then developed his own drawings. Besides holding the position of chief of artists and sculptors of the Roermond studios, Cuypers was a

The sixth station — Veronica wiping Christ's face.

member of the Academie des Beaux Arts of France, Vienna and Berlin and received an honorary degree from the University of Holland. His statues earned gold medals at world exhibitions in London, Paris, Vienna, Brussels and Antwerp, and William II, the German emperor, appointed him to complete the dome of Cologne Cathedral. Father Lavelle decided that, after the first three stations were finished, they should be sent to the Chicago World's Fair of 1893. Using clay models, Cuypers' final pieces were made of Caen stone, satisfied with the success of that material in such outstanding buildings as Buckingham Palace in London and Canterbury Cathedral. The first three sculptures, more than one-half life-size, arrived in New York in April 1893, and in June were awarded the first prize for art at the Chicago exposition. By late 1896, twelve stations were finished. When all fourteen were set in the transept walls, Archbishop Corrigan solemnly blessed them in March 1900. Cuypers had used four pieces of marble to create each scene. The final cost was between $15,000 and $17,000, much of it contributed by famous New Yorkers including the Bouviers, ancestors of Jacqueline Kennedy Onassis; the Colemans; the Hildreths; the Millses; the O'Connors; the O'Donohues; the O'Reillys; and the Marquise de San Marzano. [33]

Even before the Cathedral opened, there had been long-standing plans to erect a set of bells in the north tower. In 1878, the *American Architect and Building News* reported that bells on exhibition at the American centennial celebration in Philadelphia in 1876 would be placed in the spires of St. Patrick's.[34] That never happened. Renwick's proposals were not sent to the Board of Trustees until 1888 when he suggested bells be hung in the north spire.[35] The Board began a search for bells appropriate for the grandest church in America. They directed William Pecher, the Director of Music, and members of a special committee to carry out the search. The committee chose a bell foundry in upper New York State to do the work. It took two years, beginning in 1890, to cast fifteen bells ranging in weight from four hundred to sixty-five-hundred pounds at a cost of $11,750. When they were ready, the committee visited the foundry only to find the set was out-of-tune and uneven in quality. The company's attempts to "sharpen" or "flatten" the tones or to replace those bells they could not repair were considered unsatisfactory by the committee, which rejected them as unsuitable for the Cathedral. And so, another company would have to be found.[36]

This time, Archbishop Corrigan looked across the ocean to France. Georges and Francisque Paccard of Annecy in Savoy were fourth generation members of a family of bell-makers. A contract was signed with them in December 1895 to prepare nineteen bells at a cost of more than $25,000. Less than two years later, expert bell-hangers from Europe arrived with the bells. But the bell-hangers would have to wait to begin work. So impressed by their beauty was Archbishop Corrigan that he decided to exhibit them under the organ gallery just inside the Fifth Avenue entrances in August 1897. Unquestionably the finest set of bells on the continent, they were adorned with bas-relief sculptures of saints, Gothic ornaments and various fruits, flowers and leaves. In addition, each bell was named, most in honor of saints identified by a Latin poetic inscription; and each donor's name was inscribed as well. The bells ranged in weight from one-hundred-seventy-three pounds (Bell of St. Godfrey) to six-thousand-six-hundred-eight pounds (Bell of St. Patrick). The bronze clappers in the shape of anchors were made in the United States.[37]

The nineteen bells:

St. Patrick	B flat	6608 pounds
Blessed Virgin Mary	C	4625.5 pounds
St. Joseph	D	3260 pounds
Holy Name	E flat	2693 pounds
St. Michael	E	2319 pounds
St. Anne	F	1956 pounds
St. Elizabeth	G	1357 pounds
St. Augustine	A flat	1162.7 pounds
St. Anthony of Padua	A	971.3 pounds
St. Agnes	B flat	802 pounds
St. John the Evangelist	B	667.7 pounds
St. Bridget	C	574 pounds
St. Francis Xavier	C sharp	476.3 pounds
St. Peter	D	401.5 pounds
St. Cecilia	E flat	345 pounds
St. Helena	E	286 pounds
St. Alphonsus Liguori	F	240.9 pounds
St. Thomas Aquinas	F sharp	204 pounds
St. Godfrey	G	173 pounds

On the feast of the Assumption of Mary, August 15, 1897, five thousand congregants joined in a two-hour ceremony led by Archbishop Corrigan and fifty members of the clergy. The Cathedral was decorated with gold bunting and papal and American flags. As each bell was blessed, Fr. Lavelle struck each one with a powerful swing of a mallet and the clear tones rang out through the huge space of the building. The sounds would not be heard again until May 4, 1898, the twenty-fifth anniversary of the episcopal ordination of the Archbishop, when the thunder of chiming bells greeted the long procession entering the Cathedral for the liturgy.[38]

H. C. Champ was a Canadian living in Brooklyn, New York, who entered a competition at the Cathedral for a mechanism which would allow the bells to be rung from below the spires. The plan was to save a bell-ringer a long and dangerous climb by step ladders, since there was no staircase in the north tower or spire. Champ won the contract with his compressed air system which electrically connected a keyboard to pneumatic engines, one for each bell. The piston of each engine was fitted to a clip hung on the clapper of each bell. (The bells are stationary and are struck by the moveable clappers.) Wooden rods, one inch in diameter and one-hundred-ten feet long, ran up the spire and were attached to the levers by leather straps. The success of the invention was evident on the faces of Fifth Avenue strollers assembled on New Year's Eve to mark the arrival of the year 1900, although the official inauguration of the system did not take place until September 8, 1901. The final installation in the bell system was an automatic clock for ringing the Angeles three times daily. The E. Howard Clock Company finished that work in 1901.[39]

The huge St. Patrick's bell was donated by the Cathedral parishioners; the Catholic Club and the Holy Name societies also gave bells. The other donors were: John B. Manning; Joseph J. O'Donohue; Michael S. Coleman; Henry McAleenan; the Marquise de San Marzano; Augustine Daly; John D. Crimmins; George B. Coleman; Mrs. Thomas F. Ryan; Eleanora Keyes; Maria A. Mills; and Thomas Kelly. Other bells were offered in honor of Edward Fox; James Edward Fox; Aloysia Miniter; and John and Mary Koop.[40]

If he did not realize it during his first years as Rector, Fr. Lavelle would find during the last decade of the nineteenth century that administering the grand Cathedral bore little resemblance to administering any other church. A century later, American houses of worship, regrettably, are not immune to the caprices of demented or disenchanted individuals who find it attractive for their purposes to disrupt the order of high profile institutions such as the Cathedral.

Thus, as early as the fall of 1891, Fr. Lavelle found it necessary to request the presence at the Cathedral of a plainclothes police officer on Sundays.[41]

To counter the heat and humidity retained by the stone in the structure, the Rector arranged for a ventilation system to be installed. Four-hundred-sixty registers at the ends of the pews emitted 75,000 cubic feet of fresh air per minute, sent out by two blast wheels.[42] To care for the youth of the parish, he requested permission for the purchase of two lots on East Fiftieth Street to start a boys club, he organized the founding of a musical and dramatic society and he formed a fife and drum corps. For the adults, there were many other societies including Fr. McMahon's library which expanded its availability to the general public in 1892, having first served only Catholics. Eventually, there were eleven branches of the library in the City, and a state charter was granted in 1896. Other private libraries merged with it after the turn of the century to form the New York Public Library system.[43]

Growing immigration from Italy led to a request from the community within the parish for priests who spoke their language to minister to them. Archbishop Corrigan arranged to bring from Rome to St. Patrick's Rev. Gerard Ferrante, who stayed from 1891 until 1920. No other priest in the history of the Cathedral except two rectors, Msgr. Lavelle and Bishop Flannelly, served longer.[44]

Not the least of Fr. Lavelle's challenges was financing the maintenance of the physical plant and the cost of liturgical, charitable and social programs. Every year, the budget carried a deficit, in addition to the debt and the annual interest payments. Even though the parishioners responded generously to his pleas for donations, he found it necessary to resort to supplementary sources of income such as the two-week fair he held at the Grand Central Palace in 1894, the special collections beyond the usual ones, and the rental of pews for those able to afford the yearly cost and the initial price of an auction bid when choice pews became available. Usual annual rental cost was $150; on one occasion, pew number six in the center aisle brought a bid price of $3000, this in addition to the annual rental cost.[45]

1892 was the four hundredth anniversary of Columbus' discovery of the New World and New York City held a six-day celebration in October, including a grand naval parade in the harbor. Eager to take part in the observance, the Catholics of the City organized a parade on Fifth Avenue, moving from Fifty-ninth Street past St. Patrick's and terminating at Fourth Street. Twenty-five thousand marchers participated in the evening event on October 11th. The principal liturgical celebration was a pontifical Mass celebrated at the Cathedral by the Archbishop and called "perhaps the most impressive celebration connected with the Columbian Centennial...." Outside, a cable was stretched from spire to spire carrying three large flags, while inside, bunting, flags, shields and floral arrangements graced the building, especially the sanctuary. Palms were brought from the site in the Bahamas where Columbus was reputed to have first stepped ashore. The gallery choir sang to the accompaniment of the Philharmonic Society orchestra under the direction of William Pecher. Rev. John Kellner directed the boys chancel choir.[46]

The following spring, Christopher Columbus' eleventh-generation lineal descendent, the Duke of Verague, was an honored guest at a Mass. In May, Princess Eulalie of Spain and her suite of attendants arrived for a solemn Mass, after an honor guard escorted her carriage from Fifty-ninth Street. Her New York stop was en route to Chicago for the World's Fair where she represented the Spanish court. Obviously, world dignitaries viewed St. Patrick's Cathedral as the church of prominence to be visited in America.[47]

James Renwick did not live to see the Cathedral illuminated by electric lighting. In the year he died, 1895, the Trustees first gave thought to its use, but it took nine more years before they acted. When they did, it took 2,548 lamps of sixteen candlepower each to light the building.[48] Early that year, Fr. Lavelle boarded a steamer for a vacation in the Bahamas, seeking a respite from ever-demanding burdens. Before dawn one morning when the ship was close to Harbor Island, the terrifying sound of the ship being torn open by rocks it had struck roused him from sleep. Realizing the ship had hit a reef, the captain ordered women and children into lifeboats. Fr. Lavelle later recalled his thoughts while he awaited rescue on deck, bundled in a life jacket: he "saw clearly a small monument in New York" erected to his memory with the inscription on its face: "Lost At Sea." Several vessels came to help and, in the end, all the passengers were safely evacuated and transported in lifeboats to the island of Nassau, sixty miles from the accident scene. Once reaching the comforting shore, the survivors begged Fr. Lavelle to lead them in prayers of thanksgiving.[49]

If Fr. Lavelle was being taxed by duties of his office, the Archbishop's burdens were relieved in 1895 when Bishop John Farley was appointed his auxiliary. In the previous

I pledge allegiance to the Flag of the United States of America and to the Republic for which it stands, One Nation Indivisible, with Liberty and Justice for All.

President Benjamin Harrison made a commemorative proclamation and introduced the Pledge of Allegiance for the occasion of the Columbus centennial. The Pledge was written by a Baptist minister and avid socialist, Francis Bellamy. Some wanted to add 'equality and fraternity' after 'liberty and justice' but issues around blacks and women were too hot to handle at the time.

fifteen years, Archbishop Corrigan had confirmed almost 200,000 Catholics, and he indefatigably carried out all episcopal functions without help. After the new bishop's consecration at the Cathedral in December, the Archbishop was required to perform only several thousand confirmations each year. But his schedule at the Cathedral remained undiminished; he regularly preached at the 11 o'clock Mass on the first Sunday of each month, although he freely admitted he was not a good public speaker. Parishioners still filled the church to capacity when he was there.[50]

By the time St. Patrick's entered its second decade, William Pecher had built an impressive music program. According to one of the local newspapers, the music had "long been famous for its excellence." In the middle of the decade, the two choirs grew in number of trained voices to one-hundred-thirty, with many of the soloists "of national reputation." Pecher regularly directed the seventy-voice grand choir which was led by a double quartet of four male and four female voices. The chancel choir under James Ungerer was composed of boys from the orphan asylum, their ages ranging from five to twelve years. Both choirs sang on Sundays and on special feast days. The grand, or gallery, choir sang a different mass each Sunday, and found it necessary to repeat a mass on only three occasions during the year 1894. Masses were selected from the works of the world's great composers including Beethoven, Mozart, Haydn, Cherubini and Gounod. French composers were especially popular, including Guilmant, the organist of the Church of the Trinity; Dubois of the Church of the Madeleine; and Widor of St. Sulpice, all in Paris. During Holy Week, the masses of Palestrina were used, and music by Allegri was often included. Although some American composers' masses were sung, Pecher lamented that there was "not such a store of these to draw from." On the most glorious feasts of the year, Christmas and Easter, the choirs were joined by the Philharmonic Society Orchestra. In 1895, there was even a solemn high Christmas Mass at 4:30 a.m., celebrated by Fr. Lavelle for the benefit of those unable to attend at a more reasonable hour. Most assisting at that Mass were women servants who worked "in the great houses of the millionaire district"; they began assembling at 3 a.m. and by the start of the Mass, the church was filled to capacity. The chancel choir sang at this early service and was accompanied by orchestra and organ. The principal Mass at ll o'clock was offered by the Archbishop and admission was by ticket only. After about 8000 persons were admitted, according to Father Lavelle's estimate, those besieging the doors were required to await the next Mass. Inside, campstools were set up in the aisles and when all seats were filled, standees crowded into any place they could find. Pecher's grand choir provided the music and the famous Australian soprano, Dame Nellie Melba, sang Gounod's *Ave Maria,* "her clear, bell-like notes" ringing through the building.[51]

The following year, Fr. Lavelle proposed the formation of a choral society named in honor of St. Cecilia and consisting of at least one hundred members, well-trained in music theory and the history of liturgical music. He dreamed that the society would present one or two concerts each year under Pecher's direction, who he believed ought to hold "the first musical position in the City of New York."[52] Two years later, chancel choir director Ungerer increased the number of singers in that choir to almost one hundred; at the same time, he revived the Rector's proposal for the formation of the cathedral singing society, suggesting works like Handel's *Messiah* at Christmas and the *Stabat Mater* during Lent.[53]

In another creative move, Fr. Lavelle became President of the Catholic Summer School of America, an institution he helped found at Lake Champlain to provide recreational and educational opportunities for laymen and laywomen. He held the position until 1903; later he was its Chairman of the Board of Studies [54]

The property of the Boys Orphan Asylum between Fifty-first and Fifty-second Streets and Fifth and Madison Avenues was put on the real estate market in 1897. Two years later it was sold, and in another two years the Girls Asylum property was bought by private interests. The Archdiocese retained just a small parcel on the block after it purchased the Boland Trade School property (*above right*). The orphans moved to a new home in the Kingsbridge section of the Bronx. [55]

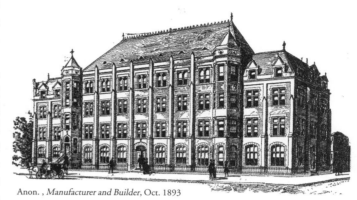

Anon. , *Manufacturer and Builder*, Oct. 1893

The building was built (ca. 1893) when an earlier attempt in 1871 to teach farming and trades at the Boland Farm near Peekskill failed when equipment costs kept rising locally. Many young men from the Boys Orphan Asylum would train here.

In the final years of the nineteenth century, many citizens eagerly supported a movement to expand the City's borders, creating a Greater New York. From 1686 until 1874, when part of the western Bronx was added, the City consisted only of Manhattan Island. In 1895, another area of the Bronx was annexed, a section formerly part of Westchester County. Many visionaries considered the additions meager and wanted to consolidate the three islands of the harbor — Manhattan, Staten Island and Long Island — into a single metropolis. Brooklyn, at the western tip of Long Island, had been a separate city since 1834;

Archbishop Corrigan's most precious project came to fruition in 1896 with the opening of St. Joseph's Seminary in Dunwoodie, Yonkers, to prepare priestly ministers to those growing millions.

indeed, by 1898, it was the fourth largest municipality in the country. Despite ongoing opposition to consolidation from many quarters, on May 4, 1897 the State legislature enacted a law creating Greater New York as of January 1, 1898. The new city was divided into five boroughs: Manhattan, Kings (Brooklyn), Queens, Richmond (Staten Island) and the Bronx. Only the western part of Long Island (Brooklyn and Queens) joined the City. But, even without the rest of Long Island (Nassau and Suffolk Counties), the population of the new New York rose to about 3,393,000 persons, an increase of 126%, making New York by far the most populous city in America.[56] The boundaries of the Archdiocese of New York did not change; all of Long Island, including the boroughs of Brooklyn and Queens, remained the territory of the Diocese of Brooklyn. Thus, two dioceses existed in one city. Yet, St. Patrick's Cathedral continued to be recognized as the principal religious institution in the largest metropolis in America.

The end of a century seemed an appropriate time for the Board of Trustees to address some unfinished business. Renwick had warned them about the possibility of fire in the ceiling area; they studied ways to protect the building from such a catastrophe. In 1899 representatives of the New York Fire Department, architects and engineers attended a board meeting to consider doing what Renwick had urged — replacing the plaster ceiling with iron. Or perhaps pour concrete over the ceiling beneath the roof to retard the spread of fire from the attic into the lower building. Agreement proved elusive, and the fire danger continued to plague subsequent boards (and rectors) for almost another century.[57]

A new century opened, and opening with it was Fa-Lavelle's school for catechists and a Catholic study club for boys. He also asked Colonel Thomas O'Donohue to form a society of honorary ushers to assist at and add appropriate dignity to the celebration of the Christmas and Easter pontifical Masses. Still today, members of the society dress in formal attire on these and other special occasions. The next year a new tradition was established, when the Cathedral School Alumni Association held its first communion breakfast. Countless such breakfasts have since fed souls and bodies, as dozens of organizations met annually establishing their own traditions. Many organizations continue the custom to the present day.[58]

For reasons unknown, the building dedicated to St. Patrick contained no statue in his honor until 1900. In the central niche of the reredos of the high altar, the logical place for a patron's image, was a statue of the Sacred Heart, there since opening day in 1879. Archbishop Corrigan told John B. Manning, one of the trustees, that Catholic rubrics required an image of the saint to whom the church was dedicated. So, Manning himself arranged for a statue (*right*) to be made. It was sculptured by Joseph Sibbel. The Sacred Heart statue was taken to the grounds of St. Joseph's Seminary in Yonkers.[59]

This statue replaced Manning's in the 1940s. "It's himself!," one visitor marvelled

Not rubrics, but Canon law, the law of the Church, specified that Cathedrals had to be consecrated, but also required that the structures be free of debt before the consecration rite could take place. The mortgage on St. Patrick's was, at $270,000, still a lofty amount in 1900.[60] The Archbishop looked for its elimination before May 1904, the twenty-fifth anniversary of the opening, a propitious time, he thought, for the consecration.[61] Ironically, a generous donation added to the debt, rather than eliminated it, because the money contributed was designated for an addition to the building, and the cost of that addition exceeded the amount given. The debt, then, was carried until 1910. The story of the donation follows.

Margaret Kelly, the wife of banker Eugene Kelly, was the niece of Archbishop John Hughes. She left a bequest of $200,000 for construction of a Lady Chapel as a memorial to her late husband.[62] Eugene Kelly had been a selfless donor to numerous charitable causes during his lifetime, especially to Seton Hall College, to the Catholic University of America, and to various other Catholic charities. He was considered one of the Catholic University's founders and was its treasurer from 1887 until his death in 1894. An immigrant from Ulster in Ireland, he entered the United States with only one hundred pounds in his pocket. After learning the dry goods business in New York, he moved west to Kentucky where he began building his fortune. In 1849, he set out for California expecting to amass new wealth during the gold rush era. With several other partners, he opened a dry goods business in San Francisco; later, he started a banking house. In 1856, a branch of his banking company came to New York, and the following year he settled permanently in the City and married Margaret Hughes. (His first wife had died in 1848.) In time, he became a director of several banks, chairman of the state electoral committee, a member of the City's Board of Education, a patron of the Metropolitan Museum of Art, and, in the course of it all, a multimillionaire. Mindful of his roots, he was an activist in Irish nationalist causes. His home was within the Cathedral parish, a short walk on Fifty-first Street from Fifth Avenue (Thirty-three West Fifty-first Street). He died following a stroke in December 1894, and the multitude at his Cathedral funeral included the Mayor of New York and fifty clergymen, notably two bishops, Archbishop Ryan of Philadelphia and Archbishop Corrigan who offered the Mass.[63]

Having received the Kelly bequest, in 1899 Archbishop Corrigan asked William R. Ware, founder of America's first school of architecture at Columbia College and an acknowledged architectural expert, to assist him and Eugene Kelly's sons in selecting an architect for the most important project since the building opened. The professor invited fourteen architects to submit plans for the chapel in a competition for the commission. Ten were from New York: Renwick and Aspinwall (the deceased architect's former firm); N. LeBrun and Sons; C. C. Haight; Heins and LaFarge; Little and O'Connor; Charles T. Mathews; George B. Post; William Schickel; Henry G. Wynn; and Stockton B. Colt. Invited also was the American firm of Cram and Wentworth of Boston and the Canadian architect, Joseph Connolly of Toronto. There were two Europeans, one English and one French, the latter probably Gousset of Rheims. The judges were Professor Ware, three sons of Eugene Kelly and Archbishop Corrigan. Criteria ranged from the best architectural considerations favored by Professor Ware, to the Archbishop's desire for ecclesiastical correctness to the personal preferences of the Kelly brothers. Judging submissions independently of each other, agreement was unanimous: design #12 was the best. Sealed envelopes marked with numbers contained the names of the architects, and inside envelope #12 was the name of Charles Mathews. His drawings portrayed a chapel in thirteenth century French Gothic style, containing some elements of the early fourteenth century, a building more ornate than the rest of Renwick's structure.[64]

Charles Thompson Mathews was born in Paris on March 31, 1863. He probably spent his early years in Europe, although his family's permanent residence was in Staten Island, New York. In 1876, his father purchased a large estate in Norwalk, Connecticut, for use as a summer home. That home is today the Lockwood-Mathews Mansion Museum. Charles was enrolled in St. Paul's School in Concord, New Hampshire, and after studies at Yale, he received his bachelor's degree in 1886. He soon published his first book, but decided to return to academia to pursue an interest in architecture. He studied under Professor Ware at Columbia and was awarded his degree in 1889. In 1891 he worked for Edward Kendall in New York. His ecclesiastical designs, including the interior of Holy Trinity Church in the City, won him rapid recognition. His most famous commission and the one which occupied the most years of his career was the Lady Chapel of St. Patrick's Cathedral.[65]

The Cathedral had space for a Lady Chapel behind its east end, without having to move the Archbishop's residence on 50th St. or the Rectory here in the foreground.

Archbishop Corrigan wanted excavation to begin in the summer of 1900, but the first spadeful of ground was not removed until July 20, 1901.[66] When the Archbishop suggested appointing an advisor to review the work prior to signing final contracts, Mathews protested, asserting that the competition rules had clearly assigned complete control of design and construction to the winner. He noted, further, that those invited to participate in the competition were men of fine reputation obviously including himself. He relented in agreeing to a review by the engineer of the Washington Bridge (Hutton), or by Professor Ware himself, but on the condition that whoever was chosen as advisor would "make his report and retire."[67] Charles T. Wills was hired as the general contractor. Wills enjoyed the confidence of many architects because he was adept at eliminating "red tape" which could decelerate steady construction progress and because he had good experience, having supervised dozens of major projects.[68] Wills estimated that the entire cost for the fifty-six-feet long, twenty-eight-feet wide and fifty-six-feet tall structure and including the two small adjacent chapels would be just over $725,000. The estimate also included connecting an ambulatory to the existing north and south aisles. Pledging an additional $165,000 beyond their mother's gift, Eugene (Jr.) and Thomas Kelly could not assume the entire cost, and the remainder would have to come from other sources. The agreement set payment of the gift by January 1, 1904, in time to complete the addition before the silver anniversary celebration planned for May of that year when, it was still believed, the Cathedral would be consecrated.[69]

The first problem Mathews had to face was remodeling the rear wall. By designing an ambulatory with two semi-octagonal chapels leading to the Lady Chapel, the architect achieved a smooth and graceful transition from Renwick's open space to the delicate beauty of the new chapels. His solution for finding sacristy and additional storage space was to excavate two levels below, even though the cost would have been reduced about $140,000 were those areas eliminated. Instead, to save money, it was decided to substitute brick for marble below ground level, and to use composition material for the ceiling rather than stone, just as had been done for the same reason in the rest of the church. This realized a savings of $200,000. Building a stairway to the sacristy and storage rooms "at first occasioned considerable anxiety. The stairway passes between the foundations of the two rear piers of the Cathedral which support the clerestory walls of the choir [sanctuary]. These were built on a solid rock, and the construction of the stairway necessitated the removal of the rock between these piers. Blasting between these foundations was a very delicate operation, for the slightest accident might have wrecked the entire Cathedral."[70]

The polished marble — unlike the earlier unpolished stone — came from the Columbian Marble Quarrying Company in Vermont.[71] Early in 1902, the Trustees gave approval to remove the original rear wall and to send the stone to the parish of Our Lady of Lourdes for use in building its new church. The pastor of that church was Rev. Joseph McMahon, the priest who had been so successful in establishing and administering the Cathedral Library. By April, the Columbian Company, overstocked with stone it had already quarried, was pleading for the work to be accelerated. Columbian officials wanted to send six cars of stone every two weeks, a total of four to five thousand feet a month. By summertime, contracts had already been let both for window glass in the basements and for heating and ventilation.[72]

Earlier that year, in February, Archbishop Corrigan had walked from his residence to the Cathedral and was near the excavation area, unaware in the dim lighting that workmen had removed part of the flooring. When he fell into the opening, he was able to cling to a beam twenty-five feet above the ground until his cries for help brought aid. He seemed at first not seriously harmed, but as time passed, his injured leg continued to bother him. Someone remarked that he had "not been himself," and shortly thereafter he was diagnosed with pneumonia after attending a meeting in Washington, D. C. That April meeting came only after he was confined to bed for several weeks. Despite the lingering weakness he showed, there was universal expectation of recovery, perhaps because many people recalled his general good health during his entire lifetime; even the Pope sent a congratulatory cablegram. But, optimism was premature; on May 5, 1902, he suffered a heart attack and died suddenly. After his body was laid in his home for one day, it was placed on a catafalque in the Cathedral and a "continual stream of people" poured into the building to pray during the two days before the funeral. At the Mass, a long procession of clergy walked from the Boland School on Madison Avenue and snaked around the Cathedral in view of some twenty thousand onlookers in the neighboring streets and the six to seven thousand inside the church. Nearly one thousand priests and numerous archbishops, bishops, abbots, monsignors and a host of civic officials joined Cardinal Gibbons of Baltimore in final prayers. At the foot of the coffin was a wreath sent by President Theodore Roosevelt. The remains were placed in the crypt after the service.[73]

If Archbishop Corrigan's episcopacy was one of controversy, the fact seemed not to have alienated him from the faithful who paid tribute to him in death. A month after his funeral, a memorial meeting was held at Carnegie Hall, arranged for and by members of the laity.[74] As could be expected, the Archbishop was remembered by clergy and laity alike for his successes. The new seminary, the new orphan asylums and the Cathedral improvements were evident. But, he also had added one-hundred-eighty-eight churches, chapels and stations to those established by his predecessors. There were two-hundred-eighty-four more priests, seventy-five more schools and thirty more charitable institutions than there had been when he took office seventeen years earlier. And the many synods held at St. Patrick's brought a code of statutes to the Archdiocese for its orderly administration. The fame of St. Patrick's Cathedral had spread world-wide; locally, its trustees included such prominent figures as Eugene Kelly, John D. Crimmins, John B. Manning, J. Coleman, William R. Grace and Hugh Grant, Catholics eminent in business and government. Like Archbishop Hughes, Archbishop Corrigan had begun work which he now left for others to complete.[75]

1. Ellis, Edward Robb, *The Epic of New York City*, Old Town Books, New York, 1960, pp. 364-365, 375, 389, 409, 411-412, 421, 422.

2. Garraty, p. 511.

3. Ellis, p. 380; Cohalan, *Popular History*, p. 105 *et passim*.

4. Cohalan, *Popular History*, pp. 105-106.

5. Smith, pp. 419, 555-559; *Memorial of the Most Rev. Michael Augustine Corrigan, D.D.*, Cathedral Library Association, New York, 1902, pp. 25-48, *passim*.

6. Catholic Review, March 13, 1886.

7. Cohalan, *Popular History*, pp. 118-138, *passim*, p. 175.

8. *Souvenir of the Centennial Celebration of St. Patrick's, New York, 1809-1909*, n.p.

9. Catholic Review, April 21, August 11, October 20, 1888; *Catholic News*, October 7, 20, 1888; Farley, pp. 140-141; New York Sun, undated letter of Fred Sutton, copy in ASPC; Sutton Report, November 17, 1941, ASPC; Maryland Geological Survey of Baltimore County, Johns Hopkins Press, 1929, pp. 243, 244. The Pennsylvania State Travel Guide in 1994 reported that only the Eiffel Tower and the Washington Monument surpassed in height the Philadelphia City Hall in the year 1901. This may not take into account the height of some cathedral spires in Europe, for example, Salisbury at 404 feet and Strasbourg at 466 feet. By any comparison, St. Patrick's masonry spires were among the tallest structures in America.

The estimated cost of the spires at $190,000 was $10,000 less than the actual cost. (*See: Detailed Statement of Specifications for Alterations to Buildings, City of New York*, 1885, ASPC.) Even though the spires were finished in October 1888, a viewer on Fifth Avenue was able to see only the tops, since the scaffolding was left in place until the Spring of 1889 to complete pointing and work on the interior (Catholic Review, October 27, 1888).

Renwick's latest addition suffered criticism just as the essential building had in 1879. A Pennsylvania architect wrote that he thought using elaborately carved high spires, which he thought seemed to imitate those of Cologne Cathedral, was to step away from the best Gothic period towards the more decadent later Gothic. He thus found fault with both Cologne and St. Patrick's. His was a solitary voice. *(See: Roth (to unknown persons),* September 6, 1886, AANY, microfilm tape C-ll).

10. Minutes of the Board of Trustees, 1888-1890, *passim; Catholic News,* October 20, 1888; Catholic Review, August 11, October 20, 1888.

11. Minutes of the Board of Trustees, December 6, 1888, April 10, 1913; Renwick to Corrigan, February 8, 1886, November 4, 1887, AANY.

12. Carthy, *Magnificence,* pp. 62-63; Catholic Review, April 28, 1887, April 28, 1888; *Catholic News,* April 17, 1887.

13. *Cathedral Bulletin,* June 1929, October 1930.

14. *Catholic News,* March 31, 1934.

15. Carthy, *Magnificence,* pp. 53-54; interview with Msgr. Florence Cohalan, December 1994.

16. New York Sun, February 12, 1888.

17. Smith, pp. 456-457, 461; Farley, pp. 150-151; *Catholic Review,* May 26, 1888; Delaney, p. 376; interview with Msgr. Florence Cohalan, December 1994. There was a Cathedral clubhouse for use by the various societies. It was blessed by Archbishop Corrigan on January 15, 1893.

18. Farley, pp. 132-155, *passim; Catholic Review,* September 22, 1888.

19. Minutes of Board of Trustees, December 1888.

20. Lavelle to Corrigan, April 17,1890, AANY; Delaney, p. 289.

21. Lavelle to Corrigan, August 25, 1890; *The World,* December 15, 1895; *New York Times,* August 26, 1890; Cathedral Bulletin, October 1960. Work began on the altar late in August 1890.

22. Contract and related correspondence of Draddy and Archbishop Corrigan, AANY, Folder 12, G-44, G-54 including Draddy to Corrigan, March through August 1892. The contract for the altar was signed in 1891. By that time, Renwick had taken on partners, and his firm was known as *Renwick, Aspenwall and Russell.* The first design used a bas-relief to show the eagle in front of the pedestal.

23. Draddy to Corrigan, (as in previous note); *Catholic News,* October 8, 1893; Cathedral Bulletin, October 1960; New York Herald, October 1, 1893; Minutes of the Board of Trustees, April 1894; contract for altar, June 24, 1891, box: St. Patrick's Cathedral, folder 6, G-43, AANY. The scene of the Holy Family in the center of the reredos was based on a painting of Raphael. The reredos is 25 feet high and sixteen feet wide.

24. Farley, p. 214; *Cathedral Bulletin,* October 1960.

25. Farley, p. 214; Cathedral Bulletin, October 1960; Delaney, p. 134; *New York Times,* December 4, 1894; New York Tribune, March 3, 1895. Daly was born in North Carolina. In 1859 he began his career as a drama critic for the New York *Sunday Courier.* His theater work began in 1867 and he opened his own theater, the Fifth Avenue, in 1869. He died in Paris in 1899.

26. Gabriel, Brother Angelus, FSC, *The Christian Brothers In The United States, 1848-1858,* New York, 1948, p. 583; Farley, p. 212.

27. Minutes of the Board of Trustees, February 2, 1899; *The World,* December 15, 1895.

28. Stoltzenberg to Rev. Joseph Connolly, informal note, 1895, AANY; *The World,* March 5, 1895; *New York Times,* Dec. 17, 1895. The following year, a statue of St. Rose of Lima was donated anonymously for placement on the facade with the other two. It was expected that others would follow in short order. Not only did no others follow, but the statue of St. Rose was not

erected in one of the niches. It is possible that the statue is the one today at the Altar of St. Rose of Lima, but that seems unlikely, since that altar was not built for another ten years. The mystery endures. *See: Catholic News*, January 19, 1896.

29. Farley, pp. 209-210; Delaney, p. 533. Incised under one of Sibbel's statues is the name *St. Alphonsus Ligori* [sic]. The misspelling of the name *Liguori* has never been explained in any available records. Rather than risk the possibility of serious damage to the statue itself by attempting to correct the error, authorities appear to have decided to allow the mistake to join other oddities at the Cathedral which add to its uniqueness. (For example, there is a window panel inserted upside-down.)

30. Draddy wrote several letters to Archbishop Corrigan from Carrara, Italy between March 30 and August 19, 1892. In one of them, he mentioned that the statues of Mrs. Drexel were nearly all pointed, and that the pedestals were nearly finished. Since Mrs. Drexel is the donor of the upper and lower tier statues, the assumption is that Draddy sculptured the statues of St. Thomas Aquinas and St. Dominic, since the lower statues were the work of John Massey Rhind. *See:* Draddy to Corrigan, 1892, AANY.

31. Farley, p. 213; contract for well, box: St. Patrick's Cathedral, folder 6, G-43, AANY. James Renwick died on June 23, 1895. His surviving company, called Renwick, Aspinwall and Owen, designed the holy water well. Renwick's funeral took place at Grace Church on Broadway at 10th Street, the building whose design was his first commission and which won international fame for him. At the funeral service on June 27th, John Crimmins represented the Trustees of St. Patrick's Cathedral. Burial was in the family plot at Greenwood Cemetery in Brooklyn. *See: New York Times*, June 25, June 28, July 2, December 15, 1895.

32. Farley, pp. 178-180, 213; *New York Times*, August 26, 1890. The League of the Sacred Heart made the presentation in honor of the bi-centennial of Blessed Margaret Mary (today, a saint), to whom Our Lord appeared (The Sacred Heart). The very industrious Father Joseph McMahon was the moderator of the League.

33. Stoltzenberg to Lavelle, April 29, 1891, folder G-43, AANY; Lavelle to Corrigan, September 30, 1891, folder GH-43, AANY; *Catholic News*, June 25, 1893, October 25, 1896; *Cathedral Bulletin*, August 1948; Smith, p. 476; estimate of Stoltzenberg Company, January 9, 1894, folder G-43, AANY. Cuypers had collaborated on a book for which he prepared drawings of doors, grills, floors and other parts of the National Museum of Amsterdam *(Le Musee National a Amsterdam)*. The Stoltzenberg Company maintained a New York office at 51 and 53 Barclay Street at the corner of Church Street. It was the Stoltzenberg Company which first proposed that three stations be made before the others, that they first be exhibited in the Cathedral for one month and that only then they be sent to the Chicago exhibition. The uncertainty about the price of the stations arises from different amounts reported by different authors. Archbishop Farley reported a final cost of $10,000 and the accuracy of other information in his history suggests that this is the likely cost.

34. *American Architect and Building News*, January 19, 1878. As late as 1952, the apparently erroneous information was still being reported. *See: Catholic News*, April 19, 1952.

35. Renwick to Board of Trustees, Minutes of the Board of Trustees, December 6, 1888.

36. Minutes of the Board of Trustees, 1893-1898, *passim,* especially, March 23, 1893, June 1, 1893, March 1, 1894, December 6, 1894; bill and related correspondence of Meneely Company, folder G-43, AANY. The long delays were not expected. The *New York Times* reported in August 1890 that the bells would be in position by Christmas. In July 1892 the bells were reported to be "corrected." Four bells apparently were acceptable, four were replaced, four were "slightly sharpened," and three were "slightly flattened."

37. Minutes of the Board of Trustees, December 5, 1895, February 3, March 3, 1898; *Catholic News*, July 18, August 8, August 15, August 22, 1897. In 1796, after the Reign of Terror in the middle of the French Revolution came to an end, Catholics in Annecy, France, asked their bishop for a parish priest to fill the vacancy caused during the persecution. The bishop set a condition that the people first replace the church bell which had been melted down for a cannon during the war years. When a bell founder arrived from Geneva to cast a new bell, the mayor of the town, Antoine Paccard, offered to help him. The gesture generated in the mayor so intense an interest in bellmaking that he decided to establish his own bell foundry. So, the Paccard family business was born. At the end of the twentieth century, the seventh generation of the Paccard family continues the tradition, the family having made more than 80,000 bells which are heard today all over the world. Every state capitol building in America has a replica of the Liberty Bell made by the firm. And a source of great pride, the twenty-ton Savoyard at Sacre Coeur in Paris is a Paccard. It is the largest tuned bell in Europe. *See: Paccard — Fonderie de Cloches*, Van Bergen Bellfoundries, Inc., Atlanta, 1985.

38. *Catholic News*, August 22, 1897, May 7, 1898

39. New York Journal, January 27, 1901; Toronto World, March 20, 1898; Farley, p. 224. An article in the *New York Times* reported that the system was tested on September 14, 1901 in the presence of Fr. Lavelle and the Board of Trustees. The controls for playing the bells on mother-of-pearl stops were in a small cabinet, the size of a writing desk. The bells could also be played electrically by using a perforated disc which revolved slowly like that used in a music box. It was programmed to peel the Angelus at 8 a.m., 12 noon and 6 p.m. and to sound the *De Profundis* at 7 p.m.. At other times, hymns were played. *See: New York Times*, September 15, 1901.

40. Farley, pp. 216-217.

41. Minutes of the Board of Trustees, October 8, November 6, 1891.

42. Minutes of the Board of Trustees, May 7, 1891; Meehan, n.p.

43. Carthy, *Magnificence*, p. 66; Lavelle to Corrigan, June 24, 1892, folder C-30, AANY .

44. Interview with Msgr. Florence Cohalan, December 1994; listing of priests of St. Patrick's Catheral, ASPC.

45. Carthy, *Magnificence*, p. 68; *New York Times*, December 18, 1894.

46. *Catholic News*, October 9, 16, 1892; Farley, p. 142.

47. Farley, pp. 142-144; *Catholic News*, June 4, 1893. Princess Eulalie was the aunt of the King of Spain and the Queen Regent's sister. Her entourage proceeded with its honor guard from the Hotel Savoy at 59th Street.

48. Minutes of the Board of Trustees, April 1895 and 1904, *passim.*

49. New York Press, November 18, 1895.

50. Cohalan, *Popular History,* p. 173; New York World, December 15, 1895.

51. New York World, December 26, 1895. Dame Nellie Melba (1861-1931) was the stage name of Helen Mitchell.

52. Lavelle to Corrigan, undated, but 1896, folder G-11, AANY.

53. Ungerer to Corrigan and Trustees, August 28, 1898, ASPC. In his letter, Ungerer gave a summary of his work, both at the Cathedral and at the seminary. He noted that his $1200 salary was not commensurate with his work, or comparable to that of "other boys' choirmasters in leading churches of this city...." Further, he said his duties precluded his employment to earn income "from outside sources."

54. *Cathedral Bulletin*, June 1929.

55. New York Evening Post, March 20, 1897; New York Herald Sun, January 23, 1898; Carthy, *Magnificence,* footnote, pp. 176, 177.

56. Ellis, pp. 451-453.

57. Minutes of the Board of Trustees, April 15, 1899.

58. Carthy, *Magnificence,* pp. 66, 74-83, *passim; The Honorary Ushers of St. Patrick's Cathedral,* unpublished booklet, no author, May 1962, ASPC.

59. Corrigan to J. B. Manning, February and March 1900, AANY; *Cathedral Bulletin,* September 1960; *The New High Altar and the Altar for the Lady Chapel,* a preliminary description prepared for the Archbishop of New York by the architects, May 9, 1942, ASPC, hereafter cited as *New High Altar.*

60. Carthy, *Magnificence,* footnote, pg. 179.

61. Corrigan to Trustees, April 16, 1900, AANY.

62. Journal of the Fair, November 22, 1878.

63. Dictionary of American Catholic Biography, p. 289; New York Sun, December 7, December 17, 1894; New York Herald, December 27, 1894; New York Times, December 20, 1894; New York Tribune, December 23, 1894. Eugene Kelly's father, Thomas Boye O'Kelly participated in the Rebellion of 1798 in Ireland. To avoid easy identification, he changed his name to Kelly. After his son came to America, he worked in New York for Donnelly & Company, the leading dry-goods business in the City. He took a train of mules to San Francisco and arrived in 1850. Among his high positions in New York in his later years was as a director of the Bank of New York, of the Emigrant Savings Bank, of the National Park Bank and of the Equitable Life Assurance Society. The coat of arms of the O'Kelly family appears in the stained glass windows of the Lady Chapel of St. Patrick's. *See: Dictionary of American Biography,* Volume X.

64. Thomas Kelly to Mathews, undated, but 1900, ASPC; Ware to architects, November 6, 1899, ASPC; Farley, pp. 163-170, *passim.*

65. *Nineteenth Century Architects: Building a Profession,* exhibition booklet, Lockwood-Mathews Mansion Museum, Norwalk, Ct., April 1 – April 29, 1990, hereafter cited as *Nineteenth Century Architects.* Mathews wrote a work entitled: *The Renaissance Under the Valois, A Sketch in French Architectural History,* and dedicated it to his former professor, William R. Ware (Watson Library, Metropolitan Museum of Art, New York). Upon his return from Europe in August 1900, Mathews released a description of what he planned for the chapel. The building would be similar to the Sainte Chapelle in Paris and to the Lady Chapels of Amiens and Beauvais Cathedrals, an "amalgamation of those two chapels." He planned an open work belfry at the peak of the roof like that on top of the Lady Chapel at Amiens. The plain lower walls were to "flower into a riot of elaborately carved pinnacles..." above. He wanted windows as close as possible to those of the 13th Century, and blue-toned in recognition of the color associated with Mary. He estimated a total cost of $240,000, more than the legacy of Mrs. Kelly, but he stated that the Kelly family planned to provide the difference. *See: New York Times,* September 1, 1900.

66. Corrigan to Trustees, April 16, 1900, AANY; *Memorial of the Most Rev. Michael Augustine Corrigan, D. D.,* pp. 25-48, *passim.*

67. Mathews to Corrigan, March 28, 1901, ASPC. Mathews lived at 30 West 57th Street and his office was at 281-283 Fourth Avenue. Mathews himself filed the application with the Department of Buildings of New York to alter the Cathedral. He estimated at the time of the original application (October 9, 1901) that the cost would be $400,000. *See:* Application to Alter, Repair, Etc., Department of Buildings of the City of New York, and amendments to application dating from 1901 to 1909, ASPC.

68. *Nineteenth Century Architects.* Wills' many buildings included the Scribner Building on Fifth Avenue; the New York Life Insurance Company Building; the Astor Residence on Fifth Avenue at 65th Street; and the Judson Memorial Church at Washington Square.

69. John Agar to Corrigan, July 12, 1901, AANY; Minutes of the Board of Trustees, 1901, *passim.*

70. Farley, pp. 163-170, *passim;* Agar to Corrigan, July 12, 1901, AANY.

71. J. F. Manning to M. C. Henry and Co., April 14, 1902, ASPC.

72. Minutes of the Board of Trustees, April 3, July 17, 1902; Manning to McHenry Co., April 14, 1902; Tiffany and Company to Mathews, December 30, 1901, ASPC. The marble used to construct the Church of Our Lady of Lourdes came from both the rear wall of St. Patrick's Cathedral and from the Academy of Design. The church was built on the site of the home of Alexander Hamilton. Nearby were thirteen trees planted by America's first Secretary of the Treasury to commemorate the thirteen original states. *See: New York Times,* May 19, 1902.

73. Carthy, *Magnificence,* pp. 71-73; *Catholic News,* April 26, 1902; Cohalan, *Popular History,* p. 174; *Memorial of the Most Rev. Michael Augustine Corrigan, D. D.,* pp. 51-56, 63-66. The Archbishop died at 11:05 p.m. After the congregation left the Cathedral following the funeral, the sculptor Joseph Sibbel took a death-mask at the coffin just before final interment. Encased in a glass container and placed with the body was a parchment with the name and a short account of the life of the Archbishop.

74. *Memorial of the Most Rev. Michael Augustine Corrigan, D. D.,* pp. 77-83. Congressman W. Bourke Cockran, considered one of the greatest orators of his time, gave one of six addresses at the memorial meeting held on June 8th.

75. Smith, pp. 452-454, 555-569; Farley, pp. 136-137; Trustees of St. Patrick's Cathedral, a listing of the trustees from 1879, ASPC. By 1902 there were more than seven hundred priests in the Archdiocese.

William R. Grace was the first Catholic Mayor of New York, elected in 1880. His enormous wealth derived from shipping, silver mines, oil, minerals and railroad properties, among other ventures. *See:* Carthy, *Magnificence,* p. 89.

CHAPTER VI

Finishing Touches: The Years of Cardinal John Farley

Eleven days after the death of Archbishop Corrigan, Fr. Lavelle wrote to Auxiliary Bishop John Farley relating events of the Archbishop's final minutes of life. His death had come quickly, within just a few minutes of a rapid decline in his pulse rate. The Rector added his impression that there was widespread hope in the Archdiocese that Bishop Farley would be named the next Archbishop of New York.[1] In 1884, the Third Plenary Council of Baltimore had approved a new method of nominating bishops for vacant sees: the bishops of the province (the area encompassing the dioceses within the purview of the Archdiocese) would submit names; the diocesan council would make recommendations; and the archbishops of the country would approve or recommend their choices. All three groups approved Bishop Farley's name for submission to the Pope for approval.[2] The appointment was announced on September 25, 1902, to the gratification of the preponderance of Catholics in the Archdiocese. The new Archbishop was "gracious in manner and dignified in bearing," a cautious man who loved peace, a hard worker and an able administrator. Although he was not a coadjutor like all previous auxiliary bishops of the Archdiocese, for seven years he had served under Archbishop Corrigan and was administrator of the Archdiocese after the Archbishop's death.[3]

He received his primary education and his preparatory seminary training in Ireland; after he emigrated to New York, he attended St. John's College, Fordham. He went to Troy for one year of seminary study and finished his work in Rome where he was ordained in June 1870. His first assignment was to St. Peter's Church in Staten Island; then he moved into administrative positions in the Archdiocese before he was appointed Pastor of St. Gabriel's parish in 1884. He became one of only about a dozen monsignors in the entire country, and in 1895 he was honored with the title *prothonotary apostolic,* the highest honor below episcopal rank. Later in the same year he moved to that rank when he became an auxiliary bishop in New York. During twelve years when he had been secretary of Cardinal McCloskey, he was at the Cathedral frequently and was knowledgeable about much of it. For seven years before the building opened and for the first five years after, he was closely associated with St. Patrick's. He first compiled a detailed description of the original windows, the source of most of what we know about them. The Apostolic Delegate to the United States, Most. Rev. Diomede Falconio, conferred the *pallium* on him at the Cathedral on August 12, 1903.[4]

The immediate task at hand for him at the Cathedral was the completion of the Lady Chapel. At first the work proceeded steadily, but by the end of 1903 labor problems were causing delays.[5] Further delays resulted from the discovery, made during excavation, that the original foundations near the apse at the east end had deteriorated; other work could not resume until they were fortified.[6] The first sections completed were the sacristies and the small crypt behind the main sacristy intended for the Kelly family. Charles Mathews personally supervised the work and was in frequent attendance at the site. Both his office and his home were within a short walk of the building. He hired John Williams to make a beautiful bronze door from Mathews' own design to separate the sacristy from the steps leading to the altar.[7] By March 1904, over $300,000 already had been spent, and the estimate for completion of all the work had risen to $650,000. By 1905, as the iron frame was being lifted for the roof, downstairs finishing touches like window glass and carpeting were being applied. Little and O'Connor, one of the architect competitors who lost the commission to Mathews, collaborated with him in some of the designs as the building neared completion. Early in 1906, steel ribs were being set in the vaulting.[8]

That year, the stress associated with the job was taking its toll on Mathews' health. He was called to jury duty and worried that he was unable to supervise the project. Finally, his physician warned him to get some rest and recommended a European trip far from the source of all his anxiety. Resigned to the vacation, Mathews nevertheless arranged to meet Archbishop Farley in Europe to visit some Cathedrals and discuss stained glass windows for the chapel.[9]

Mathews wanted Piccirilli Brothers to build a new altar for the chapel, but their estimate proved too expensive. But, in October 1906, he ordered the removal and storage of the old altar from the north aisle temporary chapel, still planning to replace it. Two months later, with the new altar plans apparently scrapped for the time being, the old altar was cleaned and renovated and brought to the new chapel, just as the partitions erected between the old and new sections of the building were being removed. At Christmas, with both floor and ceiling unfinished and with new lamps not yet installed, Msgr. Lavelle celebrated the first Mass offered in the chapel. (He had been made a *monsignor* in 1903.) Plastering and work at the rear entrances continued into the following year. The temporary lighting was used until 1908. Mathews' altar was never built, even though Eugene Kelly, Jr. offered to contribute the cost in 1907. The original altar remained in use until the present altar was erected in 1942.[10]

Mathews' health problems resurfaced in mid-1908, and he was ordered back to Europe to recuperate. He became embroiled in a dispute with the builder, Charles Wills, and he was not on best terms with Archbishop Farley after the Archbishop decided to review drawings of Paolo Medici of Rome for one of two altars planned for chapels adjacent to the Lady Chapel. When his exasperated physician shouted to him: "I say go, if the thing falls down," the architect dejectedly affirmed the high quality of his work. He sailed for Europe in June.[11]

His reluctance to leave New York was overcome by his determination to visit the studios of Paul Vincent Woodroffe, a stained glass artist of Chipping Campden, England, and to stop in Rome to examine the work of Paolo Medici.[12] Woodroffe was later selected as the artist of the fifteen windows for the new chapels. The Kelly brothers collaborated with Mathews and Archbishop Farley in selecting the subjects to be represented in the glass. Mathews was insistent that the windows be of the highest quality. He wrote to Farley in 1909: "What the right glass means to me may be judged by the fact that the whole chapel was designed merely as a shell to hold a particular kind of glass. With a mistake in this regard, nine years of work (and, at times, unspeakable anxiety) go for nothing." Mathews was looking to achieve "something as near as possible like the tapestries of jewels made in the thirteenth century at Chartres, Bourges and Tours."[13] The competition to find an artist who could achieve this goal was held in 1909. Paul Vincent Woodroffe agreed to submit his designs of one window in July 1909. The Archbishop decided to meet him in Canterbury, England, the following month to review other drawings. Mathews, Thomas Kelly and Archbishop Farley together approved Woodroffe's studies, and he began work immediately on the rest of his drawings. Kelly met Woodroffe in London in the spring of 1910, and by the following summer, all the sketches were complete.[14]

Woodroffe's commission was the most important of his career and was "probably the largest for stained glass ever given to an English artist by an overseas church." Born in 1875 in India, where his father was a civil servant, he spent his childhood in Bath, England. He studied at the Jesuit school at Stonyhurst and at London's Slade School of Art. He began his career as an illustrator of bookplates and nursery rhyme, song and poem books. After further study under Christopher Whall, the leading stained glass designer of the Arts and Crafts Movement, he began making stained glass early in this century. His first workshop employed about nine craftsmen, but World War I interrupted work when several of his assistants enlisted for military service.[15]

His quoted prices for the chapel windows ranged from $3250 to $5000 each. Woodroffe promised he would visit Chartres, LeMans and Ste. Chapelle in Paris and, of course, New York. There is no evidence that he ever managed to get to the City. His first window glass was at the chapel in 1912 and was in place early in 1913, but most of the windows were made after World War I. In subsequent years, Woodroffe's firm built nine more windows, ten in all, and he contracted with other firms for the other five. The English firm of John Hardman of Birmingham made one of them, two were made by French firms and two by Franz Mayer of Munich, Germany. Mayer was assisted by Carl de Bouche of the same city. In the years after the war, Woodroffe took on other commissions while he continued working on glass for the Lady Chapel. For example, he finished windows for the Canterbury School in New Milford, Connecticut. By late in the 1920s, he was devoting all his time to the Cathedral project. The last glass was set in the chapel in 1934. Woodroffe was seventy-nine years old when he died in 1945.[16]

Several windows depict early American missionaries who were associated with New York; one window, designed after the Communist Revolution of 1917, whimsically depicts a Russian Bolshevik wearing a peaked cap and holding a red flag as he topples a cross from the roof of a church; another panel shows Msgr. Lavelle, the Rector. The principal theme is the Mysteries of the Rosary, the medallions at the tops identifying each mystery.[17]

Long before Mathews turned his attention to the windows, he was concentrating on two altars for the chapels adjoining the Lady Chapel. In 1904, Michael C. Bouvier, a New York banker, offered to donate an altar to honor St. Michael the Archangel and St. Louis IX, King of France, in memory of Mr. Bouvier's parents.[18] His father, also named Michael, immigrated here from France and married Louise Vernoa in Philadelphia where the couple set up a home.[19] Jacqueline Bouvier Kennedy Onassis, wife of President John F. Kennedy and later wife of Aristotle Onassis, was a relative of Michael Bouvier. Mathews chose the Tiffany Company of New York to build the altar, and Bouvier hoped it would be finished within a year.[20] Sadly, the work was plagued by problems and dragged on for years. For example, when Mathews chose Paul Gunella, a sculptor who had learned his trade while sculpturing at Milan Cathedral, local New York unions forced construction to stop, since Mr. Gunella was not a local tradesman. In the end, Piccirilli Brothers of New York was employed to set the altar under the direction of the Tiffany Company. At one point, Mathews demanded that the assembled altar be dismantled and reset, because he objected to the jointing material being used. Frustrated at the delays, Bouvier said that his dominant feeling was "one of loss of interest closely allied to disgust." When all the difficulties were resolved, the altar was completed late in 1908, the finished product a jewel that generations after might consider well-worth all the construction trouble.[21]

Personal preference often trumped theology in the choice of which saint or angel got an altar. In this case, the donor's father was named Michael, but, in any case, beauty is the real winner.

A year after initiation of plans for the St. Michael and St. Louis altar (*above*), John D. Crimmins, a member of the Board of Trustees of the Cathedral, and a successful New York builder, decided to donate an altar in honor of St. Elizabeth. The gift was in memory of Mr. Crimmins' wife, mother of their fourteen children. Lily Louise Lalor Crimmins died in 1888 after a lifetime devoted to the care of orphans and destitute children.[22] Mr. Crimmins was equally devoted to charitable causes in the City, including the embellishment of the Cathedral.[23] The altar was a Mathews conception, as was that of St. Michael and St. Louis, but the Archbishop wanted Paolo Medici to submit another plan. Medici was a descendant of the famous Medici family of Florence; his company was engaged in ecclesiastical art work in Rome, especially at St. Peter's Basilica. Mathews voiced strong opposition and even Medici supported Mathews' argument that only a Gothic design was suitable. Thus, Medici built the altar following Mathews' design which Mathews

THE CATHEDRAL ALTARS DESCRIBED IN THESE PAGES, WITH CHANGES MADE SINCE THE 1940s.

1. Library pamphlet rack and large holy water font [This is now the gift shop.]

2. Altar of St. Anthony of Padua

3. Altar of St. John the Evangelist

4. Altar of St. Stanilaus Kostka [This is now the shrine of St. Elizabeth Seton]

5. Altar of St. Rose of Lima

6. South Transept Entrance

7. Altar of the Sacred Heart [A roughly 4x4 octagonal marble block stands a comfortable distance short of the altar; the block held a tabernacle for veneration until the latter was moved to the present Lady Chapel altar; today a large painting of Our Lady of Guadalupe is suspended above the block.]

8. Altar of St. Andrew

9. Altar of St. Teresa of the Infant Jesus (The Little Flower)

10. Archbishop's Sacristy

11. Altar of St. Elizabeth

12. Altar of St. Michael and St. Louis

13. Special Confessional for the Deaf and the Dumb [This space now serves as an office for ushers.]

14. Altar of St. Joseph [Before the Cathedral was extended and the present Lady Chapel was built, roughly this area was the Lady Chapel. Its altar was used for the new Lady Chapel until the present altar was built for it ca. 1943.]

15. Chancel Organ [the organ pipes, that is; the organ is farther up the aisle.]

16. Altar of the Holy Family [This is now the baptistry; the Holy Family altar itself was moved into the sanctuary when the desire arose to have the celebrant closer to the people than the High Altar was.]

17. North Transept Entrance

18. Altar of the Holy Relics [More properly the Holy Face altar, with St. Veronica in mind.]

19. Altar of St. Augustine [It had become the St. John Neumann shrine but is now the Polish Saints' altar.]

20. Altar of St. John Baptiste de la Salle

21. Altar of St. Brigid and St. Bernard [It is sometimes called the Irish altar.]

22. Baptistry [Now the shrine of St. Jude.]

23. Archbishop's throne

24. Statue of St. Patrick

25. Pulpit

26. High Altar and Baldachin (canopy)

27. Entrance to mortuary crypt and sacristies

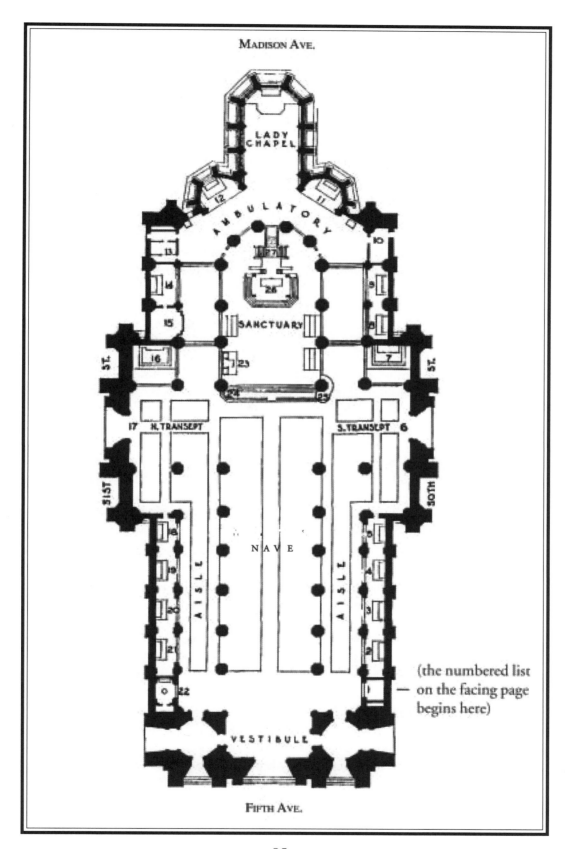

MADISON AVE.

LADY CHAPEL

AMBULATORY

12   11

13

10

14

9

15

8

SANCTUARY

ST.   16   23   7   ST.

24   25

17   N. TRANSEPT   S. TRANSEPT   6

31ST   30TH

18   5

NAVE

AISLE   AISLE

19   4

20   3

21   2

22   1

VESTIBULE

(the numbered list
— on the facing page
begins here)

FIFTH AVE.

based on sketches of Albrecht Durer. Mathews' drawing was ready by May 1907 and Medici completed his models in Rome the following month; the contract was received in September, and the sculpture arrived on Ash Wednesday 1909. Medici brought his own workmen from Rome to erect the altar which was consecrated by the Archbishop on January 10, 1910. Both of the Mathews altars are considered exquisite works of art and are favorites of visitors.[24]

The east end addition is "more refined in scale" than the Renwick building. Mathews achieved a mixture of thirteenth and early fourteenth century French Gothic style, "giving the impression of a building whose construction had extended from one century into the other." He added gargoyles to his structure, something missing in the Renwick design, and he used copper on the roof to add a patina, a light touch of color. The fifty-six-feet long by twenty-eight-feet wide and fifty-six-feet high chapel and its flanking chapels added two hundred ninety square yards of space to St. Patrick's. The interior length was measured at three hundred seventy-six feet from west front to the extreme wall of the Lady Chapel. On the outside, the length was over four hundred feet.[25]

During the final years of construction, Mathews worked closely with Archbishop Farley's secretary, Rev. Daniel McMackin, a man of exceptional talent. He had graduated from the North American College in Rome and is suspected to have been the silent author of, or at least a serious contributor to, one or both books which bear Archbishop Farley's name as author. One of those books is the first history of St. Patrick's Cathedral, published in 1908. Fr. McMackin's innate gifts were legendary. The story is told that on one occasion Congressman W. Bourke Cockran was a scheduled speaker at the Cathedral. Expecting that a written copy of his speech would be prepared for him, he arrived to learn that nobody had done so. Calmly, Fr. McMackin asked him to wait a few minutes, left and returned after a short time; he handed Cockran a speech which he, Fr. McMackin, has composed on the spot. Effortlessly, Cockran delivered the polished words without a flaw.[26]

Besides the Lady chapel, Archbishop Farley was left with several other unfinished projects within the Cathedral, projects he dispatched with the help of generous benefactors. J. Coleman traced his family history back over one thousand years to medieval Ireland. One of his ancestors was Abbot Coleman, founder of the ancient monastery of Clonmacnoise, an outstanding center of art and learning during the era when Ireland had no equal in Europe in the work of preserving ancient world manuscripts and recording history. Three miles from Clonmacnoise in County Louth was Mellifont Monastery, built in 1142. James Coleman decided that the entrance portal of St. Bernard's Chapel at that monastery would make an unusual and fitting reredos for an altar he wanted to give the Cathedral in memory of deceased members of his family. He visited Mellifont and enlisted help in having the architecture copied. The communion table of the altar was designed with reproductions of the cross of the scriptures at Clonmacnoise and crosses representing members of the Coleman family who were abbots. Henry Wynn, another of the architects who had lost the commission for the Lady Chapel in the competition with Charles Mathews, was successful this time and was designated the designer. Draddy Brothers, one last time, was chosen to build a Cathedral altar. Archbishop Farley consecrated what was popularly called the "Irish altar" in honor of St. Bernard and St. Brigid on May 30, 1903.[27]

The last of the chapel altars was donated by Msgr. Lavelle himself in memory of his father, Patrick. St. Rose of Lima, a saint of the Americas, was the patroness at the new shrine. Statues of St. Margaret, an early martyr, and St. Catherine of Alexandria were placed with St. Rose's statue. Archbishop Farley blessed the altar on August 30, 1906.[28]

When the Cathedral opened, all the lower windows contained stained glass except two on the south side of the sanctuary where the first sacristy was located. Archbishop Corrigan had begun replacing the clear glass with figured stained glass and, now, Archbishop Farley finished the task, bringing to thirty-nine the total of windows with stained glass.[29] The final "unfinished business" was illuminating the interior with electric lights. Since 1894, various schemes had been advanced for replacing the gas jets with electric lamps. Considering the novelty of harnessed electric power, there was great fear of its potential for causing fire, especially since the vaulting was not masonry, but plaster. The solution was to use a steel conduit system through which 68,632 feet of copper cable was strung. It carried current to 2,548 lamps of sixteen candle power each, hardly a sunburst by modern standards, but a marvel in 1904.[30] The expansion of the building at the east end required a new heating system. That same year saw a coal-burning system installed under the supervision of Alfred R. Wolff, a consulting engineer. It performed well until 1942.[31]

Five years after the bells were ready in the north spire, Montell Toulmin came to operate the bulky keyboard used to play hymns. Toulmin and his sister were children of an English immigrant who operated the bells of St. Thomas Episcopal Church, two blocks north of the Cathedral on Fifth Avenue. Their grandfather was Governor Mathews of Georgia. Both children were taught by their father. And so, for forty-four years on Sundays and special feast days, the younger Toulmin left his farm near Bound Brook, New Jersey at 5 a.m., to arrive in the City in time for morning Masses. On holidays, his music was broadcast by radio, and each New Year's Eve, thousands gathered on Fifth Avenue to listen to his hymns of praise and thanksgiving for God's blessings, as they welcomed the new year. Toulmin wrote most of the music he played, and, besides the bells, he mastered the organ, the violin, the mandolin and other instruments. For many years, the music of the elder Toulmin at St. Thomas and the younger Toulmin at St. Patrick's sounded over the Avenue. After her father died, Montell Toulmin's sister took charge of the bells at St. Thomas.[32]

In March 1904, Archbishop Farley was given an auxiliary, Bishop Thomas F. Cusack, who was consecrated at the Cathedral on April 25th. He was in charge of priests who specialized in parish missions, and he served in New York until his appointment to Albany in 1915.[33] Also in 1904, Joseph Rutledge, St. Patrick's verger from its early days, was succeeded by Peter Smith. Mr. Rutledge died a year later and he left his lifetime savings to help eliminate the debt on the Cathedral.[34] The next year, with an end of construction of the Lady Chapel in sight, the Archbishop and Charles Mathews held discussions about building an above-ground sacristy, as had been planned by James Renwick. Archbishop Farley favored a sacristy similar to one at Cologne Cathedral in Germany which he had visited. As Renwick had planned, Mathews designed a Gothic structure which extended from the south ambulatory towards Fiftieth Street; like Renwick's, the Mathews addition was never built. Mathews also drew plans for the iron guards over the residence windows which open on the court north of the Lady Chapel.[35]

Sometimes architectural purists are heard to argue that oil paintings are not proper for Gothic cathedrals, but there were several in St. Patrick's in the early years of the century. Pedro de Moya's *Flight Into Egypt,* copies of Raphael's *Transfiguration* and *The Sistine*

Madonna, The Doubting Thomas, The Baptism of Our Lord, The Marriage Feast of Cana, The Return of the Prodigal Son, St. Patrick Preaching at Tara, and a copy of Andrea del Sarto's *Madonna del Sacco* all hung on Cathedral walls. There was also a tripartite paint-ing.[36] Outside, Thomas Poole in 1908 created elaborate bronze enclosures for the transept doors. They contain panels with the heraldic arms of the first four Archbishops of New York. They were made by Paul Cabaret.[37]

During the early years of Archbishop Farley's administration, the face of the City changed rapidly, largely due to the many immigrants entering the Port of New York. Between 1901 and 1910, almost nine million persons entered, two million of whom were Italians. To-gether with Jewish immigrants from Eastern Europe, they brought the population of New York to nearly five million by the end of the first decade of the century. In that first decade, the tenement population alone increased by half-a-million people. Despite abject poverty, life was not hopeless as many people found employment in City improvement programs. The City fathers' plans for new parks, wider streets, modern piers and a subway system, the City's first, served the double purpose of giving employment to those in need and building a modern metropolis. Twelve thousand laborers worked for twenty cents an hour on the subway project. The first line ran from City Hall to West 145th Street. It opened in 1904.

Charles L. Ritzmann, ?1902

*The ongoing construction of the Cathedral mirrored the explosion of new building in the city during the early decades of the century. Years later, one of those nine million immigrants reflected that he had envisioned streets paved with gold, but once here found that they weren't paved at all, and that **he** had to pave them..*

Four years later, a line was built to Brook-lyn, and another ran through a tube under the Hudson River to New Jersey. In 1909, the Queensboro Bridge was opened to Queens County and the Manhattan Bridge connected with Brooklyn. Far north of the City, the Croton reservoir system was ex-tended into the Catskill watershed, assur-ing a safe and adequate water supply. The magnificent Pennsylvania Railroad Station was completed in 1910 and three years later, its rival, Grand Central Station. The same year, 1913, the imposing Municipal Build-ing and the Woolworth Building, tallest on earth, were opened.[38]

Fifth Avenue changed with the rest of New York. The famous Flatiron Building (*left*) at 23rd Street was erected in 1912 and the palatial New York Public Library re-placed Renwick's Croton Receiving Reser-voir at Forty-second Street in 1911. As-signed to nostalgia today, an identifying treasure of Fifth Avenue, the double-decked bus, was introduced by the Fifth Avenue Coach Company in 1905; two years later the last of the horse-drawn stages disap-peared from the Avenue, and the same year,

the first taxis cruised through the streets. In the Cathedral's immediate neighborhood, on the site of the female orphan asylum, the Boland Trade School was renovated in 1903 to become Cathedral College (*above*), the institution where prospective priests prepared for entry into the Archdiocesan major seminary; the Chancery Office of the Archdiocese moved into the same building. In 1905, Msgr. Lavelle opened Cathedral High School in the elementary school building on Fiftieth Street near Lexington Avenue. Beginning as a parish high school, it eventually became the first of the Archdiocesan high schools.[39]

The Cathedral, by 1908, was the mother-church for 1,200,000 Catholics under the spiritual care of Archbishop Farley.[40] As Rector, Monsignor Lavelle assumed a prominent profile readily recognized throughout the City. Appointed vicar-general in 1902, the following year he was honored with the title *monsignor,* when he became a domestic prelate. "He was much in demand as a speaker at both religious and civic affairs, was chairman of innumerable committees, and indefatigable in his attendance at functions of every kind. He was very popular with the clergy who found him kind, approachable and understanding, and always ready to fill in without notice if anything prevented the appearance of a scheduled speaker of the day." His principal concerns at the Cathedral were financial; he was hard-pressed to eliminate the debt so that the building could be consecrated. When the twenty-fifth anniversary of the opening came and passed in 1904, expenses continued to grow, rather than decrease. By 1910, borrowing had reached $175,000 and some property owned by the Board of Trustees on Thompson Avenue was sold to help pay current expenses. The board treasurer, John Crimmins, recommended that a special yearly collection be established for the specific purpose of reducing the debt. Crimmins further suggested that each church of the Archdiocese be assessed for the same purpose. Crimmins for a long time had been apprehensive about the enormous debt, but Msgr. Lavelle felt that Crimmins was "inclined to be pessimistic." The Board formed a committee to consider solutions. They recommended that wealthy members of the Archdiocese be approached for their help and that the assistance of parishes be enlisted as well.[41]

Msgr. Lavelle's office brought him prestige and civic authorities sought him out as an honored guest or guest speaker on special occasions. In 1909 he addressed the audience at the Metropolitan Opera House at a Lincoln's Birthday celebration; the following June he delivered the opening prayer at the formal inauguration of the Queensboro Bridge. The same year, although he was not appointed to the post, the Trustees of the Catholic University of America in Washington, D. C. recommended him for the rectorship of that institution. As New York's vicar-general, he directed the affairs of the Archdiocese from his Cathedral office whenever Archbishop Farley was away from the City, as, for example, during the Archbishop's trip to Europe from May through August 1909. Often he was host of the many dignitaries who came in a steady stream including Archbishop Glennon; Bishop Kennedy of the American College in Rome; the Archbishop of San Francisco; Cardinal Gibbons; and Archbishop Falconio, the Apostolic Delegate, all of whom visited in 1909.[42]

In November 1903, Pope Pius X wrote a *motu proprio,* a directive on proper liturgical practice, in which he ordered the restoration to the sacred liturgy of Gregorian Chant, the medieval music of the Church. He begged the bishops to support conscientiously both the spirit and the letter of his directive. Archbishop Farley appointed a commission to implement the changes, and by 1904 the grand choir of St. Patrick's was replaced by an all-male choir of thirty voices. The summer before the *motu proprio* was issured, William Pecher, the music director, suffered a heart attack. He was confined to his home for several months and Clement de Macchi substituted at the gallery organ until Mr. Pecher's death in February 1904. Mr. Pecher's contributions to St. Patrick's were recognized with an honor unusual for a layman. An honor guard stood at his bier in the Cathedral for two days before his funeral Mass. Msgr. Lavelle delivered the eulogy. Shortly afterwards, James C. Ungerer, a native of France who had been chancel organist and director of the chancel choir since 1893, succeeded Pecher as Director of Music. To him was left the burden of developing a new program implementing the introduction of plain chant, and training a choir to sing it. Joseph O'Connor took charge of the chancel choir for which he selected boys from both the parish school and Cathedral College. Ungerer encountered resistance from both "lovers of music" and the congregation-at-large who

It was all-out war — some liturgical leaders insisting on only *Gregorian music, others, mindful perhaps of Haydn, Mozart, Palestrina, Bach and music still being created today, rejecting that narrow interpretation of Pius X. Fortunately, Pius X sided with the latter. At a Congress of Sacred Music held in Rome in 1912, he informed the Gregorian hardliners that such intransigent and extremist views were not based on his motu proprio, and that he strongly deprecated insisting on the exclusive use of plain chant. The diehards die hard. At the Council of Trent in 1562, they had tried the same thing and were voted down with the words,* **non impedias musicam** *— don't set up roadblocks where music is concerned.*

found the ancient melodies strange to listen to and difficult to sing. Recalling the glories of the repertoire of past decades, the plain chant was a disappointment for those unfamiliar with its simplicity or those who resented change. One writer optimistically maintained: "When the singers of Gregorian have multiplied, and the choir director can gather for festal days five hundred trained voices, as they do in Montreal and Paris, the solemn and harmonious effect will efface the memory of operatic church music." Instruction in chant was instituted at the archdiocesan seminary and a priests' choir was formed to sing the chant at funerals of clergy and on other special occasions.[43]

In the early years of the century, there were normally six Masses on Sundays, the last of which was a solemn service at which both the gallery and chancel choirs sang. A sermon was always preached, frequently by guest preachers. Every day two priests were available for spiritual counseling at the rectory, and confessions were scheduled on Fridays, Saturdays, the eves of holydays, and additionally whenever needed.[44] Normal Sunday Mass attendance was about twelve thousand persons. Vespers were sung on Sunday afternoons, a tradition which continued into many decades of the century. The usual schedule was often expanded whenever there were special observances. A liturgical highlight each year was the Feast of St. Patrick in March. Other extraordinary events included the ordinations of priests and the consecration of bishops. Heavy crowds were drawn to funerals for members of the hierarchy and clergy, as well as for prominent laymen.[45] There were special services in times of disaster or crisis, and special collections were taken to aid victims of catastrophes, such as that taken for the San Francisco earthquake survivors in 1906, when a very generous response came from parishioners. In 1909, a typical year, liturgies included a pontifical Mass for victims of an earthquake in Italy; a Mass celebrated by the Apostolic Delegate for the Paulist Fathers; a Mass to honor the founder of the Blessed Sacrament Fathers; a St. Patrick's Day Mass attended by throngs including a large contingent from the Sixty-ninth Regiment (a custom still observed today); Holy Week services, some of which lasted two-and-a-half hours; a requiem Mass for the founder of Colliers Magazine; the first Cathedral liturgy of Benediction of the Blessed Sacrament; the first graduation ceremony of Cathedral High School; and the Centenary Mass for the Sisters of Charity when 1600 children's voices were raised in joyous song.[46]

The year 1909 was a busy one in New York's civic life. Many festivities were held and the Cathedral took prominent part in the celebrations. In September, there was a two-week observance, the "Hudson-Fulton" festival, beginning with a naval parade of warships and several marching parades. A grandstand was built in front of St. Patrick's and at nightfall the building was illuminated. A parade manager asked the Cathedral to suspend "peace" flags from the Cathedral spires and the Church happily complied. During one parade, 25,000 troops marched in precise formation past St. Patrick's reviewing stand; during another, fifty-two floats built by German societies added a carnival atmosphere to Fifth Avenue. In October, six thousand members of various Italian societies turned out. The idea of erecting a reviewing stand in front of the building had been sparked earlier that year when the Ancient Order of Hibernians suggested one for the St. Patrick's Day Parade. Monsignor Lavelle stipulated that he would allow it only if the Hibernains could guarantee a "first-rate" event. Archbishop Farley reviewed the parade from the stand and later remarked that the parade was "better than in many years." Woodrow Wilson was the honored speaker at the dinner sponsored by the Friendly Sons of St. Patrick after the parade.[47]

The Centenary of the Diocese of New York was a week-long tribute held from April 26 to May 2, 1908, and though it was not a civic affair, enormous numbers of citizens took part. The principal religious observance was a grand spectacle held at the Cathedral, a solemn pontifical Mass celebrated by Cardinal Michael Logue, Archbishop of Armagh and Primate of All Ireland. Virtually the entire hierarchy of the United States and many prelates from Canada heard Cardinal Gibbons deliver the sermon. A long procession took about one

hour to enter the building. 7,500 persons estimated to have filled every niche in the building heard congratulatory messages from President Theodore Roosevelt and Pope Pius X. A sixty piece orchestra added glorious sounds to the liturgy. Several other Masses followed at St. Patrick's during the week. At Carnegie Hall there was a tribute, the Catholic Club held a reception and on Fifth Avenue 60,000 marchers passed three Cathedral reviewing stands (*above*) specially built to hold 3,500 reviewers. Half-a-million spectators lined the streets.[48]

Probably the most gratifying event of the decade both for Archbishop Farley and for Msgr. Lavelle was the October 5, 1910 consecration of the Cathedral. Because the stubborn debt on the building had been carried beyond the target date for the consecration on the twenty-fifth anniversary of its dedication, the ceremony was delayed for six years. It was a laudable achievement that, within two years after the Archbishop asked for its complete eradication, the $850,000 owed was paid. A splendid five-hour ceremony was conducted by Archbishop Farley attended by a host of ecclesiastical and civic dignitaries. For the first time in the history of the United States, three cardinals were present in a sanctuary together. 50,000 people jammed the streets around the Cathedral for the blessing of the building after which there was a solemn Mass. The Archbishop decreed an annual observance of the event each October in all the churches of the Archdiocese.[49]

According to custom, twelve bronze crosses were erected on the interior walls, and on October 10th each year, candles still are placed with the crosses. It is the responsibility of the sacristan to erect the candles each year on the anniversary of the consecration. In the beginning of the century, the sacristan was Raymond B. Perez. He was the lineal descendent of the family of Rev. Juan Perez, confessor to Christopher Columbus and Queen Isabella of Spain. Raymond Perez was the son of an immigrant from Galicia, Spain.[50]

No small amount of credit for reducing the debt should be assigned to Msgr. Lavelle and the Board of Trustees. Among its members were two mayors of New York, William Russell Grace, the first Catholic to hold the office, and Hugh Grant; John D. Crimmins, who provided substantial assistance to Catholic works of charity; and J. Coleman, who generously supported both the Cathedral needs and many other Catholic charities.[51]

In the four years preceding the outbreak of World War I in Europe, slow but noticeable changes were observed both in the appearance of the midtown neighborhood and in the composition of its residents. The commercial center of the City was gradually moving northward, reflected in the construction of superb commercial and public buildings. As mentioned earlier, the Woolworth Building and the Municipal Building opened in 1913; they dramatically changed the downtown skyline; and closer to the Cathedral, Pennsylvania Station was built on Thirty-fourth Street and Grand Central Station and the New York Public Library on Forty-second Street.[52] Perhaps more contributory to the change in the character of the Cathedral neighborhood was the manifest inclination of New York society to abandon their mansions for life in luxurious apartments. Whereas 90% of the wealthy in New York lived in private homes in 1911, by 1930 the same percentage chose to live in large apartments, large enough to provide them with luxuries to which they were accustomed, including live-in servants. By 1945, more than half the residences of the 1910 Cathedral parish had been razed, and at least another 25% of them had been converted to businesses. On Fifth Avenue, traffic patterns exempli-

Board of Trustees members like William Grace were incredibly wealthy — in those times almost a boast that Catholics could compete with their Protestant forerunners in New York. Even magnanimity was competitive. Grace, for example, founded an institute which gave free tuition to women to study dressmaking, stenography, typewriting, book-keeping and/or domestic science. He was moved to do this after viewing the economic conditions of workers' families during a strike by employees of one of his enterprises. The ubiquitous Sisters of Charity were in charge of his Grace Institute.

fied a bustling business center rather than the placid, even rustic, atmosphere which had retreated into the realm of nostalgia. For the first time, there were more motor vehicles in New York than there were horses in 1917. After that year, even the two-horse streetcars disappeared.[53]

The Cathedral's appearance also changed. A new system of approaches to the building, including steps and terraces, was built in 1911, using granite from Deer Island in Maine.[54] Inside, Woodroffe's Lady Chapel stained glass arrived slowly, but steadily, except for an interruption during the World War I years when work was suspended at his studios.[55] Msgr. Lavelle was happy to receive whatever he could to pay for the glass; one donor was George F. Duval, who promised "up to $3000 and even a little more if necessary."[56] The family of one of the trustees presented a gift of a new altar of the Sacred Heart. Alfonse and Antonio de Navarro, sons of José de Navarro, approached Archbishop Farley in 1910 with the offer of a new altar for the Lady Chapel to memorialize their mother who recently had died. Mrs. Ellen Dykers de Navarro had intended to present the same gift before her death and her sons wanted to fulfill her wishes. The Archbishop suggested, instead, that the donation be for a new Sacred Heart altar. The brothers agreed, stipulating that Mrs. de Navarro's name be inscribed in the frontal base. Traditionally only liturgical Latin texts were used in altar inscriptions, but Archbishop Farley agreed to their request when he learned that Mrs. de Navarro's name had been incised in three other altars she had donated to New Jersey churches. Mrs. de Navarro's name is the only memorial inscription on a St. Patrick's altar.[57]

The sons chose Henry Bacon, one of the prominent architects of the day, to design the new altar. Bacon then was embarking on what would become his best-known work and one of the architectural treasures of America — the Lincoln Memorial in Washington, D. C. Because he specialized in strict, austere classical Greek design, not Gothic, the St. Patrick's commission was altogether unexpected for Bacon. Besides the classical, Bacon was interested in early American architecture from the earliest days of his career. As a student, it was his practice to sketch what he observed, something few of his peers were known to do. He went to Europe in 1889 as a Rotch Traveling Scholar, and returned to this country to work for McKim, Mead and White. He collaborated with Daniel Chester French and Augustus Saint-Gaudens after he entered upon his own practice in 1902. He served on art commissions in New York and Washington, D. C., and won medals, among many awards, at the World's Fairs of 1893 and 1915. A member of New York's Episcopal Church, the only Gothic piece he produced is here at St. Patrick's, and is more austere than what was to be found in Gothic art of Catholic churches of his time, possibly reflecting his preference for classical design. Cardinal Farley consecrated the altar in May 1913. The original bronze Sacred Heart altar was transferred to a chapel at St. Joseph's Seminary in Yonkers.[58]

In 1915, nine years after he has sculptured it, William Ordway Partridge presented his beautiful creation, the *Pieta*, to St. Patrick's Cathedral.[59] Robert Burns Wilson, after seeing the statue for the first time, was moved to write:

"It has all the 'bigness' that can be put into marble and it has such a feeling wrought into it that one neglects to think of it as a work of art, and knows only that he is looking upon the Mother, the Mother of the Man, the Man from whose birth the days of our years are reckoned. In absolute simplicity it is classic. It is the woman of all ages, the woman whose heart of love is stronger than even the mighty sorrow of the mother who has seen her son die on the cross. This noble work shows how fine in appreciation, how deeply penetrative is the mind that conceived it. In the treatment of the great subject, nothing has been forgotten. Here is the breadth – the avoidance of trivialities – the strength which the purely critical view demands. This dead Christ is dead; this is the body of a man who died hanging upon the cross. The strained muscles of the arms recall those dreadful hours. We note all these things, feeling that they are nothing; so perfect is the art that they seem natural actualities, and we so accept them. It is, however, not exactly within the province of words to depict what we feel when we see the Mother's unconscious action, prompted by the hunger of her breaking heart, as she uplifts and holds the body with the head on her arm; we see the instinctive effort of her being to realize, in some sense, if only for a moment, some semblance of the life that is gone. It is the cry of a mother's heart, pitiful and pitying, over the son who she knows is dead. It is also the cry of the breast, the arms, the hands which must feel once that he is alive. One looks at this group and there he realizes, if never before, that what is human is divine."[60]

A mother understands best — as a world at war was learning once again in 1915, the year this statue was displayed in the Cathedral.

Partridge was born in Paris on April 11, 1861 of wealthy parents from New England. His father was an artist and an art collector who relocated his family to Paris during the fashionable Second French Republic and Second Empire of Napoleon III, the era of the 1850s and 1860s. His mother's cousin was George Catlin, known for his paintings of American Indians. His own cousin was John Rogers. Partridge began his studies in this country and continued his training in Stuttgart, Paris, Naples and Florence. After returning to New York in 1884, he studied at Columbia College. In 1887, after a brief flirtation with the stage, he went to Rome to study sculpture under Pio Wlonski. His career as a sculptor and art critic began two years later in Milton, Massachusetts. In hopes of gaining recognition for an American school of sculpture, he helped found the Society of American Sculptors. Ironically, he is usually thought of as belonging to the beaux-arts period of the nineteenth century, even though his more than two hundred creations were made in the twentieth. A multi-talented man, he was an author, an actor, a lecturer and a poet. His *Pieta* was not signed, so after his death, his wife arranged to have a facsimile of his signature cut into the stone. The pedestal on which it rests was not added until 1952.[61]

The number of precious vestments and sacred vessels donated over several decades induced Cardinal Farley to seek a second sacristy to house them properly. Anne Leary, one of New York society's "Four Hundred," was known for extraordinary works of charity. When she offered to donate the money to build an addition, it appeared that another of Renwick's dreams – a sacristy above ground – would become a reality. Many European cathedrals have such rooms, called *treasuries,* and Charles Mathews was chosen to design a treasury-sacristy resembling those at Cologne Cathedral and Paris' Notre Dame. Mathews' drawings show the addition where Renwick planned it, extending from the south ambulatory to Fiftieth Street, but including an underground crypt.[62]

Pope Leo XIII had made Anne Leary a countess in 1902; she was the first American woman to receive a title from the Holy See. Her wealth was inherited, most from her father who had made his fortune as a hatter in New York. One of his clients was John Jacob Astor, who supplied him with beaver pelts acquired from Astor's far west businesses. Countess Anne lived in one of the grand Fifth Avenue mansions where she entertained lavishly.[63] Her brother, George, owned a house on the Avenue at 86th Street. When another mansion was built on a lot adjoining the Learys' and blocking their open view southward, George expressed his disapproval, one story relates, by having a small sculpture carved on the surface of his house facing the offending neighbor. It was a carving of a figure with a disrespectful thumb placed to the nose.[64]

Much of Anne's wealth was dispensed to worthy charities including Bellevue Hospital for a chapel. Apparently, she planned a bequest to pay for the sacristy-treasury at St. Patrick's, but after her death in 1919, her will was contested, and years of lawsuits completely consumed the legacy. Neither the sacristy nor the burial vault intended for her remains and those of her family members could be built. Her body was interred in a vault beneath Old St. Patrick's Cathedral, and buried with her, at least temporarily, was another of Renwick's dreams.[65]

Before the dark days of World War I, many happy celebrations crowned the years. One of them was an extraordinary demonstration of enthusiasm by half-a-million Catholics who lined the City streets to welcome Cardinal Farley on his return from Rome in January 1912 after he entered the College of Cardinals. There were three Americans among the nineteen named worldwide by Pope Pius X, and for the first time the new cardinals were able to travel to the Holy City to receive the emblems of their office from the Pope personally. In American Church history, only five prelates had been granted the red hat, and two were from New York.[66] The City "pulled out all the stops" for the occasion. A special ship sailed from New York to Hoboken, New Jersey, to meet the Cardinal's transatlantic steamer at its point of debarkation. Four hundred officials escorted him to the Battery where a parade was formed by scores of cars, mounted police and a horse-drawn carriage for the Cardinal. The entourage proceeded up Broadway to Twenty-third Street, then turned up Fifth Avenue to St. Patrick's. Along the path were "people jostling, crowding, waving their hats, with handkerchiefs, flags and pennants a-flutter everywhere in every hand, and from every window of the towering Whitehall Building." All along the flag-draped route, strains of "Home Sweet Home" were never out of hearing range, and at points along the way the crowds swarmed close to the carriage in frantic disregard of orders by overwhelmed police. Dazed, more than once the Cardinal felt his lip quiver, "and when the spires of the Cathedral could be seen ahead and from its chimes the notes of that homecoming melody that all the bands had been playing all along the way could be heard, those near the carriage say that the Cardinal's eyes were wet with tears." Inside the Cathedral, six thousand children and hundreds of priests awaited him. In the week following, St. Patrick's was illuminated every night by 50,000 bulbs which outlined its profile. A tribute from President Taft was read at a celebration dinner after the Cathedral welcome; New York's Governor John Dix personally delivered a tribute.[67]

Later that year, the first religious service sponsored by trade unions in the City was conducted at St. Patrick's. Msgr. Lavelle led a solemn vespers service on the eve of Labor Day for five thousand workers joined by many union leaders. The tradition continues with Labor Day services at the Cathedral to the present day.[68] Pope Pius X died in August 1914 and Archbishop John Bonzano, the Apostolic Delegate, offered a solemn pontifical Mass for his soul. In the center aisle was a catafalque displaying duplicates of the Pope's tiara and the symbol of the keys of the fisherman.[69]

Just weeks before the Pontiff's death, on July 29th, war erupted in Europe. Strong forces were at work in America to assure that this conflict remain European — that the United States stay isolated from entanglements in European alliances. Indeed, Woodrow Wilson, President since 1912, would win a second term in 1916 after he pledged to continue to keep the American nation out of the war. Fulfilling his promise proved elusive for many reasons, one of which was the emotional response of many Americans to the sinking of the British steamer *Lusitania* by a German submarine after the liner, carrying many Americans, left New York's Fourteenth Street pier and approached the coast of Ireland.

Even though America was not in the war until 1917, Jacques Ungerer, the Cathedral Director of Music, returned to France to help defend his homeland. He was in the French army from October 1914 until April 1915. During the period, John Philip Foley substituted for him at St. Patrick's.[70]

Not all Americans agreed with Wilson's stance, and sporadic acts of violence sometimes occurred to protest his neutral position. On October 4th, Cardinal Farley preached at the Cathedral in support of peace; nine days later, a bomb exploded in the Cathedral. It was supposed that the 4:45 p.m. blast was caused by dynamite, certainly dangerous, but the time of the occurrence was fortunate, since no crowds were in the building and, consequently, there were no injuries. The sound of the blast heard many blocks away brought police and clergy rushing to the scene. Auxiliary Bishop Hayes was working at his desk in the Chancery Office across 51st Street; he "did not move a muscle," but appeared some time later when he "quietly directed the closing of the Cathedral to the public, arranged other details and then with his usual calm, returned to the work that had been so violently interrupted." Two pews were destroyed, there was minor damage to the floor and some of the stained glass over the altar of St. Bernard and St. Brigid was broken, but there was no other harm to the building. That night, around 11 p.m., another bomb was set off outside St. Alphonsus Church.[71]

Both incidents were attributed to "anarchists" intent on drawing attention to the war and to the death of the Spanish revolutionary, Francisco Ferrer. The New York City Police Department managed to infiltrate organizations of suspected anarchists in the City during the following months. A plot was uncovered to unleash another bomb blast in May before the 7:30 a.m. Mass, a time when many people would be in the pews. Two of the detectives scattered around the building were disguised as cleaning women and they apprehended two conspirators, a cobbler named Carmine Carbone and his accomplice, Frank Abarno. Both men were sentenced to prison terms. Cardinal Farley expressed sorrow at the fate of one of the men whose parents he knew to be good people suffering "disgrace and affliction."

Practicing what the Church taught and what he preached, he expressed forgiveness demanded by the Gospel of Christ. [72]

These and other terrorist plots had little evident effect on political moves to draw the nation into the war, but a series of other events led to America's entry in April 1917. Fear of hostilities on home soil was almost non-existent, and the Cathedral's Board of Trustees declined the next month to insure the building against war damage. Throughout the City and the Archdiocese, there was enthusiastic support for the war effort. When the Holy See created the American Military Diocese in November to minister to military personnel, Bishop Patrick Hayes of New York was appointed Chaplain Bishop. He had been consecrated an auxiliary bishop in October 1914. Over one thousand American priests were under the jurisdiction of Bishop Hayes, including eighty-seven chaplains from New York. [73]

Support for Americans in the military and the war effort at home was strong at St. Patrick's. Shortly after America's entry, the Young Men's Clubs of the Cathedral began preparatory training for those eligible for induction. Fundraising events included a baseball game at the Polo Grounds. There were special collections for a library fund for the Army and for support of the chaplains; a drive for pledges of food conservation; war bond drives; and a special Mass on the Fourth of July to beg for "a speedy and victorious issue in the impending conflict," "impending" because Americans did not join the fighting ranks in Europe until well into 1918. In January 1918, Cardinal Farley solemnly blessed a service flag with 502 stars, one for each Cathedral parishioner in the military. The flag was hoisted at the Cathedral and flew until after the armistice ending the fighting. By May, half of the members of the Cathedral Young Men's Clubs were in military service, and a second draft promised to add many more to the ranks. Labor Day Masses were offered for military personnel and for a speedy termination of the war. At the end of September, a special Mass attended by a large deputation from the Sixty-ninth Regiment was offered for those who had given their lives. Fund raisers continued even as the war drew to a close late in 1918, since there was general expectation of a long delay in the return of those oversees. Many never returned. Private George A. Atkins was the first parishioner to fall in battle. He died in France. The funeral Mass for the poet Joyce Kilmer was offered at the Cathedral on October 14th, less than a month before hostilities ended. [74]

While the war was always on the minds of most Americans, and a source of overwhelming anxiety for many, the ordinary routine of ministry continued at the Cathedral. A Mass was offered for Emperor Franz Joseph of Austria after his death in 1916, and the following year Masses were offered for the souls of Cardinal Falconio, former Apostolic Delegate to the United States and Archbishop Thomas Kennedy, Rector of the American College in Rome. In August 1918, the Knights of Columbus opened their national convention at the Cathedral. [75] And Msgr. Lavelle had to be concerned with such mundane matters as the support of the school. He asked those who could to underwrite the expense of educating the children, $12 per child each year, about one-third the annual cost of an equivalent public school education, he asserted. He begged "those whom God has blest with ample means" to give more to balance donations of those who could afford little. Cardinal Farley continued to officiate each Sunday at the 11 o'clock Mass, often with visiting dignitaries in attendance. In May 1917, Former President Reyes of Columbia, South America, found a sermon delivered by a guest preacher "most impressive and instructive," even though the Dominican priest spoke for almost one hour extending the Mass until 1 p.m.[76]

Barely two months later, the Cardinal underwent surgery and he was rarely seen in public afterwards. Late in August 1918, his condition was critical. On August 25th, Msgr. Lavelle announced in the Cathedral that there was "just a ray of hope." In the beginning of September, his condition improved slightly, but pneumonia developed and he died on September 17th at his summer home in Orienta Point, Mamaroneck, New York. The twenty-five mile route from Orienta Point to the Cathedral was lined with the prayerful as his body was transported, accompanied by a cortege of fifty cars. On September 22nd, crowds waiting to view his remains were five deep in two lines, one on Fifth Avenue and one on Madison Avenue, from Fifty-first Street to Seventieth Street. During the next two days there were several services and the funeral was held on September 25th, attended by three cardinals, forty-two archbishops and bishops and twelve hundred priests. Crowds filled the space outside for blocks around during the Mass sung by Archbishop John Bonzano, the Apostolic Delegate. The Cardinal's red *galero* was suspended next to Cardinal McCloskey's over the crypt where his body was laid to rest.[77]

1. Lavelle to Farley, May 16, 1902, AANY.

2. Smith, p. 589.

3. Cohalan, *Popular History*, pp. 178-180.

4. *Ibid.*, pp. 178-179. Father Farley was secretary of Archbishop (and later Cardinal) McCloskey from 1872 to 1884. His description of the windows first appeared in print in the Journal of the Fair in 1878. Shortly after he became Archbishop, he gave the benediction at the laying of the cornerstone of the New York Public Library in 1902. *See:* Henry Hope Reed, *The New York Public Library, Its Architecture and Decoration*, W. W. Norton and Company, New York, 1986, p. 44.

5. By April 1903, the foundations of the chapel were complete and the walls had risen about three or four feet above ground level. *See:* New York Times, April 19, 1903.

6. Minutes of the Board of Trustees, October 1, 1903, December 3, 1903; Correspondence of Tiffany Company and Charles Mathews, 1901-1906, *passim*, Archives of Lockwood-Mathews Mansion Museum, Norwalk Connecticut, hereafter cited as ALMMM.

7. Minutes of the Board of Trustees, 1903, *passim*. The cost of the door was $2850.

8. Minutes of the Board of Trustees, November 2, 1905; estimate of costs for Lady Chapel as of March 4, 1904, ASPC; George Gillespie to Mathews, April 4, 1905; John Agar to Mathews, June 14, 1906, ALMMM. Mathews' designs for the Lady Chapel and the adjacent chapels are at the Cooper-Hewitt Museum (a division of the Smithsonian Institution) in New York. His drawings of the *lavabo* and *sacrarium* in the sacristy are among them.

The heavy work of setting huge stones at high levels of the Cathedral was not without its risks. On April 15, 1905, Andrew Brown, an expert marble worker, lost his footing above the northeast transept and fell to his death on the roof fifty feet below, dragging with him a huge turret weighing two hundred pounds which he had been setting on a base. *See:* New York Times, April 16, 1905.

9. Mathews to Agar, June 17, 1906; Mathews to Michael Bouvier, April 23, 1906; Mathews to Farley and Agar, June 17, 18, 1906, ALMMM.

10. Mathews to Wills, January 10, 1906; Mathews to Agar, October 5, 1906; Mathews to Wills, December 1, December 11, 1906, ALMMM; *Cathedral Bulletin*, October 1960; Minutes

of the Board of Trustees, 1907-1908, *passim*. Mathews approved removal of the wooden partition which had separated the original sacristy from the chapel of St. Joseph on December 11, 1906. While work continued in the chapel upstairs, downstairs carpeting was laid in the smaller sacristies (there are actually three sacristies below the chapels), and an order was placed for Tiffany glass in sacristy areas. The cost of glass for fourteen windows was set at $450 in January, 1906. *See:* Daniel Harrington to Mathews, January 11, 1906, ALMMM. It is not known where the Tiffany windows were placed in the sacristy areas, since they are no longer there; it is suspected that they were ceiling windows allowing light from the terrace above.

It is not known, also, how it was possible for Mass to be celebrated at Christmas 1906, since the marble floor was not in place. Just the day before, Christmas Eve, Mathews gave the contractor permission to lay filling over the beams of the lower sacristy, the filling necessary as a base for the marble. The cost of the marble floor including the platforms and steps for the altar was $18,353. Carrara marble had been used in the mosaic floor of the sacristy below. Traitel Brothers installed the chapel floor.

Temporary "arc lights" were used in the chapel until the permanent fixtures were in place in 1907. The permanent lamps were made by Sterling Bronze Company of New York. The exact date of completion of the Mathews addition is not known (excepting the altars of the side chapels), but the amount of work unfinished well into 1907 leads me to believe it was not completed before the end of 1907, more likely early in 1908. *See:* Mathews correspondence, 1907, ALMMM.

11. Minutes of the Board of Trustees, June 4, 1908; Mathews to Farley, June 16, 1908; Mathews to T. Kelly, February 25, 1907, ALMMM.

12. Mathews to Farley, June 16, 1908, ALMMM.

13. *Nineteenth Century Architects, Building a Profession*, exhibition booklet, Lockwood-Mathews Mansion Museum, Norwalk, Connecticut, April 1-April 29, 1990.

14. Paul Vincent Woodroffe to Farley, August 1, 1909, April 4, 1910, August 1, 1910, AANY.

15. *Paul Woodroffe, 1875-1954*, exhibition booklet, William Morris Gallery, London, November 20, 1982-January 9, 1983; *Nursery Songs*, Metropolitan Museum of Art, Thames and Hudson, 1980, preface. The Arts and Crafts Movement was founded in England in the nineteenth century by those concerned about adverse effects the Industrial Revolution was having on workers and on the quality of their products. Mass production, they felt, caused monotony because of the repetition of motions and lack of creative work. William Morris, one of the founders of the Arts and Crafts Movement, turned to the work of medieval craftsmen for inspiration to bring dignity and satisfaction to workers, something he believed machines denied their operators. Morris and others formed a company which produced goods by hand. An American, Elbert Hubbard, brought the industry to this country in the 1890s, beginning in Erie County, New York. The Movement came to fruition in the early years of the twentieth century. *See:* *Heritage Magazine*, July/August 1990; Reyntiens, Patrick, *The Beauty of Stained Glass*, Little Brown and Company, Boston, 1990, pp. 28, 148.

16. *Paul Woodroffe, 1875-1954*, exhibition booklet; Minutes of the Board of Trustees, 1913, *passim;* Paul Woodroffe to Mathews, October 1, 1907, ASPC; Robert Reiley to Cardinal Hayes, November 3, 1927, AANY; Peter Cormack to Thomas Young, October 4, 1982, July 26, 1983, ASPC. One of the craftsmen (glaziers) employed by Woodroffe between the world wars was Fred Bennett. In 1983 he said his best recollection was that four separate French and German firms were involved in building the windows, in addition to the John Hardman Company and Woodroffe's studio. He believed there were two French firms and two German firms. The name Carl de Bouche of Munich appears in a window over the altar of St. Michael and St. Louis. Gabriel Mayer of the German firm *Franz Mayer of Munich* told the author that Mr. de Bouche owned a small studio in Munich along with about a dozen other artists in the late nineteenth century, and

that he, Mr. de Bouche, collaborated with Mayer on many projects. According to Mr. Gabriel Mayer, most of the records of the Mayer Company, possibly the most famous maker of stained glass in Germany, were destroyed during World War II. Some sketchy fragments survived, but they lacked details. The Franz Mayer Company's American division is in New Jersey.

17. Farley, p. 169

18. Michael Bouvier to Mathews, January 3, 1904, ALMMM.

19. Handwritten notes of Bishop Joseph Flannelly re: altars of St. Patrick's Cathedral, 1960, ASPC. Mr. Bouvier's father, also named Michael, was born in Point St. Esprit, France on March 19, 1792 and died in Philadelphia on June 9, 1874. Louise Vernoa Bouvier was born in Philadelphia on March 29, 1811 and died in the same city on October 9, 1872.

20. Bouvier to Mathews, January 3, 1904, ALMMM. The first Tiffany estimate for the altar was $18,000, which was twice revised, settling at $14,000. Mathews wrote to Bouvier in 1906 that, because the bids for his original design were too high, i.e., apparently higher than what Bouvier planned to donate, he would have to "give up the design which I made, and begin all over again." (Correspondence of Mathews, Tiffany and Bouvier, January through March, 1906, *passim, ALMMM).*

21. Correspondence of Mathews, Bouvier and Bond Thomas of Tiffany Company, 1906-1909, *passim,* ALMMM. The Reliance Labor Club, a union of marble setters, made the objection to employing Mr. Gunella. Paul J. Gunella had worked at Milan Cathedral for over twenty-five years under his uncle who was in charge of the work there. The Piccirilli family of sculptors did carving for many of the best known artists in America including Daniel Chester French and Augustus Saint-Gaudens. Attilio Piccirilli was the best known member of the family. He studied at the Royal Academy of Fine Arts and the Academy of San Luca in Rome before coming to New York in 1888 where other members of his family were already working on East 55th Street. Independent of other sculptors, Attilio carved the sculpture for the Maine Monument at Columbus Circle, and the medallions of the Morgan Library and the Frick Collection in New York. The brothers also carved the statue of Abraham Lincoln for Washington's Lincoln Memorial, the pediment group at the New York Stock Exchange, the "Four Continents" at the United States Customs House and the lions at the New York Public Library. The studio of the family was located in the Bronx. *See:* Reed, Henry Hope, *The New York Public Library,* W. W. Norton Company, New York, 1986, p. 38; *also: New York Times*, Real Estate Section, October 17, 1999, p. 9.

Another problem arose when a subcontractor failed to follow Mathews' specifications and parts of the altar had to be dismantled and reassembled. A further delay resulted from a disagreement about the choice of jointing material. A serious difficulty was the discovery by Mathews that one of the subcontractors allowed another sculptor the use of some of Mathews' drawings. When Mathews saw a statue resembling one he had designed for the Cathedral altar, he prevailed upon his attorneys to take action. The subcontractor agreed not to allow the use of the Mathews designs and the statue was destroyed.

22. Handwritten notes of Bishop Joseph Flannelly re: altars of St. Patrick's Cathedral, 1960, ASPC. Mr. Crimmins was born on May 18, 1844 and was baptized in St. John the Evangelist Church, which was on the site of the present Cathedral. Lily Louise Lalor was born in New York on January 10, 1848. She died on March 6, 1888.

23. *See: Alive and Well Magazine,* June, 1980.

24. Rev. Daniel McMackin to unknown correspondent, April 1, year unknown, possibly 1902; Mathews to Thomas Kelly, Feb. 25, 1907; Mathews to Farley, May 3, June 13, 1907, ALMMM; *Catholic News,* January 15, 1910. The altar is Paterno marble. The niches are lined with malachite. Mathews was so distressed about the Archbishop's intention to have Paolo Medici

submit a design that he told the Archbishop that he (Mathews) would "hound the man out of the profession" if he intruded into the work which Mathews felt had been guaranteed to him.

25. Farley, p. 166; measurements of Cathedral taken on August 10, 1983, ASPC. Some publications about St. Patrick's have printed erroneous information about its dimensions. For example, Meehan in 1910 and the Paulist Press booklet in 1922 record the extreme interior length as 370 feet. In 1983, Cathedral employees measured the interior at 376 feet. Meehan and the Paulist Press publication give the exterior length as 398 feet; in other places it appears as just over 400 feet, and again as 405 feet.

26. Interview with Msgr. Florence Cohalan, December 1994.

27. Farley, pp. 210-212. John Draddy died in Italy in 1904, shortly after the altar was finished.

28. *St. Patrick's Cathedral, New York,* Archbishopric of New York, 1942, hereafter cited as *Archbishopric,* p. 52; *Cathedral Bulletin,* October 1960.

29. *Centenary of the Archdiocese of New York,* unpublished manuscript by Msgr. Walter P. Kellenberg, Chancellor, September 5, 1950, ASPC, hereafter cited as *Centenary,* pp. 52, 53

30. Farley, pp. 210, 225-227; Minutes of the Board of Trustees, January 7, February 4, February 23, 1904. The wiring was completed in February 1904. The system was installed by the Charles L. Eidlitz Company.

31. Farley, pp. 227-229; Fred Mack to Archbishop Francis Spellman, September 28, November 6, 1942, ASPC. Besides new heating equipment, a fresh air ventilation system was introduced using registers located at the ends of the pews. Two blast-wheels, eight feet in diameter, moved the air through iron ducts under the floor to the four-hundred-sixty pew registers. A separate system of heat and ventilation was built for the Lady Chapel.

32. *New York Times,* May 16, 1946; *Catholic News,* May 25, 1946, April 9, 1952.

33. Delaney, p. 131; Cohalan, *Popular History,* p. 205; Farley, p. 150. Bishop Cusack was Rector of St. Stephen's Church on East 28th Street. Rev. Edward McGlynn, who had entered into the Henry George controversy with Archbishop Corrigan, was a former Rector of this largest parish church of the Archdiocese. It is one of the few surviving New York buildings designed by James Renwick. In 1990, the parish merged with that of Our Lady of the Scapular of Mount Carmel and the building of the latter was demolished, the proceeds of the sale of the property used for a renovation of the exterior of the Renwick building. Restoration of the Romanesque Revival style interior, including art of Constantino Brumidi, master of murals in the United States Capitol Building, is currently in progress. The church has more than one hundred stained glass windows by Mayer of Munich who helped Woodroffe with St. Patrick's Lady Chapel windows. *See:* Catholic New York, July 17, 1997.

34. Carthy, *Magnificence,* p. 131; *Catholic News,* October 23, 1915. A verger was assigned to care for the interior of a church or cathedral and to act as an attendant. The term is no longer used at St. Patrick's. Instead those who help with seating, security, collections and similar duties are called ushers.

In some European cathedrals and universities, a verger took part in ceremonies, carrying a rod or similar symbol of office in processions in front of dignitaries such as bishops or university presidents. Even in this century, vergers continue to perform that ceremonial function.

At St. Paul's Cathedral and Winchester Cathedral the old spelling, *virger,* is still used. *See:* Oxford Universal Dictonary, Oxford University Press, London, 1955, pp. 2346, 2360.

35. Farley to Mathews, July 5, 1906; Mathews to McMurray, June 4, 1907, ALMMM; *Nineteenth Century Architects: Building a Profession,* photograph of Mathews' sacristy plans

36. Farley, p. 215. In 1898 there was also a painting of St. Sebastian in the baptistry. *See:* Smith, John Talbot, *Cathedral Bells,* Jenkins Co., New York, 1898, n.p.

37. Farley, p. 209, footnote; Minutes of the Board of Trustees, February 1908.

38. Cohalan, *Popular History,* pp. 182, 211-212; Lankevich, George J. and Furer, Howard B., *A Brief History of New York City,* Associated, Port Washington, N. Y., 1984, pp. 199-201. "In 1900, 36 percent of all working Irish were employed by the City; by 1930, the figure was 52 percent."

More than two million Italians arrived in this country between 1900 and 1910, most of them through the Port of New York, and nearly half of them remained in New York for a time. The vast majority of excavators and rockmen, those who dug and hauled away the rubble for subway construction, were Italian immigrants.

"The skilled trade unions in New York City barred African-Americans from membership or segregated them into their own locals." But, they were able to find work in the most hazardous jobs, working in the deep rock and underwater tunnels, where others shunned employment. *See: Steel, Stone and Backbone, Building New York's Subways, 1900-1925,* exhibition pamphlet, New York Transit Museum, March 26-July 6, 1997.

39. Lankevich, p. 206; Ellis, pp. 462, 494; Carthy, *Magnificence,* pp. 74-83 *passim,* 87

40. Farley, appendix.

41. Cohalan, *Popular History,* p. 181; Journal of Msgr. Lavelle, October, November, December 1909, *passim;* John Crimmins to Board of Trustees, April 7, 1910, AANY, folder I-13

42. Carthy, *Magnificence,* pp. 104-107, *passim;* Journal of Msgr. Lavelle, 1909, *passim.* Msgr. Lavelle celebrated the silver jubilee of his ordination to the priesthood in 1904.

43. Farley, p. 152; Smith, pp. 612-613; *Cathedral Bulletin,* March 1947; *Catholic News,* February 27,1904. Pecher was buried in Calvary Cemetery.

44. Smith, p. 438. "The regular staff of the cathedral parish" consisted of the Rector and five assistant priests.

45. An example of an extraordinary liturgical service was a pontifical Mass of requiem offered for the deceased Pope Leo XIII on July 29, 1903. All seats were filled and there was an abundance of standees. A catafalque was in place at the entrance to the sanctuary. Besides the two hundred priests and seminarians in the procession, veterans of the Papal Guard who had fought for Pope Pius IX also walked at the head of the line. Many foreign governments sent representatives. William Pecher directed the music. *See: New York Times,* July 30, 1903.

46. Smith, p. 438; Carthy, *Magnificence,* p. 98; Cathedral announcements, *passim;* Journal of Msgr. Lavelle, 1909, *passim.*

47. Journal of Msgr. Lavelle, 1909, *passim.*

48. *Catholic News,* May 2, May 9, 1908; *Parish Monthly,* Church of Our Lady of Good Counsel, New York, June 1908; *New York Times,* April 29, May 2, May 3, 1908. The grand parade began at Washington Square and ended at 57th Street. The excitement engendered by the presence of Cardinal Logue and the determination of many to catch a view of him almost created panic near the Cathedral. As the last contingents of the parade passed the crowds in the streets of the Forties along Fifth Avenue, spectators fell in behind the end of the marchers in order to see the Cardinal on the Cathedral steps. An immense crowd developed with each passing street, so that when the police at the Cathedral were faced with an immense throng rushing forward, they formed a human box around the Cardinal and Archbishop Farley to protect them from injury. They managed to press through the crowds to the Archbishop's residence on Madison Avenue, but the mass of people continued to press so that one of the mounted police officers and his horse toppled to the ground. A near-stampede broke out, and ambulances rushed to the scene to aid the many injured. Police finally managed to disperse the crowds by forming a wedge of mounted officers moving along the Avenue.

49. Cohalan, *Popular History*, p. 96; *Catholic News*, October 8, 1910.

50. Richard N. Fastiggi to Thomas Young, April 4, April 14, 1997, ASPC.

51. Listing of Trustees of St. Patrick's Cathedral, ASPC. William Russell Grace was born in Ireland and went to sea as a boy. He worked in Peru for a shipping firm as a young man and, while still in his twenties, he formed W. R. Grace and Company in New York. He became an advisor to the Peruvian government, and supplied the country with materials for building railroads and equipment for building an army and navy. He helped the country resolve its national debt in return for concessions of silver mines, railroads and other benefits. He then expanded his business to other countries in South America. He founded the New York and Pacific Steamship Company and operated service to the west coast of South America. As New York's mayor, he opposed Tammany Hall with a program of reform. He was a generous benefactor of workers and the poor. He died in 1904.

John Daniel Crimmins helped make his father's contracting firm one of the largest in the city. He constructed most of New York's railroad lines, and built many skyscrapers, hospitals and churches and the City's first underground telephone and telegraph lines. He was a trustee of several Catholic institutions, including the Cathedral. *See:* Delaney, pp. 124, 221-222; *Alive and Well Magazine,* June 1990.

52. Cohalan, *Popular History*, p. 211

53. Carthy, *Magnificence,* pp. 93-94; Ellis, p. 509; *Cathedral Bulletin*, February 1956.

54. Application, Bureau of Buildings, Borough of Manhattan, 1911, ASPC. An application was filed on July 1, 1911 for work including new granite retaining walls, and new marble platforms and steps. The architect was T. H. Poole and Company of Thirtieth Street.

55. Minutes of Board of Trustees, February 13, 1913.

56. Lavelle to Farley, November 21, 1911, AANY.

57. Correspondence of de Navarro brothers, May 6, 1900, April 3, April 4, April 10, April 14, April 18, May 9, May 31, 1910, AANY. Ellen Dykers de Navarro donated altars to Holy Cross Church in Rumson and Our Lady Star of the Sea Church in Long Branch, New Jersey. José de Navarro, her husband, had been a contributor to the building of Holy Cross Church in 1883. The de Navarros maintained a home near Sea Bright, New Jersey. José was president of Ingersoll-Rand Company. He was succeeded in that office by W. R. Grace, Mayor of New York City.

Antonio de Navarro was married to Mary Anderson, a famous actress. Alfonse de Navarro was a member of the Board of Trustees of St. Patrick's. He died in 1926 in Scotland, leaving a considerable amount of his estate to charitable causes. *See: New York Times*, September 19, 1926; Eric Beerman to Thomas Young, June 5, 1996, ASPC.

58. Christopher Thomas to Thomas Young, September 9, 1993, November 19, 1993, ASPC; *Pencil Points Magazine,* May 1924. The images of two saints are at each end of the altar. It is not known whom they represent. In the *Cathedral Bulletin*, October 1960, is the statement: "At each end of the reredos stand two saints particularly devoted to the Sacred Heart."

59. Tour of St. Patrick's Cathedral, 1982; *Cathedral Bulletin*, August 1948, August 1966; Minutes of the Board of Trustees, March 11, 1915; Catalog of Works of William Ordway Partridge, exhibition booklet, State University College at Plattsburgh, New York, October 20-November 20, 1974.

60. Robert Burns Wilson, *William Ordway Partridge*, International Studio Magazine, Volume 31, 1907.

61. Catalog of Works of William Ordway Partridge. Partridge died on May 22, 1930.

62. Minutes of the Board of Trustees, April 10, 1913 *et passim 1911-1921*; Carthy, *Magnificence,* p. 65; *New York Times*, September 3, 1990. Miss Leary earlier had offered to donate an

altar at the intersection of the choir and the south transept, possibly a Sacred Heart altar which later was donated by the de Navarro family.

63. Carthy, *Magnificence,* p. 65; *New York Times,* September 3, 17, 1990; index for missing correspondence re: Anne Leary, AANY.

64. Interview with Msgr. Florence Cohalan, December 1994

65. *New York Times,* September 3, 17, 1990; index for missing correspondence re: Anne Leary, AANY.

66. Cohalan, *Popular History,* pp. 197-198.

67. *Catholic News,* January 20, 1912.

68. *Catholic News,* September 7, 1912.

69. *Catholic News,* September 5, 1914. The Pope had died on August 20th.

70. Notes of Msgr. Flannelly re: organists, 1944, ASPC; *Cathedral Bulletin,* March 1947

71. Carthy, *Magnificence,* p. 99; *Catholic News,* October 17, 1914; *New York Times,* September 5, 1938.

72. Carthy, *Magnificence,* pp. 98-99; Farley to Bishop McFaul, March 8, 1915; Farley to Bishop Shahan, March 5, 1915; Farley to Father Walsh, March 6, 1915, AANY; Burton, Katherine, *The Dream Lives Forever,* Longmans, Green and Co., New York, 1960.

73. Minutes of the Board of Trustees, May 10, 1917; Cohalan, *Popular History,* pp. 213, 217.

74. Cathedral announcements, 1917-1919, *passim.* In March 1918, there was a Catholic war drive to raise $2,500,000; the Cathedral was assigned a goal of $50,000. It was estimated that at least 35% of American fighting men were Catholics. Approximately one thousand were members of the Cathedral parish.

75. Cathedral announcements, 1916-1918, *passim.*

76. Lavelle to "My Dear Friends," October 15, 1917, ASPC; R. Reyes to Farley, March 16, 1917, AANY.

77. *Catholic News,* September 21, September 28, 1918, February 15, 1919; Cathedral announcements, September 22, 1918; Cohalan, *Popular History,* p. 214.

CHAPTER VII

A Wounded Time: the 'Cardinal of Charity', Patrick Hayes

During Cardinal Farley's funeral Mass, Archbishop Bonzano, the Apostolic Delegate, revealed that it was the Cardinal's "earnest wish" that his Auxiliary Bishop, Patrick Hayes, become his successor. If the choice was to be from local clergy, Bishop Hayes was the obvious choice for many reasons: he had served almost as "Cardinal Farley's other self" during many years as his secretary, chancellor and auxiliary bishop; he was readily recognized in Catholic circles and by civic authorities in the City; and his performance as Chaplain Bishop of the Army and Navy had made his name familiar nationally. His appointment was announced on February 16, 1919, and he was installed in the presence of six thousand on March 19th. Archbishop Bonzano conferred the *pallium* on May 8th.[1]

He was born in St. Andrew's parish near City Hall, in the Five Points section of New York, a neighborhood notorious for its high crime.[2] When he was four years old, his mother died, leaving him in the care of an aunt and uncle who raised him. When not attending the local public school, and later the parochial school of Transfiguration Parish, he helped in the family grocery store. He continued his education at La Salle Academy on Second Street, then at Manhattan College, both under the direction of the Brothers of the Christian Schools. A diligent student, he was called the "Little Pope" by schoolmates until, according to one report, he put an end to the sobriquet with "an effective left hook."[3] His ordination was in September 1892, followed by study for two years at Catholic University in Washington, D. C., the only time in his life when he was out of the City for an extended time. His first pastor was Monsignor Farley, the future Cardinal, at St. Gabriel's Church. When Farley became a bishop one year later, Father Hayes was his secretary. He followed Archbishop Farley to the Cathedral when he took over reins of the Archdiocese in 1902 and he lived in the Archbishop's residence. He became Chancellor of the Archdiocese and the first President of Cathedral College, with his office located on Fifty-first Street across from the Cathedral. In 1906, the Holy Father made him a domestic prelate, and he was consecrated an auxiliary bishop in 1914; a year later he was named Pastor of St. Stephen's Church, the Renwick architectural treasure formerly in the charge of Bishop Cusack and, earlier, Rev. Edward McGlynn. When America entered World War I, he was made the first bishop of the military diocese. Administering the new diocese of one million souls in a wide network was a formidable task, especially since the sudden appointment allowed him little time to organize it. He set up his chancery headquarters in New York, but travelled throughout the country visiting as many bases as he could. Cardinal Farley's illness and death interrupted his plans to visit the troops at the front in France. As a member of the National Catholic War Council, formed to coordinate Catholic war-related efforts, he was closely acquainted with Franklin Delano Roosevelt, then the Assistant Secretary of the Navy. As Archbishop of New York, he "had one major, overriding and almost exclusive interest, Catholic Charities, to which he was drawn by a strong natural attraction, by experience, by his recognition of its great and growing importance, and above all, by a deep religious conviction that after divine worship, the preaching of the Gospel, and the proper administration of the sacraments, it was the primary work of the Church."[4]

Having lived at the Archbishop's residence and served at Cathedral College and the Chancery across the street for thirteen years before his appointment, he was a familiar figure at the Cathedral long before he became Archbishop. His close association with Cardinal Farley and Msgr. Lavelle made him privy to the ordinary activities of the Cathedral and its problems. One of the first he had to address as Archbishop was the danger of fire, especially after the bombing incident of 1914 and the war in 1917 and 1918. With the Board of Trustees, he sought estimates for systems of fire protection such as plate wire glass over the stained glass windows, standpipes with hoses in the galleries and a sprinkler system over the ceiling. Several measures to reduce the risk of fire were taken, but the Board of Trustees deferred purchasing a sprinkler system. The prevailing opinion was that, since there had been no fire in nearly forty years, the Cathedral was relatively safe. One common-sense measure was cleaning four decades of accumulated dust from the attic and triforium areas. Removing seven tons of dust reduced anxiety, but did not offer a permanent solution.[5]

A far more pressing problem was the condition of the stone fabric of the exterior. On St.

In an hour of prayer each night, he reviewed in his mind each work and problem of his Archdiocese which required God's help, and mentioned it by name. Then, he would fold his hands across his chest holding a crucifix until he fell asleep. That was how he was found the morning after he died

Patrick's Day 1918, a section of stone fell from the north tower to the ground. An inspection revealed serious deterioration, especially on the finer carvings of the north spire and on some of the pinnacles around the building. After repairs were completed in the fall of 1920, another inspection found the rest of the building in "surprisingly good condition." Nevertheless, periodic inspections were ordered, since continued deteriorization of the stone was considered inevitable.

Authorities also considered replacing the aging wooden floor, fragile steam pipes and early electric wiring, the last probably impelled by a gnawing worry about fire.[6]

The spiritual life of the parish was not so decrepit. As the Cathedral entered its fifth decade, spiritual activity flourished, supported by dedicated laymen privileged to be on the staff. Peter Smith was the verger appointed to succeed Rutledge in 1904. He died in 1914. The sexton was Thomas Dunne who was followed in 1918 by Joseph Boyle. Owen McCormick became sexton in 1921 and remained in that position until his death in 1944. He had begun work at St. Patrick's as an usher.[7]

After the war ended, a distinguished visitor to St. Patrick's was Cardinal Desire Mercier, Primate of Belgium. When the war had begun on the western front, German troops had swept through Belgium towards France. They had occupied Belgium for the rest of the war.

During the occupation, Cardinal Mercier "had received worldwide acclaim for the moral leadership he gave the people in occupied Belgium." In New York, his reception was exultant. His arrival coincided with the parade of American Expeditionary Forces held on September 10, 1919 to mark the victory in Europe. There was an enormous turnout of citizens to honor the troops, and General John J. Pershing, the American commander in France, led one division up Fifth Avenue. When he reached the Cathedral, Pershing dismounted from his horse out of respect for Cardinal Mercier who was reviewing the parade. In several events during the following weeks, honors were heaped on His Eminence. He celebrated a solemn pontifical Mass at the Cathedral on October 8th.[8]

Late that year, the great Irish patriot and later President of the Irish Republic, Eamon de Valera, came to America where he actually had been born. He was the honored guest of Archbishop Hayes in the reviewing stand (*below left, with the Cardinal and Governor Al Smith*) during the 1920 St. Patrick's Day Parade.[9]

During the traditional Mass before the parade, Rev. Francis Duffy, the famous chaplain of the old "Fighting Sixty-Ninth" Regiment, was the preacher. Father Duffy's image was preserved for posterity in a statue erected on one of the central traffic islands at Times Square, later named Duffy Square in his honor. After the war, he was Pastor of Holy Cross Church, just west of Times Square. The statue was the first erected to honor a Catholic priest on public property in New York State.[10]

The picture shows its age. Fresh from the British prison from which he escaped, De Valera spent many months raising money for the cause. He would return to Ireland to find a civil war unleashed. The story below shows that the battle wasn't over here either.

The Irish Independence Movement was in high gear during the last years of World War I and into the decade of the 1920s. Mayor Terence MacSwiney of Cork had died in an English prison during a hunger strike, and on Thanksgiving Day 1920, a Mass was offered at the Cathedral for his soul. Across the street from St. Patrick's at Fifty-first Street and Fifth Avenue was the Union Club. On the day of the Mass, three flags were flown from the facade of the Club, the American, the French and the British banners. Fearing a confrontation over the flying of the Union Jack, Catholic officials had asked the Union Club to remove the flag until after those attending the Mass had left the neighborhood, but officials refused, asserting that it was being displayed in honor of the tercentenary of the landing of the Pilgrims on American shores. The worst fears were realized as some in the crowd exiting the Cathedral attempted, by one method or another, to remove what they considered an affront to Irish sensitivities. As more people left the Church, the disturbance grew, and many windows at the Union Club were broken. Monsignor Lavelle rushed to the steps on Fifth Avenue to try to quell the disturbance, but his pleas were ignored.

Days later, sixty New York Catholics signed a letter and arranged to have it printed in several local newspapers in protest of what they considered the infusion of politics into the religious affairs of the Church. They clearly implied that responsibility for the riot lay at the doorstep of the Catholic clergy. In a rare display of indignation, Archbishop Hayes issued a statement chastising those Catholics who had arranged for publication, for not extending him the courtesy of consulting him before making an erroneous judgement. He denied that Church authorities were in any way responsible for the disturbance, and he offered no apology.[11]

Early in the century, Archbishop José Ignacio Montes de Oca y Obregon of San Luis Potosi, Mexico, had been exiled during the political disorders in his country. In 1921, he was returning from Spain where he had lived for seven years, and stopped at St. Patrick's to visit his friend, Msgr. Lavelle. On August 18th, he died suddenly in the rectory. His body lay in state in the Cathedral for three days, and Archbishop Hayes offered his funeral Mass before his body was temporarily interred at Calvary Cemetery.

Happily, disturbances like that of Thanksgiving Day were virtually unknown in Msgr. Lavelle's ordinary course of activities. In his role as spiritual guide, he founded the Catholic Theatre Movement in 1912 and, the following year, became moderator of *Theta Pi Alpha*, an association of Catholics teaching religion to public school students. Also in 1913, he was placed in charge of a council formed for the spiritual and material welfare of Italian immigrants in the Archdiocese. During the war he was chairman of the New York Association for the Care of Troops, and he helped establish the Soldiers and Sailors Club and a hospital to care for soldiers suffering the effects of poison gas. After the war, the Trustees urged him to increase revenue. He added two extraordinary collections each year to those usual for Sundays. He was pleased to realize a small surplus during the 1920s. Greater contributions allowed for increased service for his charges in the parish. The Boys Club, for instance, was able to present shows under the direction of Rev. John Quinn with about one-hundred-fifty children participating. In 1922, the boys held their performance in the Grand Ballroom of the Waldorf-Astoria Hotel. Their motto was: "Genius may inspire, but hard work brings results." The hard work was rewarded by a "steadily increasing host of admirers that patronize our entertainments."[12]

The Rector had long hoped to establish an official bulletin for the Cathedral. As early as 1890, he had suggested that an organ be published by the League of the Sacred Heart, but the first issue of the *Cathedral Bulletin* was not printed until 1920. Publication continues to the present, but the magazine is now entitled, *Alive and Well at St. Patrick's Cathedral*. Msgr. Lavelle was ably assisted in his many Cathedral duties for twenty years by a priest considered his "right arm," Rev. Henry Hammer. The gracious priest served at the parish from 1917 until 1937.

As related earlier, much of the land in the blocks around the Cathedral had been sold to raise needed money. In 1921, St. Patrick's lost some of the property on the Cathedral block itself. The City needed to widen the road bed on Madison Avenue by twelve feet. Six feet were taken from the sidewalk in front of the Archbishop's Residence and the Rectory, and the buildings' entrance steps which extended beyond the wall lines were removed and reset within the building lines. The entire terrrace wall behind the Lady Chapel had to be moved a few feet closer to the building. The work was completed in November.[13]

The prosperity of America in the 1920s may have helped Msgr. Lavelle build a revenue surplus in that decade. Prosperity was just one mark of the era. During the decade, there was widespread fear, commonly labeled the "Big Red Scare," that the Communist Movement born in Russia would spread through the United States. Many considered the labor strikes, so frequent at the time, as a prelude to a Communist-inspired revolt. A resultant xenophobia led to changes in immigration laws, so that by the end of the decade, America's "melting pot" theory yielded to demands for preserving a homogeneous population, despite a history of generations of immigrants. Jewish and Catholic immigrants became the new scapegoats of such groups as the Ku Klux Klan which was then enjoying a rebirth. The 1920 census revealed that most Americans were living in urban communities. Rural forces reacting to the "evils of city life" led successful efforts to ban the sale of alcoholic beverages. "Prohibition," in turn, created further problems for cities, as words like "bootlegger" and "speakeasy" entered ordinary conversation.[14]

The responsibilities of his office required the attention of Archbishop Hayes to all these changes in American life, but they affected the daily life of the Cathedral very little. The building's fiftieth anniversary in 1929 was fast approaching. Except for some windows and a few statues, the physical structure was virtually complete. During the decade, Mrs. Etta Phillips, a benefactor of many charities, especially causes for the blind, donated two statues, that of St. Augustine in 1920 and St. Monica in 1925, the two mounted on each side of the ambulatory. The exquisite bronze paschal candle holder used during the Easter season was presented in memory of her son. When Mrs. Phillips died in 1934, Msgr. Lavelle accorded her an honor rare for a lay person. Her body reposed in the Cathedral, in the chapel of St. Rose of Lima, before her funeral. She is the only woman ever to have received this honor.[15]

During the war, the American government needed space in Bronx County for a hospital for the wounded, and it requested the Roman Catholic Orphan Asylum. The Archdiocese agreed. In the chapel of the building there was a Renaissance marble altar which was brought to St. Patrick's in 1922 and placed in the north ambulatory. It was dedicated to St. Joseph, replacing the original altar in his honor which was sent to St. Joseph's Seminary in Yonkers, New York. Today, some viewers find the Renaissance design inappropriate for a Gothic building, but, for others, its simplicity is fitting to honor a saint whose life was a model of that virtue. Joseph O'Donohue's family donated the altar in his memory. The first St. Joseph altar had been in the south ambulatory. In its place was erected a beautiful Gothic altar to honor St. Andrew. It was a gift of Amelia Dougherty Hildreth in memory of her father, Andrew Dougherty.[16]

It was Archbishop Hayes' custom to celebrate pontifical Masses at the Cathedral only on special occasions. But, he regularly presided at high Masses from the *cathedra*, the episcopal throne, while another priest offered the Holy Sacrifice. The music at these liturgies was the responsibility of Jacques Ungerer. John O'Connor was his assistant at the changel organ until Mr. O'Connor's death in July 1918. Ungerer was born in France, and when World War I broke out in the summer of 1914, he immediately enlisted in the French army. John Philip Foley was chief organist and music director during Ungerer's absense. Ungerer resumed his duties in April 1915. The music adhered strictly to Pope Pius X's *motu proprio* of 1903, and was presented by many outstanding singers. Beginning in 1916 and continuing for twenty-eight years until he accepted a position in Hollywood to train singers for Metro Goldwyn Mayer Company, the Cathedral's baritone soloist was John van Bommel. Before his arrival in the United States, he had sung in the Royal Opera Company in the Netherlands where he was born and where he once gave a command performance for Queen Wilhelmena. A familiar face belonged to the great Irish tenor, John McCormack, who was a regular parishioner. In 1918, Mr. McCormack sang at a fund-raising concert for the benefit of the Catholic Orphan Asylum.[17]

Early in March 1924, Archbishop Hayes received word that he would be elevated to the Cardinalate at the end of that month. His welcome home from ceremonies in Rome was almost a repetition of the one extended to Cardinal Farley twelve years earlier. A barrage of boat whistles greeted his ship as it entered New York Harbor. A delegation of bishops, priests and prominent laymen in formal attire provided his escort to his car which joined a line of forty in procession past his boyhood home near City Hall to Broadway and finally to Fifth Avenue. The parade continued north to St. Patrick's, mobbed with well-wishers outside and thousands of children inside. The formal welcome was a Mass two days later, attended by archbishops, bishops and other clergy joined by New York Governor Al Smith, the mayor and several ambassadors. Members of the Philharmonic Society and the New York Symphony Orchestra accompanied the choir under Jacques Ungerer's direction.[18]

In June 1926, a World Eucharistic Congress assembled in Chicago. From many places on the globe, Catholic prelates arrived in the Port of New York enroute to the meeting. Seven Cardinals and a host of archbishops and bishops arrived including the Pope's legate, Cardinal John Bonzano, the first time a papal legate visited this country. The Governor and the Mayor extended a formal welcome at City Hall following a ticker-tape parade on Broadway. At the Cathedral, specially erected thrones were in the sanctuary for the largest contingent of Cardinals ever present in the building at one time, eight including Cardinal Hayes.[19] The same month one year later, the City prepared a festive parade for Charles Lindbergh after his historic non-stop transatlantic solo flight. His journey of thirty-three and one-half hours made Lindbergh probably the best-known figure in aeronautical history, and his "Spirit of St. Louis," the most famous plane. The motorcade stopped in front of the Cathedral where Lindbergh offered a handshake to Cardinal Hayes who gave the hero a blessing.[20]

Some of the special liturgies at St. Patrick's during the 1920s included a pontifical Mass celebrated by Bishop Januarius Hayasaka, the first Japanese bishop in Church history. The following year, the Holy Father signed the Lateran Treaty, and a special Mass recognized the event at St. Patrick's. Since the pontificate of Pius IX, the popes had refused to leave the Vatican to protest confiscation of papal territory by the Italian government, and were called "prisoners of the Vatican." The new treaty established the Vatican State, independent of Italy. When Marshal Ferdinand Foch, the commander-in-chief of all allied forces during World War I, died the same month, a memorial Mass was offered for his soul.[21]

Fulton J. Sheen, a priest who taught at the Catholic University of America, and who became "the outstanding preacher in the history of the Church in America," made his first appearance as a preacher in St. Patrick's in 1929 when he presented a series of sermons during Advent. He would continue his association with the Cathedral until his death as an archbishop fifty years later. The scholarly, ascetic figure was born in Illinois in 1895, and was ordained in 1919. By 1924 he had received an S. T. D. degree from the Catholic University of America, a Ph. D. from the University of Louvain, Belgium, and an S. T. D. from the Collegio Angelico in Rome. By the time of his first series at St. Patrick's, he was well-known in academic circles in this country and abroad.[22] Many other clerics associated with the Cathedral during those years moved to positions of high office in the American Church. Rev. Edward V. Dargin, at St. Patrick's from 1924 to 1927, became an auxiliary bishop of New York, and was head of the first full-time marriage tribunal. Rev. Bryan J. McEntegart worked at St. Patrick's from 1923 to 1925, and again in 1941 and 1942. He became Bishop of Ogdensburg, New York, and President of the Catholic University of America. He died as Bishop of Brooklyn, with the honorary title of archbishop.[23]

Kaiden-Keystone

Pietro Yon, known internationally as the composer of many liturgical works including *Gesu Bambino,* a favorite Christmas hymn, was associated with St. Patrick's from the 1920s until his death in 1943. He came to the Cathedral as organist in 1927, and in 1929 succeeded Jacques Ungerer as Director of Music.[24] Born in SettimoVittone in the northern Italian area of Piedmont, he was already in love with the piano at the age of six. His parents, poor people who struggled to provide for their large family, recognized in him a tenacity which one day would lift him to great heights. Hard work and determination earned him entry to the Royal Conservatory in Milan where he excelled; he moved on to the prestigious St. Cecilia's Academy in Rome to complete his music studies. A brilliant student, he finished a course of eleven years in just five. At graduation ceremonies, when he won every prize being awarded, King Victor Emmanual III summoned him for a command performance.

Yon's childhood home looked down on the town of Ivrea, where St. Patrick stopped on his way from Rome to Ireland to drive out the druids there. He decided to tell the saint's story in music. The world premiere of his oratorio, The Triumph of St. Patrick — which he dedicated to Cardinal Hayes — was held in the Cathedral in 1934.

After graduation, he played on occasions at the Vatican and he was the regular organist at the Royal Church in Rome. His opportunity to come to America came from Rev. John B. Young, founder of one of the finest boys choirs in the world at St. Francis Xavier Church in New York. Fr. Young was a Jesuit who led the effort to raise standards of church music in the United States. He offered Yon a position at St. Francis Xavier, and the young musician immigrated here in 1907. Soon, Yon had a studio at Carnegie Hall and was teaching at the College of Mt. St. Vincent. His national concert tours built him a strong reputation. In New York he became a close friend of Enrico Caruso and Arturo Toscanini, under whom he played in the NBC Symphony Orchestra. The Vatican made him an honorary organist, an honor awarded only once before — to the

Yon played an original composition for Leopold Stokowski's Philadelphia Orchestra in the Wanamaker Store's Grand Court in that city. He stands at Stokowski's right.

great Franz Liszt. In 1929, King Victor Emmanuel called him to the Royal Palace where the king conferred knighthood on him. Back in New York, he headed the committee of organists to design the organ at Carnegie Hall, a place he loved so deeply he called it "an oasis ... like a temple of music."[25]

Like Fr. Young, Yon was dedicated to raising the standards of religious music in America. He abhorred the popular craving for "cheap and jazzy music in the churches," and wanted to help enforce Church rules regarding selection of proper music. He was ably assisted in his first years at St. Patrick's by a humble and talented musician, Msgr. Joseph Rostagno, who came from Rome to train Cathedral College students in Gregorian Chant. He was vice-director of music at the Cathedral from 1929 until 1935. Called "one of the greatest living authorities on the ancient polyphonic music of the Church," Msgr. Rostagno's self-effacing demeanor left most people unaware that he was a prelate, since he never wore the robes of a monsignor and did not use the title. Before coming to St. Patrick's, he had been choirmaster of the college of Turin and of the Turin seminary, while editing the music magazine *Santa Cecilia,* and working as artistic manager of a publishing house, *Marcello Capra.* As second Director of the Vatican Choir beginning in 1919, he toured the countries of Europe and the United States.[26]

In the late 1920s, some fine art pieces came to St. Patrick's, some historically significant. In 1926, Mrs. J. L. Marshall donated a vestment which had belonged to Pope Clement X, pontiff from 1670 to 1676.[27] In observance of the seventh centenary of the death of St. Francis of Assisi, the Franciscan Tertiaries of New York presented a statue of the saint. It is a reproduction of a sculpture in the Cathedral of Assisi by the French artist Dupré, and stands about fifteen feet high, made of Carrara marble. It was blessed by Cardinal Hayes on October 7, 1928 and set in the north ambulatory near the Rector's entrance.[28] Mrs. Nicholas F. Brady, a papal duchess, in January 1927 donated an altar in honor of St. Therese of Lisieux, filling the last unoccupied chapel of the Cathedral in the south ambulatory, previously used to house a book and pamphlet rack. Genevieve Brady and her husband were wealthy Catholics who had close ties with many high-ranking officials at the Vatican. They maintained a home in Rome on the Janiculum Hill where they often entertained Vatican prelates, among whom were several cardinals including Eugenio Pacelli, later Pope Pius XII. Their generosity in the cause of religion was almost legendary. In New York, their apartment was at 910 Fifth Avenue, not far from St. Patrick's. The new altar was unveiled in time for Christmas 1927; Cardinal Hayes dedicated it the following April.[29]

The design of the chapel was by Maginnis and Walsh. The artist chosen to make the shrine, Mario Korbel, had earlier sculptured a wood statue of St. Therese for the Bradys' private chapel on their Long Island estate. Korbel was born in a small village in Bohemia in 1882, and he studied under several masters in Munich, Berlin and Paris. He had a studio in Czechoslovakia and two in the United States, in Chicago and New York. His works are exhibited worldwide, including in the Metropolitan Museum of Art in New York, in the Vatican Museums and at the University of Havana. He was best known in New York for his sculptured heads of prominent citizens. The shrine at the Cathedral was erected by the Alexander Pelli Company. The relic displayed at the altar was also a gift of Mrs. Brady who had received it from Cardinal Pietro Gasparri, the Vatican Secretary of State. The wrought iron case which houses the relic was made by Samuel A. Yellin, one of the finest craftsmen of wrought iron in America. He was born in Poland in 1886, studied in Europe and in Philiadelphia, and won numerous awards for his works which are found mostly in this country, notably at Yale University, The National Cathedral in Washington, D. C., and the Metropolitan Museum of Art.[30]

The inscription at the Little Flower's altar reads: I want to spend my heaven doing good on earth.

For several years before the May 1929 golden anniversary of the Cathedral's opening, Msgr. Lavelle was planning extensive improvements, hoping to finish them before the event. Even though much of the exterior remained unfinished, and despite speculation which persisted about the razing of the residences to allow for expansion of the east end of the Cathedral, Cardinal Hayes had his sights focused on restoring the interior.[31] Msgr. Lavelle considered maintaining the exterior fabric as routine business, even after such unusual occurrences as lightning strikes which required replacing the cross on the north spire.[32] But, inside, he scheduled the largest program of improvements since the building opened: completion of the nine Lady Chapel windows not yet built; new altars for the main sanctuary and the Lady Chapel; a marble floor throughout; an updated heating system; a modern amplification system; new lighting; a greatly enlarged sanctuary; a new baptistry; new pews; a marble communion railing; a book rack replacing the holy water well; bronze doors at Fifth Avenue; and two new organs, one of which, the gallery organ, he expected to be the finest in America.[33]

Midway through the decade, he initiated a drive called the Cathedral Golden Jubilee Improvement Fund.[34] By 1927 preparations were in place to begin the first projects. The architectural firm, Maginnis and Walsh of Boston, was selected to oversee the work. Collaborating with them and executing many of the designs was architect Robert J. Reiley, whose office was first on Forty-first Street and later on Forty-fifth Street in Manhattan. Charles Maginnis directed the work. Maginnis had emigrated from Ireland to England in 1885, and studied in London before moving to Boston to work for William Wentworth and Edmund Wheelwright. He established his own firm in that city in 1898. His numerous buildings, mostly ecclesiastical and collegiate, are found in the United States, Canada, Mexico and China. One of his outstanding designs is the National Shrine of the Immaculate Conception in Washington, D. C. Throughout his life, he was in demand as a lecturer, and the American Institute of Architects awarded him many medals. Robert Reiley was a consulting architect for St. Patrick's for about twenty years in the decades of the 1920s and 1930s.[35]

The wooden floors had long been regarded as inherently risky for fire, and the danger increased because of a covering of carpet. In 1924, Msgr. Lavelle suggested to Cardinal Hayes that a marble floor be tested in one of the vestibules to ascertain its suitability for the rest of the building. Apparently pleased with the result, he ordered that the entire floor be replaced, beginning in April 1927. Reinforced concrete was laid under Tennessee marble throughout the entire building, except under the pews where terrazzo was used, and in the Lady Chapel which already had a marble floor. At intervals, mosaic religious symbols selected by Reiley, whose inspiration came from Cardinal Hayes' breviary, were inserted into the marble. Near the entrances, mosaics of the heraldic arms of the archbishops and cardinals were set. That of Cardinal Hayes was placed at the entrance to the Lady Chapel. Before the new floor was finished, a complete heating system was installed with its pipes running in the crawl space below the floor to new radiators along the walls.[36]

In the meantime, Reiley journeyed to Europe to visit some Cathedrals. In Paris, he met one of the Kellys, donors of the Lady Chapel, and the two discussed a new altar for the chapel which would not obstruct the view of the windows. Woodroffe, the window artist, was making every attempt to finish the windows as soon as possible, so he was accepting no other commissions until the work was done. Reiley wrote to Cardinal Hayes from Biarritz, France, that he was hoping both the Lady Chapel altar and a new main altar would follow the pattern of northern French Cathedrals in allowing an unobstructed view through the Cathedral to the chapel windows. This would mean removing the towering reredos of the high altar and replacing it with a baldachin over a low table, allowing an open view from the nave to the east.[37] Unfortunately, the replacement altars would have to be postponed for many years after the Great Depression of the 1930s struck the American economy, although work on the chapel windows continued until the last was installed in 1934.

The floor was finished by Christmas 1927. The following year work began on the organs, including a redesigned gallery to house the grand organ. By Easter, the sanctuary was being extended into the nave to a length of seventy-five feet, the entire area lifted six steps above the nave floor. Its marble pavement was gray and green with red and dark green borders. The figure of a pelican feeding its young was inlaid in the center, a symbol of Christ in the Eucharist. Other symbols representing the four evangelists were at the four corners of the open area in front of the high altar. Enclosing the entire sanctuary was an oak screen of exquisitely carved Gothic design. Inside the sanctuary the old moveable chairs were replaced by permanent sedilia, seating for the clergy, enough for seventy clerics. Although the earliest studies for a new sanctuary had been made as early as 1922 by Irving and Casson, the final drawings were those of Robert Reiley and Maginnis and Walsh.[38]

It became obvious, as the date for the jubilee drew nearer, that the renovations would not be complete by May 1929, so official celebrations were postponed. Work continued slowly as some of the original gas fixtures, still in place, were finally removed. In September 1929, a new *cathedra,* the episcopal throne, was being erected on the north side. To signify the apostolic succession of the archbishop, statuettes of Sts. Peter and Paul were on the back of the chair; between them were the heraldic insignia of the archbishop. A magnificent spired canopy with statuary and open tracery rose over the seat, its pinnacle thirty feet from the floor. By this time, the improvement cost had reached one and one quarter million dollars.[39]

The first of the two new organs to be completed was the chancel organ. A concert and a service of Benediction of the Blessed Sacrament were held at the dedication in January 1928. With 1462 pipes and 114 ranks, it proved suitable for accompanying congregational singing. The gallery organ could not be built until the entire gallery itself was reconstructed. Its two levels were reinforced with steel beams and supports before reinforced concrete was poured. Alfred Kilgen of the George Kilgen Company of St. Louis designed the instrument under the watchful eye of Pietro Yon and with his assistance. The firm's beginnings traced back three centuries in Derlach, Germany, when the founder, Johann Sebastian Kilgen, a French Huguenot, fled to Baden, Germany to escape religious persecution. Finding refuge in a monastery, he helped the monks build organs until he was able to establish his own company in 1640. It is still in existence. The American branch was begun in New York by George Kilgen in 1851 on East 34th Street. In 1873, the company relocated to St. Louis. Because Pietro Yon had headed a committee of organists to plan the Carnegie Hall organ, which also was built by Alfred Kilgen, it is likely that it was at his urging that the Kilgen Company was selected for the Cathedral organs. Yon had played at the dedication concert of the Carnegie instrument, attended by Franklin D. Roosevelt, then New York Governor.[40]

After three years' preparation in St. Louis, the first section arrived in May 1929. For the next eight months, five electricians and a staff of tuners labored day and night using 10,000 magnets and fifty miles of wire. When it was finished in January 1930, the seven-division instrument, called the finest church organ in the world and the largest in America, could reproduce the sounds of a seventy-five piece string orchestra, and contained seventy-five chimes, an overpowering brass section, and numerous other marvelous features. Its powerful blowers could force almost 31,000 cubic feet of air through the pipes each minute. The initial estimate of $135,000 reached $250,000 by the time it was finished. There were 7855 pipes, the smallest only ½ inch in length, the largest thirty-two feet, and that one equipped with a device to produce the sound of a sixty-four-feet-long pipe.[41]

On the evening of February 11, 1930, seven thousand persons came to the Cathedral for the dedication ceremony, while five thousand had to be turned away at the doors. Cardinal Hayes conducted the service, and Pietro Yon thrilled the huge assemblage and those listening via radio with both the roaring blasts and the pure soft tones of the grand instrument. It was especially gratifying for Msgr. Lavelle, because his friend John Whalen, a New York attorney, had donated the entire cost. Thus, the organ was built in his memory. Whalen had intended to leave a gift of millions of dollars to Msgr. Lavelle personally, but the Rector persuaded him to give it in the name of Cardinal Hayes. The Cardinal was delighted at Msgr. Lavelle's magnanimous gesture.[42]

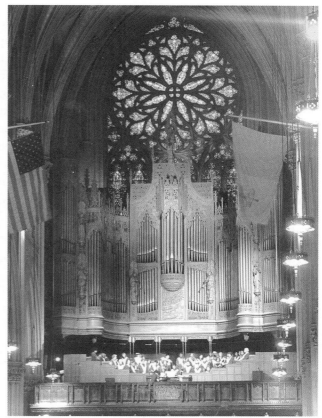

The gallery organ.

As impressive as the organ sounded, the beauty of its case is no less stunning. The carvings were done by Irving and Casson from drawings of Robert Reiley and Maginnis and Walsh. The panels on the front of the gallery show carved oak singing angels, while the case above displays eleven figures of angels, each over six feet in height. Each one holds a musical instrument.

On the new floor of the church, new pews were also a Reiley design. They were finished in 1929 and a modern ventilating system was introduced at the ends of each pew, just as had existed in those they replaced.[43] The following year, the last section of the sanctuary, the altar railing, was finished. Discussions had been taking place since 1927, but not until 1930 was a donation made by Mrs. Marion McMillan, a member of the parish. Maginnis and Walsh and Robert Reiley prepared the scheme, and Albert H. Atkins, an American who taught at the Rhode Island School of Design, was the sculptor of the statuettes. The railing itself was made in Italy from Tavernelle and Swiss Cipolin marble. Atkins worked very quickly and the fifty-feet-long railing was ready in time for the First Sunday of Advent at the end of the year. There are thirteen statuettes of saints associated with the Eucharist.[44]

The renovation program, expected at first to be finished in 1929, continued into 1931. The last elements were changes in the small chapels at the western end of the building, and an entirely new lighting system. The last bay of the south aisle contained a Gothic holy water well. It was removed and sent to Gate of Heaven Cemetery and Robert Reiley designed a carved oak case along the walls of the room for pamphlets and other Catholic literature, earlier housed in the south ambulatory. After a full decade of planning, new lighting was completed throughout the entire building in January 1931. Later in the year, the last bay of the north aisle, opposite the pamphlet rack bay, received a new baptistry. Mr. and Mrs. Bruno Benziger, members of the Catholic publishing family, gave the gift. The walls were lined with carved limestone and the floor was made of marble. The marble of the font was similar to what had been used to build the altar railing, and a marble altar like those found in the Roman catacombs was set against a wall near the font. Above the table an image of Our Lady of Einsiedeln was carved into the limestone. Einsiedeln, Switzerland, was the ancestral home of the Benziger family, where, in the ninth century, St. Meinrad had brought the original statue of the virgin, considered miraculous. An eight-feet-high cover of intricately carved oak was suspended over the font. At the entrance were wrought iron gates made by the Ferro Studios of New York. Robert Reiley, once again, was the architect of the baptistry. He also had begun studies for a baldachin over a new high altar, but, as mentioned earlier, fears of a worsening depression caused a postponement until 1939.[45]

The year of the fiftieth anniversary of St. Patrick's, 1929, was also the golden jubilee of Msgr. Lavelle's ordination to the priesthood. His testimonial banquet at the Hotel Biltmore several days after June 5th, the actual anniversary date, was planned by priests of the Archdiocese. The principal celebration, however, was a solemn Mass celebrated by the jubilarian with Cardinal Hayes presiding. Just before the Mass, the Cardinal surprised him by investing him with a mitre, ring and pectoral cross, the pontificals which he now was permitted to wear four times each year as he celebrated a pontifical Mass. The special honor, called *prothonotoary apostolic,* elevated him to the highest rank of prelate below a bishop.[46]

Just four months later, on October 20, 1929, the stock market crashed, and during the following years, panic spread over the country. Until mid-1930, Cathedral contributions continued at the same level as before, but by that summer, ordinary revenue had dropped by about 25%. Money donated for improvement programs was insufficient to cover the cost of work already done, so it was necessary to arrange loans for the balance. Thus, the decision was made to suspend further renovations until the financial climate of the nation improved.[47] Because of the Depression, the Church was more concerned with widespread unemployment and the poverty resulting from it than it was about improving the physical plant of the Cathedral. For many years, Msgr. Lavelle had employed widows with no other means of support, since government social programs did not come into existence until later in the 1930s during Franklin Delano Roosevelt's administration.[48] And he reminded those who were employed that they had a moral duty to help their suffering brothers and sisters during a time of "the greatest need since the institution of Catholic Charities." In 1934, a year after Roosevelt's "New Deal" programs went into effect, there were about one million New Yorkers on relief. Cardinal Hayes, known as the Cardinal of Charity, had ample opportunity to earn the title during those years of suffering. In addition to special collections for the care of the needy, volunteers went from door to door in parishes, including the Cathedral, begging for funds to help the poor. The Rector was hard-pressed to provide basic necessities for parishioners when many sources of ordinary income such as pew rents and vigil light donations were lower than normal by about one-third. In 1932, the annual special collection was $5000 lower than in earlier years. The budget for the music program had to be cut by 20%, and Cardinal Hayes suggested that protective services be terminated in order to save money. Above all, parishioners were asked for prayers for divine assistance by participating in novenas and begging the intercession of St. Patrick and St. Joseph, patron of workers.[49]

Former New York Governor and presidential candidate Al Smith was a great help in those difficult times. Except for two years, he had been Governor from 1918 until 1928, the year he lost the election for president to Herbert Hoover. During the following depression years, he headed the Cardinal's Special Gifts Committee to provide relief through Catholic Charities. Frequently seen in the pews of the Cathedral, he also launched the Cardinal's annual charity drive at the Waldorf-Astoria Hotel in 1932. The dinner at the hotel later was named in his honor and it continues annually to the present.[50]

Helping provide work during the Depression were transportation improvement programs such as construction of the Eighth Avenue and Sixth Avenue subway lines. The population of Manhattan was falling, as more people moved to surrounding counties both within and immediately outside the City limits. The new subway lines reached out into the outlying City counties. The Triborough Bridge, which opened in 1936, also facilitated passage by commuters from Queens and Long Island into Manhattan. Bridges linking New Jersey and Staten Island built earlier also helped.[51]

Many of those fortunate enough not to suffer during the Depression extended helping hands to those who did. Some tried to alleviate the general dreariness of living conditions by improving the quality of civic life. Each spring, for example, the Outdoor Cleanliness Association conducted a flower mart on the steps of the Cathedral, a custom which continued into the 1950s.[52] And hard times could not afford the luxury of neglecting repairs at the expense of more costly work at a later time. After some ornamental pendant stones in the arches around the doorways began to disintegrate, several pieces fell to the pavement. Robert Reiley conducted an inspection of the entire building. He found it in only fair condition at best, due to deleterious elements in the urban air. There was worry that falling stone might destroy the glass roofs over the north and south transept entrance enclosures; roof patching caused water to seep over the flashings and inside the building when snow accumulated; and the droppings of pigeons which had found a home on high perches on the building caused considerable deterioration. Mortar joints were in a poor state of repair and some of the stained glass and the exterior protective glass was cracked or broken.[53] Al Smith inaugurated a three-year repair program when he took part in a formal ceremony in September 1935, posing with a spray gun to apply a chemical preservative to the stone. Joints on all sides of the building were repointed or grouted and the marble was waterproofed up to the fifty-feet level during the course of the repairs. The final work, in 1938, was the replacement of all the steps at Fifth Avenue with Deer Island granite.[54]

If it is true that in time of trouble people draw closer to God, that seemed evident at the Cathedral during the Depression, when large crowds often filled the pews. An estimated seven to eight thousand attended the Christmas midnight Mass in 1933, the largest crowd in the church's history. The following Easter, four thousand waited outside the doors to enter for the solemn Mass when all available space inside was taken. A daily Mass was added at 12:15 p.m. for the first time in 1931 for those unable to attend the morning Masses.[55] The devotion of the faithful was especially ardent during Lent and particularly during Holy Week. Throughout the decade, Rev. Fulton Sheen preached at the Sunday Lenten high Masses, at the Good Friday Three Hours Meditations and at the Easter solemn pontifical Mass celebrated by Cardinal Hayes. Stationed at the Catholic University of America in Washington, D. C., Fr. Sheen made the journey to New York each week where his spellbinding oratory drew throngs of penitents to the Church, many of them converts to Catholicism. Not only during Lent, but throughtout the year, Father, later Monsignor Sheen, conducted classes for those seeking instruction in the Catholic faith in the rectory, in the school or, as numbers grew, in an auditorium. One of his converts was Heywood Broun, at whose funeral in the Cathedral he preached the eulogy, not long after Broun became a Catholic.[56]

The solicitude of the clergy for the faithful during this period is reflected in a typical Lenten program which included confessions during the Mass hours, daily praying of the rosary and night prayers, long confession hours on Saturdays, stations of the cross, vespers, daily instructions after the noontime Mass, weekly lectures, and devotions and Benediction of the Blessed Sacrament throughout the week. The faithful were encouraged to pray for themselves, "for those near and dear, for our country, for the Church, and for relief from the Depression."[57] Stationed at St. Patrick's from this time until 1946 was Rev. Walter Kellenberg. He was made Chancellor of the Archdiocese and later moved to the See of Ogdensburg, New York. Ultimately, he became the first Bishop of Rockville Center on Long Island.[58] Although he was never assigned to St. Patrick's, Rev. Francis Duffy, chaplain of the Fighting Sixty-ninth Regiment during World War I, was often in attendance. The announcement of his death was made at the Cathedral in July 1932, and five years later his statue was unveiled in Duffy Square at Times Square.[59] Still today, its company is bustling traffic and scores of pigeons.

God's glory is not diminished by human conditions, and the rites of the Church are celebrated in good times and bad. So, special services were held in the difficult depression years in honor of holy men and women, including celebrations of the beatification in 1930 and the canonization in 1934 of St. John Bosco, the founder of the Salesian Order, and the canonization of St. Isaac Jogues, the New York martyr, in 1931. Other liturgies marked civic events such as the centenary of Simon Bolivar in 1930; the bicentennial of George Washington's birth in 1932; and the twenty-fifth anniversary of the Boy Scouts of America in 1937. Cardinal Hayes offered a pontifical Mass in November 1931 in honor of the dogma of divine maternity of Mary, defined at the Council of Ephesus fifteen hundred years earlier; in 1934, he welcomed two thousand servicemen of the American fleet, and warned against unpreparedness in the face of a growing menace on the European horizon. He asserted that "unpreparedness on the part of our defense arms of service, on sea and land, at the critical period of these fermenting, fomenting and seething times, amid openly avowed hatreds abroad and disloyalties at home, would be supreme folly." Two months later, the death of German President von Hindenburg was announced in the Cathedral with the plea that parishioners pray that "God may raise up men of wisdom and judgement to lead [the German people] through this emergency." The Cardinal's voice raised in alarm against the growing power of Hitler's Nazis five years before the outbreak of the worst war in human history went largely unnoticed. But four years after von Hindenburg's death, President Franklin Delano Roosevelt requested that Americans pray for peace in the world, and that message was urged on the faithful at St. Patrick's. On the very day, September 3, 1939, when Great Britain and France declared war on Germany, the international peace organization Pax Romana was sponsoring a pontifical Mass in St. Patrick's.[60]

Bishop John Dunn, the auxiliary bishop of Cardinal Hayes since 1921, died in August 1933. The Cardinal had only one auxiliary bishop at a time and Monsignor Stephen Donahue was consecrated in the spring of 1934 to succeed Bishop Dunn. Earlier in the year in which he died, Bishop Dunn had offered a funeral Mass for Thomas Kelly, the son of Eugene Kelly and an eminent benefactor of St. Patrick's. One of his pall bearers was Charles Mathews, the architect of the Lady Chapel. Mathews himself died the following year. Another funeral which drew "great attendance" was that of Jacob Ruppert, owner of the New York Yankees and of the Ruppert Beer Company, which produced a favorite local brand of beer. He died in January 1939, the month before Msgr. Lavelle offered a memorial Mass upon the death of Pope Pius XI. Besides these special liturgies, traditional services instituted in previous years became part of the ordinary schedule, such as the annual solemn Mass each New Year's Day attended by the Holy Name societies of the Archdiocese, the weekly chanting of vespers on Sundays, and the four-week course of sermons during Advent in preparation for Christmas. In 1936, Rev. Leonard Feeney, a Jesuit who years later was excommunicated for his teaching at variance with Church doctrine, was the Advent series preacher. After many years of separation, Father Feeney returned to communion with the Church before his death.[61]

Until 1931, few guidebooks had been published about St. Patrick's Cathedral. The last complete history of the building was published in 1908, and booklets printed in 1910 and 1922 merely used excerpts from the earlier work with a few additions. In 1931, Augustin McNally wrote, *A Guide to St. Patrick's, New York* which he revised in 1935. More a description of the building and its furnishings than a history, it was, nevertheless, current. McNally had immigrated from Scotland at a very young age, and after growing up in Pennsylvania, he became a journalist, working in St. Louis, Pittsburgh, Washington, Rome and New York. He worked with Herbert Hoover in the Food Administration during World War I, and accrued wide experience as a theatrical reporter later. He served as dramatic editor of the New York Tribune and wrote on a variety of topics. The McNally guide was used at St. Patrick's until Maginnis and Walsh prepared their book when the new altar was dedicated in 1942. McNally was often seen in the pews of the Cathedral and inspired many by his piety.[62]

Another close friend of St. Patrick's, James A. Farley, rose to national prominence during the first two terms of President Franklin Roosevelt. He was chairman of both the New York State Democratic Committee and the Democratic National Committee during those years, and was appointed Postmaster General by the President in 1933. He helped Roosevelt secure both the nomination and the election as President in 1932, and he directed the 1936 presidential campaign leading to Roosevelt's landslide victory. When the president decided to run for an unprecedented third term in 1940, Farley opposed him and sought the nomination for president himself, with virtually no hope of securing it. Although the President asked for his help in the 1940 campaign, Farley declined and resigned his national offices. He returned to New York where he remained active in politics for many years. He served as a trustee of St. Patrick's Cathedral from 1960 until 1974, two years before his death.[63]

The individual associated with St. Patrick's longer than anyone else except Msgr. Lavelle came to find "temporary" employment in 1936. Bernard Carroll became sacristan and remained for over fifty-six years until sickness necessitated his retirement in the fall of 1992. He knew parishioners by name and served the clergy, from newly-assigned curates to visiting popes. Many distinguished civic and ecclesiastical leaders addressed him by his first name. He rarely had need to refer to manuals, as he knew all the ceremonies of the church from long experience, and oversaw details with precision and care.[64]

Few contrasting elements of parish life at St. Patrick's could be more striking than the desperate conditions of those in need and the peace and comfort afforded them by the liturgy. No small contribution to that liturgy came from the music provided under the unsurpassed direction of Pietro Yon. Hailed in the press of the world as the "very finest organist of today," the "master of masters," the "king of the modern organists" and "the greatest and most skillful master of the organ of the entire world," his very name brought people from far and near to St. Patrick's to hear "the organ under his fingers and feet...with a beauty and depth of tone seldom associated with it." The performance of the sacred music was matched by the excellence of the compositions selected, including many created by Yon himself. His genius produced a prodigious output – more than thirty Masses, more than one hundred religious songs and carols, fifty ballads, an oratorio and six orchestrated concertos or sonatas with choral arrangements. Those who could afford the price of admission attended the master's Carnegie Hall recitals or those he gave in many cities of the world, over fifteen hundred in all. But devout parishioners had only to walk into the Cathedral each week to have their spirits lifted to God by the beautiful sounds from the gallery.[65]

In 1933, after assistant organist Paolo Giaquinto left, Yon brought in as chancel organist one of his students, Edward Rivetti. Rivetti received his earliest training from Baron John von Festnick of Austria. Except for two years during World War II, when he served in the United States Navy, Rivetti was assistant organist at the Cathedral until he retired in 1972. His students at Cathedral College described him as one who had "the patience of Job, a love for his Church and her music, and a genuine regard for his 'college boys.'"[66] Yon was a friend of Giovanni Martinelli, a tenor of the Metropolitcan Opera Company, who, like John McCormack, the famous Irish tenor, was a regular parishioner. For many years, Mr. Martinelli was the soloist at the Christmas midnight Mass. Another Metropolitan Opera soloist was the basso Nicola Moscona.[67]

In 1934, Yon's oratorio dedicated to Cardinal Hayes, *The Triumph of St. Patrick,* had its debut at Carnegie Hall and was received with praise, both for the composition and the performance. Written for chorus, orchestra and organ, its soloists were members of the Metropolitan Opera Company. The Chicago premiere two years later met with equal encomiums from music critics. Yon's other work outside the Cathedral included performances under Arturo Toscanini in the NBC Symphony Orchestra. In 1939 he was music director of the religious pavilion of the World's Fair. A year earlier, he had prepared the ceremonies for installation of Pope Pius XII, who made him a Knight of St. Sylvester, his second Vatican honor.[68]

Visitors during the decade included Cardinal Jean Verdier, the Archbishop of Paris; high ranking Italian military officers; and the Prince Regent and Crown Prince of Luxembourg. In October 1936, the highest ranking Vatican official ever to visit this country,

Cardinal Eugenio Pacelli, Secretary of State, arrived in New York. He stayed at the home of Mr. and Mrs. Nicholas Brady, donors of the St. Therese shrine in the Cathedral. His guide on a month-long cross-country tour was the auxiliary bishop of Boston, Francis Spellman, destined for greatness in the New York Church in years to come. In the Cathedral, Cardinal Pacelli presided at the solemn Mass commemorating the consecration of the building, and he presented a candle as a remembrance of his visit. The candle was affixed to a pillar near the altar of St. Therese where it remained for many years. Three years after his visit, Cardinal Pacelli became Pope Pius XII.[69]

With Cardinal Pacelli, Monsignor Fulton Sheen, whose words gave hope to people in hard times, and former Governor Al Smith, who was practically a one-man army for Cardinal Hayes in raising money for Catholic Charities during the depression.

In June 1932 while attending the International Eucharistic Congress in Dublin, Cardinal Hayes was striken by a massive heart attack. During the next six years, his public appearances were infrequent as he had to restrict his activities. On Sunday, September 4, 1938, Msgr. Lavelle received newspaper reporters in the Cathedral rectory after the eleven o'clock Mass and told them: "The word of the passing away of our beloved Cardinal Hayes came as a terrific shock. He retired to his room early last evening at St. Joseph's, Monticello, New York, where he usually spent the summer days. Death came upon him peacefully in his sleep." The summer home was on the grounds of a sanitarium and summer camp about one hundred miles from Manhattan. The next day, a cortege of several cars accompanied the Cardinal's body on a three-hour journey to the Cathedral where Msgr. Lavelle conducted a brief prayer service. During the next several days, there were three requiem Masses and about 250,000 people waited on lines for up to three hours to pay their respects at the bier. At a Mass for school children, "probably the largest congregation ever assembled in the Cathedral" filled every inch of space. The Cardinal's boyhood friend, Cardinal George Mundelein, celebrated his burial Mass, and another friend from early years in New York, Archbishop Joseph Rummel, gave the eulogy. His galero was placed next to those of Cardinals McCloskey and Farley over the high altar and his tomb in the crypt below it.[70]

As could have been expected, the man who had earned the title, "Cardinal of Charity," was mourned deeply by the poor who felt "a genuine sense of personal loss." In a special radio broadcast of *The Catholic Hour* a month later, Monsignor Fulton Sheen paid a moving tribute to the deceased prelate revealing details of the life of the devout Cardinal. It was his custom to remove a flower from his dining table after meals and place it at the feet of the statue of the Blessed Mother in his room. He customarily spent two-and-a-half hours daily kneeling on a hard floor in prayer and meditation until his physicians forbade the practice in his later years. His bedroom, fourteen feet by sixteen feet, was sparsely furnished, and his housekeeper used to place notes in his shoes urging him to buy new ones to replace those beyond repair. Never in his life did he ring a bell for a servant. Once, when he paid a visit to a poor elderly lady — a very normal part of his schedule — he removed her from her cold gas-lit hovel to St. Vincent's Hospital, where he cared for her until she died. In an hour of prayer each night, he reviewed in his mind each work and problem of his Archdiocese which required God's help, and mentioned it by name. Then, he would fold his hands across his chest holding a crucifix until he fell asleep. That was how he was found the morning after he died.[71]

1. Cohalan, *Popular History*, p. 216; *Catholic News*, March 22, 1919.

2. *New York Times*, September 5, 1938.

3. *New York Daily News*, September 5, 1938.

4. Cohalan, *Popular History*, pp. 216-219, 221; *Cathedral Bulletin*, October 1938; *New York Daily News*, September 5, 1938.

5. Minutes of the Board of Trustees, November 9, 1916, January 11, February 8, April 12, 1917, April 21, November 13, 1919, March 11, 1920.

6. Minutes of the Board of Trustees, 1911-1921, *passim.*

7. *Catholic News*, October 23, 1915, June 1, 1918, September 9, 1944; program of *Piccaninny Minstrels*, Boys Club of St. Patrick's Cathedral, January 20, 1922, ASPC.

8. Cohalan, *Popular History*, p. 232; Cathedral Announcements, October 8, 1919, ASPC.

9. *New York Times*, September 5, 1938. When Catholic dignitaries review the parades at St. Patrick's today, chairs are arranged on a carpet on the steps, often with a canopy above. The reviewing stands used earlier in the century were built above the steps. One of them built in 1919, as a typical example, was 210 feet long, 53 feet deep and almost 14 feet high. *See:* Application for reviewing stand, Bureau of Buildings, Borough of Manhattan, May 3, 1919, ASPC.

10. *Catholic News*, March 20, 1920. Father Duffy was Canadian by birth. He came to New York to teach philosophy at St. Joseph's Seminary which he did from 1898 until 1912. As a chaplain of the "Fighting 69th" during the War, he was decorated by the governments of France, Canada and the United States. After the War until his death in 1932, he was Pastor of Holy Cross Church near Times Square.

11. *Catholic News*, December 4, 1920.

12. *Catholic News*, October 21, 1939; *Cathedral Bulletin*, June 1929; Carthy, *Magnificence*, pp. 101-102; program of *Piccaninny Minstrels*, January 20, 1922, ASPC.

13. Minutes of the Board of Trustees, 1921, *passim;* Eggers and Higgins to E. J. Murray, June 5, 1947 and related correspondence, ASPC; interview with Msgr. Florence Cohalan, December 1994; record of priests of St. Patrick's Cathedral, ASPC.

14. Garraty, pp. 681-682, 684, 685, 688-689, 690.

15. *New York Times*, December 25, 1934; Etta Phillips to Hayes, October 22, 1920; Hayes to Phillips, November 4, 1920; Phillips to Hayes, undated, but 1925, AANY, folder Q-ll. Mrs. Phillips is buried in a family mausoleum in Salem Fields Cemetery in Cypress Hills, New York, owned by Temple Emanuel of Manhattan. She was a convert from Judaism and was buried with

her husband, who was not a convert. During her lifetime, Mrs. Phillips treasured mementos given to her with personal notes by various popes and other high Church officials.

16. *Cathedral Bulletin*, October 1960; notes of Bishop Flannelly, 1960, ASPC; Cathedral Announcements, 1920-1939, *passim; St. Patrick's Cathedral, New York,* guide book published by The Paulist Press, New York, 1922.

17. *Cathedral Bulletin*, March 1947; Cathedral Announcements, May 12, May 18, July 1, 1918 and 1920-1939, *passim*; *Catholic News*, September 30, 1944; Flannelly to Bennett, May 17, 1944, ASPC. The John McCormack concert was on Sunday, May 26, 1918.

18. Cohalan, *Popular History*, p. 234; *Catholic News*, May 3, 1924.

19. *Catholic News*, June 12, 1926. Police estimated that 300,000 spectators lined the parade route along Broadway. 10,000 soldiers, cadets and members of Catholic organizations escorted the cardinals to the City Hall reception.

20. *Catholic News*, June 18, 1927.

21. Cathedral announcements, March 1928; *Catholic News*, February 25, 1928.

22. Cohalan, *Popular History*, p. 262; Cathedral announcements, December 1929; Cathedral schedules, 1920s, 1930s; Alive and Well Magazine, March 1994.

23. Interview with Msgr. Florence Cohalan, December 1994.

24. Ungerer to Flannelly, March 17, 1953; Lavelle to Ungerer, August 4, 1928, ASPC. Ungerer retired just before Yon became Music Director. He lived for many years afterwards, and in 1953 applied for admission to the Mary Manning Walsh Home. At the same time, he requested an increase in his pension from the Cathedral to pay costs of the retirement home.

25. Biographical information on Pietro Yon, special file, 1943, ASPC. Father Young was born in Alsace, France in 1854. He was appointed to the Papal Commission for the Revision of Church Music and compiled the Roman Hymnal. *See:* Delaney, pp. 607-608.

Caruso died in Naples in 1921. *See: Catholic News*, August 6, 1921.

Yon became an American citizen, but he continued to travel to Rome to play at the Vatican during summers. His Vatican appointment was made on December 11, 1921. *See: Catholic News*, January 7, 1922.

Yon shared his studio at 853 Carnegie Hall with his brother, Constantino, Music Director of the Church of St. Vincent Ferrer. Their first studio was so small their small pipe organ had to be squeezed under a staircase. Eventually they moved to a studio on the eighth floor with the organ mechanisms built into a specially designed chamber outside the studio. The large Kilgen organ had fourteen stops. In order to muffle the volume so as not to disturb neighboring musicians, the walls around it were three feet thick. Across from the studio was his apartment. One of the musicians who taught at the Yon studio was Jacques Ungerer, Yon's predecessor at St. Patrick's. All students were required to master both Italian and French, and those languages were taught in the studio. *See: Catholic News*, October 7, 1916; *Alive and Well Magazine*, January 1987; Yon to Lavelle, October 1, 1929, AANY; Peyser, Ethel, *The House That Music Built — Carnegie Hall,* McBride and Co., New York, l936, pp. 141-142.

26. *Catholic News*, February 2, 1935. Monsignor Rostagno left New York on February 2, 1935 and returned to Italy. He lived in Torino. *See:* Anne Golden to Flannelly, October 23, 1952, ASPC.

27. Handwritten note of Cardinal Hayes, September 8, 1926, ASPC; Cheetham, Nicolas, *Keepers of the Keys,* Charles Scribner's Sons, New York, 1983, p. 320.

28. *Cathedral Bulletin*, August, October 1960; *Catholic News*, April 14, September 2, 1928.

29. Hayes to Brady, January 24, 1927, AANY; Gannon, Robert I, *The Cardinal Spellman Story,* Doubleday and Co., New York, 1962, p. 52, hereafter cited as *Spellman; Catholic News*, April 14, 1928. Mrs. Brady asked Cardinal Hayes to offer the first Mass on the altar on her birthday.

30. International Studio Magazine, Volume 57, 1915, Volume 84, 1926; *Catholic News*, January 7, 1928; Brady to Hayes, undated, probably April or May 1927, AANY; *Cathedral Bulletin*, October 1960. Korbel's father was a Bohemian clergyman who was described as one "whose views of life were something stricter than those of the most conscientious Quaker." Because his father limited his son's study of art, Mario decided to come to America. His father came here later. His mother was a Roman Catholic. During World War I, he worked to gain independence for Bohemia from Austria-Hungary. After the war, he returned to Prague where he worked on statues for the gardens of the Bradys and others. He spent a year preparing studies for his figure, "Saint Therese" for the Bradys. The first such statue was given to the Vatican, and the second, carved in wood, was for the Bradys' private chapel on Long Island. After the wood statue was finished, the Bradys intended that other statues would be presented to churches and cathedrals, presumably St. Patrick's among them.

The Alexander Pelli Company was located in Elmhurst, Queens County, New York. Samuel Yellin was born on March 2, 1886 and died in New York on October 3, 1940.

31. In 1928, Augustin McNally wrote an article in which he stated that Catholics in the future might "witness the passing of the domestic structures on the eastern front of the site." *See: Catholic News*, September 8, 1928.

32. *Catholic News*, August 22, 1925. The replacement cross weighed ½ ton. It was blessed on August 19, 1925.

33. *Catholic News*, September 8, 1928.

34. Cathedral announcements, December 15, 22, 25, 1929. By Christmas 1929 the fund had raised $700,000, still $175,000 short of its goal.

35. Charles Maginis' first firm was called Maginnis, Walsh and Sullivan. It became Maginnis and Walsh in 1908 and in the last years of Mr. Maginnis' life it was Maginnis, Walsh and Kennedy. Mr. Maginnis died in 1955.

Robert J. Reiley's offices were at 12 East 41st Street and 62 West 45th Street. *See:* Placzek; Reiley to Msgr. Stephen J. Donahue, June 21, 1927, AANY; Reiley to Fred Mack, May 16, 1940, ASPC.

36. *Catholic News*, July 2, July 23, 1927, September 8, 1928; Lavelle to Hayes, July 17, 1924, AANY; Reiley to Hayes, September 22, 1927, AANY. Initially, D. H. McBride Company of 41 Park Row, New York was expected to replace the floor. The actual contractor was the Edward S. Murphy Company.

37. Reiley to Hayes, November 3, 1927, AANY

38. *Catholic News*, March 10, 1920, September 8, 1928; *Archbishopric,* pp. 78, 79; Julia Grant to Maginnis and Walsh, March 14, 1947, ASPC.

39. *Catholic News*, July 8, 1928, September 7, 1929; *Archbishopric,* p. 78.

40. *Catholic News*, July 23, 1927, February 4, 1928; *New York Evening World*, February 3, 1930; *Archbishopric,* p. 76; Peyser, Chapter 9, *passim*. Rev. Philip Furlong of Cathedral College assisted Yon and Kilgen in the design of the organ. Fr. Furlong later became a bishop of the military ordinariate.

The manager of the eastern district for the Kilgen Organ Company was Ludwig Zentmaier. According to his wife, Mr. Zentmaier was in charge of the installation at St. Patrick's, overseeing the work of thirty-five men employed on the job. Mr. Zentmaier came to America from Frankfort, Germany and settled in St. Louis. He moved to New York to assume management of the Kilgen Company business in the City. *See:* Robert L. Zentmaier to St. Patrick's Cathedral, January 7, 1997, ASPC.

41. New York Evening World, February 3, 1930; *Catholic News*, July 2, 1927, February 15, 1930; information supplied verbally by organ curators Mel Robinson and John Peragallo to author, August 1983 and August 1995.

42. *Catholic News*, February 15, 1930; interview with Msgr. Florence Cohalan, December 1994. The gallery organ was scheduled to be used for the first time on Christmas Day 1929, even though the formal dedication would not take place until the following February. *See: Catholic News*, December 21,1929.

43. *Archbishopric*, p. 77

44. Reiley to Donahue, June 21, l927; *Catholic News*, September 20, December 13, 1930; *Archbishopric*, pp. 79, 80. Atkins was born in Milwaukee in 1899 and died in 1951.

45. *Cathedral Bulletin*, August, September, December 1930, January 1931, July 1948, September 1960; *Catholic News*, July 11, 1931; *Archbishopric*, pp. 47, 75; Minutes of the Board of Trustees, January 8, 1920; *Centenary; The New High Altar and the Altar for the Lady Chapel*, preliminary description by the architects, May 9, 1942. Before the pamphlet rack was moved to the southwest bay, it had been located in the chapel used for the new Shrine of St. Theresa. *See: Catholic News*, April 23, 1927; *Cathedral Bulletin*, August, September 1930.

Joseph Charles Benziger founded the Benziger firm in Einsiedeln in 1793. The New York branch opened in 1853. The baptismal font the family donated was made of Bottocino marble. *See:* Delaney, p. 45; *Catholic News*, July 11, 1931.

46. Carthy, *Magnificence,* p. 104.

47. *Ibid.,* p. 181, footnote #26.

48. Interview with Msgr. Florence Cohalan, December 1994.

49. Cohalan, p. 253; Cathedral announcements, April 26, 1931 and l930s, *passim;* Lavelle to Hayes, April 18, 1932, AANY. At the Catholic Charities dinner at the Waldorf-Astoria on October 4, 1933, more than 3600 persons were present, including 42 archbishops and bishops; the Apostolic Delegate to the United States, Archbishop Cicognani; Al Smith; and President Franklin Delano Roosevelt. John McCormack sang for the occasion. *See: Catholic News*, October 7, 1933.

50. Cohalan, *Popular History,* pp. 246-255, *passim.*

51. Carthy, *Magnificence,* pp. 108-109; Cohalan, *Popular History,* p. 263.

52. Flannelly to Outdoor Cleanliness Association, 1952, ASPC.

53. Reiley to Lavelle, April 24, 1935, ASPC. Reiley found that the mortar joints were in worse condition around the lower portions where the Pleasantville marble had been used. The upper areas of the Lady Chapel needed considerable work, as did the arches of the doorways. The west front and Fifty-first Street walls were found in worse condtion than those on Fiftieth Street.

54. *Catholic News*, September 21, 1935; *New York Times*, September 19, 1935; Report of Fred T. Sutton of Vermilya-Brown Company, November 17, 1941, ASPC. The chemical was intended to harden the stone. The work was divided into three phases with two months required for each phase. But there were to be intervals between the phases, so that the work was expected to take three years and be completed in 1937. The Nicholson and Galloway Company was the contractor.

55. *Catholic News*, February 14, 1931, December 30, 1933, April 7, 1934.

56. Cathedral schedules, 1930s; Sheen, Fulton J., *Treasure In Clay,* Doubleday and Co., Garden City, New York, 1980, pp. 253-254, 260-26l.

57. Schedule for Lent and Easter, 1932, ASPC.

58. Records of priests, ASPC; interview with Msgr. Florence Cohalan, December 1994.

59. Cathedral announcements, July 10, 1932, May 2, 1937.

60. Cathedral announcements, February 16, December 14, 1930, May 17, November 15, 1931, February 21, 1932, June 10, August 5, 1934, October 2, 1938; *Catholic News*, February 13, 1937; New York Herald Tribune, June 4, 1934; Gannon, p. 176.

61. Cathedral announcements, September 3, 1933, November 29, December 6, December 13, December 20, 1936, and 1930s *passim;* Cohalan, *Popular History,* pp. 222, 259-260; Journal of Msgr. Lavelle, 1939, *passim; New York Times,* February 2, 1933. The pontifical Mass celebrated for the deceased Pope Pius XI was one of the occasions on which Msgr. Lavelle was permitted to wear the vestments of a bishop as prothonotary apostolic. Cardinal Hayes had died the previous September, and a new archbishop had not yet been appointed for New York. Msgr. Lavelle noted in his journal that American Cardinals Mundelein and Dougherty had left for Rome two days earlier to take part in the election of a new pope.

St. Patrick's Cathedral was not in possession of the drawings of the Lady Chapel made by Charles Mathews. Two years after his 1934 death, a collection of the drawings was donated by Florence Mathews to the Cooper-Hewitt Museum on East 91st Street where they remain today.

62. McNally memorandum to Major Edward Bowes, Tuesday of Holy Week 1941, and related information, ASPC.

63. Delaney, pp. 176-177; records of Trustees, ASPC. Farley died on June 9, 1976.

64. Mr. Carroll provided the author with some details. The author worked at the Cathedral for several years when Mr. Carroll was sacristan.

65. Biographical information on Pietro Yon, special file, 1943, ASPC.

66. *Chimes,* yearbook of Cathedral College, 1963; Cardinal Terence Cooke to Rivetti, July 12, 1972, ASPC. After the death of Pietro Yon in 1943, Paolo Giaquinto applied to Msgr. Flannelly for the position as Yon's successor. In his letter of application, he stated that he had been chancel organist for many years. *See:* Giaquinto to Flannelly, May 2, 1943, ASPC.

67. Flannelly to Bennett, May 17, 1957, ASPC; *Catholic News,* December 4, 1943; press release, Chancery office of Archdiocese of New York, December 21, 1939, ASPC.

68. Peyser, pp. 141-142; *Musical America Magazine,* May 10, 1934; *Alive and Well Magazine,* June 1993; biographical information on Pietro Yon, special file, 1943, ASPC.

69. *Cathedral Bulletin,* September 1932, October 1941; Cathedral announcements, July 23, 1933; *Catholic News,* October 10, November 7, November 14, 1936; Kelly to Eggers and Higgins, September 2, 1943, ASPC.

70. Cohalan, *Popular History,* p. 259; special file on death of Cardinal Hayes, 1938, ASPC.

71. *Catholic News,* October 15, 1938.

~ 128 ~

CHAPTER VIII

A World Redefined: The Years of Cardinal Francis Spellman

For eight months following the death of Cardinal Hayes, the vacancy in the See of New York remained unfilled, the long hiatus caused in part by the death in February 1939 of Pope Pius XI. Bishop Stephen Donahue, auxiliary bishop of the Archdiocese, was administrator until the appointment of a new archbishop. In Rome, the conclave of cardinals to elect a new pope opened on March 1st, and on the following day, Cardinal Eugenio Pacelli, the Vatican Secretary of State, was elected Bishop of Rome. He chose the name Pius XII. On April 24th, the official announcement was made that the new pontiff had chosen Auxiliary Bishop Francis J. Spellman of Boston to be Archbishop of New York. It was the same Bishop Spellman who had accompanied Cardinal Pacelli on his journey through America in 1936, including his visit to St. Patrick's.[1]

Francis Joseph Spellman was born on May 4, 1889 in Whitman, Massachusetts, the oldest son of William and Ellen Spellman.[2] After elementary and secondary education in the local schools, he entered Fordham University in New York in 1907, and graduated four years later. He decided to study for the priesthood, and was sent to the North American College in Rome where two future cardinals were members of the faculty, men who later helped advance their student's career in the Church. Despite a serious illness, the young seminarian recovered, was ordained in 1916, and offered his first Mass at St. Peter's tomb. His first Mass in this country was celebrated in New York on July 23rd in the Lady Chapel of St. Patrick's Cathedral.

From 1916 until 1925, Fr. Spellman worked at various assignments in the Archdiocese of Boston. In the latter year, through the efforts of Monsignor Borgognini-Duca, a friend and former teacher in Rome, he was sent there to work in the Secretariat of State, the first American ever to work at that office. After he became a monsignor in 1928, he met Cardinal Eugenio Pacelli, the future Pope Pius XII, and the two became close friends. In 1932, he was appointed an auxiliary bishop of Boston, and Cardinal Pacelli consecrated him in St. Peter's Basilica, the first American accorded that privilege. During the next six years in Boston, he became acquainted with Joseph P. Kennedy, father of future president John F. Kennedy, and he met President Franklin Delano Roosevelt for the first time. When Cardinal Pacelli came to America in 1936, the young bishop arranged all the details of his itinerary, and accompanied his friend on every step of his journey, including a meeting with President Roosevelt.[3]

Following Archbishop Spellman's appointment to New York, Bishop Donahue and Msgr. Lavelle welcomed him at the border of the Archdiocese on May 22, 1939, and arranged a luncheon for him.[4] A twelve-car procession from the Archdiocesan line at Portchester to the Archbishop's residence followed, greeted by a large gathering of the curious faithful along the way. On the next day, nearly half the hierarchy of the United States attended a glittering installation ceremony at the Cathedral, with an estimated seven thousand inside and over thirty thousand in the streets around the Cathedral. The ceremonies were broadcast by radio for the inauguration of an administration which was to become "the longest and most active in the history of New York."[5]

The population of the Archdiocese in 1939 was vastly larger than it had been at the beginning of the Hayes administration two decades earlier. The City had grown by almost two million residents to almost seven-and-a-half million, many of them still suffering the ill effects of the depression. But, even though the Great Depression was nearing its end, just around a bend was the near certainty of war in Europe, as the tentacles of Adolf Hitler's monster war machine reached farther and farther outside the borders of Germany. In the City, because 1939 was the one-hundred-fiftieth anniversary of the American constitution, a world's fair opened, the first in the City since 1853, five years before St. Patrick's cornerstone was blessed. The fair drew forty-five million visitors, whose spending for the event created jobs which helped ease the financial pressures on many New Yorkers, even though the event itself lost money before its closing in 1940. In September 1939, World War II broke out in Europe, and the Depression ended, as the European democracies flooded American businesses with orders for war materials. The business boom brought unemployment to a standstill.[6]

That year, there were enormous changes in the Church and in the world at large. The Church of New York suffered the end of the exceptional life of St. Patrick's famous Rector, Msgr. Lavelle. In May, his strength waning, he had pontificated at a Mass in the Cathedral at which Archbishop Spellman presided, a celebration of the Rector's sixty years as a priest. At a grand dinner in his honor at the Hotel Commodore, there were accolades from Pope Pius XII and President Roosevelt among a host of other tributes. The affair was reminiscent of the testimonial given three years earlier on his eightieth birthday, a dinner attended by over 5,000 guests.[7] The day after the anniversary, as his strength continued to diminish, he retired to his bed. By October, he realized he was close to death. He expressed joy when he learned that Archbishop Spellman had ordered his remains to be interred in the crypt of the Archbishops. He died in the rectory at 8:34 p.m. on October 17th in the presence of Archbishop Spellman and some close friends. The Archbishop presided at almost all the services held on the following days, including Masses arranged for the children of the Catholic schools and for the religious of the Archdiocese. He also celebrated the solemn pontifical requiem Mass, and Bishop Donahue delivered the eulogy. Then, the body of Msgr. Lavelle was laid to rest with those of the Archbishops of New York.[8]

Local newspapers showered copious tributes on the deceased prelate, as did Church and political dignitaries around the country. Many recalled his dedication to charitable and civic causes, ranging from the spiritual care he extended to members of the Italian apostolate to his work with Catholic teachers in the public schools, to his association with the Catholic Theatre Movement, to his care for troops during the First World War, to his work with the blind, with religious communities, with the Catholic Summer School of America (*below*), with the Catholic University of America and with scores of other groups.[9] The day after his death, he was eulogized in the House of Representatives.[10] Archbishop John Mitty of San Francisco, a former New York priest, recalled his zeal, his energy, his ready sympathy and heartfelt loyalty, and made note of his "colorful character."[11] In so doing, he reminded New Yorkers of stories which abounded about him. A few, as related by the New York Archdiocese's eminent historian, Msgr. Florence Cohalan, are worth relating.

Yes, it had boating, swimming, golf, tennis, quoits, euchre games, dancing, plays, singing, visiting performers, not to mention side trips to Montreal or Vermont. Yes, the accommodations were primitive. But, as James Addison White tells it in his history of the founding of the Cliff Haven Catholic Summer School of America, the school (1892-1940) represented a hunger that welled up — mainly among Catholic lay groups and especially the Reading Circles — to discover more about the riches of their faith and its place in the new world. Msgr. Lavelle saw this coming. Three-week 'courses' were a series of lectures by a variety of experts on teaching methods, poetry, anthropology, history, trade unions, literature, school administration, tax policy, free will and hypnotism, science and more. Lecturers included President Taft (vacationing nearby) and Gov. Theodore Roosevelt.

As a much-in-demand speaker, he was often present at banquets, and prided himself on eating anything placed before him at the table. But, on one occasion over dessert, he raised some eyebrows when he confessed his aversion to a condiment — cinnamon. On another occasion, when delivering a eulogy for a brother priest, he caused mild hysteria in the congregation when he recalled that one of the "eccentricities" of the deceased was his deep devotion to the Holy See in Rome. Perhaps most "colorful" of all was the occasion when a loudspeaker was brought for the first time to the Cathedral. It was controlled by a shut-off switch behind the reredos of the old high altar. In an effort to keep sermons within the bounds of reasonable time constraints, Msgr. Lavelle informed his staff that the system would be disengaged after a set number of minutes. On the first day the system was in use, and Msgr. Lavelle was delivering a sermon, the current was suddenly cut off. Nobody ever learned who the culprit was, but the next day the new system was summarily removed.[12]

Major Edward Bowes, a Cathedral benefactor, had decided to donate ornamental shade trees for planting around the Cathedral. As a special honor in memory of Msgr. Lavelle, he arranged to have them in place before the funeral Mass. By working in pre-dawn hours, workers were able to complete the project six hours before the liturgy began. Since the trees were fully grown when planted — about thirty-five feet in height — the work was considerable, requiring blasting to remove rock below ground level to provide a thirteen-feet diameter of space for the roots. The trees were taken from an estate in Westchester County, and were thought to be about fifty years old when moved. Eleven maples and three dogwoods were planted on the terraces, and four English elms were set in front of the building. Seventeen oleanders, about ten feet high, were placed in tubs on the terraces at Fifth Avenue. The instant beautification of the gardens brought praise from many quarters. Major Bowes was a convert to Catholicism, and was known nationally for his syndicated radio program, "Major Bowes and His Original Amateur Hour," one of the most popular shows of the era. Born in 1874, he had made a fortune early in his life in San Francisco, only to lose it during the 1906 earthquake there. But, just as that city was rebuilt, so he rebuilt his fortune. His title "major" was carried from World War I. He came to New York in 1909, and became active as a theatre owner and executive. His gift of the trees was the first of several donations without which St. Patrick's would have been sorely burdened to meet its needs.[13]

The priest who assumed the direction of the Cathedral's everyday affairs during the final illness of Msgr. Lavelle was his senior assistant, Rev. Joseph Flannelly, who had been transferred to the Cathedral only one year earlier. On the day after Lavelle's funeral, Archbishop Spellman appointed Father Flannelly *Administrator,* the title which is the English language equivalent of the Latin *rector.* He continued to use the title during his entire tenure. He was born near the Cathedral on West Fifty-first Street in 1894, and was the first graduate of Blessed Sacrament School to become a priest. His education continued at Cathedral College and St. Joseph's Seminary. After ordination in 1918 until he came to St. Patrick's, his only assignment was at Our Lady of the Rosary Church in Yonkers, New York where his work centered on youth activities and supervision of the school. He belonged to the Archdiocesan priests choir, and was a chaplain of the Yonkers Fire Department and of the Knights of Columbus.[14]

Beginning with Christmas 1939, Fr. Flannelly's first as Administrator, the midnight Mass was broadcast on radio station WOR. The broadcast continued annually thereafter.[15] One of his first duties as administrator was making preparations for the ceremony of the *pallium* investiture of Archbishop Spellman. This sign of an archbishop's authority was conferred by Cardinal Dennis Dougherty of Philadelphia on March 12, 1940.[16] The same year, Fr. Flannelly undertook the remodeling and modernization of the rectory, a program of electrical renewal, new plumbing, the installation of an elevator and the conversion of office space. During the eight month construction period, the clergy lived at 35 East 51st Street. Early in his tenure, Father Flannelly realized that, as the character of the neighborhood changed from residential to commercial, so the closing of the Cathedral school was inevitable; 1942 was its last year in existence.[17]

The beautification of the Cathedral begun by Cardinal Hayes in pre-Depression days was resumed almost immediately after Archbishop Spellman and Father Flannelly began their administration. As early as December 1939, the Archbishop authorized Charles Maginnis to approve designs for a new altar in the Lady Chapel, a scheme unfulfilled for

Our Lady of New York: Is she praying, or just excited at the prospect of welcoming her devoted visitors?

twenty years. Robert Reiley supervised its installation in 1941. The Archbishop estimated the cost at about $20,000, and a donation by George J. Gillespie made it possible.[18] Hildreth Meiere, a New York artist, was its designer. She lived on Park Avenue and had a studio on Fifty-seventh Street. She enjoyed the reputation of a great mural painter and in 1927 received the New York Architectural League Medal. Her most notable work was at the Nebraska State Capitol where she painted the murals of the domes, ceilings and floors. She also designed the rotunda doors of the National Academy of Sciences in Washington, D. C.[19] The Alexander Pelli Company, builders of the St. Theresa altar, also executed this altar. The statue of Mary, sculptured in an unusual pose of outstretched hands, a position called *orans*, meaning praying, was portrayed in many images in the Roman catacombs.[20] The statue was the work of Oronzio Maldarelli, who headed the Department of Sculpture of Columbia University. He received other commissions for art at Columbia, at the New York World's Fair of 1939 and at the U.S. Department of the Treasury, and was the recipient of many awards.[21] Piccirrilli Brothers did the carvings in their New York studios. The altar was erected between February and April 1942, and at its dedication on April 13th, Archbishop Spellman named it *Our Lady of New York*. The altar was the first that Archbishop Spellman ever consecrated and he personally celebrated its first Mass in thanksgiving for the chapel's benefactors. The original altar was removed to the convent chapel of the Daughters of Mary, Health of the Sick, at Cragsmoor, New York, and its reredos was given to the convent of the Parish Visitors in Monroe, New York.[22]

Even before the Lady Chapel was ready, Archbishop Spellman announced that an anonymous donor had made possible the fulfillment of another dream, the erection of a new high altar. The donor was Julia Grant, the wife of Hugh Grant, a member of the Board of Trustees of the Cathedral.[23] Ever since Robert Reiley in 1927 had suggested a low table under a baldachin to allow a view open from east to west ends of the interior, Cathedral authorities entertained the hope that this would happen, all, that is, except Msgr. Lavelle. He was wont to say that the old altar would be removed and a new one built "over my dead body," in his own words.[24] And so it happened, since, by this time, his remains reposed in the crypt below. Mrs. Grant had proposed her donation to Cardinal Hayes in 1930, but she withdrew it in 1931 when she learned that there were plans to combine parts of the original altar with the new baldachin, a scheme she opposed. But she retained the pencil drawings of Charles Maginnis and copies of other preliminary studies. Correspondence

The original High Altar (above) yields to the 1942 altar, allowing a see-through passage to the Lady Chapel beyond. The word 'baldachin', originally a canopy of brocaded silk, actually is derived from the place it came from — Baghdad.

between the two resumed in May 1940, and in February 1941, the General Bronze Company signed a contract for the baldachin, and the William Bradley Company one for the altar. Estimates for cost approached $115,000. Construction was set to begin in February and be completed in April 1942, the same schedule as that for work on the Lady Chapel altar.[25]

Between the planning of the new altar and its construction, Pearl Harbor, Hawaii, was attacked on December 7, 1941, bringing the United States into World War II. The Archbishop was concerned that materials for the altar or baldachin might be needed for defense purposes, so he conferred with government officials. They told him the materials could not be reprocessed advantageously. He also saw the advantage of providing employment to "men who would otherwise be idle." There was also a symbolic reason for proceeding, as he saw that "in our country altars are being erected, while in other countries they are going down together with freedom and civilization."[26] And so, on February 15, 1942, the final liturgies were celebrated on the beloved old altar. Monsignor William Scully preached at the last solemn Mass sung by Monsignor Flannelly (he had been made a monsignor in October 1941); Bishop James McIntyre celebrated the last low Mass; and Bishop Thomas McDonnell sang the last vespers. In time, Msgr. Flannelly became a New York bishop, Msgr. Scully became Bishop of Albany, Bishop McDonnell was made Coadjutor Bishop of Wheeling, and Bishop McIntyre became Cardinal Archbishop of Los Angeles.[27]

A temporary altar was used on Sundays for the duration of the construction period, and Mass was offered on weekdays at the Sacred Heart altar. Careful dismantling lasted until late March when the marble of the altar was crated and moved by truck to Fordham University for rebuilding in the college chapel, which once had been the chapel of the diocesan seminary. The statue of St. Patrick was removed to the grounds of the archdiocesan seminary in Yonkers, New York, and the statues of Sts. Peter and Paul were sent to a church in their honor in the Bronx, New York. Marble salvaged from the reredos went to Fordham University.[28] In April, the new, free-standing altar was erected on a predella, or platform, five steps above the pavement. The Tavernelle marble frontal contained a sculptured panel of a ship, representing the Church guided by St. Peter. There was no tabernacle, the Blessed Sacrament being reserved at the Sacred Heart altar. A bronze baldachin soared to a height of fifty-seven feet, the canopy supported by four piers decorated with figures of both the Old and New Testaments. The statuettes were designs of John Angel, who also sculptured a statue of St. Patrick which was erected on a pier at the north side of the sanctuary. Angel was born and trained in Devon, England, but his works are found principally in the United States, including at the Cathedral of St. John the Divine in New York. In England, he designed many war memorials. Exhibitions of his works were held at the Royal Academy in London and at the Pennsylvania Academy of Fine Arts.[29]

Archbishop Spellman set May 9th for the altar's consecration. The honor of offering the first Mass was given to the oldest surviving priest who had served at St. Patrick's, Rev. William Daly. He had been at the Cathedral from 1886 until 1902 and his parents had donated the St. Veronica altar. The first pontifical Mass was offered by the Archbishop on May 13th in observance of the twenty-fifth anniversary of the episcopal consecration of Pope Pius XII. The following December, the Archbishop rededicated the original altar in its new home at Fordham University.[30]

Mrs. Grant was careful to include in her donation many appurtenances to enhance the beauty of the altar. A four-and-a-half feet high bronze crucifix and accompanying candlesticks graced the low reredos behind the altar. In addition, she gave a new gold chalice studded with jewels; a bronze thabor, or exposition throne, over seven feet high; a sterling silver monstrance in the form of a Celtic cross, designed by Charles Maginnis and gilded by Tiffany and Company; stunningly crafted altar cards for use during the celebration of Mass (the cards were used before reforms of the Second Vatican Council); candelabra; a fabric dossal; and altar cloths of finest linen. Her gift also included the John Angel statue of St. Patrick which portrayed the patron saint vested in a chasuble, the chief Mass vestment, and holding a Gospel book and a shamrock. On the opposite south pier over the pulpit, a new canopy replaced the original one which, in the absense of electricity, had the form of a shell to project the preacher's voice.[31]

But besides the baldachin, no other part of her gift changed the appearance of the sanctuary as much as the five apsidal windows over the altar which replaced those of 1879. The new windows were made by Charles J. Connick, who was said to know "more about stained glass, ancient and modern, than anybody else." He was acknowledged on both sides of the Atlantic to be a leader in the revival of the medieval art of stained glass making, one who rejected the proclivity of nineteenth century artists to use large painting-like portrayals of saints or other religious themes like those in the lower windows of the Cathedral. He wrote: "My critical sense is never very keen when I enter a great structure like St. Patrick's Cathedral, but my imagination soars to great heights. I speculate about what might have happened to that great interior if the picture windows had never been invented. What a mighty symphony of color and light a master craftsman could have achieved in those great clusters of window openings with St. Thomas Aquinas, St. Francis and Abbé Suger at his elbow to encourage him!" Connick was called a man of prodigious talent with no equivalent on the European scene during his lifetime. "His designs were impeccably crafted and within their terms of reference were almost unassailable. They were the fine flowering of a movement that had persisted for well over a century." He was born in Pittsburgh, and studied in both the United States and Europe. Early in his career he worked with the famous architect Ralph Adams Cram. His windows are found at Boston University, Princeton University, the Cathedral of St. John the Divine and other cathedrals, churches and educational institutions throughout the United States. Not surprisingly, he considered the sun the greatest of God's gifts to humanity, and his devotion to St. Francis led him to adopt the Franciscan "Canticle of the Sun" as a favorite prayer.[32] His association with St. Patrick's began when Charles Maginnis commissioned him to replace the five apsidal windows in 1941. In September, he submitted his drawings, choosing as a subject the parables of Our Lord. The next month, the contract set a cost of $23,000. They were completed and installed rapidly, and all were ready by the time the new altar was consecrated in May 1942. That

A slice of Connick's apsidal windows, this one the parable of the sower. The birds seem to think it's feeding time.

spring, the entire aesthetic appearance of the interior was changed. Someone entering at Fifth Avenue had his or her eyes drawn immediately to the sanctuary where the strong blue tones of Connick's windows and the sharp noble lines of the Maginnis baldachin focused all attention. And beyond the sanctuary, for the first time, the soft colors of the Lady Chapel windows provided a glass reredos for the altar, instead of a massive stone wall.[33]

Virtually everyone was so pleased with the new windows that it was decided to add four more like them on the east wall of the transept clerestory facing west, so that a wider vista of blue met the eyes of those looking east towards the sanctuary. Connick was commissioned to remove the four already in that location, those dedicated to St. Monica and St. Augustine; St. Paul; The Sacred Heart and St. Margaret Mary; and St. Louis. From August to October 1943, they were transferred to the facing west wall at a cost of $4800, and in their place Connick created windows with subjects almost identical to those moved. A figure of St. Denis was added with St. Paul and one of St. Bernard with St. Louis. The new glass cost $26,600, a gift of Mrs. Patrick McGovern. Each of the new windows received protective exterior glass, and the following year, all the other clerestory windows were given the same protection.[34]

From 1904 until 1942, the church and residence buildings had been heated by coal. In the winter of 1942-43, Monsignor Flannelly learned that it was unlikely the aging burners would survive until spring and he was faced with a dilemma: how to find replacement equipment when materials needed were required for the war effort. He decided to request permission from the War Production Board to purchase steam from the New York Steam Corporation. This required only about one-third the critical material which would have been used if the boilers were replaced. The plan yielded a bonus of additional savings, because there was no need to purchase the six hundred tons of coal used by the old system.[35]

Shortly after the war began, a statement appeared in advertisements carried in the City's subways contending that the Cathedral site had been sold to the Church by the City for one dollar. The old canard had been revived from time to time since early in the century, but this time, Msgr. Flannelly vehemently denounced it as scurrilous.[36] Why the splenetic attack reemerged at that time is unknown. It is ironic that it appeared during the tenure of an archbishop whose patriotism and loyalty to his country is indisputable. Even before Pearl Harbor, Spellman had not shared the prevailing abhorrence of most Americans for American intervention. He believed the war was inevitable "and thought it necessary in defense of liberty." The war helped make him the most visible of American church leaders, since he had succeeded Cardinal Hayes as Military Vicar of the Armed Forces of the United States in 1939. In that capacity, he made numerous journeys to all continents of the world both during the war and in the decades afterwards. In his absence from New York, his Auxiliary Bishop and later Coadjutor Archbishop, James McIntrye, administered the Archdiocese, and was regularly at the Cathedral. Over several decades, Spellman travelled more than half a million miles, including six trips around the world. On one of those journeys, in 1943, he was gone from the City from February until August. During his travels he often met with world leaders, among whom were prime ministers, ruling members of royal families, and, of course, high ranking military officers.[37]

He would visit three wars before it was all over — this one, Korea and Vietnam. His biographer, Fr. Robert I. Gannon, S.J., tells how he said Mass for the grunts in all weathers; how, in World War II alone, he was the Ordinary of 3,270 chaplains, of whom 38 were killed in action, another 90 wounded, and 33 died in non-battle circumstances; how he published a meditation, The Risen Soldier, *to console families that lost a son or daughter to the war; and how he protested American attacks on Vatican City personnel and property and pressed the case for keeping Rome itself an open city.*

While he was attending to the spiritual needs of the troops abroad, the Archbishop did not neglect the war effort on the home front. In August 1941, even before the Pearl Harbor attack, he opened the Cathedral canteen at 17 East Fifty-first Street in the Cathedral College building. By 1944, the center had provided refreshments and relaxation for 630,000 men and women of the armed forces. The canteen closed in 1947, but was reopened during the Korean War; in later years, it was at Lexington Avenue and Fifty-fourth Street, and still later, on Park Avenue. From its start to its closing, over two million members of the military services were served. Msgr. Fulton Sheen referred to the canteen as "another cathedral, one built of devoted acts and acts of sacrifice," recognizing the dedication of many volunteers.[38]

Participation in the sacred liturgy was much stronger during the war than earlier. In fact, even just before the war started, it was decided that Mass would be offered on the various altars around the Cathedral on the feast days of the saints whom the altars honored.[39] Msgr. Flannelly found it necessary in 1943 to request an additional Mass on Sundays, and attendance at the Masses was "considerable." A year earlier, 53,174 Catholics of the Archdiocese were serving in the armed forces. A service flag recording that number hung over the west portal on Fifth Avenue, while, inside, another flag with thirty-seven gold stars honored those who had given their lives. By January 1944, when the Archbishop rededicated the flags, there were 149,157 in the services, and inside the Cathedral, a banner with 1,396 gold stars was a vivid reminder of the horrible cost of the war. Archbishop Spellman rededicated the flags for the last time on January 1, 1945 during a military vespers service.[40]

Even before the war ended, there were fears that this worst of all wars in history was but prelude to another, and that the next might involve current allies on opposing sides. There was abundant suspicion of the Soviet Union's future intentions; vandals painted a red hammer and sickle on the walls of St. Patrick's, of the Cathedral of St. John the Divine and of several Jewish synagogues. But suspicions did not diminish the exuberance of the celebrations on V-E (victory over Europe) Day in May 1945 after the German armies were defeated. Throngs crowded into the Cathedral to give thanks, as church and cathedral bells throughout the City sang out; ship and factory whistles added to the cacophony. Three months later, V-J (victory over Japan) Day brought over 50,000 people into the Cathedral in the few hours between 7 and 10 p. m., after world peace was announced. The next day, the Feast of the Assumption, special services drew large numbers of grateful worshippers.[41]

The sacrifices required of Americans at home during the war "had almost no adverse effect on the standard of living of the average citizen...." True, there was rationing of gasoline, meat, sugar, shoes, butter and other scarce goods, and many items simply disappeared from store shelves; automobiles were not manufactured, and metal was replaced by plastics in some goods, but except for some minor inconvenience, life continued much as it had been before the war.[42] Church contributions were no less generous than they had been previously. The people of the Cathedral parish, for example, presented the Archbishop with almost $10,000 to furnish a science laboratory at the new Cardinal Hayes High School just a few months before the attack at Pearl Harbor. In the month the United States entered the war, Major Bowes paid the cost of renovating the chancel organ platform and he paid for new kneelers, prie-dieus, votive stands and chairs for the ambulatory; Mary Young Moore, later named a papal countess, gave a new chalice, crafted by Patrick Gill; and Julia Grant assumed the costs of a new faldstool for Archbishop Spellman to use at liturgies when he was not presiding at the *cathedra*. There was even a donation from a group of Polish soldiers exiled in Iraq. They gave it to Archbishop Spellman when he visited them to offer a Mass.[43]

It was another gift of Mrs. Grant in 1943 which fulfilled the desire of many Catholics for a devotion at the Cathedral to the Child Jesus. Archbishop Spellman wanted a statue of the Christ Child based on an American tradition. There was a popular devotion to the Child under the title *The Infant of Prague,* but the Archbishop learned of another devotion practiced among New York Indians in 1640. The Jesuit missionary martyr, St. Jean de Breboeuf, had written a poem in Huron, *Jesous Ahatonhia (Jesus is Born),* to honor the holy Child represented in a wax statue robed in a rabbit skin, and presented by missionaries to Indian catechists (ones preparing for baptism). "The whole village fell in love with it and wanted to honor it...," so the statue was passed from home to home of the Indian families who sang hymns. "So lavish were the Indians in giving to the Lord Jesus the things which they most valued, that the priest had sometimes to restrain their generosity."[44] The poem (*right*) referred to the Child as *The Holy Child of Earth and Heaven,* and this was the title assigned to the new statue enshrined behind the high altar, just above the entrance of the crypt. Designed by Charles Maginnis, the figure was carved from bass wood by Ernest Pelligrini and blessed by the Archbishop in August 1943. Encircling the head was a golden nimbus encrusted with garnets, sapphires, pearls and diamonds, and a brooch with the same stones was attached to the robe. The stones were chosen for the colors of the American flag, and both nimbus and brooch were made by Tiffany and Company in New York.[45]

During the long war years, Pope Pius XII had not named any prelates to the College of Cardinals, and the membership was "the lowest it had been in centuries." Archbishop Spellman was one of four Americans called to the consistory in Rome in February 1946. The red hat which had belonged to the Pope himself when he was a cardinal was given to his friend, Cardi-

'Twas in the moon of wintertime
When all the birds had fled.
That mighty Gitchi Manitou
Sent angel choirs instead.
Before their light the stars grew dim
And wand'ring hunters heard the hymn,
Jesus your King is born
Jesus is born, in excelsis gloria!
Within a lodge of broken bark
The tender Babe was found,
A ragged robe of rabbit skin
Enwrapped his beauty 'round.
And as the hunter braves drew nigh
The angel song rang loud and high,
Jesus your King is born
Jesus is born, in excelsis gloria!
The earliest moon of wintertime
Is not so round and fair
As was the ring of glory on
The helpless infant there.
The chiefs from far before him knelt
With gifts of fox and beaver pelt.
Jesus your King is born
Jesus is born, in excelsis gloria!
O children of the forest free
O sons of Manitou
The Holy Child of earth and heaven
Is born today for you.
Come kneel before the radiant boy
Who brings you beauty, peace and joy.
Jesus your King is born
Jesus is born, in excelsis gloria!

nal Spellman. Three years earlier, he had given the Archbishop his own pectoral cross and chain.[46] Spellman told Cardinal Conrad von Preysing of Berlin that he was concerned about the cost of scaffolding required to suspend his hat from the ceiling of St. Patrick's after his death; an unsympathetic Cardinal von Preysing remarked: "I have no trouble of that kind. I have no ceiling!"[47] New York's new Cardinal arrived in the City on March 5th at LaGuardia Aiport where Mayor William O'Dwyer led a large contingent of dignitaries. A motorcade passed through crowd-lined streets to Cardinal Hayes High School and then to the Cathedral where American flags and a gilded shield bearing Spellman's coat-of-arms were at the entrance. Inside, five thousand school children sang the national anthem as the procession passed up the center aisle. At a public reception at the Metropolitan Opera House, Governor Thomas Dewey and Mayor O'Dwyer welcomed him on behalf of the citizens. Several religious services were conducted in the following days at the Cathedral.[48]

In May 1945, Best and Company decided to build a store at Fifth Avenue and Fifty-first Street, north of the Cathedral. The initial stages of construction required extensive blasting operations. Because of fear that the blasting might cause damage to the Cathedral, an inspection of the entire structure was made, and earlier suspicion that the building needed extensive repairs was confirmed. Marble in sections of both the Cathedral and the rectory was found to have deteriorated, the wooden roof trusses were in precarious condition, many pinnacle stones were poorly fitted to their bases, some of the stone had actually fallen from the building during the previous winter and decorative stone all over the building was cracked or broken. In July, after blasting began, a crocket on the facade over the Fifty-first Street entrance fell to the pavement. Another inspection was ordered immediately, this time carried out by the George Fuller Company. Their report confirmed that extensive repair was essential and needed immediately. Maginnis and Walsh were called in as architectural advisors for the work.[49]

The architects did not recommend that much of the damaged marble be replaced. Rather, they suggested its removal and a concomitant change in the design of some areas, since they believed urban conditions would cause new stone to deteriorate like the old. They considered some of the ornamental stone a hazard to the public and to the safety of the building itself. Elimination of Renwick's ornamentation was a difficult decision, since it detracted from the richness of the architecture. Renwick had assigned cusped molding to all the arched entrances and expected that statues of the Apostles would be affixed to the coves of the jambs at "some future time." Elaborate crockets and finials were all about the building. The new plan called for both the cusped molding and many finer carvings to be replaced by simpler designs. Open pinnacles along the tower buttresses and in several other places were to be filled with solid masonry. At the same time, any defective stones on all sides of the building were to be replaced. The architects recommended Georgia white marble for the project.[50] Even though the Lady Chapel had been built long after the rest of the building, some of its marble was "actually crumbling in the hands of the workers," and it was learned subsequently that some of that stone had been quarried as surface marble which was called "markedly unsound."[51] Thus, the decision was made to eliminate the gargoyles from the walls of the chapel (*page right*) and the finials on the spires and flying buttresses. The gargoyles on the chapel were the only ones on the entire building. The three-year program was placed in the hands of the Fuller Company with the collaboration

The offending gargoyles would not have scared off anyone anyhow.

of Maginnis and Walsh. The stone selected was from the Georgia Marble Company, but cut by the Rockwood Alabama Stone Company.[52] The Trustees initially authorized a loan of up to $2,000,000, but in June 1946, Major Edward Bowes, who by then was a close friend of Cardinal Spellman, died. "Of his $4,500,000 estate, he left $3,000,000 to the Major Bowes Fund of St. Patrick's Cathedral..." to be used as the Cardinal needed it. Since the total cost of repairs would rise to well over $3,000,000, the bequest paid for the greatest part of it. Before the work began, it was resolved that the daily routine of the Cathedral must not be upset. The building "had never been closed for a single day since first its doors opened," and this tradition was to continue unbroken.[53]

One of the first things replaced was the cross on the north spire. Archbishop Spellman blessed a new twelve-and-one-half-feet-high bronze cross weighing one ton in December 1945. After that, work concentrated on the stone replacements for which about three hundred fifty men were employed. A strike interrupted the progress in August 1946; by that time about half the project had been completed including repair of the roof supports and windows, and much of the stone work. Almost $1,000,000 had already been expended. Costs reached almost $2,500,000 by October 1947. When the restoration was completed in July 1948, there were new crosses on both spires, new copper louvres and spire window glass, a complete new roof, a lightning rod system, four new tower entrances and partial new transept entrances, a new main west portal, stone replacement on the surface of the entire facade, and a roof support system with steel reinforcing the wood beams, especially at the crossing of the nave and transept.[54]

Several other improvements were made simultaneously. The most beautiful, by far, was the rose window. The original cathedral glass with geometric designs was still in place in the frame of the rose window when, in March 1945, Charles Connick began designing what he claimed was to be the "crowning glory" of his career. "The material and workmanship ... shall be equivalent to or better than the best I have done in any other windows," he boasted. He chose an angelic theme with symbols representing the eight beatitudes in the hands of the angels in the eight petals of the rose. He portrayed six angels in the lancets below. But, Mr. Connick died suddenly before he began assembling the window, leaving the architects to ask: who could possibly have the skills to build so fine a work of art? The fretting was unnecessary, as one of Connick's craftsmen made the templates in October, and Orin Skinner, Connick's successor at the company's helm, was eager to finish the window "in the spirit of a memorial to our leader...." "Many of us," he wrote, "have been with him from twenty-five to thirty years, and we were in sympathy with his every thought. He often said that his windows should be signed by many names, for the men and women who worked with him are like an extension of his own spirit, as well as of his hands and brain." After he visited the Boston studios to see the work in progress, Msgr. Flannelly agreed. So did Charles Maginnis, who called Connick's company "an organization closely resembling a medieval guild with all its attendant mastery of the art." By March 1946, the full-size cartoons of the window were under way, and when it was installed the following year, it was hailed as a marvel. The final cost was $25,000, most donated by Clendenin Ryan.[55]

Another project completed in this period was a connecting passageway from the Archbishop's residence to the sacristy. Although the Trustees had approved the addition in 1942, the Eggers and Higgins structure was not built until 1946. Shortly afterwards, a room for choir practice was added in the north tower off the choir gallery. The additional space was a blessing for the new Music Director, Charles Courboin, even though access still required a climb of forty-two stairs from the Cathedral floor.[56]

In the late 1940s, the Cathedral was approaching its seventieth birthday (its ninetieth measuring from when the cornerstone was laid). Msgr. Flannelly found that time and ordinary use were wearing away more than just the exterior stone. Almost ten thousand dollars were required to repair the Lady Chapel windows, and additional expenditures went for new sidewalks, repair of the small exterior doors and replacement of kneeler pads in the pews. The Rector believed that damage to several altars was the result of blasting on Fifty-first Street. The blasting and water seepage wreaked havoc on the altar of St. John Baptiste de la Salle and the altar of St. Anthony. Lesser damage was inflicted on several other altars, as well. After repairs were made, Msgr. Flannelly had all the altars cleaned, as well as the statues of St. Francis, the Pieta and the Doctors of the Church, and the baptistry and stations of the cross. Next, he had the sacristy restored and replaced part of the Lady Chapel marble pavement, which he said "had to give way to a more practical paving after forty-three years of constant and very heavy traffic." About one quarter of the chapel floor was replaced with Tennessee marble identical to that in the adjoining ambulatory. At the same time, new marble floors were set in the tower vestibules at Fifth Avenue, and the original wooden doors with black leatherette covering between the vestibules and the church were replaced by wooden and glass doors.[57]

In April 1897, the Trustees had declined an offer made by a local company to create for the Cathedral new "bronze pictorial doors."[58] Forty eight years later, the idea was revived in earnest. New York was not alone in making the change from wood to metal; the cathedrals of Milan and Cologne were engaged in the same process. With the great bronze doors of the Baptistry of Florence Cathedral held high as an ideal, even the portals of St. Peter's Basilica in Rome were destined to receive bronze. The motif selected for New York was the missionary and cosmopolitan character of the Church here. Charles Maginnis was chosen to design the replacements, and John Angel, who had completed the figures of the baldachin and the statue of St. Patrick, received the commission to prepare figures for the doors. Mr. Maginnis wanted to include a trumeau, a supporting pillar dividing the two leaves of the central door, but Msgr. Flannelly preferred a wide unobstructed opening which ultimately was chosen. The Rector also wanted a figure of St. Patrick in the center of the tympanum, the space above the doors at the top of the arch, but tradition dictated that an image of Christ the Savior occupy that place of honor. Instead of St. Patrick's image, two shamrocks with a dove, the symbol of the Holy Spirit, were chosen to be above the other sculpture, accompanied by the quotation: "The Holy Spirit, Whom the Father will send in My Name, will teach you all things."[59]

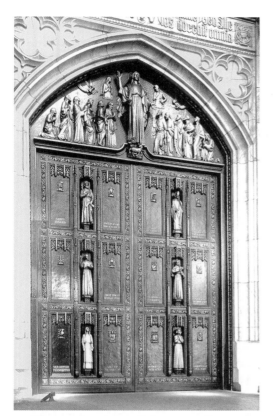

The panel statues tell the story all over: an Italian peasant woman who became the Church's patroness of immigrants by her work with Italians abroad; the wealthy convert whose nuns transformed New York in too many ways to count; the Native American who proved once again that salvation, even sanctity, is an option for everyone; a Celtic Welshman who brought the same faith to Ireland that the Irish brought to the new world; a French missionary martyred by the fear of competition of the entrenched; and Joseph the breadwinner, which was what most immigrants were trying to become themselves.

Anticipating criticism about his decision to sculpture his figures in a Gothic style instead of a more modern design, John Angel quoted the axiom: "Always make your sculpture conform to the style of the architecture." He believed that no style was more appropriate for divine worship than thirteenth century Gothic architecture.[60] By July 1948, he had finished three sculptures: St. Frances Cabrini; Mother (today Saint) Elizabeth Seton; and Blessed Kateri Tekakwitha.[61] The three remaining figures were St. Patrick, St. Joseph and St. Isaac Jogues. They represented holy men and women of special significance to New York. Above the doors were the figures of Christ and the Apostles. Both exterior and interior sides of the doors are decorated, so inside, the heraldic arms of Cardinal Spellman were on the tympanum over the doors.[62] The Halback Company of New York employed forty-four men for eighty-two weeks to construct the doors. Unveiled at the end was a set of central doors weighing 40,580 pounds, over twenty-three feet high and over fourteen feet wide, and four doors for the towers. The tower doors weigh 16,700 pounds each, and are twenty-nine feet high and over seven feet wide. Cardinal Spellman blessed and officially opened them for the first time two days before Christmas 1949.[63] Part of the nearly $300,000 cost was paid by Countess Mary Young Moore of Los Angeles. For a long time, the Young family had distinguished themselves by their generosity to the Catholic Church. Mary Young Moore, with residences in both Los Angeles and New York gave Pope Pius XII large sums of money to help relieve war victims as well as for other causes. The Pope conferred her title on her in March 1950, and Cardinal Spellman named a Catholic high school in the City in her honor.[64]

A number of special gifts became part of the Cathedral's growing patrimony during the 1940s. Major Bowes and his wife presented a beautiful painting of the Holy Family by Del Sarto, and it was hung on the Lady Chapel wall.[65] Of great sentimental value for Cardinal Spellman was the war-torn flag of the American battleship, *USS New York,* which had been presented to him on V-J Day after he offered Mass for the crew aboard the ship. The flag had received its scars during the battles of Iwo Jima and Okinawa, and had survived the destructive power of the atomic bomb dropped during tests in 1946 at Bikini in the Marshall

Islands. The old ship had been built at the New York Naval Shipyard in Brooklyn in 1912, and commissioned in 1914. It had pounded Okinawa from close range for seventy-six days — a record period for any ship in a single engagement in history. Yet it survived unscathed during its entire lifetime. But it suffered an ignominious death many years later when it sank under a barrage of 500-pound shells during fleet exercises. Cardinal Spellman blessed the flag in the spring of 1947 and had it enshrined in a case on the south wall of the narthex of the Cathedral, in memory of men and women of the armed forces from New York. A bronze plaque identified it.[66]

Two years later, Michael Kelleher, as Boston friend of the Cardinal, donated the American and Papal flags which were suspended from the nave triforia. The year before, Major General Sosa Molina, the war minister of Argentina, had donated to the Cathedral a replica of the statue of Our Lady of Lujan. The original is in the Basilica of Lujan. And in February 1949, Cardinal Spellman was presented with a reproduction of the bell of St. Joan of Arc from the people of France. It was one of the gifts of the French Gratitude Train. Made of bronze, the 500-pound bell was two-and-one-half feet high. It was placed directly under the *USS New York* battle flag. Another precious gift, one not readily visible in the Cathedral, was a group of drawings of the Cathedral by James Renwick. They were given in 1948 by Mr. S. Guard, who had worked in Renwick's firm.[67]

Across Madison Avenue from the Lady Chapel were six magnificent Renaissance buildings, the Villard Houses, the work of McKim, Mead and White and one of the City's treasures. Built on land which the Cathedral had sold to Henry Villard in 1882, they were purchased in 1886 by Whitelaw Reid, the editor of the New York Tribune. In 1948, the Archdiocese of New York purchased half of the buildings from the Reid family estate, and the following year most of the rest of the complex, except the north corner wing, was bought from Mrs. John Hubbard. In May 1949 there was a solemn dedication, and Archdiocesan offices including the Chancery moved in. Eventually, the north corner wing was acquired from Random House Publishers. In 1968, the New York Landmarks Preservation Commission designated the entire complex a landmark.[68]

Balancing its good fortune in acquiring the Villard property, was a bedeviling problem across the street — the pigeons which had found roosting havens in high places all about the Cathedral. For many years, Msgr. Flannelly had been confounded in his attempts to find a humane solution to the destruction, not to mention the hazards, the birds were causing. Suggestions came from many people who seemed to feel challenged to succeed where others had failed. The Rector rejected a host of proposals including schemes to simply chase after them and snatch them up one-by-one; to transport them to distant locations; to use pigeon hawks; and even to de-stroy their eggs. One prominent businessman told Cardinal Spellman that "stuffed owls did the trick" for his firm, suggesting the presence of an owl, stuffed or otherwise, might frighten the birds. But, Msgr. Flannelly was convinced that strict enforcement of the City ordinance forbidding the feeding of pigeons was the only solution. The problem was never solved. [69]

The winner and still champion: a New York City pigeon.

A popular attraction at St. Peter's Basilica in the Vatican is the plaques spaced in the floor with the measurements of cathedrals of the world. The locations and measurements indicate their lengths relative to each other and to St. Peter's. St. Patrick's is the only American cathedral represented, and American visitors have been heard expressing surprise at how small St. Patrick's is compared to many others. But, when the St. Patrick's markers were installed at the end of 1949 in readiness for the Holy Year 1950, the dimensions used were incorrect. Somehow, information that the extreme interior length of St. Patrick's was three-hundred-thirty-two feet was forwarded to Rome, and that figure ranked the Cathedral last in size of the sixteen buildings then honored. The true length is three-hundred-seventy-six feet.[70]

Many Cathedral curates of the 1940s later achieved high status in the American Church. Rev. George Guilfoyle became an auxiliary bishop of the Archdiocese of New York and he died as Bishop of Camden, New Jersey. Rev. Francis Reh was made Bishop of Charleston and later of Saginaw, Michigan. Two Cathedral priests, Rev. William Scully and Rev. Edwin Broderick, served as bishops of the Albany Diocese, and Rev. Thomas Donnellan became Bishop of Ogdensburg and later Archbishop of Atlanta. Two Cathedral priests were appointed as bishops for the military, Rev. James Griffiths and Rev. Philip Furlong. An assistant at the Cathedral for fifteen years was Rev. Michael Deacy, a truly devout, even saintly, priest, whose holiness attracted many to the Church. He is said to have had an almost magnetic attraction to the poor and homeless and, being "utterly without pretensions," he seemed unaware of his considerable spiritual gifts. Struck by his humility, Cardinal Spellman assigned him to St. Patrick's when he learned of the young cleric's intense desire to serve in a pastoral role, rather than to pursue further study which was planned for him.[71]

The music program of the Cathedral sustained a heavy loss when the great Pietro Yon died in 1943. For the three years before his death he had maintained a grueling schedule. For example, his March 1940 choir concert of sacred music featuring Giovanni Martinelli, tenor of the Metropolitan Opera company, was broadcast to Italy. Yon himself composed the music entitled "Passion, Death and Resurrection," and the program was introduced by the Consul General of Italy, Gaetano Vecchiotti. After America became engaged in the war, Yon began a tour of concerts with the American Red Cross to entertain the troops. The demands proved too taxing, and he suffered a paralyzing stroke during Lent in 1943. Under orders to rest in a quiet place near Huntington, Long Island, he died on November 22, 1943. Cardinal Spellman presided at his funeral Mass celebrated by Msgr. Flannelly and attended by great musicians of the world, hundreds of priests and nuns, and admirers who filled the building. Yon's own "Mass of Requiem" was sung by his choir whose members formed an honor guard and escorted his coffin to the steps of Fifth Avenue where they sang his "Tenebrae of Good Friday."[72]

Pietro Yon had made the music of St. Patrick's famous. There was no dearth of talented musicians vying to succeed him. Applications poured in from composers and organists who had been trained in England, Italy, France, Belgium and Poland and whose reputations were international.[73] The artist chosen was Charles Marie Courboin who originally came as a substitute for Yon "during the duration of the illness...." From April, when Yon was first stricken, until October, when Courboin arrived, it was hoped that rest and care would allow for Mr. Yon's return. In the interim, Yon's assistant, Edward Rivetti, directed the music. Courboin was born in 1886 in Antwerp, Belgium, where, from an early age, he evidenced his considerable musical talent. He wrote his first composition at age twelve. By 1902 he was the organist at Antwerp Cathedral and he began recital tours in major cities including London, Paris, Rheims, Lille, Boulogne, Lubeck, Hamburg and Moscow. He was twice knighted by the Belgian government. He entered this country in 1904, settling in Oswego, New York, where he played the largest pipe organ in the state outside New York City. Beginning in 1919, he was concert organist for Wanamaker's in Philadelphia and New York. His advice was sought on the design and construction of pipe organs throughout the country. He also made recordings for RCA Victor Company, and was appointed to head the Peabody Conservatory of Music in Baltimore. An associate of great musical figures, he had played for Saint-Saens in Paris and was a close friend of Marcel Dupré. At the time of Rachmaninoff's death, the great composer was writing an organ concerto for Courboin.[74] Just after Courboin's arrival, Edward Rivetti was called into service in the Navy. He served for two years until the war ended and Charles Lauria replaced him during that time. When the blasting for construction of Best and Company which had caused damage to other parts of the Cathedral was found to have harmed the organs as well, Courboin oversaw the extensive repairs by the Kilgen Company. Some of the work continued until 1948. When Courboin was satisfied with the quality of repairs made up to April 1947, he recorded three albums at the Gallery organ that month. The same month he arranged for the first visit of the choir of the United States Military Academy. Eighty cadets sang during the Sunday Mass on April 13th, eighty others joined in the procession and several were altar servers. The cadets continue the tradition annually to the present time.[75]

During the war, the boys' choir which had sung since 1908 had to be suspended. In order to rebuild it in 1948, Rev. William Greene held auditions for boys of the grade school of St. Ann's Academy. Fifty-five were selected. After an intensive program of rehearsals, the resurrected choir sang for the first time in mid-December, a kind of dress rehearsal for Christmas. They were next heard at the Christmas Eve midnight Mass and again on Christmas Day. Thereafter, the boys sang every Sunday during the scholastic year. Both the adult and boys choir appeared on television during midnight Mass that year, the first time the service was televised. The next year, the boys choir recorded an album of Christmas music.[76]

The purpose of music in liturgy was to assist the faithful to give prayerful praise to Almighty God. But it is the Mass, not the music, which is the center of Catholic worship. And, like the music, the ceremonies surrounding the Mass liturgy were sublime. The finest preachers addressed the congregation. Monsignor Fulton Sheen continued to deliver the Lenten series and the Three Hours Meditations on Good Fridays. He also preached the Easter Sunday sermon during the high Mass. Once he recalled that "an hour before Mass, a gentleman came in and said: 'I will give fifty dollars for a ticket to hear Bishop Sheen.' [Monsignor Sheen was made a bishop and received the honorary title *archbishop* in later years.] I said to him: 'You can have the pulpit for fifty.' That was clue enough for him to recognize me."[77]

In 1941, Monsignor Flannelly announced that, beginning in November, Mass would be offered on the side altars on feast days of saints whom each altar honored. Earlier that year, before the Pearl Harbor attack, the Archbishop had celebrated or presided at several

Masses for those suffering during the Nazi conquests and those engaged in the life-and-death struggle in progress in Europe. In March, a Mass for the people of France was described by the French ambassador as "magnificent and impressive." In May, the Archbishop consoled those attending a Mass for the Polish people when he asked them not to lose hope, as "we look forward to the glorious day when peace and justice for all will prevail in this world." In June, there was a solemn pontifical Mass for Great Britain, the lone European defender of democracy. Lord Halifax and New York Governor Herbert Lehman attended.[78] Shortly afterwards, the Archbishop presided at the funeral of Ignace Jan Paderewski (*below*), the famed pianist who had been Poland's first President until he resigned late in 1919. He had arrived in America in November 1940 after the invasion and defeat of Poland. An ardent Catholic who supported the work of the sick, Paderewski suffered a failure of his own health in May 1941. He was unable to rally from an attack of pneumonia and died at the Hotel Buckingham in New York on June 29th. His body lay in state in the Cathedral for two days until the solemn funeral Mass on July 3rd. Archbishop Spellman made a rare appearance in the pulpit where he delivered a eulogy in English. The capacity crowd in the Cathedral watched the casket borne outside where a military caisson awaited. Then, a military band accompanied it to Pennsylvania Station for the trip to Arlington National Cemetery outside Washington, D. C. He was buried with full military honors at a temporary grave where his remains would rest until a free and independent Poland could welcome him home.[79]

His funeral Mass in St. Patrick's Cathedral in New York in 1941 was attended by 4,500 inside and 35,000 outside, It included statesmen and leaders of the political and musical world. By presidential decree (an action taken only once before in U.S. history) he was buried at Arlington Cemetery in Washington, D.C. He was laid to rest under the mast of the battleship Maine until his body could be transported to a free Poland for burial.

The first non-Latin rite Mass ever offered at the Cathedral took place in March 1942. Archbishop Spellman presided at the Byzantine-Slavonic liturgy. The next year, three thousand people were present for a Byzantine-Melkite, or Syrian, liturgy. Owen McCormick, St. Patrick's sexton for twenty-four years, died the next year, and his funeral Mass was attended by countless friends made over the years including former Roosevelt aide James A. Farley who regularly attended services and knew him well. Late that same year, the "happy warrior," former Governor Al Smith, died in New York. Archbishop Spellman cabled from Rome a blessing of the Holy Father, and arranged for the governor's body to join the number of the honored few who had lain in state in the Cathedral. An honor guard of the Fighting 69th Regiment stood at his bier, while nearly 250,000 mourners passed. Mrs. Eleanor Roosevelt, Governor Thomas Dewey and high government officials joined the substantial number of prelates, clergy and laymen at the funeral Mass for the four-time governor and presidential candidate.[80]

In April 1945, as the war was nearing its end, President Franklin Delano Roosevelt died in Georgia. Msgr. Flannelly celebrated a solemn votive Mass and the Archbishop presided. There were prayers "for the preservation of the nation"; for President Harry Truman, Roosevelt's successor; and for the deceased President's soul. On July 28th, an Army B-25 bomber was passing over the City in bad weather and crashed into the seventy-eighth and seventy-ninth floors of the Empire State Building. America was weeks away from the end of the war as the disaster occurred. A few days later, a Mass for the fourteen who died was offered by the Archbishop at the Cathedral. Eleven of them were staff members of the War Relief Services of the national Catholic Welfare Conference, whose office was in the building. In the fall, John McCormack, the Irish tenor who was a close friend of St. Patrick's, died in Dublin. Msgr. Fulton Sheen and many friends from the world of music were among the two thousand who prayed for McCormack's soul at a Cathedral liturgy. In October, Bishop William Arnold, the first American major general to enter the episcopal ranks, was consecrated by Archbishop Spellman.[81]

Knowledge of Monsignor Sheen's work with converts to Catholicism was widespread in America. Early in 1946, he received into the Church the playwright, author and lecturer, Clare Boothe Luce. He baptized her at St. Patrick's Cathedral, as he did Louis Budenz, the former editor of the Communist *Daily Worker*.[82] It should be noted that the everyday work of evangelization was carried on by the Cathedral priests less visibly, but with wider influence. Besides the famous people mentioned above, there were seventy-one converts received into the Church at the Cathedral in 1944. In addition, there were one hundred eighty-three baptisms, one hundred sixty-eight confirmations, six hundred seventy eight marriages and vast numbers of sick calls.[83] In 1946 there were Cathedral funerals for Major Edward Bowes and for former Mayor James Walker, who had returned to the practice of his faith several years before his death, having been alienated earlier due to marital difficulties. In October that year, not a few heads turned in surprise at the appearance in the Cathedral of the Soviet Ambassador to the United States and the Vice-foreign Minister of the Soviet Union, joining United Nations colleagues for a Mass at the opening of the second General Assembly of the United Nations. United Nations representatives from thirty-four nations joined the 3500 in attendance. The funeral of one of American's greatest sports figures, Babe Ruth, also took place at St. Patrick's, on August 19, 1948. Cardinal Spellman offered a special prayer he had composed for the Mass: "May the Divine Spirit that inspired Babe Ruth to overcome hardships and to win the crucial game of life animate many generations of American youth to learn from the example of his struggles and successes, and loyally to play their positions on all-American teams, and may his generous-hearted soul, through the mercy of God, the final scoring of his own good deeds, and the prayers of his faithful friends, rest in everlasting peace."[84]

Cardinal Spellman raised to episcopal rank the only rector of St. Patrick's so honored when he consecrated Monsignor Flannelly an auxiliary bishop on December 16, 1948. The Cardinal presented him with the pectoral cross of Archbishop Hughes, and for the ceremonies of consecration the new Bishop wore the vestments which Pope Pius XII had worn at his own episcopal ordination at the hands of Pope Benedict XV. They were the same vestments the Cardinal himself had worn when he was consecrated by Pope Pius XII when the latter was a Cardinal. The vestments were later sent to Fordham University to be preserved.[85]

The Cathedral was an expected stop, even for someone whose country was taking a battering in the brand new war.

A large number of distinguished guests at St. Patrick's in the 1940s included Winston Churchill who visited on March 20, 1940, and the Grand Duchess Charlotte of Luxembourg, who was seated in the sanctuary during a service in February 1941. The presidents of Peru, the Philippines and Ecuador were honored guests in 1942, and the next year, Poland's General Sikorsky and Paraguay's President attended Masses. The Duke of Windsor, formerly King Edward VIII of England, attended midnight Mass, and in 1947, the Vice-president of the Philippines took part in a liturgy. A special visitor of a different kind was the pilgrim statue of Our Lady of Fatima, which was carried into the Cathedral in December 1948 where devotions in her honor were held. The Portuguese statue was taken worldwide from city to city to encourage prayer among the faithful in accord with the message of the Fatima apparitions of 1917. A very special relic from Goa — the arm of St. Francis Xavier — was put on public view in the Cathedral the following December.[86]

In June 1950, divisions of North Korean troops crossed the thirty-eighth parallel separating North Korea from South Korea; sixteen member nations of the United Nations responded with troops, more than 90% of them Americans, all placed under the command of American General Douglas MacArthur. By the time the Korean War ended in 1953, more than one-and-a-half million Americans had taken part, and 24,000 had been killed. Cardinal Spellman resumed his World War II practice of spending Christmas with the troops, so that he was not at the Cathedral for midnight Mass during several years in the early 1950s.

At the same time, the local population was experiencing another in a series of changes which had defined its character throughout history. A new wave of migrants came after World

Now 65, the snow shoes might be getting heavier, but he's still there.

War II from Puerto Rico, most of them in search of jobs to alleviate the poverty they had endured in their homeland. Like those before them, they encountered severe discrimination and resentment, and almost one million white, middle-class New Yorkers left the City and settled in the suburbs. Although some Puerto Ricans returned to their island home in the early 1960s when economic conditions improved, more than 700,000 remained in the City, and Spanish became the City's second language. Most of the newcomers were Catholics, and both the Archdiocese in general and the Cathedral in particular responded to their spiritual needs by offering special services in Spanish, although the Mass was still required to be in Latin throughout the world. Numerous liturgies with devotions popular among Puerto Ricans were held, and increasingly as they years passed, others in honor of national patrons of other Latin American countries were introduced.

While the population of the City continued to grow, albeit at a slower pace than in previous decades, the number of people in Manhattan declined for the first time in modern history. In the Cathedral neighborhood, office buildings continued to replace already scanty numbers of residences. The new towers of steel and glass caused the number of parishioners to dwindle drastically. But, attendance at religious services did not decline, since more and more workers were required for the increasing numbers of businesses, and many of them became daily participants at Mass before or after the work day or during lunch hours. By the 1960s, "nearly two-and-a-half million people were converging daily to jobs in the central business district of Manhattan." The attraction of one of the world's greatest cities also brought more tourists, and St. Patrick's became a mandatory stop during their visits.[87]

The cultural and religious discrimination against the new arrivals was accompanied by a surprising recurrence of anti-Catholic charges in some quarters. A book written with what was described as hollow scholarship maintained that the Church "was not entirely unwilling to receive from the public treasury favors which ... seem questionable," a false reference, once again, to the Church acquiring the land on which the Cathedral was built by unethical means. And, once again, Catholic periodicals responded with an account of the history of the site as registered in official City records and exposing the charge as "wholly without foundation or justification."

More mundane concerns occupied much of Bishop Flannelly's time as he labored to eradicate the debt incurred in the 1950s. From 1910 until 1943, the Cathedral was free of debt, but when the three-year restoration began, even though much of the cost was paid from the bequest of Major Bowes, additional loans had to be assumed. Inflation and increased ordinary expenses added to the difficulty. In 1944, the normal cost of maintaining the Cathedral was $553 a day; by 1952 it had risen to $835 a day. Finally, in January 1958 the Rector was able to write to the Cardinal "with great pleasure" that the final payment of the loan had been made. The word reached Spellman in India; he expressed satisfaction that the Cathedral's priests were wholehearted "in the care of souls and the administration of the parish."[88]

A small part of those ordinary expenses was the cost of the electrification of the bell-ringing system. Montell Toulmin died in May 1946. He had played his own compositions on Sundays and special occasions for forty-four years. But in the five years after his death, the bells were played only occasionally when Bishop Flannelly was able to engage the services of Charles Henry. He could not find a permanent replacement for Toulmin. After

Cardinal Spellman read about an automated bell-playing system at Trinity Church on Broadway at Wall Street, he suggested a similar arrangement for the Cathedral. A bequest from Mrs. Maren Fellowes in 1951 made the project possible and the installation was completed during Holy Week the following year. During preparation of the system, it was learned that only sixteen of the nineteen bells had ever been played. The $9290 cost of electrification included connecting the other three bells to the system. It took fifteen weeks for the I. T. Verdin Company to finish the job. The old tower clock which had controlled the playing of the Angelus since 1902 was disconnected.[89]

Meanwhile, trees were planted along the street on Fifth Avenue. Locating a variety able to endure the harsh treatment inflicted by urban pollution had proved elusive, but Nelson Rockefeller wrote to Cardinal Spellman in 1952 that he "would consider it a privilege" to present the Cardinal with some honey locust trees, a variety which he was convinced were disease-proof and fume-resistant. He stated that "after many years of experimentation...we at Rockefeller Center have found the right ones for Fifth Avenue."[90]

When William Partridge's *Pieta* was given to the Cathedral early in the century, it did not rest upon a platform. The base was added in 1952. Partridge had not chiselled his initials into the stone and as early as 1932 his wife had requested that this be done. She repeated her request in a letter to Bishop Flannelly almost two decades later. The name Ordway Partridge, without his given name William, was cut in one-inch high letters in the form of his signature near the bottom of the statue.[91]

When the choir practice room was built in the north tower in 1947, access was by the stairway in the south tower. The climb was difficult and time-consuming. In 1952, the James Mitchell Company installed an Otis elevator in the north tower. The contract was the first of many for the company for construction work in St. Patrick's extending into the 1990s. In the 1970s, on the recommendation of W. Knight Sturges, the consulting architect of the Cathedral, Philip Mitchell, President of the Mitchell Company, was named *Keeper of the Fabric of St. Patrick's Cathedral.* He held the office into the 1990s.[92]

1954 was declared the *Marian Year* by Pope Pius XII in honor of the Immaculate Virgin Mary. Since it was also the seventy-fifth anniversary of St. Patrick's, and because

The Archbishop graced the Alfred E. Smith Dinner. In 1954 the speaker was President Dwight Eisenhower. Charles Silver (l.), a Jewish philanthropist, chaired the dinner and was a major friend of Catholic Charities.

Earlier, in 1948, President Harry S. Truman attended the Friendly Sons of St. Patrick dinner. Needless to say, his upcoming opponent, Thomas E. Dewey was there, too.

Mary Immaculate is patroness of the United States, Bishop Flannelly appealed to parishioners for donations of their old gold and silver to be melted and rolled to make a new ciborium for the sacred Hosts distributed during reception of the Eucharist. He hoped the memorial would represent the gifts of many, rather than a donation from a single benefactor.[93] Until that time, the ciborium used at the noontime Masses was the same one Cardinal McCloskey had used when the Cathedral opened, and it was now too small for the numerous communicants.[94] The design of the new ciborium was adapted from the *Ardagh Chalice*, unearthed in Limerick, Ireland in 1869. Scholars believed it had been buried about a thousand years earlier to protect it from pillage by invaders. An anonymous craftsman offered his talent to fabricate the new vessel which contained four matching stones and four enamels showing images of the Immaculate Conception, Our Lady of the Miraculous Medal, the Sacred Heart and St. Patrick.[95]

After the rose window was made in 1947, all the window frames were filled with stained glass except the twelve nave clerestory windows high above the center aisle. Bishop Flannelly and Orin Skinner of Connick's stained glass company, began discussing subjects and style of new windows in 1952. Skinner liked the treatment in St. Cecilia's Cathedral in Omaha, Nebraska, where each window portrayed a well-defined figure in its center with symbols appropriate for the figure around it. For the subjects, Bishop Flannelly chose the twelve fruits of the Holy Spirit. Two saints, one male and and female who exemplified each of the virtues (fruits of the Holy Spirit), were chosen for each window. A gift from John R. Morron in memory of his wife, the Marquesa Isabelle G. Morron, paid for the six south windows which were installed in 1954. Antoinette Lindsay bequeathed the cost of the six on the north, added two years later. The color scheme matched that of the Connick windows in the apse and the transept. By the summer of 1956, all the windows of St. Patrick's contained figured stained glass.[96]

In June 1955, the long-contemplated St. Patrick's Information Center became a reality when an office was opened on East Fiftieth Street. Father Charles McManus, assisted by a staff of lay persons, directed the program. Anyone interested in learning about the Catholic Faith could meet individually with a priest or staff member or could join an instruction class. The center was open daily until 9 p.m. and for several hours on Saturdays. New classes began every six weeks, retreats and days of recollection were held, a library was maintained and study groups were formed. Volunteers who helped with instruction were both older Catholics and students of Cathedral High School. After a modest beginning, telephone calls for information soon reached one thousand a month and about nine hundred came in person for instruction or information each year. Some came to learn, some to listen, some to dispute, some to pray. Their composition varied from business executives who worked in the neighborhood to those who identified with the "beat generation," societal rebels of the day. Many new converts emerged from their experiences at the center; and others became open-minded and well-disposed towards Catholicism.[97]

In a colorful ceremony in Rome in May 1954, Pope Pius XII proclaimed Pope Pius X a saint in Heaven. In June 1957, the last unoccupied niche in the north transept of the Cathedral was filled with a statue of Saint Pius. As Pope in the early years of the twentieth century, the Saint had made participation in the Eucharist available to young children and he had encouraged Catholics to receive the sacrament frequently. Thus, he was portrayed in the new statue administering Holy Communion and wearing the vestments of the Mass. Joseph Piccirilli of Luisieredi, Italy sculptured the statue from photographs of the saint. A bequest from Maria Louisa Fernandez Criado Richards made it possible.[98]

Another figure, somewhat unexpected in a church building, a wax image of the recently deceased Pope Pius XII, was brought to the Cathedral in 1959. According to current accounts, perhaps hyperbole, the figure was so lifelike that individuals were seen kneeling before it for a blessing, and, on at least one occasion, asking to confess. Cardinal Spellman succeeded in acquiring the personal cassock of the deceased Pope for the statue; the pectoral cross and the ring used were those the Pope had given the Cardinal personally. In 1965, a former mental patient shattered the glass case around the statue and it was removed temporarily. In 1968 the Apostolic Delegate to the United States suggested it should be removed, after which it was destroyed, the prevailing view being that it held no intrinsic artistic value. Inquiries from visitors who once saw the image still are made today.[99]

The boundaries of St. Patrick's parish encompass a large area. By the 1950s many office buildings and hotels had risen, especially in the northern and northeastern fringes. A survey of a twenty-block area indicated "an overwhelming mandate" for another church within the parish somewhere northeast of the Cathedral. Cardinal Spellman decided that a Cathedral chapel ought to be opened at Fifty-ninth Street and Park Avenue because of the large number of parishioners and business people who were unable to travel the long distance to the Cathedral. The Marquis George MacDonald was a Trustee of St. Patrick's who had offered Bishop Flannelly his help in "some big project" which might be planned in the future. The Bishop gave him an opportunity to help establish the chapel. MacDonald sent a check for $1,000 to initiate a fund-raiser. August 1958 was the centenary of the blessing of the Cathedral cornerstone, a suitable occasion for a "new daughter" to be opened. The Bishop asked for contributions from the "first founders of the Cathedral's chapel," that is,

whoever wished to support the effort. An ideal building was found at 487-495 Park Avenue at Fifty-ninth Street. It had been erected in 1887 for the Arion Society, a singing group. Later it became the Liederkranz Music Hall, home of another singing society. The Anderson Galleries, antiques dealers, occupied the building after that, followed by a bank and still later the Park Avenue Theatre until it was purchased by St. Patrick's. A meeting to enlist the help of area residents attracted six hundred people; that number gradually grew to six thousand who expressed

interest. So, a support guild was formed. The theatre was transformed into a beautiful replica of the Italian Renaissance Pitti Chapel of the Princes in Florence (left). Its three altars were made by the Gasparri Studios in Italy. The same company also built mosaic stations of the cross. On the ground floor there was room for 510 people, and there was a mezzanine level for 200 more. Offices of the chapel guild and other Catholic organizations were above the chapel, and on the top floor were the living quarters of the clergy.[100]

The chapel was named after three second century child martyrs, Sts. Faith, Hope and Charity. Cardinal Spellman celebrated its first Mass in December 1958, and in the days following there was one daily Mass and four on Sundays. Large attendance rapidly required the addition of other Masses. Counted among other celebrities who were parishioners was Ed Sullivan, the newspaper columnist and television show host. The chapel, like its Cathedral parent, became an oasis for prayer among business people in the neighborhood.[101]

Catholics in the post-war years maintained strong faith and devotion exemplified in the widespread practice of communion breakfasts held after participation at Masses. They were very popular at St. Patrick's and often luncheons or dinners were arranged, as well as breakfasts, after Masses or vespers services. The services were sponsored by Catholic groups as diverse as department store employee associations, ethnic organizations, youth groups, college councils and civil service societies. So many organizations applied to Bishop Flannelly for special liturgies, usually held on Sundays, that often he had to rearrange schedules to accommodate as many as possible. The most frequent requests were for the Sunday high Mass at which Cardinal Spellman usually officiated when he was in the City. Some of those participating had established a tradition decades earlier, but it was in the 1940s and 1950s that the special liturgies became the norm rather than the exception. Cardinal Spellman readily responded to requests that he be in attendance, but always with one stipulation — sermons were limited to fifteen minutes.[102] Often sponsoring groups invited a special preacher for the services, and if the Cardinal's edict dampened the hopes of speakers granted a rare opportunity to demonstrate their elocution skills in the queen of American churches, it undoubtedly enhanced his popularity among the listeners in the pews. Even to the present, many of the groups continue to sponsor Masses, notably the Holy Name societies of the New York City Police and Fire Departments; the Guild of Catholic Lawyers; the Scouts; the Knights of Columbus; the Ladies of Charity; the Catholic Teachers Association; the Society for the Propagation of the Faith; the Knights and Ladies of Malta; the Knights and Ladies of the Holy Sepulchre; and the United States Customs Service, to mention just a few. There were groups with government association such as the Catholic War Veterans; the Dongan Guild of New York State employees; the United States Coast Guard SPARS; the Parks Department employees; workers of the Department of Public Works; the Port of New York employees; and the staff of the United States Immigration and Naturalization Service. From the business sector came Catholics employed by W. and J. Sloan Company; Arnold Constable Company; the New York News; the Continental Can Company, the Greater New York Cartmen's Association; Faber, Coe and Gregg, Inc.; Sperry Gyroscope Company; McCreery Company; Gimbel's Department Store; Lord and Taylor; Schrafft's; Sak's Fifth Avenue; Bloomingdale's; Stern Brothers; Bonwit Teller; Best and Company; Macy's; Colgate-Palmolive Peet Company; the National Broadcasting Company; Metropolitan Life Insurance Company; the New York Telephone Company; the New York Naval Shipyard; and the Railway Express Agency.

Professional organizations included the Pasteur Guild; the Catholic Institute of the Press; the Ozanam Guild; the Catholic Nurses Association; the Catholic Court Attaches Guild; the Genesian Guild of Actors, Actresses and Writers; the Catholic Poetry Society of

America; the New York Catholic Physicians' Guild; the Catholic Business Associates; the American Catholic Sociological Society; and the Fordham Law Council. Newman Clubs, alumni associations and other college societies represented Cathedral College; the College of New Rochelle; the Catholic University of America; the College of Good Counsel; Notre Dame University; Hunter College; City College of New York; the United States Military Academy; and Mt. St. Vincent College. Religious societies included the Catholic Daughters of America; the Vincentia Guild; the Carroll Club; the Catholic Youth Organization; the Catholic Young Women's Club; the Sodality of the Immaculate Conception; the Spanish Catholic Action Association; the Catholic Benevolent League; the Edith Stein Guild; the McAuley Guild; the Daughters of Isabella; the Order of Seville; the Union of Holy Name Societies; the Third Order of St. Francis; the Catholic Women's Benevolent League; and the National Catholic Community Service. There were also high school alumni-alumnae associations and union groups such as the Catholic Men's League of the United States Naval Supply Depot; employees of the New York Air Procurement District; the Longshoremen; and the Motion Picture Industry employees. Among ethnic groups holding liturgies were the Pulaski Memorial Committee and the Hungarian Catholic League.[103]

Whether the Cardinal was in attendance or not, the fifteen-minute rule applied. Cardinal Spellman himself very infrequently was seen in the pulpit. In almost thirty years as Archbishop of New York, he preached in St. Patrick's fewer than a dozen times.[104] Msgr. Fulton Sheen, on the other hand, even after he was raised to the episcopacy and had his own weekly television program, continued to return to the Cathedral to preach the Lenten series. Sometimes his talks were broadcast by radio, once as far away as Montreal. In 1952, both Holy Week and Easter services were telecast.[105]

The celebration of non-Latin rite liturgies in St. Patrick's, begun some years earlier, continued from 1951 until 1957, and Cardinal Spellman regularly presided. Lenten services were held in the Byzantine-Melkite Rite; the Byzantine-Russian Rite; the Chaldean Rite; the Maronite Rite; the Syro-Malabar Rite; and the Byzantine-Hungarian Rite. In June 1953, the emotional departure ceremony for missionaries of the Maryknoll order was held for the first time at the Cathedral.[106] In 1957, conductor Arturo Toscanini's funeral Mass was attended by many famous musicians, some of whom joined the Mayor of New York as honorary pallbearers. Two years later, three of the four American cardinals gathered for a formal greeting for the new Apostolic Delegate to the United States in a colorful Cathedral ceremony.[107]

Two special anniversaries were marked by especially joyful celebrations in 1958: the centenary of the blessing of the cornerstone and the sesquicentennial of the Diocese of New York. The 150th anniversary of the Diocese was observed on Easter Sunday, and on the cornerstone blessing anniversary in May, Cardinal Spellman brought to the Cathedral the chair (*right*) which Archbishop Hughes had used during the 1858 ceremony. The intricately carved wooden chair was displayed in the sanctuary with a green ribbon from arm to arm to dissuade the more adventurous from putting it to practical use. During the day, Mass was offered at sixteen altars and over 30,000 people attended them.[108]

Pope Pius XII died in October of that year. Cardinal Spellman blessed a catafalque erected in the Cathedral to symbolize the bier of the Pope, his close friend. Governor Averell Harriman, Mayor Robert F. Wagner, United Nations Ambassador Henry Cabot Lodge and UN Secretary General Dag Hammarskjold came to a special pontifical Mass. When the Cardinal returned from Rome after attending the obsequies there, he found the Cathedral still draped in black and purple, and still crowded with mourners. But, before the end of the month, after a consistory was held to elect a successor, Monsignor John Maguire announced from the pulpit that Pope John XXIII was the new Supreme Pontiff. Shortly afterwards, an especially happy Christmas midnight Mass at the beginning of a popular pontificate was televised on about one-hundred-fifteen stations nationwide.[109]

Following his successes in the Pacific theatre during World War II and his command of United Nations Forces during the Korean War, Douglas MacArthur was one of the most popular of American generals. In 1951, he issued public statements critical of the Korean War policies of the Truman administration. Truman ordered him to refrain from making public policy remarks, and when the general refused, the President dismissed him from his command. Cardinal Spellman, a long-time friend of the general, considered him one of the greatest living Americans. The City arranged a huge welcome home parade for MacArthur and Spellman reviewed the march from the steps of St. Patrick's. As the general's car reached Fiftieth Street, he ordered it to stop, approached the Cardinal and remarked: "I thought I'd see you in Tokyo again before we'd meet in New York."[110] Several other political figures came to St. Patrick's in the 1950s. Both President Battle Berres of Uruguay and President Giovanni Gronchi, the first head of state of Italy to visit this country, were visitors. And, as in 1946, once again officials of the Soviet Union — this time Andrei Vishinsky and Ambassador Nicolai Novikof — attended a Mass for peace at St. Patrick's, together with delegates of other member nations of the United Nations.[111]

In 1950, the reinstituted boys choir, very popular with worshippers, cut a record of sacred music with singer Perry Como, accompanied by Charles Courboin at the organ. The next year the boys gave a concert at Town Hall and made two more recordings. Another record followed in 1952. Later in the decade the boys group and adult choir combined for a recording of Christmas carols. Guest choirs continued to sing at services, including those of the United States Air Force Academy and the Naval Academy which followed the earlier lead of the cadets from West Point.[112] In the music world, the reputation of Dr. Charles Courboin grew steadily. Many were willing to pay his fee of $75 per hour for private lessons, even though he often waived the cost when he recognized real talent in those unable to afford it. He used to improvise at the gallery organ while Edward Rivetti challenged him at the chancel organ, each deferring to the other in alternating fashion to allow their exceptional skills to blossom. Courboin was not beyond raising adamant objections to interference by those he considered unqualified in musical matters. He once complained to Bishop Flannelly about a colleague's lack of adequate training and "correspondent deficiency in musical taste." He made revisions in the gallery organ producing new sounds not envisioned by those who had built it in 1930. And he secured the services of Joseph Pastore as an independent organ curator. Pastore had worked for the Kilgen Company.[113]

Several publicly recognizable personalities were pewholders during the decade. John A. Coleman, whose family had been associated with St. Patrick's for generations, was a prominent member of New York's business community. The Grants, the Benzigers and James A. Farley remained parish members, and Fulton Oursler, the editor, playwright and novelist was a pewholder until his death in 1952. When he died, he was senior editor of *Reader's Digest.* Several film stars added excitement for visitors when Warner Brothers obtained permission to film part of *Miracle in the Rain* at the church in 1955. The scenes were shot between 10 p.m. and 6 a.m. when the Cathedral was closed, so there was no interruption of normal activity or disturbance to churchgoers.[114]

When elected pope, John XXIII was advanced in years and was considered an "interim pope." So, his call for the first church council since 1870 was a great surprise. The Second Vatican Council of 1962-1965 was to bring sweeping changes in the life and practices of the Catholic Church at the same time as upheaval was taking place in American political and social life. President John F. Kennedy was assassinated in 1963, and during the administration of his successor, Lyndon Johnson, the country was divided into vociferous camps in opposition to or in support of the Vietnam War. Racial tensions erupted in urban riots, and college students and other young people took part in demonstrations all over the country. A culture of sexual license and drug addiction, and a concomitant spurning of religious values proliferated in America. Within the church and in other parts of the world there was great upheaval; some Catholics resisted any change in the liturgy and traditional practices recommended by the Council; others raced to change the Church far beyond what was approved or even suggested by the Council. And sound teachings of the Church were often disregarded or ignored.

In spite of Cardinal Spellman's reservations about liturgical changes, the first parts of the vernacular Mass which had replaced the traditional Latin, or Tridentine, Mass were introduced to New York in the fall of 1964, before the Council ended. The rest of the revised Mass went into effect in March 1966, long before many other dioceses were ready. Pope John had died in June 1963 when most of the Council's work was unfinished. At the news, the bells of St. Patrick's were tolled, mourning wreaths were hung inside and outside, and a catafalque was erected in the center aisle in honor of the pontiff beloved by people of all religions for his gentleness. Cardinal Spellman, visibly moved, spoke of the "warmth and fatherly charity" of Pope John, recalling how "he loved everybody." He noted that "often he spoke ... fondly of the United States and her generous people." After the funeral in Rome, the Cardinal offered a solemn pontifical Mass in the Cathedral and Bishop Sheen preached.[115]

The demands of his office were burdensome on the Cardinal as he entered his third decade as Archbishop. He was over seventy years old in 1960, but did not relax his efforts both in the Archdiocese and at St. Patrick's. In that year he began the annual awards service for married couples reaching their golden wedding anniversary. At the first ceremony, twelve hundred couples were honored before their friends and relatives. Many of them had never participated in such a pageantry-filled event. The human face of the Cardinal was apparent in his gentle gesture of stooping to "lift a man of his own age who was trying to kiss" his ring.[116] Equally comfortable with those of high office, he received the President of Italy who presented him with a chalice as a token of his visit. While he was faithful to presiding at the Sunday pontifical Masses, he was committed to his Christmas visits to the troops abroad. He travelled to Vietnam each year from 1962 to 1966 except when he went to the South Pole in 1963. Bishop Sheen, who had been appointed to his own diocese in 1966, was not normally at the Cathedral until he resigned, returned to New York and received the honorary title *archbishop* in 1969. In 1967, the Cathedral again was the site, and Cardinal Spellman the host, for the welcome to the United States of the new Apostolic Delegate, Archbishop Luigi Raimondi. Five American cardinals and about seventy archbishops and bishops were in attendance.[117]

Bishop Flannelly was nearing the end of his rectorship and faced rising costs as the buildings aged with him. The $12,000 cost of air conditioning the parish house in 1963 and many other ordinary repairs used much of the gift from the estate of Lucille P. Borden. She left a bequest of almost $500,000.[118]

The growth of the drug culture and the growing crime problem in the City required a heightened level of security at the Cathedral and the residences. In August 1962, a self-described drug addict broke into both Cardinal Spellman's and Bishop Flannelly's offices and escaped with some cash. A few weeks later when he returned, he was apprehended by detectives who were "staking out" the buildings. In April 1965 a woman kneeling in prayer at the altar railing was seriously injured, and another person slightly burned, by a fire bomb thrown at her by an intruder. Two nearby witnesses extinguished the flames using their own clothing, as people fled the smoke-filled church in panic. The altar railing was heavily damaged. The incident followed by less than a week the destruction of the glass case enclosing the wax statue of Pope Pius XII. A former mental patient hurled a five-pound chunk of concrete at the glass. Similar attacks on religious buildings and churchgoers throughout the city were becoming a disturbingly common occurrence.[119]

In contrast to the pain occasioned by events like these, those who loved St. Patrick's had their spirits lifted when a laudatory book about St. Patrick's was published, *The Dream Lives Forever,* by Katherine Burton. The author was a convert to Catholicism who had written over twenty books, mostly biographies of Catholic figures. She had been editor of McCall's and Redbook magazines.[120] Another happy occasion was the designation of St. Patrick's as a New York City landmark in October 1966. This followed a surge of popular support for preserving the City's architectural treasures after the demolition of Pennsylvania Station and the Metropolitan Opera House.[121]

The fire bomb incident focused attention once again on the need for a fire suppression system. City fire officials pointed out a number of hazards including combustible materials in attic areas, open voids in the attic and triforia and limited accessibility to some parts of the building. The installation of a sprinkler system, however, was considered a cure worse than the malady, since its use could cause extensive water damage to the ceiling. Although authorities were satisfied that safety precautions in place fulfilled the requirements of the law, worry about harm to the magnificent structure persisted.[122]

W. Knight Sturges, an architect of the Shanley and Sturges firm, took part in the fire protection discussions. He and Mr. Shanley, his partner, prepared a complete survey of the building, and Sturges designed a dry sprinkler system for possible future installation. The survey was a broad study, not restricted to fire precautions alone, but bearing in mind changes either suggested or required by decisions of the Second Vatican Council. Mr. Sturges had graduated from Harvard University and received his architectural training at Yale. He specialized in church architecture and was a contributing writer for religious and architectural journals. He taught at Notre Dame, Yale and Columbia Universities. His association with St. Patrick's was the beginning of a twenty-year term as consulting architect, much as Robert Reiley and Charles Maginnis had been in the decades before him.[123]

The survey was completed in August 1963 and Sturges made several recommendations for improvements the following month. In addition to constructing elevators to connect the sacristy and parish house to the Cathedral, he proposed that the Cathedral be air conditioned, and that the beauty of the interior be enhanced by the installation of "downlites." He further proposed new altars to honor American patrons, specifically recommending Mother Elizabeth Seton and Mother Frances Cabrini, both of whom had strong New York connections. The advantage of air conditioning was not only for comfort, but to allow closing the doors, thus eliminating distracting noise whose decibel levels rose each year from emergency vehicle sirens, horns of vehicles and general traffic. His most urgent suggestion was that the plaster vaulting be examined for stability followed by a restoration of the entire interior wall and ceiling surface. He strongly believed some of the chapel altars and original windows ought to be replaced. For two years after the survey was issued, discussions continued on their implementation, leading to further suggestions such as a complete renovation of the sanctuary to better conform to norms of Vatican II, and even the installation of removable television sets for those unable to see the high altar. A portable arrangement was suggested, so that the sets could be used during "great ceremonies," but not during regular daily or Sunday Masses.[124]

None of what Sturges suggested was effected during the 1960s. One reason may have been so as not to have anything detract from the most spectacular event in the history of St. Patrick's and of the entire American Church up to that time — the first papal visit to the United States in October 1965. Cardinal Spellman was the "prime mover behind the arrangements" for the fourteen-hour visit on the occasion of the twentieth anniversary of the United Nations. Pope Paul VI chose that time to plead with world leaders to work for a lasting peace on earth. The papal visit, the first to the Western Hemisphere, not just the United States, began at 9:23 a.m. on October 4th, when an Alitalia Airlines jet landed at Kennedy Airport. On hand for the official greeting were Secretary General U Thant of the United Nations, United States Secretary of State Dean Rusk, New York Governor Nelson Rockefeller, New York City Mayor Robert F. Wagner, Speaker of the House of Representative John McCormack, Senators Robert and Edward Kennedy, Cardinal Spellman and Bishop Bryan McEntegart of the Brooklyn Diocese where the Airport was located. As 100,000,000 Americans watched via television, the Pope addressed them on their own soil in their own language. With him were six cardinals, ten papal aides and fifty press representatives. His motorcade wound through the highways and streets of Queens County and Manhattan, all lined with spectators. When it arrived at the Cathedral, bells chimed and 50,000 New Yorkers shouted words of welcome. The Pontiff could only utter to Cardinal Spellman: "I am amazed." Inside, the crowd broke into applause as His Holiness walked up the center aisle to the sanctuary where he knelt to pray, joined by nine cardinals. He responded to Cardinal Spellman's words of welcome with a blessing:

"Welcome to you from Rome with the blessings of those great saints, Peter and Paul, whose blood sanctified it, and the blessing of Christ whose Vicar on earth we are.

"Today we feel a common citizenship with you because we are here in your city and your country and because you are citizens of the Church of Rome. We truly are one in sentiment. The patron of this great Cathedral, St. Patrick, once said: 'As you are Christians, so be you Romans'. This we feel in a special sense because we are all citizens of Rome.

"Asking your prayerful support of our message of peace, we extend to all of you and your dear ones at home — the aged, the sick and the children, in a special manner — our fraternal apostolic blessing."

Leaving the Cathedral on the arm of Cardinal Spellman, he greeted the crowds on all sides of the terraces and steps, those waving from windows of skyscrapers, from rooftops of nearby buildings and from the crush of humanity on all the surrounding streets.[125]

President Lyndon Johnson met with the Pope in New York during the papal visit. At the very same time, the country was engaged in the most divisive war in its history except for the War Between the States. The United States government had been supporting the government of South Vietnam since 1954, but in 1964, Johnson sent the first combat troops. By the end of 1965, the American troop commitment had reached almost one-half million. Cardinal Spellman approved of American intervention, but "he deplored the Kennedy Administration's involvement in the coup that led to the overthrow and murder of President Diem," the South Vietnam leader. He believed the event would have "very unpleasant consequences for Vietnam, America and the Church." By 1967 there was a deep chasm dividing Americans who supported or opposed involvement in the war. In January that year, twenty-three protestors interrupted a Mass at St. Patrick's when they stood and displayed placards suggesting the Church was supporting an immoral conflict. The next year, two Jesuit priests who had been denied permission to celebrate a Mass of protest in the Cathedral, offered a Mass on the sidewalk across Fifth Avenue for about thirty-five supporters. The Cardinal visited the troops in Vietnam at Christmas just after the papal visit, and did the same the following year. Just before his last trip, he announced in the Cathedral that he had sent the Pope his letter of resignation as Archbishop of New York, in obedience to Vatican II age directives. He added that Pope Paul had declined to accept his resignation.[126]

Thus, he planned another trip to Vietnam at Christmas 1967. On December 1st, he attended a benefit event at the Waldorf-Astoria Hotel, his last public appearance. The following day he suffered a massive stroke and died in St. Vincent's Hospital after being anointed by Bishop Terence Cooke. His body was received at the Cathedral the following evening by his Coadjutor, Archbishop John Maguire, and it remained for viewing until the funeral Mass. On the days preceding the funeral there were Masses for laity, students, religious and military personnel. At the funeral liturgy, President Johnson led the delegation of civic officials including Vice-president Hubert Humphrey, Senator Robert Kennedy, Senator Jacob Javits, Governor Nelson Rockefeller and Mayor John Lindsay. The assembly of prelates concelebrating the Mass was led by Archbishop Luigi Raimondi, the Apostolic Delegate. All six American Cardinals and the Cardinal Primates of England, Ireland and Canada attended. There were two archbishops, fifty bishops and a multitude of Catholic and non-Catholic clergy. Spellman's friend and biographer, Rev. Robert Gannon of Fordham University, delivered the eulogy. The sixth Archbishop of New York and America's best-known high churchman was laid to rest in the crypt under the high altar, and his *galero* was lifted to the ceiling over his body. When this red hat was suspended, the tradition ended.[127]

Cardinal Spellman's remarkable career on the world stage sometimes clouded his equally remarkable achievements advancing the work of the Church in his own Archdiocese. By the time of his death, there were over 5000 beds in Catholic hospitals, and the enrollment of Catholic schools was almost a quarter of a million students. He had left New York a system of expertise in administration, and by reason of his own character, he had defended the Church and its people, never succumbing to intimidation by critics. St. Patrick's Cathedral came to be for many in the world a symbol of Catholicism in America, as did the Archdiocese of New York. One auxiliary bishop for New York in 1938 became ten in 1967, with three more auxiliary bishops in the Military Ordinariate and Catholic Relief Services. The Cardinal exerted great influence over the American Church outside New York, having consecrated many bishops who became leaders of other great dioceses and archdioceses all over the country.[128] Not a few of them were priests of the Archdiocese of New York. His love of St. Patrick's was obvious, and none of his predecessors did more to improve the physical structure. That love was shown no more pointedly than when he learned that a bishop from Reno, Nevada had described St. Patrick's as ostentatious. He retorted: "He must want to stay in Reno." [129]

1. Cohalan, *Popular History,* pp. 265-267; Carthy, *Magnificence,* p. 111.
2. Program of Installation of Archbishop Spellman, 1939, ASPC.
3. Cohalan, *Popular History,* pp. 267-275, *passim*; *Catholic News,* April 29, 1939. In Rome, the young priest became an assistant to Cardinal Gasparri, the Secretary of State and was made a monsignor. In 1930 he became an assistant to the new Secretary of State, Cardinal Pacelli. The two became close friends. He translated into English the first broadcast from Vatican City and helped publicize Pope Pius XI's encyclical protesting the Italian government's ban on Catholic Action groups. He travelled to Dublin with Papal legate Cardinal Lorenzi Lauri for the Eucharis-

tic Congress of 1932. *See: Action Magazine,* July 1939.

4. Journal of Msgr. Lavelle, 1939. This information comes from the last entry made in his journal before his death.

5. *Catholic News,* May 27, 1939; Cohalan, *Popular History,* p. 276.

6. Cohalan, *Popular History,* p. 295; Garraty, p. 736; Ellis, p. 554.

7. Guests included Cardinal Hayes, former Governor Al Smith, Mayor Fiorello LaGuardia and James Farley.

8. Seating list, testimonial dinner, June 10, 1936; Cathedral announcements, May 24, 1936; Carthy, *Magnificence,* p. 114; *Catholic News,* October 21, 1939; Journal of Msgr. Lavelle, 1939. The information in Msgr. Lavelle's journal was written by Father Flannelly.

9. *New York Times,* October 18, 1939; *Catholic News,* May 25, 1929; New York Post, New York Sun, New York Mirror, 1939, *passim.*

10. *Proceedings and Debates of the 76th Congress,* Second session, 1939.

11. Carthy, *Magnificence,* p. 114.

12. Interview with Msgr. Florence Cohalan, December 1994. As he reached the end of his life, Msgr. Lavelle reminisced for a reporter of the *New York Times.* He recalled: " I have seen Fifth Avenue change from a street of farms to one of first families and then to a street of business. And, of course, the rest of New York has changed just as much. When I was a young man, the Bowery was a shopping center, no better and no worse than other thoroughfares. It was a song which caused it to lose its reputation.

"It was only wealthy people who could afford horses and carriages. When I came here, even if I had been rich enough to keep a horse and buggy, I should not have done so because it would have looked as if I were trying to be high hat."

The reporter added: "He still reads without glasses; he celebrates Mass daily, goes out to attend sick calls and hears confession." *See: New York Times* Magazine, June 4, 1939.

13. Delaney, p. 56; *Catholic News,* September 26, October 28, 1938; correspondence file: Major Edward Bowes and Father Flannelly, 1940, ASPC. The trees had graced the estate of Edgar Price in Westchester County before their arrival at St. Patrick's.

14. Notes of Father Flannelly, 1939, ASPC; Carthy, *Magnificence,* pp. 114-116; *Cathedral Bulletin,* November 1969; Tribute to Bishop Flannelly, 1973, ASPC; *New York Times,* May 25, 1973.

15. *Catholic News,* December 15, 1945.

16. Program of Conferral of Pallium, 1940, ASPC.

17. *Catholic News,* December 14, 1940; *Cathedral Bulletin,* May 1940, January 1941; Carthy, *Magnificence,* p. 83. As part of the remodeling of the rectory, a sprinkler system was installed in the basement areas of the rectory. *See:* Application for Sprinkler System, Dept. of Housing and Buildings, April 26, 1940, ASPC.

18. Gannon, p. 266; Gillespie and O'Connor to Flannelly, March 18, 1941, ASPC; Cathedral announcements, January 18, 1942.

19. *The Arts Magazine,* Volume 14, 1928, pp. 106-107.

20. Archbishopric, pp. 158-159.

21. Exhibition catalog, Paul Rosenberg Gallery, New York, March, April 1957.

22. *Cathedral Bulletin,* February, May 1942, October 1960; *Catholic News,* June 27, 1942; George Morton to Thomas Young, August 1995, ASPC; Archbishopric, p. 158; *Activities of Archbishop Spellman* recorded by Father Flannelly, 1939, ASPC.

23. *Catholic News,* February 15, 1941; *Activities of Archbishop Spellman,* 1939.

24. Gannon, p. 266; interview with Msgr. Florence Cohalan, December 1994.

25. Grant to Hayes, February 16, February 28, 1931; Maginnis to Hayes, March 6, 1931,

AANY; correspondence file: Maginnis and Walsh with Julia Grant, 1941, ASPC; Conference report re: new high altar, December 23, 1941, ASPC.

26. *Activities of Archbishop Spellman*, 1939, ASPC.

27. Administrator's notes on original altar, 1942, ASPC.

28. William Beard report on work progress, May 1942, ASPC; Fred Mack to Maginnis, February 24, 1942, ASPC; Gannon, p. 266.

29. Archbishopric, pp. 88, 89. St. Peter is portrayed on the altar frontal seated at the stern of the ship whose rudder he is guiding. He carries two keys signifying apostolic primacy. A chalice appears on the sail of the ship and from the mast is the Resurrection banner. The inscription above reads: "This is eternal life, that they may know Thee, the only True God, and Jesus Christ Whom Thou has sent" (*Archbishopric*, pp. 85-90; The New High Altar and the Altar for the Lady Chapel; *Catholic News*, May 16, 1942).

The baldachin is cast bronze of an alloy consisting of: 81% copper; 2% tin; 2% lead; 15% zinc (Maginnis and Walsh and Kennedy to Fabrico Ltd., July 17, 1961, ASPC). The decorative theme of the baldachin is the redemption of humanity. The nine statuettes facing the rear represent figures in salvation history prior to the Redemption: Christ the Messias, Melchisedech, Abraham, Moses, David, Isaias, Simeon, John the Baptist, Peter. Figures facing the front are associated with the New Testament: Christ the King and High Priest, St. Athanasius, St. John Chrysostom, St. Ambrose, St. Augustine, St. Benedict, St. Dominic, St. Francis of Assisi, St. Ignatius Loyola. St. Michael the Archangel's statuette is at the peak of the baldachin.

The carving of the John Angel statue of St. Patrick was by Robert Baille (Maginnis to Flannelly, November 19, 1942, ASPC).

30. *Cathedral Bulletin*, May 1942; Interview with Msgr. Florence Cohalan, December 1994; Carthy, *Magnificence*, p. 117; *Catholic News*, May 9, December 12, December 19, 1942.

31. Archbishopric, pp. 136-139, 140, 142, 144; The New High Altar and Altar for the Lady Chapel; correspondence file, Maginnis and Walsh with Julia Grant, 1941, ASPC.

32. *Stained Glass Magazine*, Spring 1946, Autumn 1946, Spring 1987; Boston Globe, December 29, 1945; Connick, Charles, *Adventures In Light and Color*, Random House, New York, 1937, p. 355; Reyntiens, Patrick, *The Beauty of Stained Glass*, Little Brown and Co., Boston, 1990, p. 165.

33. *Catholic News*, April 25, 1942; contract for windows, 1941, ASPC; Connick to Maginnis, September 16, 1941, ASPC. The parables of Our Lord is the subject of the five windows. Symbols of the seven sacraments appear in the tracery at the tops (The New High Altar and Altar for the Lady Chapel).

34. Centenary, p. 53; contract for windows, 1942, ASPC; Thomas A. Kelly to Kellenberg, January 9, 1943, Kelly to Flannelly, August 2, 1943, Kelly to George Gillespie, November 10, 1942, ASPC. Thomas A. Kelly was a central figure in the construction at St. Patrick's for many years. He was a consultant at the Chancery office whose approval was needed for all work. When Archbishop McIntyre was transferred to the Archdiocese of Los Angeles, Kelly followed. Archbishop, later Cardinal, McIntyre placed him in charge of all construction operations and procedures. *See:* Weber, Francis J, *His Eminence of Los Angeles*, Volume I, Saint Francis Historical Society, Mission Hills, CA, 1997, pp. 242-243.

35. Mack to Spellman, September 28, 1942, ASPC; Memorandum of meeting re: heating system, November 6, 1942, ASPC.

36. Statement of Msgr. Flannelly, August 13, 1942, ASPC. Msgr. Flannelly believed the erroneous information traced to a book published in 1905 entitled: "Nooks and Corners of Old New York." He stated that in June 1882, Col. William Stone had written an article for the Journal of Commerce in which he traced the title of the site, and that Henry Beekman had done the same

in 1893. He referred those interested to the records at the Registry Office of the City of New York in Liber 620 of Conveyances, page 360.

According to the New York Evangelist of December 14, 1893, Beekman was the former corporation counsel, and carried out the trace at the request of Mayor Ely in order to squelch the rumors forever. Beekman traced the transactions to their beginnings in 1796.

Even before Colonel Stone's article, the history of the acquisition of the property had been printed in the Journal of the Fair, on October 24, 1878, and the first Cathedral guide by Msgr. Quinn, printed in 1879, repeated the same information.

37. Cohalan, *Popular History,* pp. 285-326, *passim,* especially pp. 284, 285-287, 294.

38. Cohalan, *Popular History,* p. 285; Carthy, *Magnificence,* p. 120; Gannon, p.196; Burton, p. 177.

39. *Cathedral Bulletin,* November 1941

40. Flannelly to Spellman, October 18, 1943, ASPC; Burton, p. 169; Carthy, *Magnificence,* pp. 118-119; Centenary; *Activities of Archbishop Spellman,* 1939, ASPC.

41. Burton, p. 175; Carthy, *Magnificence,* p. 120; special Cathedral announcement for V-J Day, ASPC; *Catholic News,* August 18, 1945.

42. Garraty, p. 761.

43. *Activities of Archbishop Spellman,* ASPC; Flannelly to Spellman, December 3, 1941, ASPC; correspondence file: Maginnis and Walsh with Julia Grant, 1942, ASPC; *Catholic News,* May 16, 1942; Gannon, p. 213. The soldiers were so grateful for the special effort of the Archbishop to visit them that they saved the money from their pay to commission a silversmith in Baghdad to make the chalice. They presented it to him just as he was about to begin the celebration.

44. Maginnis to Grant, November 6, 1942, ASPC; *The Holy Child of Earth and Heaven,* memorial booklet of St. Patrick's Cathedral, March 17, 1944. The poem, which became a hymn, was the first American Christmas carol (Correspondence file: Maginnis and Walsh to Julia Grant, 1942, ASPC).

45. *Catholic News,* August 21, 1943; *New York Times,* August 14, 1943; *The Holy Child of Earth and Heaven;* correspondence file: Maginnis and Walsh to Julia Grant, 1942, especially November 6, 1942, ASPC; *Activities of Archbishop Spellman.*

46. Cohalan, *Popular History,* pp. 294, 295; Spellman, Francis, *Action This Day,* Charles Scribner's Sons, New York, 1944, p. 38.

47. Gannon, p. 294. The Pope had given his good friend the chain and pectoral cross on March 2, 1943. The Archbishop had revealed his closeness to Pope Pius at a luncheon in New York on January 8, 1941, almost two years after his arrival in New York as Archbishop (*Activities of Archbishop Spellman,* 1941, ASPC).

48. Centenary; *Catholic News,* February 23, 1946.

49. Report of the Inspection of St. Patrick's Cathedral, April 26, 1945, ASPC. The blasting in July was so severe that the Cardinal's office twice called the George Fuller Company to investigate, expressing concern about the effects on the Cathedral. The Fuller Company added that the blasts were felt as far away as their own office on the 19th floor of their building at 57th Street and Madison Avenue. *See:* Fuller Company to Prentiss B. Reed, July 28th, 1947, ASPC.

50. Maginnis and Walsh to Kelly, September 13, 1945, ASPC. Despite the deterioration of the delicate carvings, most of the stone was in excellent condition. The United States Department of Commerce tested some of the marble removed during renovations. It found that the blocks which had "tremolite veins" ought to be replaced "because tremolite weathers rapidly and it is believed to be the cause of cracks in several blocks in this cathedral." But, the marble without the veins could expect a slow rate of weathering. The conclusion of the study was that "if the same

rate [of weathering] continues, it will require over 400 years for the weathering to reach a depth of one inch." *See:* E. U. Condon to Fuller Company, December 26, 1945, ASPC.

51. Vermont Marble Company to Fuller Company, April 24, 1946, ASPC. The Vermont Marble Company was of the opinion that the Lady Chapel marble came from the area of Dorset, Vermont. *See:* James F. Murphy to Kelly, May 9, 1946, ASPC. A chemical analysis of a sample of the Lady Chapel stone revealed it was a calcite marble, not dolomitic marble. It contained bands of alternating coarse and fine crystals, very uncharacteristic of good Vermont marble. The company found "what was undoubtedly the source. An old marble man in [the Dorset area] identified the fine and coarse crystal bands as characteristic of a small opening well up the mountain near East Dorset." It was believed the quarry, identified as the Freedley-Garwood Quarry, had a short-lived operation before it was abandoned. It was on a sharp slope with a shallow opening. The marble was called "markedly unsound" and "not of commercial quality," because "only after surface material is removed can sound durable marble be secured." Thus, there was an inherent lack of durability and good weathering characteristics. *See:* Vermont Marble Company to Maginnis and Walsh, May 3, 1946, ASPC. So, the assurance of the Department of Commerce of the innate durability of the original marble used, as specified in *endnote #50 above,* could not be given for the Lady Chapel stone, even though it was added to the building many years after the original stone.

52. James Murphy to Georgia Marble Company, October 24, 1945, ASPC; Fuller Company to Spellman, December 10, December 11, 1945, ASPC.

53. Gannon, pp. 267-268; Carthy, *Magnificence,* p. 122; Burton.

54. *Catholic News,* December 8, 1945; *Cathedral Bulletin,* August 1946, October 1947, September 1949; Report of the Architects, Maginnis and Walsh, for Thomas A. Kelly, September 13, 1945, ASPC; Fuller Company to Kelly, November 6, 1945, July 7, 1946, July 19, 1946, ASPC. The strike was called by the stonecarvers union. There were only about forty-five members of the union and about twenty-five of them were in New York. Of that number, sixteen were at the Cathedral. *See:* Crandall to Kelly and related memorandum for Cardinal Spellman, July 17, July 19, 1946, ASPC.

An ingenious use of United States Navy surplus material, pontoons used by the Seabees during World War II, was made by the Fuller Company in order to lift up and support the transept roof while the masonry below was being cut out and replaced. Workers built "a fulcrum of H-beams and angle braces on the adjacent solid wall, installing at each corner a pair of 51'6" long lever beams, and the necessary pick-up hangers and angles at the ends of the trusses. At the outer end of the lever beams were secured counterweights made by filling with water standard Navy steel pontoons – surplus from the needs of the Seabees in the war. The system was tightened and maintained during the work to just such a degree as would permit a piece of paper to be slid beneath the timber trusses at their bearing points." *See:* report entitled: " St. Patrick's Cathedral Repairs," by Jere J. Sullivan, Vice-president of George A. Fuller Company, March 27, 1947, ASPC.

While scaffolding was in place for repair of the stone at the north transept, emergency repairs were made to the large Life of Mary window because much of the glass was cracked and actually bulging. The cost was $4000. *See:* Fuller Company to Kelly, May 22, 1946, ASPC.

55. Maginnis to Flannelly, March 7, 1945, ASPC; Kelly to Maginnis and Walsh, January 19, 1946, ASPC; contract for rose window, April 5, 1945, ASPC; *New York Times,* February 20, April 2, 1947; *Catholic News,* April 5, 1947; Orin Skinner to Kelly, September 24, 1945 and related information, file on rose window, 1946, ASPC; Clendenin Ryan file, 1946, ASPC; *Cathedral Bulletin,* April 1946. The six archangels depicted in the lancets are identified as: St. Michael, St. Gabriel, Uriel, St. Raphael, Chamuel and Jophiel. *See: New York Times,* February 20, 1947, April 2, 1947.

The Seraphim portrayed in the leaf forms of the window hold symbols of the beatitudes: a dove for the poor in spirit; a lamb for the meek; scales for the just; a lily for the clean of heart; a crown for the persecuted; an olive branch for the peacemakers; a broken sword for the merciful; and an inverted torch for those who mourn. *See: Catholic News*, April 5, 1947.

56. Minutes of the Board of Trustees, June 11, 1942; Fuller Company to Kelly, May 21, 1946; Kelly to Flannelly, June 1, 1946; Kelly to Fuller Company, January 22, 1947; Murphy to Kelly, February 19, 1947, ASPC. When the connection between the Cathedral and the Archbishop's residence was under consideration, there was a proposal to extend the passage along the entire length of the Cathedral on the Fiftieth Street terrace from the residence to the tower door near Fifth Avenue. Although the projected cost of just under $31,000 was small in comparison to the enormous cost of the repairs, the plan was rejected in order to keep costs to a minimum. The Cardinal had approved the plan, and Msgr. Flannelly had suggested a covered passage, but open on the street side in imitation of a cloister, like that at St. Joseph's Seminary. The purpose of the passage was to allow ceremonial processions in inclement weather.

57. *Cathedral Bulletin*, September 1949, November 1949; Flannelly to Kelly, May 20, 1947; Kelly to Fuller Company, August 6, 1947; Fuller Company to Kelly, May 5, 1947; V. W. Gasparri to Fuller Company, January 2, 1947; Gasparri to Kelly, January 2, 1947; Flannelly to Maginnis, November 29, 1949, ASPC. Joseph Cacioppo of Corona, New York repaired one of the stations of the cross in the summer of 1947. He wrote that he had carved the main altar of the Cathedral when he worked for William Bradley and Son earlier in the decade. He mentioned, further, that he also did work for the Pelli Company, makers of the Lady Chapel altar.

58. Minutes of the Board of Trustees, April 1, 1897.

59. Maginnis to Flannelly, February 19, 1945; Flannelly to Maginnis, March 5, 1945; Maginnis to Flannelly, March 22, 1945; J. Quasten to Maginnis and Walsh, January 27, 1947; Flannelly to Maginnis, February 19, 1946; Maginnis to Flannelly, March 5, 1946, ASPC; *A Description of the New Bronze Doors*, memorial booklet prepared by Maginnis and Walsh, December 23, 1949.

J. Quasten was Dean of the Faculty of Theology of the Catholic University of America. He wrote to the architects that it was contrary to tradition to place the figure of St. Patrick in the tympanum over the bronze doors rather than that of Christ. Other experts whose opinions were solicited were Dom Anselm Strittmatter of St. Anselm's Priory in Brookland and Rev. Damian of Holy Name College in Washington, D. C. *See:* Strittmatter to Maginnis and Walsh, February 24, 1947; Maginnis and Walsh to Flannelly, February 25, 1947; Damian to Flannelly, March 22, 1947, ASPC.

60. *A Description of the New Bronze Doors*, December 23, 1949.

61. John Angel to Flannelly, July 13, 1947, July 10, 1948, ASPC.

62. The heraldic arms of Cardinal Spellman were never inserted into the marble floor, as were those of the other Archbishops of New York.

63. A. W. Nelson to Kelly, December 16, 1949, ASPC; *Catholic News*, December 24, 1949; *Cathedral Bulletin*, January 1950. Incomplete records do not tell us about the disposal of the wooden doors which were replaced. Some may have been sent to the Old St. Patrick's Cathedral on Mott Street.

In 1988, Richard J. Kohler wrote to the Rector of St. Patrick's informing him that he, Kohler, had been the craftsman in charge of building the bronze doors in the Halback Company's workshop in Greenpoint, Brooklyn. *See:* Kohler to Dalla Villa, February 22, 1988; Kohler to Young, May 1, 1991, ASPC.

The Halback Company was located at Banker Street in Brooklyn. Rochette and Panzini of East 25th Street prepared the plaster casts. *See:* contract for bronze doors, March 15, 1948, ASPC.

64. Certificate of payment, January 3, 1949, ASPC; contract for bronze doors, March 15, 1948, ASPC; file: correspondence of Countess Mary Young Moore and Msgr. Flannelly, 1948, ASPC; *Catholic News*, May 5, 1962, August 12, 1950; Msgr. Francis Weber to Sr. Elizabeth, October 7, 1991, AANY. *Also see:* Gannon, p. 97. Mary Young Moore was born in Los Angeles on November 7, 1882. She received the *Pro Ecclesia et Pontifice* medal from Pope Pius XII in 1940, was made a Dame of the Holy Sepulchre in 1946, and at the request of Archbishop Spellman was made a papal countess in 1952. She moved from Los Angeles to New York where she became a confidant of Cardinal Spellman. She died on October 23, 1971, and Cardinal Terence Cooke, successor to Cardinal Spellman, offered her Requiem Mass in California. She had been Vice-president of the National Conference of Catholic Charities and Vice-president of the American Catholic Historical Society. Moore Catholic High School in Staten Island was named in her honor. *See: Catholic News*, August 19, 1950; Weber, pp. 507-508.

65. Archbishopric, p. 64.

66. *Catholic News*, June 6, June 21, 1947; *Cathedral Bulletin*, June 1947; A. G. Borden to Reverend Fathers, August 13, 1968; Kelly to William Somerville Company, March 5, 1947, ASPC. The flag was blessed on Decoration Day (renamed Memorial Day), May 30, 1947.

67. Maginnis to Kelly, January 13, 1949; Maginnis to Michael Kelleher, June 7, 1949, ASPC; *Catholic News*, October 2, 1948; *New York Times*, February 25, 1949; speech of Msgr. Flannelly to Friendly Sons of St. Patrick, March 1, 1948, ASPC. The original statue of Our Lady of Lujan has been venerated in Argentina since 1630. The bell of St. Joan of Arc was decorated and contained the inscription: "From the City of D'Annecy, I am the ambassadress who sings recognition and friendship."

In November 1954, additional drawings of James Renwick were presented to the New York Public Library by James Leftwich whose wife was a grandniece of Mr. Renwick. Other Renwick drawings of the Cathedral are at the Avery Library of Columbia University.

68. Shopsin, William, et al., *The Villard Houses*, Viking Press, New York, 1980, *passim*.

69. Msgr. Flannelly file re: pigeons, 1941, ASPC.

70. Rev. Matthias Cremer to Flannelly, September 28, 1948; Flannelly to Cremer, October 1, 1948, ASPC; *New York Times*, October 6, 1949.

71. Interview with Msgr. Florence Cohalan, December 1994.

72. *Catholic News*, March 23, 1940, November 27, 1943, December 4, 1943. Yon died in the home of Richardo San Vero, father-in-law of Yon's son, Mario.

73. The letters of application are in the Archives of the Cathedral.

74. *Catholic News*, October 9, 1943, April 5, 1947. Some information was provided by Ray Biswanger of Reader's Digest, author of an unpublished biography of Charles Courboin, August 1993. Courboin's honors included that of Chevalier of the Order of Leopold I and Chevalier of the Order of the Crown of Belgium.

75. *Catholic News*, April 5, 1947, April 19, 1947; Flannelly to Courboin, May 25, 1944; Kilgen Organ Company to Flannelly, February 12, 1947, ASPC. During part of the time when Mr. Rivetti was serving in the Navy, Charles Lauria substituted for him at the organ. At the time, Serafino Bogatta was the assistant music director and also sang in the choir. *See:* Courboin to Lauria, and Flannelly to Courboin, April 13, 1945, ASPC.

76. *Catholic News*, December 11, December 18, 1948, January 1, 1949; *New York Times*, May 25, 1973; *Cathedral Bulletin*, December 1948; file: choir recordings, 1949, ASPC. It appears that Father Greene, who was a member of the Cathedral staff and Chairman of the Music Commission of the Archdiocese, directed the choir, while Edward Rivetti was organist, an arrangement unlike that in earlier years when the chancel organist also directed the chancel choir.

77. Cathedral Lenten schedules, 1940-1949, ASPC; Sheen, pp. 299-300.

78. Gannon, p. 188.

79. *Catholic News*, October 21, 1941; Cohalan, *Popular History*, p. 325; *Activities of Archbishop Spellman*, 1941, ASPC; Rev. Vincent Raith to John Ryder, May 9, 1951, ASPC.

80. *Catholic News*, March 14, 1942, April 10, 1943, September 9, October 7, 1944; *Activities of Archbishop Spellman*, 1942, ASPC; Gannon, p. 257; Cohalan, *Popular History*, p. 325; Carthy, *Magnificence*, p. 119.

81. *Catholic News*, August 4, 1945, September 20, 1945, October 13, 1945; *Activities of Archbishop Spellman*, 1942-1945, ASPC.

82. *Catholic News*, February 23, 1946; Sheen, pp. 265-266. Archbishop Sheen received Mrs. Luce into the Church on February 16, 1946.

83. Flannelly to "Dear Friend," February 26, 1944, ASPC.

84. Gannon, pp. 267-268; *Catholic News*, November 2, November 23, 1946; prayer for Babe Ruth, August 19, 1948, ASPC.

85. *Catholic News*, December ll, December 18, 1948. Cardinal Spellman customarily allowed those he ordained to episcopal ranks to select rings and pectoral crosses which had belonged to earlier bishops, archbishops and cardinals of New York. *See:* Gannon, p. 146.

86. Gannon, photograph caption; *Activities of Archbishop Spellman*, 1941, ASPC; Spellman, p. 76; *New York Daily News*, June 2, 1943; *New York Times*, May 1947 (date uncertain); *The Honorary Ushers of St. Patrick's Cathedral;* Flannelly to Msgr. Murphy, June 7, 1949; Flannelly to Catherine Quirk, October 28, 1949, ASPC.

87. Garraty, p. 785; Cohalan, *Popular History*, pp. 296, 320; Carthy, *Magnificence*, pp. 109, 124; Ellis, pp. 580, 584.

88. Spellman to his family, December 1957; Flannelly to "Dear Friends," February 26, 1945; Flannelly to Spellman, January 7, 1958; Spellman to Flannelly, February 4, 1958, ASPC; *Cathedral Bulletin*, October 1953.

89. *Catholic News*, May 26, 1946, April 19, 1952; *New York Times*, May 16, 1946; memorandum of Cardinal Spellman, September 10, 1946, ASPC; file: electrification of bells, 1946-1954, ASPC.

90. Nelson Rockefeller to Spellman, June 2, 1952, ASPC.

91. *Cathedral Bulletin*, August 1952; Lavelle to Partridge, January 26, 1932, Partridge to Flannelly, January 26, 1950, ASPC.

92. Kelly to Flannelly, August 9, 1951; Kelly to Otis Elevator Company, February 6, 1952, ASPC; *Cathedral Bulletin*, August 1952; Philip Mitchell to author (verbally), March 1995.

93. *Catholic News*, October 9, 1954.

94. Burton, p. 217.

95. *Catholic News*, October 9, 1954.

96. *Cathedral Bulletin*, April 1956; *Catholic News*, July 17, 1954; contract for clerestory windows, 1954, ASPC; Flannelly to Hunt, June 25, 1952; Flannelly to Fleming, July 19, 1954; Flannelly to McGrath, May 20, 1954, ASPC; Hunt to Flannelly, June 24, 1952, AANY.

97. Carthy, *Magnificence*, p. 121; Burton, pp. 212-214; file: St. Patrick's Information Center, 1971, ASPC. The Information Center was located at 31 East 51st Street. Rev. Francis X. Duffy, not to be confused with Father Duffy, the Chaplain of World War I, joined the staff of the Center. Later he became its director. *See:* Carthy, p. 124..

98. *Cathedral Bulletin*, August 1966; Cohalan, *Popular History*, p. 189; file: Statue of St. Pius X, 1960, ASPC; Flannelly to Criado, July 14, 1955, ASPC. Some time between the early 1900s when most of the statues were installed, and 1949, the second last to arrive – the Statue of St. Peter Canisius — was placed in the north transept. *See: Cathedral Bulletin*, September 1949; Flannelly to Regan, August 30, 1950, ASPC.

99. Spellman to Mother Pascalina, May 26, 1959; Msgr. Rigney to Mary McLoughlin, December 6, 1982, ASPC; *New York Times*, April 17, 1965.

100. Burton, pp. 224-226; Carthy, *Magnificence*, p. 185, footnote #9; Minutes of the Board of Trustees, May 16, 1957; Flannelly to McDonald, July 1,1957; Brady to Flannelly, September 18, 1957; Costello to Flannelly, November 7, 1958; Gasparri to Mitchell Company, March 29, April 14, April 18, 1958, ASPC.

101. Dinner dance program, November 18, 1958, ASPC. The first Mass in the Chapel was offered by Cardinal Spellman on December 10, 1958. Bishop Flannelly celebrated the second Mass the next day and the Chapel opened for divine service on December 21st. *See:* Rev. Leo F. Halpin, *History of the Chapel of Saints Faith, Hope and Charity,* unpublished information sheet, 1983, ASPC.

102. Flannelly to Lehr, November 10, 1948, ASPC.

103. files: Special liturgies, 1941-1960, ASPC.

104. Cohalan, *Popular History,* p. 325.

105. file: Guest preachers at St. Patrick's Cathedral, 1950-1970, ASPC; *Catholic News,* April 8, 1952; Flannelly to Breen, March 30, 1951, ASPC.

106. *Catholic News*, March 17, 1951; April 5, 1952; March 28, 1953; June 6, 1953; April 10, 1954; April 9, 1955; April 13, 1957.

107. Burton, p. 217; New York Herald Tribune, May 9, 1959; *Catholic News*, May 9, 1959. Early in the decade, for the first time in history, a Palm Sunday Mass was televised. It was Cardinal Spellman's Mass at St. Patrick's. *See: Catholic News,* April 5, 1952.

Three Cardinals welcomed the new Apostolic Delegate on May 8, 1959, Cardinals Spellman of New York, O'Hara of Philadelphia and Cushing of Boston.

108. *Catholic News*, April 12, 1958, August 10, 1958; *New York Times*, August 16, 1958; Carthy, *Magnificence*, p. 125; press release, Archdiocese of New York, undated, but August 1958, ASPC. The cornerstone chair of Archbishop Hughes is used by the celebrant of Masses in the chapel in the Archbishop's residence.

109. Burton, p. 222; Listing of television stations, December, 1958, ASPC.

110. Garraty, p. 786; Gannon, p. 382; *Catholic News*, April 28, 1951.

111. Gannon, pp. 337, 396; Carthy, *Magnificence*, p.123.

112. files: Choir and Musicians, 1944, 1949; Military Choirs, 1958, ASPC.

113. Information from Ray Biswanger of *Reader's Digest*, August 1993; Courboin to Flannelly, June 25, 1953; Pastore to Zentmaier, April 25, 1958; Flannelly to Kilgen Organ Company, September 22, 1958, ASPC.

114. Records of Trustees, Records of Pewholders, 1940-1970, ASPC; Delaney, p. 454; file: film, "Miracle In the Rain," 1955, ASPC; Msgr. Timothy Flynn to *New Yorker Magazine*, September 11, 1958, special file on St. Patrick's Cathedral, AANY. Fulton Oursler died on May 24, 1952. He was a convert to Catholicism.

115. *New York Daily News*, June 6, 1963; press release, Archdiocese of New York, June, 1963, ASPC; Cohalan, *Popular History,* pp. 311, 323; Kelly, George A., *In My Father's House,* Doubleday, New York, 1989, pp. 81-82.

116. Kelly, *In My Father's House,* pp. 72-73.

117. Cohalan, *Popular History,* p. 320; Carthy, *Magnificence*, p. 128; press release, September 19, 1967, ASPC; Spellman to Dr. Victorio di Monte Zamolo, January 20, 1964, ASPC.

118. file: Bequests and Donations, 1960-1969, ASPC; contract for air conditioning, 1963, ASPC; Clancy to Institutional Air Conditioning Company, July 16, 1963, ASPC.

119. *New York Daily News*, September 8, 1962, April 23, 1965; *New York Times*, April 23, 1965.

120. Delaney, p. 73.

121. file: Landmark: St. Patrick's Cathedral, 1966, ASPC.

122. Chief George Kelly to Flannelly, November 23, 1965; Hunt to Spellman, January 28, 1966, ASPC; file: sprinkler system, 1965, ASPC.

123. *Curriculum Vitae* of W. Knight Sturges, file: Architects, ASPC; file: sprinkler system 1965, ASPC.

124. blueprints file, 1963, ASPC; Minutes of meetings re: renovations, September 12, 1963, December 17, 1965, ASPC; Architect's Preliminary Report, November 21, 1963, ASPC; Shanley to Msgr. F. Costello, August 22, 1963, ASPC.

125. Cohalan, *Popular History,* 323, 324; *Fourteen Hours,* Dell Publishing Company, New York, 1965, *passim;* Fleming et al., ed., *An Instrument of Your Peace,* official documentary report of the visit of Pope Paul VI to the United Nations and New York, Commemorative Publications, Inc., New York, 1965, p. 36 *et passim;* file: Visit of Pope Paul VI, October 4, 1965, ASPC. In commemoration of his visit to St. Patrick's and at the request of Cardinal Spellman, Pope Paul donated a bronze bust made from a casting of an original by Lello Scorzelli of Naples. The original had been made in 1963, and the copy was unveiled by Cardinal Spellman at St. Patrick's on December 20, 1965. *See: New York Times,* December 21, 1965.

126. Garraty, p. 859; Cohalan, *Popular History,* p. 320; file: report of Msgr. McGovern re: "Demonstrations and Arrests in St. Patrick's Cathedral," special file on St. Patrick's Cathedral, AANY; *New York Times,* October 11, 1966, November 4, 1968.

127. Cohalan, *Popular History,* pp. 325-326; *Catholic News,* December 14, 1967; *New York Daily News,* December 8, 1967; Archbishop John Maguire to Clergy, December 2, 1967, ASPC.

128. Between 1939 and January 1958, twenty cardinals, archbishops and bishops were ordained at St. Patrick's. Many more followed before the death of Cardinal Spellman in 1967. *See:* Monsignor Thomas Donnellan to Msgr. Terence Cooke, January 13, 1958, ASPC.

129. Kelly, *In My Father's House,* pp. 70, 71, 82, 83; Cohalan, *Popular History,* p. 313.

To Find God
in All Things

The blind, the crippled, the prisoners ...

... all those hard years.
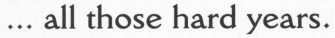

The
Cathedral
has seen
seven
wars
in its day ...

Nancy Sirkis

... and warriors
for peace like Paul
VI at the UN.

One day in Your courts.

And among our many visitors ...

That the thoughts
of many hearts
may be laid bare.

Rose windows — like people — simply don't
work if there's no source of light behind

A fitting splendor ...

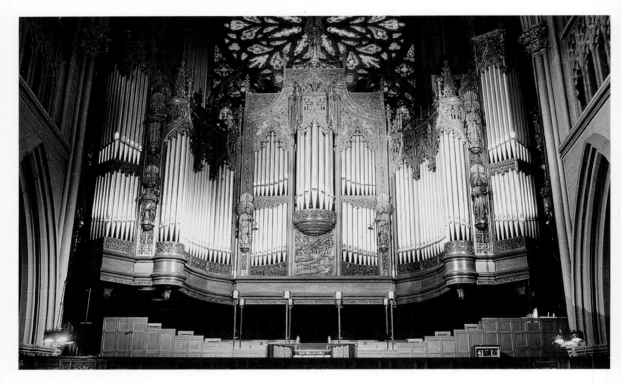

but when all is said and done ...

CHAPTER IX

Getting to the Next Hundred Years: Cardinal Terence Cooke

During several months after Cardinal Spellman's death, the business of the Archdiocese was directed by Archbishop John Maguire, Coadjutor Archbishop since September 1965, just before the visit of Pope Paul VI. He had been made Vicar General in 1953, and was consecrated a bishop by Cardinal Spellman in 1959. His role was that of a trusted assistant, like Archbishop McIntyre before him, until he, McIntyre, became Archbishop of Los Angeles. And like Cardinal McIntyre's, his face was a familiar one at the Cathedral, dating to 1950 when he was Chancellor and maintained an office just across the street on Madison Avenue.[1] Rumors were abundant during the early months of 1969 about who Cardinal Spellman's successor was likely to be, just as there was conjecture about the future of the Archdiocese itself, i.e., would or should it be divided?, would the other New York City diocese, the Diocese of Brooklyn, be joined to the Archdiocese?, would there be physical changes to the Cathedral to conform to suggestions of the Second Vatican Council?, and other possibilities either coveted or feared. There was "general astonishment" early in March when it was announced that the youngest of the auxiliary bishops, Bishop Terence Cooke, was appointed the new Archbishop. "He had not been on any of the published lists, and he had neither the Roman experience and contacts, nor the national or international standing some prophets had judged necessary or desirable." And the Archdiocese remained intact, neither gaining nor losing territory. Also, the office of Military Ordinariate remained attached to the Archbishopric of New York.[2]

The youngest of three children of Irish immigrants, Terence Cooke was born in 1921 in Corpus Christi Parish on Manhattan's upper west side. After elementary education in

the Bronx, he entered Cathedral College and went on to Dunwoodie Seminary. An accelerated course of studies due to World War II moved his ordination date forward to December 1, 1945. He was engaged briefly in parish work, and then attended the University of Chicago and the Catholic University of America in Washington, D. C., from which he received a master's degree in social work. He was then assigned to the Catholic Youth Organization and the youth division of Catholic Charities. He also taught at Fordham University. In 1954, he was assigned to St. Joseph's Seminary and three years later he joined Cardinal Spellman's staff, first as secretary, then in succession as assistant chancellor, as chancellor and ultimately as vicar general. He was made a monsignor in 1957, and received the very special honor of *prothonotary apostolic* in 1964, the same honor Monsignor Lavelle had been given decades earlier. That same year, he learned that he had contracted cancer, but he decided to keep the diagnosis a secret except from those closest to him. Although some of those close to him feared he would die, one of his friends was moved to say: "He's not going to die because he is a saint. God has some very special work for him to do." And for the next nineteen years, the saintly priest did exactly that, all the time hiding the state of his health, even while undergoing blood transfusions to enable him to continue working. In 1965, he became a bishop.

The grand ceremony at which he was installed as Archbishop of New York took place on April 4, 1968. In attendance were six American cardinals, about fifty bishops and many non-Catholic clergy, an innovation encouraged by the Vatican Council. For the first time in history, a President of the United States, Lyndon Johnson, attended, as did many civic leaders. On the very same day, a sign of troubles to follow, Dr. Martin Luther King, Jr. was murdered, the act setting off riots in cities all over the land.[3]

In 1968, New York City, with almost 8,000,000 residents, was still the most populous city in America and the third most populous in the world. The metropolitan area contained more than twice that number. New York was the financial, communications and entertainment capital of the world, home to the largest corporations, containing the busiest subway system and the largest harbor on earth. Except for the federal government, it had the largest government in the country. But its attributes were tarnished by its overwhelming problems: crime and violence were increasing; unemployment was mounting, producing an ever-widening gulf between the rich and poor, while the number of citizens receiving welfare grew steadily; drug abuse was out-of-control; conditions in public housing were abominable; and government's dealing with these and other problems was often ineffective.[4]

The Archdiocese contained close to two million Catholics in about four hundred parishes. Every day about 2,500,000 workers converged "in the central business district of Manhattan, the area south of Fifty-ninth Street." For many of them the Cathedral was their weekday parish, and the life of the Cathedral was not divorced from the life around it. Many looked to the new Archbishop of New York for direction in living Christian lives in an increasingly antagonistic anti-Christian world.[5]

Two months after the death of Dr. Martin Luther King, Jr., New York Senator Robert Kennedy was shot and killed in California, while campaigning for the Democratic nomination for President. His funeral Mass was offered at St. Patrick's before one of the largest assemblages of combined Catholic and civic dignitaries in American history. Archbishop Cooke concelebrated the liturgy with four priests close to the Kennedy family. Participating in the sanctuary were six cardinals, Agnelo dell'Acqua representing Pope Paul VI, Cody of Chicago, Krol of Philadelphia, McIntyre of Los Angeles, O'Boyle of Washington and Cushing of Boston; numerous archbishops and bishops; and a large delegation of ecumenical clergy. Among the 2500 invited mourners were President Lyndon Johnson, Vice-president Hubert Humphrey, Secretary of State Dean Rusk, United Nations Ambassador Arthur Goldberg, Chief Justice of the Supreme Court Earl Warren, Prime Minister of Ireland John Lynch, Secretary-General of the United Nations U Thant, Governor of New York Nelson Rockefeller, New York City Mayor John Lindsay, members of the United States Senate and House of Representatives, and foreign ministers from around the globe. This occasion was the third time President Johnson visited the Cathedral; he was the first American president ever to attend liturgies at St. Patrick's. Millions watched the Mass which was televised

Senator Eugene McCarthy pays his respects at the funeral. The very day he was shot, Robert Kennedy beat McCarthy in the California primary for a chance to run for President. Cardinal Cooke said a brief graveside prayer in Arlington Cemetery. It was the first burial held at night there.

internationally. For many it was their first opportunity to view the Catholic funeral liturgy according to reformed regulations of the Second Vatican Council. The presence of non-Catholic clergy in the sanctuary surprised some, as did the selection of hymns which included *The Battle Hymn of the Republic.* Richard Tucker of the Metropolitan Opera Company sang, and Leonard Bernstein conducted thirty-two members of the New York Philharmonic Orchestra.[6]

Archbishop Cooke was named to the College of Cardinals one year after his appointment to head the See in April 1969. The time between appointments was the shortest ever for a New York Archbishop. Typical of his self-effacing character, he declined a large celebration upon his return from the consistory in Rome. Instead, after an early Mass, he made himself available on the steps of the Cathedral to greet all who wished to speak with him. "Well into the night," he stood gratefully receiving congratulations and promises of prayers, while the priests accompanying him took half-hour shifts at his side. During the rest of his life, he regularly followed the same practice on special occasions with kindness and patience, both at the Cathedral and around the Archdiocese.[7]

After the interment of Cardinal Spellman's remains, it was decided to renovate the crypt of the Archbishops under the high altar, to improve ventilation and to insure adequate space for inscriptions on the entrance doors. The doors were reconstructed and given a verde antique finish, the stairway and corridor leading into the burial chamber were lined with Carrara marble, and new lighting was installed. The same year — 1968 — the beautiful historic Villard Houses which housed the Chancery and other archdiocesan offices on Madison Avenue were designated a landmark.[8]

In September 1969, the Cardinal-Archbishop of Cracow, Poland received an enthusiastic welcome at St. Patrick's during a visit to the United States. Nobody at the time could know that one day he would become the first non-Italian pope in hundreds of years. Cardinal Cooke presided at a Mass celebrated by Cardinal Karol Wojtyla and concelebrated by several bishops and priests in front of a large congregation, with delegations from Polish parishes of the City. Homilies were delivered in Polish by the Cardinal and in English by Rev. Robert Gannon, who had eulogized Cardinal Spellman at his funeral. This event was one of the last major ceremonies under the administration of Bishop Flannelly.[9]

The Bishop reached his seventy-fifth birthday on October 22, 1969, on which day he submitted his resignation as required by Vatican II regulations. He was accorded the honorary title *Rector Emeritus,* and chose to live in retirement in the parish house of St.

Patrick's. On November 9th, Cardinal Cooke appointed his secretary, Monsignor James F. Rigney, as the fourth Rector of St. Patrick's Cathedral.[10]

Regular parishioners at the Cathedral knew Monsignor Rigney well. He had been Cardinal Spellman's secretary from 1965 until the Cardinal's death, and he continued in the same office under Cardinal Cooke. In 1963, following the lofty path paved by Archbishop Sheen, he had delivered the Lenten series at St. Patrick's. His easy, cheerful style of delivery brought smiles to the faces of congregations for many years during his rectorship.

Blackstone-Shelburne N.Y.

His successor as Rector of the Cathedral, Msgr. Anthony Dalla Villa, described Msgr. Rigney in the words Rigney himself used at Cardinal Cooke's funeral: "Our thoughts of him are better than our words, and he was better than both."

James F. Rigney was born in New York City in 1922, and was baptized at Sacred Heart Church on Fifty-first Street, not far from the Cathedral. His elementary, secondary and college training was completed in Catholic institutions in Manhattan. After graduation from Manhattan College in 1942, he entered St. Joseph's Seminary and was ordained by Cardinal Spellman on March 1, 1947. Following a brief assignment at St. Aloysius Church in Livingston Manor, Father Rigney enrolled at the North American College in Rome, where he was awarded a doctorate in sacred theology. In 1949, he was assigned to teach at Cathedral College, and four years later he became Professor of Dogmatic Theology at the seminary. Concurrently, he was Chairman of the Theology Department of Mt. St. Vincent's College, retaining the post until 1965. He also contributed extensively to Catholic journals, including a weekly column in the Archdiocesan newspaper; articles in the New Catholic Encyclopedia and the New Catholic Youth Encyclopedia; and contributions to *Catholic Theology of America,* a scholarly journal. In addition, he was a regular commentator on the Westchester County Catholic Hour, a radio broadcast; held a position on the Archdiocesan matrimonial tribunal; and was a member of the Board of Trustees of Cathedral College Seminary in Douglaston, New York. He became a theological consultant during the Second Vatican Council. Pope John XXIII elevated him to the rank of papal chamberlain in 1963, and in 1966 he was made a domestic prelate, both offices bearing the title *monsignor.*[11]

During Msgr. Rigney's nineteen-year rectorship, extensive improvements were made to the physical plant, some required by the ravages of time, others in order to conform to recommendations of the Vatican Council relating to the liturgy. Still others, such as air conditioning the building, were considered necessary because of the exigencies of modern living. Shanley and Sturges' 1963 survey had recommended the air conditioning because of the distractions caused by outside noise when the doors were open. There were other reasons supporting the project: higher power lighting had raised the air temperature, and soot from pollution had darkened the stone. In 1970, the firm of James E. Mitchell and Son, under Philip Mitchell, was awarded the contract for installing a system of air conditioning. The construction consulting and management company was family-owned, and had been in business in the metropolitan area since 1888, long associated with the construction of Archdiocesan offices, schools and hospitals. Philip Mitchell had joined the firm after establishing a record as an heroic fighter pilot in World War II, when he was wounded during combat and received the Distinguished Flying Cross. Creating an ideal comfort level in so huge a space was a daunting task, and since air supply units had to be placed in the triforia, fifty-five feet above the pews, rather than at the recommended twelve-foot level, it was understood that "what was being done was far from ideal, but that it would be helpful." Short of defacing one of the most beautiful buildings in America, no other solution presented itself. Work began in March 1970, and upon completion the next year, cost just under $350,000, some of which was from a bequest of the Borden family. As expected, conditions improved, but the system was sometimes ineffective when temperatures outside soared over ninety degrees and large congregations were crowded inside.[12]

Before Vatican Council II, it was not permitted for several priests to offer the Mass together, a practice known as concelebration. Thus, altar platforms were not large enough to provide room for several priests. In order to accommodate the new liturgical requirements at the Cathedral, in the summer of 1970 the high altar at the Cathedral was reduced in size slightly and moved to the center of the platform under the baldachin, both to allow more room and to permit concelebrants to face the congregation. At the same time, the baldachin received a thorough cleaning and a handsome finish. In 1971, the fire danger was partially addressed when standpipes were placed in all the triforia, and the triforia walls were sprayed with a fire-retardant paint, both measures taken at the recommendation of the City Fire Department. The stop-gap measures still did not eliminate the need for a permanent solution which once again had to yield to other needs because of lack of funds. Later that year, a donation from Mr. And Mrs. Arthur Roth made possible for the first time the illumination of the Fifth Avenue facade. The light source was on the setback of 630 Fifth Avenue in Rockefeller Center. To witness the first lighting, Cardinal Cooke joined the Roths in the rooftop gardens of the Rockefeller Center building. Beginning that November, the lights were turned on from dusk to midnight every day.[13]

The next improvement came in 1972 when the Sacred Heart altar was altered to become a new Blessed Sacrament altar. The Rambusch Company, specialists in ecclesiastical design, introduced a medieval-style pillar on top of which was the tabernacle which had been refinished and moved from the Lady Chapel. Under the pillar a marble platform was erected. The pillar was placed several yards from the Sacred Heart altar and its reredos which were left in place. Because Cardinal Cooke felt uneasy about the attention drawn to himself by the richly carved oak canopy over the throne, he asked Msgr. Rigney to have it transferred to the Blessed Sacrament chapel. It was gilded and lifted high above the tabernacle, attaching suitable decoration to the most sacred location in the Cathedral. All the work was supervised by the Mitchell Company at a cost of $55,000. W. Knight Sturges designed the bronze railing made by Anthony Minervini. Mr. Minervini served his apprenticeship in the metal working trade in Italy, and studied in Venezuela before coming to the United States. Some of his work is found in places as distant as Saudi Arabia and as close as the Garden State Art Center in Holmdel, New Jersey.[14]

Msgr. Rigney's attention next went to providing for the needs of the disabled who had no easy access to the Cathedral. Every entrance is several steps above street level, a difficult climb for the elderly, and one impossible for those dependent on wheelchairs. In 1972, a ramp was cut through the north gardens near the Fifty-first Street door at Fifth Avenue.[15]

Less than thirty years after blasting for Best and Company led to the restoration of the exterior, news that the store would be demolished and a new building erected caused considerable apprehension, because blasting again was required for construction. Of special concern was the almost century-old Cathedral ceiling which, from the floor, appeared to be cracked in several places. In July 1972 it was decided to erect scaffolding as a protection from possible falling plaster, and to inspect the entire ceiling. Six miles of steel pipe and about 500,000 board feet of lumber and 1,200 linear feet of bridge material made it one of the largest interior scaffolds ever built in New York. The inspection found the ceiling in good condition, with only some minor problems. What had appeared from below to be cracks was soot which had accumulated over decades from candle smoke and pollution entering the open doors and windows.[16]

The scaffolding provided an opportunity to restore the entire interior. A compressor was used to blow inches of dust from the decorative bosses, capitals and crevices. Then,

Jo-ann Price

loose plaster due to water damage was removed — found mostly on the upper walls rather than on the ceiling — and new plaster was applied before it was all painted. Ten painters used about 2,200 gallons of paint applied in two coats. The ribs received an off-white color, the ceiling a soft white and the purest white outlined the stone courses and block lines. Bright red highlighted the bosses, and the bolder designs, such as the dove and the sunburst at the crossing, were covered in gold. The painters were unable to find the elusive preserve jar embedded in one of the bosses by the Power family when the ceiling was built, but they were surprised to find the initials of one of the plasterers carved into the underside of one of the bosses. They left the small spot unpainted as a tribute to their fellow-tradesman, since the small defect was indiscernible from the floor below. Meanwhile, Masses, weddings, and devotions continued uninterrupted during the restoration.

Besides painting, the job entailed repair and cleaning of all the marble, including the pillars, and cleaning the stained glass windows. The restoration, planned by W. Knight Sturges, was completed in time for Easter 1973. Before the scaffolding was removed, Cardinal Cooke climbed to the top and later remarked: "I thus became the first Archbishop to touch the roof of the Cathedral." When the scaffolding was removed, the full glory of the Cathedral as it must have looked on opening day in 1879 brought a common response from churchgoers. According to Monsignor Rigney, a single word said all: "Wow!" And at the unveiling, the red galeros of the deceased cardinals, cleaned and treated with a preservative, produced a striking contrast to the pure white ceiling over the crypt. The cost of the entire project was about $1,100,000.[17]

While the scaffolding was still in place, Leland Cook, the chief photographer of Tiffany and Company, asked permission to examine and photograph the windows at close range. This was the only time in almost one hundred years when anyone could take advantage of the opportunity to do so. One Saturday, Mr. Cook found himself incredulously observing one of the original windows, part of which was set in place incorrectly. The window of the Three Baptisms contained an inscription in one lancet identifying the Baptism of Our Lord. But, a small section was upside-down. The wording which resulted read: *Bapto wsif Our Lord*. The *o wsi* panel, if turned upright, would have read *ism o*, yielding the correct spelling. It was decided to leave the panel in place as it had survived for almost a century. Mr. Cook presented many of his photographs in a centennial book published in 1979.[18]

Two final elements of the restoration were the setting in the marble floor of the heraldic arms of Cardinal Cooke and restoring the pews. Gasparri Studios placed the coat-of-arms between the new Blessed Sacrament chapel and the pulpit.[19] The forty-five-year-old pews were cleaned, stained and coated with varnish during the summer of 1973. The work was done a small section at a time over a six-week period so that services were not interrupted; on weekends the entire church could be used.[20]

Since 1946, when a connecting passage was built between the lower sacristy and the Archbishop's residence, it was no longer necessary to exit the building to the street in order to enter the Cathedral. A second connection was made in 1974 at the upper level through a door built in the chapel of St. Elizabeth. A year earlier a similar connection had been made between the parish house and the upper level of the Cathedral when an elevator was built allowing access through the chapel of Sts. Michael and Louis. Another improvement addressed a serious need for more space for meetings and classes.[21] Msgr. Rigney had the storage areas below the terraces around the Lady Chapel converted to conference rooms, creating two new areas with a connecting corridor. The cost was about $85,000. He also arranged for the construction of a new entrance for the parish house from Fifty-first Street. The new space under the north terrace contained a reception area and some small offices, and allowed passage directly from the street to the meeting rooms and the sacristy, an arrangement which eliminated constant interruption of workers in the parish house by those entering and leaving. An attractive granite facade was built at the entrance, all the work supervised by the James E. Mitchell Company.[22]

In 1975, Pope Paul VI canonized Mother Elizabeth Bayley Seton. Thus, the foundress of the American Sisters of Charity became the first native-born American to be declared a saint. New Yorkers were overjoyed that this daughter of the Archdiocese — born and raised in lower Manhattan — re-

ceived the great honor, especially the members of her order who have long labored in the City. Her home near the Battery is still lovingly preserved as a shrine. Cardinal Cooke wanted another shrine at St. Patrick's in her honor. John Bundschuh pledged resources for the purpose, and in September the altar of St. Stanislaus Kostka was demolished in preparation for a shrine at the altar's location. The statue of the Polish Jesuit was stored awaiting a suitable shrine in his honor in another location. Gasparri Studios was chosen to construct the Seton shrine. Frederick Charles Shrady designed and executed the statue and screen (*above*). The estimated cost was about $60,000.[23] Shrady was one of the most highly regarded of twentieth century sculptors. Born in New York, he traced his family roots to the colonial period when his great-great grandfather helped establish King's College, Columbia University today. By a remarkable coincidence, St. Elizabeth Seton's father also was one of the college founders. Since Shrady's father was a sculptor, young Frederick spent long periods observing his father at work. He once posed for his father who captured his image in the drummer boy of the Grant Memorial located in Washington, D. C. Frederick studied in Oxford, Paris and New York, and before World War II he achieved success as a painter with his art exhibited in museums throughout Europe and at the Metropolitan Museum of Art in New York. He married Maria Likar-Waltersdorff, a Catholic scholar and author, and he began a new career as a sculptor after serving in Bavaria during the War. His very first work was acquired by the Metropolitan Museum of Art, after which numerous pieces appeared in public buildings and churches around the world, including in the Vatican Museums and Gardens, the Basilica of the Incarnation in Nazareth, St. Stephen's Cathedral in Vienna and at Lincoln Center for the Performing Arts in New York. Mr. Shrady died in 1990. The five-and-one-half-feet high statue of St. Elizabeth was made at Mr. Shrady's studio, the Renaissance Art Foundry in Norwalk, Connecticut. Cardinal Cooke blessed the shrine during a ceremony just before the Midnight Mass at Christmas 1975.[24]

The following summer, Cardinal Cooke wrote to Msgr. Rigney that he was expecting "further news of the canonization of Blessed John Neumann," another American, and that he wanted to erect a shrine in his honor at the Cathedral. Four artists were considered for the project, and in March 1977 a model made by Herbert Gunther was selected. Mr. Gunther incorporated in his design a likeness of Old St. Patrick's Cathedral where this first American male saint was ordained on June 25, 1836. The $60,000 cost of the sculpture group was the gift of the Coleman family in memory of John Coleman. The new shrine replaced the altar of St. Augustine, who was further represented in the Cathedral by another statue and two windows. The altar statue of St. Augustine was given to the Augustinian Fathers who wanted it for their monastery at Marylake, Ontario, Canada.[25]

Herbert Gunther was born of Austrian parents in Bohemia. He studied sculpture in Prague, Germany, Holland, Greece and Italy. In the United States he became chief designer of ecclesiastical interiors at Bernardini Studios for which he directed restorations in almost three hundred churches. In 1969 he opened a studio in New York City, and maintained other studios on Long Island, New York, and in Italy. His other sculptures depicting St. John Neumann are in Saratoga Springs, New York, and at the national shrine of the saint in Philadelphia. At the Cathedral, he portrayed St. John as he appeared at age thirty, and he placed small children in the group, the inspiration for whom came from Gunther's own children. The four-ton statue was brought to St. Patrick's in February 1978, and Cardinal Cooke blessed it after it was in place. There was high praise within art circles for both the Seton and Neumann additions, although visitors sometimes expressed dissatisfaction about a modern treatment within a Gothic setting. Others found justification for such arrangements in other Gothic buildings in Europe.[26]

One more improvement was completed before the beginning of the centenary celebration of the Cathedral. A statue of the Virgin Mary for the roof of the Lady Chapel was included in Charles Mathews' drawings, but had never been made. Anthony Minervini made an eight-feet-high copper figure which was placed on the roof in September 1978, its smiling face overlooking Madison Avenue. The "completion" of the chapel was duly proclaimed.[27]

Just as the interior of the building had accumulated soot over almost a century, so the exterior facade looked dreary because of age and pollution. Cardinal Cooke and Msgr. Rigney were so pleased with the results of the interior restoration that they wanted to renew the outside. They sought the opinions of experts in stone preservation in 1977. The consultants suggested that a prolonged flow of pure water over the surface be used to clean it rather than chemicals or sand-blasting. The Nicholson and Galloway Company began work after Easter 1978, treating strollers on Fifth Avenue to the spectacle of twenty daring

workmen suspended by ropes and belts from the ten-story-high spires carefully washing a century of grime from crevices of the intricate stone carvings. The flow of water over the flat surfaces provided what architect W. Knight Sturges called "the best show in New York." Work was suspended during the winter, resuming with the return of good weather so that almost the entire Cathedral was returned to its original white color when the one-hundredth anniversary Mass was celebrated in May 1979, although some work continued into the following summer. The cost was over $1,300,000.[28] The next year, the Victorian Society in America presented its yearly award to the Archdiocese of New York in appreciation of the Cathedral's contribution to the beautification of the City; Jacqueline Kennedy Onassis presented a similar award for the Municipal Art Society in 1981, as Mayor Edward Koch joined society members in the Cathedral for the ceremony.[29]

The altar of St. Anthony was the most popular at the Cathedral. By general agreement of devotees of the saint and Cathedral authorities, the statue at the altar could only be described as uninspiring. Herbert Gunther was called upon for one more work and he produced an attractive bronze statue in July 1979. He made the clay model in his studio in Italy. Because of the popularity of the saint, new votive light stands with additional candle space were among other improvements made at the altar. The cost of the work was about $23,000.[30]

The single unfinished project of the decade was the re-establishment of a shrine in honor of St. Stanislaus Kostka to replace the one disassembled when the St. Elizabeth Seton chapel was added. From earliest years, the location of the baptistry in the last bay of the north aisle was considered only temporary; the space was thought to be ideal for a chapel of St. Stanislaus. Late in the summer of 1979, the baptismal font was moved to an open area in front of the Holy Family altar, and its oak cover was gilded and suspended above it, setting it in balance with the canopy over the tabernacle on the opposite side of the building. The baptistry table became a platform for the statue of St. Stanislaus in the former baptistry. The beautiful gates which enclosed the front of the chapel were removed and sent to the Craft Center Museum in Wilton, Connecticut under the care of Kenneth Lynch, until a decision could be reached about their future use. Mr. Lynch had made and donated the gates many years earlier. Eventually, the gates were sold at an auction conducted by Guernsey's, the auction company.[31]

Monsignor Rigney, like Cardinal Cooke, impressed those who knew him by his obvious interest in and charity towards people. He once said that he tried to avoid ever saying anything which might cause someone to blush, that he wanted people to feel always welcome at the Cathedral. Early in the 1970s, in order to fashion a fitting spiritual program for the faithful, and looking ahead to the end of the decade to prepare for a suitable centennial celebration of the Cathedral's opening, he decided to arrange a survey to learn "who comes to St. Patrick's." Volunteers conducted the random survey in the summer of 1973, questioning about 10% of those entering the building. It was learned that about one in four lived in the metropolitan area, but that almost 75% came from places outside the region. Almost half were first time visitors and only 15% made more than ten visits a year. Two months earlier, before the heavy attendance usual during the summer began, a count had been taken during one week to determine Mass attendance and numbers of visitors during hours when services were not being conducted. From the results, Msgr. Rigney projected that nearly 60,000 visitors entered the building each week and nearly 3,000,000 each year. Weekly Mass attendance was estimated at almost 13,000, and yearly attendance at over 660,000 with about 500,000 of them receiving Holy Communion during the Masses. Another survey confirmed what was strongly suspected — that those who attended Mass on Sundays were not the same people who attended on weekdays, and that the Cathedral had, in effect, two groups of "parishioners," those who came to Mass daily who considered the Cathedral their "workday parish," and the weekend tourists who came on rare occasions, perhaps once in a lifetime.[32]

A parish advisory committee was formed to help plan for the future, especially for the 1979 centennial celebration. In 1974, fifteen people formed the core of volunteers which would develop into a group of hundreds serving in several programs. At first, there were three programs: the *Young At Heart Club,* consisting of about two hundred elderly men and women engaged in social activites; the Information Service, a corps of men and women who provided visitors with a friendly welcome and information about the Cathedral; and

the staff of a new Cathedral magazine called *Alive and Well and Living in New York City.* The publication replaced the Cathedral Bulletin. Mrs. Penelope Ryan was engaged as Director of the Volunteer Program in 1975, and she administered the program until 1989. By the end of the decade, a program known as *Our Neighbors* was started, expanding the scope of the *Young At Heart* group, and enlisting scores

of volunteers (*like these at the left*) to assist the elderly in the community with ordinary activities like shopping, visiting physicians and cleaning apartments. Sometimes the volunteers simply provided companionship for the lonely homebound or brought them a friendly voice on the telephone.[33]

Monsignor Rigney was chairman of the Archdiocesan ecumenical commission and a member of the liturgical commission. He worked to instill a more ecumenical spirit into liturgical services and helped foster close relations with many other denominations. Throughout the decade, many ecumenical services were held at the Cathedral. In the spirit of the Second Vatican Council, Cardinal Cooke encouraged the effort. His Eminence was particularly close to Archbishop Iakovos, the Metropolitan of the Greek Orthodox Church in North and South America, and to Fr. John Andrew, Rector of St. Thomas Episcopal Church, whom he called his "co-pastor on Fifth Avenue."[34]

The diversity of background of New York Catholics was reflected in the languages used during Masses. The Second Vatican Council had allowed the use of the vernacular in the liturgy; in New York this did not necessarily mean English. Spanish-speaking Catholics, especially, found St. Patrick's a welcoming home when special services to honor national patron saints were celebrated in front of often-overflow congregations containing many immigrants from foreign countries. The Council had also strongly urged the use of Latin in Cathedral churches. At St. Patrick's, this exhortation was most often fulfilled through Latin musical selections sung by the choir.[35]

Several prominent sports and entertainment figures died in the 1970s, and often their funerals were held at St. Patrick's. Vince Lombardi, whose Green Bay Packers had won five National Football Conference championships, succumbed to cancer in September 1970. His funeral Mass was offered by Cardinal Cooke on September 7th. It was called the largest funeral at St. Patrick's since that of Robert Kennedy in 1968. The three thousand mourners included the entire Washington Redskins team whom Lombardi had been coaching at the time his illness forced him to retire the previous July.[36] Since Cardinal Cooke was visiting American troops as Military Vicar of the United States, Archbishop John Maguire, presided at a memorial Mass for Roberto Clemente, former Pittsburgh Pirates star, early in 1973. Baseball Commissioner Bowie Kuhn was among the sports figures and two thousand others who attended.[37] In the spring that year, Bishop Flannelly, the retired Rector of St. Patrick's, died at the age of seventy-eight after a short illness. His body lay in the Lady Chapel for three days until the Mass of the Resurrection was sung by Cardinal Cooke concelebrating with eighteen bishops and sixty-two priests. The third Rector was accorded the honor of interment in the crypt of the Archbishops of New York under the high altar.[38] A year-and-a-half later, Msgr. Rigney sang the Mass and Cardinal Cooke presided at the funeral of news journalist and television host Ed Sullivan who had lived in the parish. His *Ed Sullivan Show* had been telecast for twenty-three years to audiences sometimes as large as fifty million. He had been an active member of the Catholic community, involved with charitable causes; annually he had been master of ceremonies at the Christmas party given for the benefit of the Foundling Hospital by the Archbishops of New York.[39] Another popular local journalist, Bob Considine, died in the fall of 1975. A daily communicant at the Cathedral, he was mourned at his funeral by friends including Bob Hope, Walter Cronkite, Jack Dempsey, Bowie Kuhn, General Carlos Romulo and William Randolph Hearst.[40] In November, a memorial service was held for Casey Stengel, beloved in local and national baseball circles.[41] Fifteen hundred friends and associates of one of St. Patrick's most cherished parishioners, James A. Farley, came to his funeral on June 12, 1976. Archbishop Fulton Sheen was one of the bishops who concelebrated. Farley had faithfully attended the 9 A.M. Mass every Sunday until his death at age eighty-eight.[42] After the death of Pope Paul VI during the summer of 1978, New York Governor Hugh Carey, Senator Edward Kennedy and Mayor Edward Koch joined 3500 mourners at a memorial Mass for the only pope who, to that time, had ever visited this country and St. Patrick's Cathedral.[43]

After his retirement, Archbishop Fulton Sheen returned to live in New York, and he often appeared at the Cathedral. He delivered the Three Hours Reflection on Good Friday both in 1971 and in 1974, he was the homilist at the Mass of the Bicentennial of the United States on July 3, 1976 and he concelebrated at the Midnight Mass at Christmas 1977. At the Bicentennial service, the lay lectors were the First Lady of the Theatre, Helen Hayes, and the news commentator, Roland Smith. Cardinal Cooke was the principal concelebrant.[44] Other churchmen who came to New York's mother church during the 1970s included Cardinal Joseph Mindszenty, imprisoned by the Communist government of Hungary from 1948 until 1956;[45] Cardinal John Willebrands, President of the Vatican Secretariat for Promoting Christian Unity;[46] Cardinal Pio Taofinu'u of Samoa;[47] and two years before his election as Pope John Paul II, Cardinal Karol Wojtyla offered Mass for the City's Polish-American community, the second time he had done so at St. Patrick's.[48] And, for the first time ever, a Jewish rabbi, Ronald Sobel, addressed the congregation from the pulpit of St. Patrick's; ninety minutes later, Msgr. Rigney spoke at Temple Emanu-El on Fifth Avenue. The cause of ecumenism

An ecumenical gathering hosted by Msgr. Rigney at the Cathedral. If churches can't be ecumenical, how can a world be?

advanced considerably as, for the next several months, lectures and discussions followed the appearances at both locations.[49]

A nine-month celebration marking the centennial of the opening of St. Patrick's was scheduled to begin in August 1978 and to end on the anniversary of the opening in May 1979. The death of Pope Paul VI caused the beginning of the celebration to be postponed until October 18th to allow Cardinal Cooke enough time to attend a conclave in Rome to elect a new pope. But the sudden death of the newly-elected Pope John Paul I, just one month after he was chosen, caused another postponement. The opening ceremony finally took place on the steps of the Cathedral at noon on November 1st, 1978. Governor Hugh

The original cornerstone laid in 1858 was never found in all the excavations that went on at the Cathedral down the years. This plastic box would have to do. Parishioners and visitors could place in it any message they wanted to send to people looking back a hundred years from now.

Carey joined Cardinal Cooke, Msgr. Rigney, Mayor Edward Koch and Master of Ceremonies Walter Cronkite, the nationally-known news commentator. The Cardinal dedicated a symbolic *cornerstone of the future* and proclamations issued by both city and state inaugurating the celebration were read. Alton Marshall, President of Rockefeller Center, reminded the large assemblage in front of the building that St. Patrick's was "a place of hopes, dreams and aspirations." Long after the ceremony, dancers and singers representing varied ethnic and cultural traditions of the City's people performed for passers-by on the Fifth Avenue Cathedral terraces. A concert followed in the Cathedral that evening.[50]

To share in the joy of the centenary, Msgr. Rigney invited delegations of parishioners, choirs, lectors and clergy from around the Archdiocese to prepare, in the months ahead, their own liturgies at the Cathedral. Cathedral volunteers gave them tours of the building and served as guides. There were frequent ecumenical services and concerts during the seven months of celebration and non-Catholics took an active part.[51] Even foreign states caught the spirit. Monaco became the first foreign country to issue a stamp in honor of an American church in the one-hundred-thirty-year history of postage stamps. The November 12, 1978 limited edition issue depicted the Cathedral in a rural setting with horse-drawn carriages on Fifth Avenue.[52] As a sign of friendship from a sister church, Germany's Cologne Cathedral presented a one-hundred-thirty-six-year-old finial stone which had been taken from a buttress one-hundred-thirty-one feet from ground level. The stone had been quarried in Swabia in the south of Germany and was among those immortalized by Heinrich Heine in a poem he wrote: "It will not be completed, the Cologne Cathedral, although the fools in Swabia have sent a whole ship full of stones for its construction." Heine was wrong; Cologne Cathedral *was* finished six centuries after its construction started.[53]

The dizzying pace of celebration activity reached its apogee on May 12, 1979 at the Centennial Mass offered by Cardinal Cooke before the thousands fortunate enough to gain

entrance. In the sanctuary were Archbishop Jean Jadot, the Apostolic Delegate to the United States; five cardinals; nine archbishops; fifty bishops; over two hundred priests; and representatives of many religious denominations. The appearance of Archbishop Sheen, who spoke at the end of the service in spite of his poor health, delighted the congregation which included the governor, the mayor and scores of civic officials.[54]

Cardinal Cooke was not one to hog the stage. His entry gave due recognition of a great man, Archbishop John Hughes, whose vision made possible the century that was being celebrated.

The following September, there was a prayer service welcoming the fourteenth Dalai Lama, spiritual leader of millions of Tibetans. Possibly no other occasion could better illustrate the strong ecumenical movement in the Church at the time. Newscaster Lowell Thomas echoed the thoughts of most when he reflected: "Who ever would have thought the Dalai Lama would be at St. Patrick's Cathedral?" Over 5000 in the congregation overflowed into the streets for the hour-long service. The Cathedral event was the exiled Buddist leader's first stop on a twenty-two city tour of America. His enthusiastic reception at St. Patrick's was an extraordinary expression of good will by an extraordinarily diverse mixture of clergymen representing Armenians, Jews, Protestants and Catholics applauding sounds of clanged cymbals and horns, so unfamiliar to western ears, and never heard in western liturgies. The Dalai Lama's words were of compassion and love; Cardinal Cooke called the event "one of the dramatic 'movements of the Spirit' in our time."[55]

The decade of the 1970s at St. Patrick's was capped by the visit on October 2 and 3, 1979 of His Holiness Pope John Paul II. Elected to succeed Pope John Paul I one year earlier, the Pope already had made pastoral visits to several countries, and it was apparent that world-wide travel in the service of the Church was to be a mark of his papacy. As Cardinal-Archbishop of Cracow, Poland, he had visited St. Patrick's twice; his first visit as Pope was the second time a pontiff was stopping at the Cathedral during a stay in the City. The New York visitation had a two-fold purpose: to address the General Assembly of the United Nations, and to extend pastoral care to the Church of New York. The papal tour of this country began in Boston, continued to New York and moved on to Philadelphia, Des Moines, Chicago and Washington, D. C. Arriving from Boston in the morning of October 2nd, the Pope proceeded by motorcade to the United Nations Building where he spoke about justice and human rights. His official welcome took place at the Cathedral later in the day when Monsignor Rigney greeted him at the great doors and Cardinal Cooke was his host in the name of about three thousand well-wishers including Cardinal Medeiros of Boston and metropolitan area bishops and civic leaders. The Cardinal noted that the Holy Father came as a shepherd; the Pope replied that he came to confirm the faithful in their faith and to invoke the joy and strength Christians needed. An emotional highlight for many New Yorkers was the warm embrace the Pontiff accorded the beloved eighty-four-year-old Archbishop Sheen. A further indication of the pope's humanity brought laughter

when he used his handkerchief to wipe the brow of the young priest directing the sanctuary choir with all the intensity he could muster. That night, there was a Mass for 70,000 at Yankee Stadium televised to millions of viewers.[56]

Early on October 3rd, the religious and clergy of the Archdiocese assembled with the Vicar of Christ at the Cathedral for a prayer service, after which he met with Catholic youth at Madison Square Garden, called for peace in an address to a rain-soaked crowd in Battery Park, and bid farewell at Shea Stadium before departing from LaGuardia Airport in the afternoon. A familiar television image during the visit was that of Cardinal Cooke sheltering the Pontiff with an umbrella from wind-swept rains, whether riding through streets lined with greeters, or entering the Cardinal's residence on Madison Avenue where he was an honored guest. Msgr. Rigney proudly arranged for plaques commemorating the visit to be erected on the exterior walls of the Cathedral and the Archbishop's residence, companions of those marking Pope Paul VI's 1965 visit.[57]

When the Pope singled out Archbishop Sheen in the Cathedral for recognition, the old prelate's frailty was evident to onlookers witnessing his humble acceptance of the tribute. The Holy Father called him "a loyal son of the Church" who had "written and spoken well of the Lord Jesus." Two months later, the esteemed Archbishop died at his home in Manhattan. Nothing less than full ecclesiastical honors due the best-known figure in the history of American Catholicism could be expected when his body was brought to the doors of St. Patrick's on December 10th, the day after his death. Cardinal Cooke escorted his remains to the Lady Chapel to receive the prayers of the faithful passing his bier. Masses were offered on two days before his funeral Mass was concelebrated by five cardinals, forty-eight bishops and almost one hundred priests in front of dignitaries too numerous to name. The great preacher had stipulated in his will that he be buried at Calvary Cemetery in New York. That was not to be. The tradition of interment in the crypt of the Cathedral only for Archbishops of New York and Rectors of St. Patrick's was broken after one hundred years, as he was laid to rest under the high altar. One of the most beautiful possessions of the Cathedral treasury is the magnificent chalice the Archbishop bequeathed to St. Patrick's, a stunning work of art of Russian Jasper stone made by Kieber, the jewelry craftsman of the Russian czars.[58]

As in generations past, several 1970s Cathedral staff priests deserve note. Rev. James Mahoney, who served from 1971 to 1973, was ordained an auxiliary bishop of New York; Rev. Edwin O'Brien, who arranged details of the papal visit, was assigned as Rector of the

North American College in Rome, as an auxiliary bishop of New York, as Coadjutor-Arch-bishop and ultimately Archbishop of the United States Military Archdiocese; and Rev. Thomas Nielson was one of the privileged few who were stationed at the Cathedral for more than twenty years; he was master of ceremonies at many of the outstanding liturgies during his tenure, and a was competent assistant upon whom Msgr. Rigney relied with confidence.[59]

Monsignor Rigney announced in September 1970 that the organist of the Metropolitan Opera Company, John F. Grady, was appointed Director of Music at the Cathedral. The first native New Yorker to hold the position since William Pecher, he was born in Great Neck, Long Island, and began his musical career at the age of ten as a professional choir member at New York's Church of the Blessed Sacrament. He graduated from Fordham University and pursued graduate studies at Columbia University and at the Juilliard School of Music; he also studied organ intensively under Virgil Fox. His professional career began as Director of Music of the Fordham University radio station; often he was a guest organist at churches in the City, including the Cathedral, and he became the music director of the parish church of the United Nations, Holy Family Church, in 1965. He conducted the music at that church when Pope Paul VI visited there the same year, and he played the organ at the papal Mass at Yankee Stadium. Early in his career, he began concert tours in Europe, playing at Westminster Cathedral in London and at Notre Dame in Paris. He was appointed organist for the Metropolitan Opera Company in 1965, and continued in that position until his death. Three years before he came to St. Patrick's, he moved from Holy Family to St. Agnes Church where he founded the Concert Chorale; meanwhile he conducted concerts in the metropolitan area.[60]

In January 1971, Mr. Grady brought on his staff one of the most talented organists in the country, Donald Dumler. A native of Okeene, Oklahoma, Mr. Dumler graduated from the Juilliard School of Music after undergraduate study at the University of Oklahoma. He was associated with the Manhattan School of Music, and performed on national tours including appearances at Carnegie Hall and Avery Fisher Hall at Lincoln Center in New York, and at the National Cathedral in Washington, D. C. Gifted with perfect pitch – the ability to hear a sound and immediately to identify what note it is – from earliest years he was able to play music by ear, and he became a master of improvisation. One of his students was Prince Ali-Reza Pahlevi, the son of the Shah of Iran.[61]

Eight years before John Grady took up his post at the Cathedral, his predecessor, Charles Courboin, had begun a face-lifting of the gallery organ. The large pedal pipes were moved from a section behind the facade to the north and south triforia to help them blend better with the other pipes and to provide work room for repairs. Some ranks were added, and the pipes were revoiced on lower pressures.[62] John Grady continued making improvements, engaging the Delaware Organ Company to recover the reservoirs and chest pneumatics, to repair electrical relays and to fine-tune the entire instrument. He also hired an organ curator for routine maintenance once each week.[63]

Grady was determined to increase the size of the choir to produce fuller sounds which would carry better through the cavernous interior. He held auditions each September and invited singers from all over the metropolitan area to join. The number of choir members grew to one-hundred twenty, and at times to even more, so that all the singers could not be accommodated in seats in the gallery and some had to stand, sometimes for hours, during special liturgies. Grady introduced Sunday afternoon recitals or concerts with guest musicians; they came from local churches and from churches and cathedrals all over the world.[64]

James Heffernan

Monsignor Rigney urged his music director to develop a program of special concerts featuring great performers in an effort to make the Cathedral a haven of welcome to all. Classical religious music concerts began at the end of 1970-71, the first of which was a program in November featuring Leopold Stokowski conducting members of the Metropolitan Opera Orchestra offering a Bach cantata and other works. The following March, Zubin Mehta, conductor of the Los Angeles Symphony Orchestra (and later of the New York Philharmonic), led members of the Metropolitan Opera Orchestra in a performance of Verdi's *Te Deum* and Saint-Saens' *Symphony #3*. The Camerata Singers were directed by Abraham Kaplan. Stokowski returned the following December to conduct a program of Christmas music by Bach and Handel sung by the Cathedral choir accompanied by the American Symphony Orchestra.[65]

The early success of the concerts resulted in frequent presentations throughout the decade. Among many others were Richard Yardumian's Mass, *Come Creator Spirit* and Alan Hovhaness' oratorio, *The Way of Jesus,* a world premiere. Among the many groups performing were the American Symphony Orchestra and Chorale; the Fordham University Chorus; the Metropolitan Opera Orchestra; the choirs of Fifth Avenue Presbyterian Church, Plymouth Church of the Pilgrims and St. Bartholomew's Church; the world famous St. Thomas Church Boys Choir; the National Orchestral Association; the choir of the Cathedral of St. John the Divine; America's Youth In Concert Band and Symphonic Choir; the Riverside Orchestra; C. W. Post College Chorus; the choir of the Cathedral of Sts. Peter and Paul of Philadelphia; London's Salvation Army Band; and the Vienna State Opera Chorus.

Sometimes there were recitalists such as Enrico Arndi-condo, the first organist of the Vatican and Philippe Lefebvre, the organist of the Cathedral of Chartres, France. Annual programs in March in honor of St. Patrick, and in December for Christmas attracted large crowds. After several years, Msgr. Rigney found it expedient to engage a small firm headed by Mr. Richard Cassidy to handle concert arrangements and publicity.[66]

Concerts were also arranged to promote close cooperation with non-Catholic institutions in a spirit of ecumenism. St. Patrick's choir sang jointly with non-Catholic choirs both at the Cathedral and at other churches, either in concert or during religious services. In fact, many members of the Cathedral choir were non-Catholics.

During the 1970s there was an increased number of disoriented persons, some of them former mental patients, in the neighborhood of the Cathedral. Many were homeless people who sought out the warmth and peace of St. Patrick's, fearful of shelters or subways where they were sometimes attacked. The policy of the Cathedral was to allow them to remain in peace, so long as their behavior was not disruptive; since their attention to personal cleanliness was often non-existent, it became necessary at times to ask them to leave the building when bodily odor overwhelmed those in nearby pews. At other times, they might erupt in loud, even abusive, behavior. Thus, a neighborhood police officer became necessary.

These unfortunate persons rarely inflicted physical harm on others either inside or outside the building, although in January 1973 the courts ordered a hospital examination for a man who severely damaged the bronze doors with a sledge hammer and marred them with graffiti.[67] On another occasion, intruders smashed a small section of a stained glass window through which they gained entry into the building.[68] And so, a modern security system was installed. In 1972 a disruption stemming from an utterly unexpected source occurred. Seven religious sisters and a Catholic laywoman lay prostrate on the floor of the Cathedral during a Mass to protest American involvement in the war in Indo-china. When several nuns some time later asked permission to sponsor a Mass for peace in the Cathedral, Msgr. Rigney granted permission. But, the day of the Mass, Rev. Daniel Berrigan, a well-known opponent of the war, refused to concelebrate since he was not permitted to preach. He led a group from the building and conducted a service on the Fifth Avenue steps.[69]

The Cathedral's identification by some as a symbol of Catholicism in this country undoubtedly encouraged them to use it as a stage for publicizing their disagreement with teachings or policies of the Church. On the other hand, the Cathedral's prominence, enhanced after its designation as a landmark, was helpful in raising funds needed to defray steadily mounting expenses. Monsignor Rigney instituted the Cathedral Landmark Preservation Fund and the Friends of St. Patrick's Cathedral Fund to which both individuals and corporations responded generously. Rockefeller Center, Incorporated, always a good neighbor, was most unselfish with help, and several other companies were very supportive. A bequest from the estate of Antoinette Lindsay topped a long list of donations from individuals who gave substantial sums. Small donations from large numbers of the non-wealthy who wanted to help preserve the beauty of an important part of New York's religious heritage were received with heartfelt gratitude, as important as the "widow's mite" of the biblical parable.[70]

New York City granted landmark status to the Cathedral in October 1966. Ten years later, the National Park Service notified Msgr. Rigney that the Cathedral buildings had been designated a National Historic Landmark. New York State followed in 1981 when St. Patrick's was added to the New York State Register of Historic Places.[71]

By late in the 1970s it was discovered that the Chapel of Saints Faith, Hope and Charity was structurally "in desperate shape," and had to be razed. A new location was found on East Fifty-eighth Street between Lexington and Park Avenues, and the renovated theater was opened as a new chapel in November, 1978. Cardinal Cooke dedicated it on December 23rd.[72] Another building, the landmark Villard Houses on Madison Avenue, used for Archdiocesan offices, was proving very expensive to maintain, and the wisdom of using needed funds for its upkeep was questioned, especially since it did not afford enough space to house all the administrative divisions of the Archdiocese. But Cardinal Cooke was intent on preserving this treasure for the City, and so was elated when Harry Helmsley of Helmsley-Spear, Inc., one of the City's largest real es-

Alas, the building would meet the fate of its predecessor and have to be vacated in 1987. Several years ago, a group of Persian Sephardic Jews who had left Iran earlier opened a synagogue on the spot.

tate firms, began negotiations in 1974 to build a new hotel behind the houses, making use of the houses for parts of the new building. The design of the proposed Helmsley Palace Hotel was approved by the City's Landmark Preservation Commission which stated that with "good will and imagination, such as the Archdiocese has shown, old buildings can be adapted to viable new uses without impairing their architectural integrity." The Archdiocese retained ownership of the land and leased it to Helmsley for ninety-nine years, guaranteeing one million dollars annually to the Archdiocese. A new administrative office building with adequate space was opened on First Avenue at Fifty-fifth Street.[73]

While workmen were preparing the landmark buildings for restoration, they discovered stored in one of the Archdiocesan offices a treasure long-forgotten: forty-eight drawings of the Cathedral by the architect, James Renwick. Two of the larger renditions were treated to insure preservation, framed and hung in the Hughes Room of the parish house. The others were assigned to the Archdiocesan Archives where they were stored in receptacles designed to protect them from harmful exposure to deleterious elements, and to control levels of humidity and temperature.[74]

Two of St. Patrick's outstanding trustees died during the 1970s, John Coleman and James A. Farley. Mr. Coleman was an active supporter of Catholic charities all his life, to the extent that Cardinal Spellman had named a high school in his honor. He began his career at the New York Stock Exchange as a page boy at the age of sixteen. In time he formed his own Wall Street house and became Governor of the Exchange and chairman of its board of governors. He served as a Cathedral trustee intermittently for twenty years.[75] James A. Farley was associated with the Cathedral most of his life. It was said that Franklin Delano Roosevelt ran the country and James Farley, Democratic Party Chairman, ran the Hill (the Congress) during the Depression years. Joseph Connolly, chief usher at St. Patrick's for many years, recalled that he had been an employee of the Post Office Department when Farley was Postmaster General. He used to chuckle recalling how he would enlist the services of his "top boss" to pass the collection basket at Cathedral Masses.[76] Farley was one of the last pewholders. By 1978 there were only thirty-one pewholders remaining, so the tradition was discontinued after that.[77]

On one occasion, Msgr. Rigney was heard to lament that whenever he seemed to be making headway in his struggle to keep pace with rising costs, some unexpected expense gave a leading edge to the debts. The cost of insurance, for example, took a giant leap in the 1980s, and ordinary expenses continued to creep higher with growing maintenance costs. The heavily used pew kneelers were over half a century old in 1980, and attempting to stretch their life was considered almost stretching the power of faith. They were replaced at a cost of over $30,000. Some relief came from donors. The Brothers of the Christian Schools, who had donated the altar of St. John Baptist de la Salle, their founder, paid for its restoration in 1981 on the occasion of their tercentennial celebration. In August that year, the newly-opened Helmsley Palace Hotel on Madison Avenue assumed the cost of illuminating the facade of the Lady Chapel, installing a light source on the fifty-first floor of the hotel. The same month, the daughter of a famous American cabinetmaker, Karl Schmieg, presented Cardinal Cooke with a Chippendale chair handcrafted by her late father. It was one of only three he had made from a priceless beam of mahogany, one of the oldest in the world. Seasoned over four hundred years, the wood came from a house in Santo Domingo built between 1509 and 1515 in the city founded by Don Bartolome Colon, the brother of Christopher Columbus.[78]

After Pope Paul VI's 1965 visit, Cardinal Spellman had requested a remembrance of the occasion for the Cathedral; the Pope presented a bronze casting of a bust sculptured by Lello Scorzelli of Naples, which was erected near the northwest entrance. After the visit of Pope John Paul II, Msgr. Rigney decided to examine some of the work of Joy Buba, an American sculptress, considering a commission for her to commemorate the visit. He travelled with W. Knight Sturges, the architect, to Mrs. Buba's studio in Mt. Pleasant, South Carolina, after which she was commissioned to sculpture a bust of Pope John Paul II to complement that of Pope Paul VI. When she lived in New York, Mrs. Buba had created many bronzes including portrait sculpture at the American Museum of Natural History, the Audubon Society and the Metropolitan Museum of Art. Rockefeller Center's portrait plaque of John D. Rockefeller at the entrance to its skating rink in the promenade gardens is another of her works. Her bronze of Pope John Paul II was placed in the Cathedral in October 1982.[79] The same year, two Marian tapestries were suspended from pillars at the entrance of the Lady Chapel and were blessed by Cardinal Cooke. The handcrafted images of Our Lady of Guadalupe and Our Lady of Lourdes were made by Benoit Gilsoul, a New York artist.[80] Another of his creations, a massive bronze sculpture, is in the view of thousands emerging from Pennsylvania Station each day at the Thirty-first Street entrance of the Church of St. John the Baptist. Another 1983 project, one not visible to worshippers, was a third meeting room added to meet the need of expanding parish activities. Built above storage and work areas under the terrace, the room helped alleviate what was becoming a serious problem: scarcity of space for staff and volunteers.[81]

When the Cathedral opened in 1879, statues of Sts. Peter and Paul, given by Pope Pius IX, rested upon pedestals at the Sacred Heart altar. They had been removed decades earlier. Cardinal Cooke wanted new images in honor of the saints, and Adlai S. Hardin of Lyme, Connecticut, was awarded the commission for bronzes. Eighty years old at the time he made the statues, Mr. Hardin began his career in sculpture after a successful career as a senior executive of a major advertising agency. Despite his nearly sixty years of age when he began his new work, he received many awards and his work was exhibited in several permanent collections. His St. Patrick's statues were blessed by Cardinal Cooke after they were placed on corbels in the narthex in March 1983.[82]

In 1981, Georgiana Ioli was hired to direct the *Our Neighbors* program, assisting the Director of Volunteers. In order to identify elderly who might be in need of help, she conducted a survey of the parish; then, volunteers were recruited and a schedule of regular and special events was planned. Each week senior citizens able to walk to the Cathedral enjoyed a hot luncheon followed by entertainment or some social activity. Both those able to attend the luncheons and those confined to home became part of a network with volunteers who kept in constant touch with them, providing assistance both for emergencies and for ordinary needs. In addition, Msgr. Rigney employed social workers to assist the priests in helping the needy, the homeless and others requiring counseling for non-spiritual problems.[83]

When an international commission of Catholics and Lutherans announced that they had reached "a common mind on basic doctrinal truths," the Rector joyfully expressed his hope that in the 1980s St. Patrick's Cathedral would assume a leading role "in responding to the impulse of the Spirit," and encourage more ecumenical participation.[84] Accordingly, in June 1980, five thousand enthusiastic worshippers endured ninety-degree heat, the result of an inopportune malfunction of the air-conditioning system, to offer praise in word and song during a joint Catholic-Lutheran service.[85] A crowd estimated to be of equal size welcomed Brother Roger, the founder of the ecumenical monastery of Taizé, France in October. The son of a Swiss minister, Brother Roger was on a world-wide pilgrimage scheduled to end in Rome. On the New York occasion, groups of pilgrims who had gathered at points around the City converged at St. Patrick's.[86]

Under the direction of John Grady, the sounds of the Cathedral choir continued to dignify the rites of the Church. By 1980, there were one hundred thirty-eight choir members, making St. Patrick's the largest volunteer choir in the metropolitan region.[87] Renata Scotto, soprano of the Metropolitan Opera Company, sang with the choir for a recording in 1981; later the choir made another recording with the Canadian Brass Ensemble.[88] The next year, Msgr. Rigney expressed the hope that he could establish a permanent Cathedral orchestra and a second choir consisting of boys' voices. It was the success of the Sunday afternoon concerts and recitals which raised his hopes that an orchestra could become a regular feature of those concerts and recitals, and that the boys' choir or a choir of mixed boys and girls voices might sing each week at the 4 p.m. Sunday Mass.[89] Meanwhile, Grady continued to make professional tours in France, playing in the great Cathedrals and on French national radio. In recognition of his contributions to the fine arts, the French Ministry of Culture decorated him with the Order of Arts and Letters in October 1981. American Ambassador Arthur Hartman and Archbishop Lustiger of Paris honored Mr. Grady by their presence at the presentation ceremony in Paris. Among other special guests were conductor and pianist Daniel Barenboim, flutist Jean-Pierre Rampal and Mme. Sergei Prokofiev, widow of the Russian composer. In New York, to enrich the music program, Grady acquired the services of professional musicians as leaders of song, including James Javore and Harry Danner. Both sang with opera companies in New York and on tour in the United States.[90]

At the same time, the number of special concerts increased as a wide range of talent was introduced to St. Patrick's. The Cathedral choir accompanied by orchestra presented several religious programs, and the annual St. Patrick's Feast concert attracted guest musicians including the Irish tenor Frank Patterson. With increasing frequency, visiting groups performed inspiring music; in April and May 1982, thirty-three choirs sang at the Cathedral.[91] Guest soloists included some of the greatest from the world of music. José Carreras sang at the 1981 Christmas concert and he returned for other appearances later. In March 1981, Luciano Pavarotti sang several hymns at the World Day of Peace service before an ecumenical congregation. The Secretary-General of the United Nations delivered remarks at the conclusion of the service. Placido Domingo sang at the 1982 World Day of Peace service. And on the eve of the United Nations special session on world disarmament in 1982, over four hundred voices accompanied by an orchestra composed of members of the New York Philharmonic Orchestra, the Japan and Tokyo Philharmonic Orchestras and the Symphony for the United Nations kept listeners spellbound by their powerful presentation of the *Ode to Joy* from Beethoven's Symphony #9. Actor Barnard Hughes gave a fitting rendition of the accompanying text.[92]

The joy which filled the air during the last years of Cardinal Cooke's episcopacy was sometimes marred by unpleasant episodes. Beginning in 1970, a "gay pride" parade had taken place each year on Fifth Avenue. During the 1981 event some participants exited the line of march when they reached the Cathedral and staged a demonstration on the steps. The group included members of a local organization of Catholic homosexuals called *Dignity*. The protest was in opposition to Catholic teaching forbidding homosexual practice. One counter-demonstrator who attempted to disrupt the protest was arrested by police. The following year's parade brought more demonstrators to the Cathedral steps. Descriptions of the incidents in local and national news accounts resulted in a barrage of letters addressed to Church officials arguing that protestors should not have been permitted on the steps. By 1983, the police had cordoned off the steps and kept anti-parade demonstrators separated from marchers who again stopped the line of march in front of the building. As he did all his life, Cardinal Cooke continued to extend a kind hand to friend and foe alike, but his defense of Catholic teaching was unequivocal.[93]

In a painful incident months before his death, the Cardinal again took a strong position, this time against violence to rid Northern Ireland of British rule. Organizers of the St. Patrick's Day Parade in 1983 had chosen as Grand Marshal Michael Flannery, a supporter of aid to groups in Ireland linked to violence. The Cardinal issued a statement explaining that he disagreed with Mr. Flannery's position and that he could act in no way which might appear to condone violence. He met with Flannery privately, attempting to persuade the grand marshal to change his views, reportedly to no avail. When the parade began, the Cardinal and Church officials were not in their usual place for reviewing the parade on the steps of the Cathedral. When Flannery reached the building, he stopped the line of march waiting for the Cardinal to appear so he could give the customary greeting. After a brief time, he moved on; then the doors opened, and the Cardinal appeared on the steps. Many parade spectators gave the Cardinal a hostile reception, a response which hurt him deeply. But Flannery himself applauded the Cardinal's courage while adamantly clinging to his own position. Typically, Cardinal Cooke did not fault those who booed him; he considered himself to blame for not making his position clearer.[94]

There was one final event of exceptional happiness in the final year of Cardinal Cooke's life, the one hundred seventy-fifth anniversary of the Diocese of New York in April 1983. The Cardinal presided at a solemn pontifical Mass and made an appearance in the pulpit, something he seldom did. Among the honored guests were the Spanish Infanta Doña Pilar and New York Governor Mario Cuomo.[95]

In August 1983, Monsignor Rigney received an unexpected summons to return to New York from vacation. The same day, he announced to the staff of the Cathedral that Cardinal Cooke had received a medical diagnosis of acute terminal leukemia. What had been kept secret for eight years was quickly revealed — that His Eminence had been suffering during that period from lymphoma cancer and had been treated by regular blood transfusions. During the next six weeks, millions in the City and the nation came to realize what those close to him had always known: he was truly a holy man. He accepted his illness as God's will and the pain which accompanied it as a gift from God. The last pain-filled days of his life he called a "grace-filled" time; refusing pain-easing medication, he seemed more concerned about the grief of others than about his own suffering. On his deathbed in his residence, he struggled to receive President and Mrs. Ronald Reagan who departed deeply moved by his courage. As he was leaving, the President was heard to repeat again and again: "What a remarkable man!" It was the Cardinal's attending physician, Dr. Kevin Cahill, who first suggested he was witnessing the death of a saint. He proposed the Cardinal's cause for canonization.[96]

Death came early in October.[97] During the three days following the arrival of the Cardinal's body at the Cathedral, long lines of mourners passed the bier and Masses were offered attended by the military, the young, members of religious orders, Archdiocesan employees and other groups. For the funeral Mass, seven cardinals, seventeen archbishops, eighty-eight bishops and almost nine hundred priests filled the sanctuary and pews, together with a large contingent of non-Catholic clergy and representatives of civic government. After the Mass, the Cardinal's body was laid in the crypt under the high altar, but for the first time, a *galero* was not suspended from the ceiling above. The Second Vatican Council had discontinued the custom of cardinals being given galeros by the pope at the time of their elevation. Instead, Cardinal Cooke's wood-carved coat-of-arms was removed from the Archbishop's throne, and affixed to the wall of the Lady Chapel; thus, a saintly life ended and a new tradition was born.[98]

1. *Alive and Well,* September 1975; Kelly, *In My Father's House,* p. 67.

2. Kelly, *In My Father's House,* p. 119; Cohalan, *Popular History,* p. 327.

3. Groeschel, Benedict J. and Weber, Terrence L., *Thy Will Be Done,* Alba House, New York, 1990, pp. 87, 257; Cohalan, *Popular History,* 328; program of installation of Archbishop John O'Connor, March 19, 1984, ASPC.

4. Ellis, pp. 590, 594.

5. Kelly, *In My Father's House,* pp. 128-129; Carthy, *Magnificence,* p. 124.

6. *Catholic News,* June 13, 1968; file: Funeral of Robert Kennedy, 1968, ASPC. The Senator died on June 6th. At the funeral, eulogies were delivered by his brother, Senator Edward Kennedy, by Archbishop Cooke and by Cardinal Richard Cushing of Boston. Archbishop Cooke and Cardinal Cushing travelled to Arlington National Cemetery in Virginia for the burial service after the funeral Mass.

7. Groeschel and Weber, pp. 107-108; Cohalan, *Popular History,* p. 328.

8. Report of the Trustees of St. Patrick's Cathedral: *The Archbishops' Crypt,* March 1984, ASPC; file: Villard Houses, 1968, ASPC. The crypt report describes the chamber as containing twenty-one crypts numbered from left to right, top to bottom. Earliest information about the crypt had indicated there was room for forty-two burials. It is not certain if each burial chamber has space for two interments. The locations of those buried is as follows: #1: Archbishop John Hughes; #2: Cardinal John McCloskey; #3: Archbishop Michael Corrigan; #4: Cardinal John Farley; #5: Cardinal Patrick Hayes; #6: Msgr. Michael Lavelle; #7: Cardinal Francis Spellman.

Since 1967 the following have been interred: #8: Bishop Joseph Flannelly; #9: Archbishop Fulton Sheen; #10: Cardinal Terence Cooke; #11: Archbishop John Maguire; #18: Pierre Toussaint, #12: Cardinal John O'Connor. Information about the interments of the last five listed follows in the narrative history.

9. copy of Mass program, 1969, ASPC.

10. Tribute to Bishop Joseph Flannelly, 1973, ASPC; *Cathedral Bulletin,* November 1969.

11. file: Lenten Series, 1940, ASPC; Registration of Diocesan Clergy, 1969, ASPC; *Cathedral Bulletin,* November 1969; Minutes of meeting of Friendly Sons of St. Patrick, March 2, 1970; Rigney to Bishop Joseph O'Keefe, September 28, 1984; Rigney to Cooke, February 10, 1972, ASPC. In addition to his other offices, Msgr. Rigney was a member of the Archdiocesan Priests Senate. His weekly column in The *Catholic News* was entitled: *Why Not Ask?.*

12. Rigney to Cooke, July 26, 1971, Rigney to O'Connor, June 2, 1986, ASPC; file: Air Conditioning, 1970, ASPC. Philip Mitchell told the author in March 1995 that his appointment as Keeper of the Fabric was made upon the recommendation of W. Knight Sturges, the consulting architect.

13. Rigney to Cooke, July 26, 1971, Cooke to Rigney, July 27, 1971, ASPC; *Center Scope,* magazine of Rockefeller Center, November 11, 1971; agreement with Rockefeller Center, November 1, 1971, ASPC.

14. Rigney to Cooke, June 26, 1972, Minervini to Young, September 13, 1990, ASPC; file: Blessed Sacrament Altar, 1970, 1971, 1978, ASPC. Total costs of the renovation of the Blessed Sacrament altar were $54,681. *See:* Frank Woodruff to Rigney, June 21, 1972, ASPC. The actual name of Anthony Minervini was Mauro Antonio Minervini.

15. *Cathedral Bulletin,* January 1972; Rigney to Cooke, July 26, 1971, ASPC; file: Ramp for Handicapped, 1971, ASPC.

16. file: Restoration of Cathedral Interior, 1970, 1972, 1973, ASPC; *Cathedral Bulletin,* February, May 1973; Pittsburgh Paint News, undated issue c. 1973, copy, 1973, ASPC; When a column in the north transept was washed, it was found to be many shades lighter. Because of that, the decision was made to paint the plaster portions of the walls in shades as close as possible to

that of the marble piers.

17. *Ibid.;* Rigney to Cooke, October 31, 1972, ASPC; cost report of James E. Mitchell Company, December 7, 1973, ASPC.

18. *Alive and Well* magazine, February 1979.

19. Gasparri Studios to Sturges, May 7, 1973, ASPC.

20. Rigney to Cooke, July 11, 1973, ASPC.

21. memorandum of Archdiocesan Building Commission, May 28, 1974, ASPC; Mitchell Company to Burlington Elevator Company, September 27, 1973, ASPC.

22. cost report of James E. Mitchell Company, December 7, 1973, ASPC; Mitchell to Rigney, July 2, 1974, ASPC; architect's drawings and blueprints, 1973, ASPC.

23. file: Shrine of St. Elizabeth Seton, 1975, ASPC.

24. Hartford Courant, March 14, 1976; *The Critic* magazine, April/May 1967; *Catholic Twin Circle* magazine, August 10, 1980; *Time* magazine, April 4, 1969; *New York Times*, January 22, 1990; *curriculum vitae* of artist, 1990, ASPC; Who's Who In America, 1988; *Catholic News*, January 1, 1976; file: Shrine of St. Elizabeth Seton, 1975, ASPC. Neither Frederick Shrady nor his father, Henry, had formal training in sculpture. The statue is 5 ½ feet high and the screen is 18 feet long and 8 feet high.

25. file: St. John Neumann shrine, 1976, 1977, ASPC.

26. Gunther to Young, October 15, 1990, ASPC; *Alive and Well* magazine, July 1977, January, March, April 1978. The four-ton statue of the saint was moved into the Cathedral by placing logs under the crate encasing it.

27. *Alive and Well* magazine, August, October 1978. The statue was constructed from four feet by eight feet sheets of copper welded together.

28. *Alive and Well* magazine, *passim,* 1978 *and* October 1979; file: Restoration of Cathedral Exterior, 1977, 1978, 1980, ASPC.

29. award citation, June 4, 1980, ASPC; Carthy, *Magnificence,* p. 138; interview with Msgr. Rigney, May 1990; *Alive and Well* magazine, July 1981

30. file: Statue of St. Anthony, 1978, 1979, ASPC

31. file: Move of Baptismal Font, 1978, ASPC; file: Sale of Baptistry Gates, 1973, ASPC. The gates were sold for $28,000 in December 1985.

32. Survey of Visitors, 1973, ASPC; Rigney to Cooke, May 29, 1973, ASPC; General Report on Initial Questionnaire, June, 1972, ASPC.

33. file: Parish Advisory Committee, 1972, ASPC; *Alive and Well* magazine, February 1978. In conjunction with the *Our Neighbors* program, the Midtown Information for Senior Citizens program (MISC) was established at the Cathedral in cooperation with the New York City Department for the Aging. It provided information and referral services for the elderly and in its first year helped more than one thousand persons. *See:* Carthy, *Magnificence,* p. 144.

34. *Cathedral Bulletin*, November 1969; Groeschel and Weber, p. 120.

35. The Archives of the Cathedral contain printed programs of liturgies celebrated for a wide variety of groups.

36. *New York Times*, September 4, September 8, 1970; Delaney, p. 326. Lombardi was born in Brooklyn and attended Fordham University in New York. Early in his career, he coached the Fordham freshman football team.

37. *Catholic News*, January 11, 1973.

38. *Catholic News*, May 31, 1973; file: Funeral of Bishop Flannelly, 1973, ASPC. The bishop died in St. Clare's Hospital on May 23, 1973. His funeral Mass was offered on May 28th.

39. *Catholic News*, October 17, 1974; press release: Funeral of Ed Sullivan, 1974, ASPC. Mr. Sullivan was a columnist for the *New York Daily News* for forty-two years. The funeral was

on October 16, 1974.

40. *Catholic News*, October 21, 1975. Msgr. Rigney was the principal celebrant and eulogist at the funeral where Cardinal Cooke presided on September 29, 1975. Mr. Considine's column was syndicated by King Features.

41. file: Funeral of Casey Stengel, 1975, ASPC. The service was held on November 4th. Stengel had managed the New York Yankees to ten pennant championships and seven World Series championships between 1949 and 1960. *See:* World Almanac and Book of Facts, 1997, World Almanac Books, Mahway, N. J., 1996.

42. *Catholic News*, June 17, 1976.

43. *New York Times*, August 8, 1978.

44. file: Holy Week, 1971, 1974, ASPC; program of Mass of the Bicentennial of the United States, July 3, 1976, ASPC; McDonagh to Rigney, Dec. 14, 1977, ASPC.

45. New York Post, May 13, 1974. After his imprisonment, the Cardinal found refuge from 1956 until 1971 in the American legation headquarters in Budapest. He was at the Cathedral on May 12, 1974.

46. press release, Office of Communications of the Archdiocese of New York, 1974, ASPC. Cardinal Willebrands celebrated Mass at the Cathedral on November 24, 1974 on the occasion of the 10th anniversary of the promulgation of the Decree on Ecumenism of the Second Vatican Council.

47. file: Visit of Cardinal Taofinu'u, 1975, ASPC. Cardinal Taofinu'u preached during the weekend of October 16-17, 1976.

48. file: Visit of Cardinal Wojtyla, 1976, ASPC. Cardinal Wojtyla's visits were on September 30, 1969 and September 5, 1976.

49. file: Jewish-Catholic dialogue, 1975, ASPC.

50. file: Centenary of St. Patrick's Cathedral, 1978, ASPC; *Alive and Well* magazine, October, December 1978; Carthy, *Magnificence,* p. 140.

51. file: Centenary of St. Patrick's Cathedral, 1978, ASPC.

52. press release: Monaco stamp, 1978, ASPC. The stamp was a 2.10 fr stamp engraved by Pheulpin. Prince Ranier III approved the issue.

53. Press release: Finial of Cologne Cathedral, August 30, 1978, ASPC.

54. *New York Daily News*, May 13, 1979; *Alive and Well* magazine, May, June 1979.

55. *Time* magazine, September 17, 1979; *New York Times*, September 6, 1979. The interfaith service took place on September 5, 1979.

56. file: Visit of Pope John Paul II, 1979, ASPC; *Catholic News*, October 4, 1979.

57. *Ibid.;* file: Commemorative Plaques, 1979, ASPC.

58. Cardinal O'Connor granted permission for the first step in the process of the Archbishop's canonization to be initiated in December 1999. It consisted of a study of the life, writings and teachings of the Archbishop, a study which sometimes requires five years. *New York Times,* December 19, 1999; file: Funeral of Archbishop Fulton J. Sheen, 1979, ASPC; *Catholic News,* December 13, December 20, 1979; Carthy, *Magnificence,* p. 128; copy of will of Archbishop Fulton J. Sheen, 1979, ASPC; authentication papers of chalice of Archbishop Fulton J. Sheen, special file, ASPC

59. In December 1999, Father Nielson became the first priest on the staff of the Cathedral who was not Rector to be honored with the title *monsignor.* Decades earlier, a monsignor from Italy had served on the staff, but he had received the honor before arriving at the Cathedral. Catholic New York, December 13, 1999; interview with Msgr. Florence Cohalan, December 1994.

60. *Cathedral Bulletin*, October 1970; *Alive and Well* magazine, October, 1975, November

1990; information about the papal Mass at Yankee Stadium was provided to the author by Bishop Patrick V. Ahern and Msgr. Richard Curtin to author, July 1993.

61. *Alive and Well* magazine, October 1975; Sunday Oklahoman, August 11, 1991; information provided by Donald Dumler to author, 1991.

62. Remsen, Allan H., *Saint Patrick's Gallery Organ Revisited,* article of unidentified journal, copy in Archives of St. Patrick's Cathedral, 1962.

63. file: Organs, 1971, ASPC.

64. Carthy, *Magnificence,* p. 130; some information provided by John Grady to author, 1985.

65. file: Concerts, 1970, 1971, ASPC. The first Stokowski concert was held on November 29, 1970 and the second on December 29, 1971. The Mehta concert was on March 21, 1971.

66. program files, *passim,* 1972-1980, ASPC; file: Concerts, 1972-1980, ASPC. The Yardumian Mass was presented on March 5, 1972; the Hovhaness oratorio on February 23, 1975; the cantata *Berruecos* on December 17, 1978; and the Williams jazz Mass on April 22, 1979. Enrico Arndt-Condo played on June 25, 1979 and Philippe Lefebvre on November 16, 1980.

67. *New York Daily News,* January 8, 1973.

68. *New York Times,* October 25, 1979.

69. file: Demonstration in St. Patrick's Cathedral, 1972, ASPC.

70. file: Donations and Bequests, 1970-1982, ASPC; file: Landmarks Preservation Fund, 1979, ASPC.

71. file: Landmarks Designation, 1966, 1976, 1981, ASPC.

72. Carthy, *Magnificence,* pp. 125-126; *Alive and Well* magazine, December 1978; Halpin, *History of the Chapel of Saints Faith, Hope and Charity;* information provided by Msgr. James Rigney to author, June 1995.

73. file: Villard Houses, 1968, ASPC; Shopsin et al., *passim,* pp. 125-139; Kelly, *In My Father's House,* pp. 124, 190.

74. Inventory of Renwick drawings by W. Knight Sturges, 1978, ASPC.

75. Delaney, pp. 105-106.

76. file: Death of James A. Farley, 1972, ASPC; *Alive and Well* magazine, November 1982. Farley had helped Roosevelt in the latter's bid to secure the governorship of New York. In Washington, he was influential in generating much of the legislation of Roosevelt's New Deal. Later in life, he was Chairman of the Board of the Coca-Cola Export Corporation.

Joseph Connolly was succeeded by Richard Yosca who was an usher, then chief usher, for almost two decades in the 1970s and 1980s.

77. Rigney to Cooke, February 8, 1979, ASPC.

78. file: Kneelers, 1980, ASPC; file: Restoration — Altar of St. John Baptist de la Salle, 1978, ASPC; *Alive and Well* magazine, September 1981; file: Illumination of Lady Chapel, 1978, ASPC; authentication papers, Chippendale chair, special file, ASPC. The Santo Domingo house was built after the original city was destroyed by a hurricane in July 1502. After the building was demolished in 1929, some beams and boards were shipped to New York. The chair was made in 1935.

79. Joy Buba to Sturges, January 21, 1981. Mrs. Buba carved her signature on the left shoulder of the figure.

80. *Alive and Well* magazine, August 1982; file: Tapestries, 1978, 1980, ASPC.

81. blueprint file, 1983, ASPC.

82. file: Statues of Sts. Peter and Paul, 1981, ASPC; *Alive and Well* magazine, January, June, 1983; The Day, October 19, 1989; Door County Advocate, October 25, 1989. The blessing ceremony was on March 25, 1983.

83. Information supplied by Georgiana Ioli to author, July 1990; file: Social Workers, 1980, ASPC.

84. Carthy, *Magnificence,* p. 143.

85. file: Catholic-Lutheran Ecumenical Service, 1980, ASPC. The service was held on June 22, 1980.

86. file: Taize Ecumenical Service, 1980, ASPC.

87. Cooke to Rigney, undated memorandum, but 1980, ASPC.

88. Rigney to Thomas Z. Shepard, June 3, 1981, ASPC.

89. file, Music Program, 1981, 1982, ASPC.

90. *Alive and Well* magazine, November 1981; *curricula vitae* provided to author by Mr. Grady, Mr. Javore and Mr. Danner.

91. programs of concerts, *passim,* 1980-1982, ASPC

92. *Ibid.;* press release, World Disarmament Concert, 1982, ASPC

93. Catholic New York, June 30, 1983; *New York Times,* June 29, 1981; June 28, 1982

94. files: Demonstrations, Parades, 1981-1983, ASPC; Groeschel and Weber, pp. 127-129.

95. *Alive and Well* magazine, May 1983.

96. Groeschel and Weber, *passim,* especially p. 212.

97. Cardinal Cooke died at 4:45 a.m. on October 6, 1983.

98. file: Funeral of Cardinal Cooke, 1983, ASPC; Groeschel and Weber, p. 217.

CHAPTER X
The World Stops By: Cardinal John O'Connor

Bishop Joseph O'Keefe, the Vicar General, conducted the administrative affairs of the Church of New York during the last months of 1983 and early in 1984. He officiated at many events in the Cathedral which normally would have expected the presence of the Archbishop. Speculation about who would be selected by Pope John Paul II to succeed Cardinal Cooke grew with the passing months; one name frequently mentioned was that of Bishop Bernard Law of Missouri. But, when he was appointed to fill the vacant see in Boston, there was no consensus either in the press or among the clergy as to the Pope's choice. On January 31, 1984, the news came that Bishop John O'Connor of Scranton, Pennsylvania was to be the new Archbishop of New York.[1]

John Joseph O'Connor was born in Philadelphia, Pennsylvania, on January 15, 1920, the son of Thomas J. O'Connor, a craftsman in the gold-leafing trade, and Dorothy M. O'Connor. The five O'Connor children were raised in an atmosphere of deep Catholic tradition, and the future Cardinal was educated in the local public and Catholic schools. After attending West Catholic High School, conducted by the Brothers of the Christian Schools, he entered St. Charles Borromeo Seminary. He was ordained a priest of the Archdiocese of Philadelphia on December 15, 1945. For the first seven years of his priesthood, Father O'Connor taught and served as a guidance counselor at Catholic high schools; a work of special predilection was teaching the mentally retarded.

Chris Sheridan

For all his enormous talent and experience — still the priest. Here he confirms a handicapped boy.

During the Korean War, he responded to a call for chaplains by Cardinal Spellman, the American military vicar, and he entered the Navy. He served on land and sea for the next twenty-seven years in various assignments including service with the Marines in Vietnam. He earned many decorations and awards, and retired with the rank of rear admiral in June 1979, completing his last four years as Chief of Chaplains. While in the military, he earned several advanced academic degrees including a doctorate in political science. Expecting to return to his home diocese of Philadelphia in 1979, he was surprised to receive the charge from Pope John Paul II to serve as an auxiliary bishop to

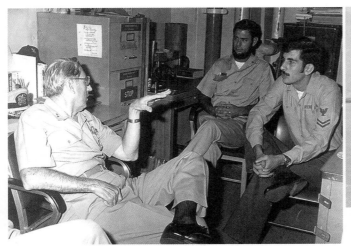

Duty might call him to the North Pole, but he could make friends anywhere!

the Military Vicar of the United States, Cardinal Terence Cooke. He was Vicar General of the Vicariate with offices in New York from 1979 until 1983, during which period he also served on the Committee on War and Peace of the National Conference of Catholic Bishops, and helped draft the pastoral letter, *The Challenge of Peace: God's Promise and Our Response.* His work on that panel brought him national attention, and in May 1983, he was made Bishop of Scranton, Pennsylvania, his first appointment in thirty-one years not associated with the military.[2]

Archbishop O'Connor took canonical possession of the Archdiocese during a March 18, 1984 ceremony at St. Patrick's, attended by thousands of priests and religious; the following day he was installed as Archbishop of New York in the presence of five cardinals, eighteen archbishops, over one hundred bishops, more than one thousand priests, and crowds of dignitaries. Many could not be accommodated even with additional temporary seating providing space for almost 3300; thus, in a spirit of ecumenism, St. Thomas Church on Fifth Avenue accepted some of the overflow crowd to view the ceremonies on closed-circuit television. A light-hearted moment of the event was when the Archbishop invited his namesake, one of the altar servers, to join him in the pulpit. To the delight of both the boy and the congregation, he placed his new miter on the the ten-year old's head, reminding listeners that he had another hat — a Mets baseball cap awarded him by that team. [3]

The Archbishop also was named Apostolic Administrator of the Military Vicariate. This was a temporary arrangement until an archbishop of a not-yet-created military archdiocese could be appointed, thus separating the Military Vicariate from the office of the Archbishop of New York, where it had been since its creation. In June, Pope John Paul II called Archbishop O'Connor to Rome to receive the *pallium,* the symbol of his office.[4]

The large space of the sanctuary in the Cathedral between the high altar and the altar rail placed the celebrant quite distant from the congregation. Because he wished to conduct the liturgy closer to the people, Archbishop O'Connor arranged for a temporary altar to be erected nearer the altar rail for the installation Mass. Afterwards, determined to remain near the congregation during future liturgies, the Archbishop ordered it to be left in place until a more permanent arrangement could be made. He announced his intention to celebrate personally the Cathedral solemn Mass each Sunday, as well as an early Mass each morning as often as his schedule allowed. At the daily Masses he delivered a short homily, and on Sundays he spoke at length. Within a short time, large numbers flocked to the Sunday solemn pontifical Mass to hear a new strong voice of the American hierarchy supporting the Church's ageless tradition. Each time he addressed important issues without vacillating from Church positions, the local press viewed him as playing "hardball on tough issues."[5] No other New York archbishop in history had so regularly appeared in the pulpit of St. Patrick's and so personally assumed a leadership role in defense of Catholic perspectives and authentic dogma. So strongly and consistently did he proclaim the sanctity of all human life and the evil of abortion, that his words reverberated in newspapers and periodicals around the country, and even beyond. Both supporters and opponents of his positions discovered a new conspicuous figure as, week after week, he applied the words of the Gospel to problems of the modern world: poverty, war, abortion, homelessness, sickness, sexual promiscuity, discrimination and many others; and week after week representatives of the media gathered inside the Cathedral recording his comments. If there were people in the nation who had never heard of St. Patrick's Cathedral, the extensive news coverage of Archbishop O'Connor's Sunday homilies rapidly reduced their number. When the Archbishop reiterated Catholic positions on abortion and homosexuality with wide coverage in the press, there was often heavy dissension and equally strong support from many quarters.

A frequent guest in the Cathedral when the Archbishop spoke was Mayor Edward Koch who became a close friend. The Archbishop's high public profile was enhanced by his custom of reviewing almost all the parades which passed the Cathedral, to the delight of both the sponsoring organizations and spectators fortunate enough to get viewing space.

In August 1984, Archbishop O'Connor appointed Rev. Benedict Groeschel, founder of the Franciscan Friars of the Renewal, as postulator and promoter for the cause of beatification of Cardinal Cooke. Father Groeschel, who had been the personal confessor of Cardinal Cooke, revealed that the Archdiocese was investigating the apparent miraculous recovery of a woman stricken with cancer, after prayers for the intercession of Cardinal Cooke were offered for her. Father Groeschel also revealed information about the Cardinal previously unknown to most people. Even the Cardinal's "closest associates were unaware that, for the last year of his life, he was in excruciating pain," which he suffered silently. In October, the Cardinal Cooke Guild was established to propagate information about and gain devotees to the cause.[6]

The following April, the Military Vicariate was formally separated from the Archdiocese; Archbishop Joseph Ryan became the first ordinary of the Military Archdiocese of the United States, and his installation ceremony took place at the Cathedral.[7] In the same week, an announcement was made that Archbishop O'Connor had been chosen by Pope John Paul II to become a cardinal. Before he left for the consistory in Rome, the Cardinal-elect, speaking tongue-in-cheek from the pulpit and referring to a directive he had received to wear red socks during the Vatican ceremonies, offered fifty dollars to anyone who might ever again discover him so brightly attired. And in a gesture of economizing, he ordered that Cardinal Cooke's red cape and cassock be reduced in size to fit him.[8]

Cardinal O'Connor received the red *biretta*, the square cap worn by ecclesiastics, from Pope John Paul II in a pageantry-filled ceremony in St. Peter's Square on May 25th. The new Prince of the Church later expressed his happiness at how smoothly the ceremonies were carried out, except when he happened to sit on his "new hat." About four thousand Americans, including Mayor Koch, made the journey to Rome; six days later, the Cardinal was welcomed joyfully at the Cathedral by other thousands including many religious and government leaders.[9]

The temporary altar which the Cardinal had ordered moved to the front of the sanctuary in 1984 was still being used at the end of 1985. Meanwhile, Msgr. Rigney investigated the feasibility of relocating the high altar and baldachin to where the temporary altar was. In fact, W. Knight Sturges, the consulting architect, had presented studies to do exactly that in 1966, a year before the death of Cardinal Spellman. Now, with Philip Mitchell, Keeper of the Fabric, Sturges revived those plans in cooperation with the architectural firm of Swanke, Hayden and Connell. The cost proved too heavy, however, and at the Cardinal's request, the beautiful altar table of the Holy Family altar was moved to the sanctuary in December 1985. It became the principal liturgical altar of the Cathedral. The reredos of the altar was left in place and restored in the summer of 1986, when the baptismal font was set in front of it on the former altar platform; the baptismal canopy was suspended over it.[10]

Chris Sheridan

The picture gives a sense of the distance between the altars.

For many years, little attention had been given to the upkeep of the Archbishop's residence and in 1985 extensive repair work was required, causing a sharp rise in ordinary maintenance expenses that year. The work took several months to complete. At the same time, Msgr. Rigney arranged for a restoration of the original wooden doors of the Cathedral transept entrances, which had not been included in the interior or exterior renovations of the 1970s. In fact, the doors were more than a century old. The wood was stripped and refinished, and broken and missing decorative bronze pieces were replaced. All the work was done by hand.[11]

In the fall, a new bronze statue of St. Jude, one of the Cathedral's most popular saints, was set on the platform of the Holy Face altar. The smaller figure it replaced was sent to Caracas, Venezuela. Adlai Hardin's earlier sculptures of the statues of Sts. Peter and Paul were so well-received that Msgr. Rigney gave the octogenarian the commission for the St. Jude statue which was received with equal enthusiasm. The $24,000 cost of the four-feet-eight-inches-high figure was a donation of Mr. and Mrs. Caswell F. Holloway, Jr.[12] In December, the stunningly life-like wood-carved figures of a Christmas creche arrived from the studios of Vincenzo Demetz Figlio in Val Gardena, Italy. The set was missing an angel which Mr. Figlio later donated in memory of his daughter, the tragic victim of an avalanche. Mr. Figlio carved the image of his daughter in the face of the angel.[13]

In 1986, the Museum of Fine Arts in Houston, Texas included in its exhibition of American presentation silver the St. Patrick's Tiffany monstrance. Before it was placed on display, the sacred vessel, made in 1942, was appraised at $100,000 by J. Shrubsole of London. It was forty inches high and made of silver set with twenty-two amethysts. According to a Tiffany publication, silver is associated with purity which has guaranteed the precious metal "an important role in Christian liturgy."[14]

The second Chapel of Sts. Faith, Hope and Charity suffered the fate of its predecessor when it was closed in March 1986. Part of one wall was discovered separated from the ceiling, and several cracks were found in the floor and walls. The severe structural damage rendered it unsafe for any future use. The two chapels had served the northeast sector of the parish for twenty-eight years.[15]

Ten years after it began, the Cathedral volunteer program was "alive and well" and growing by 1985. At the end of 1984, there were over three hundred volunteers, not including volunteer choir members. There were ten separate programs in which volunteers contributed more than one thousand hours each week. "Our Neighbors" volunteers assisted the elderly; forty others provided service for visitors at the Cathedral information desk; forty-one were tour guides; one hundred eleven helped at special events including concerts and major religious services; twenty-four served on a communications team as photographers, designers and public relations specialists; young adults provided social and cultural activities and worked with children of welfare recipients; administrative aides helped to train new volunteers; others helped with a cooperative midtown information service, with the homeless in shelters, with YWCA cooperative programs, with the students of the Juilliard School of Music who played at the Cathedral and with art education programs. By 1987, the number of volunteers had grown to four hundred seventy-one, including one hundred thirty members of the choir. In addition, dozens of volunteer ushers regularly assisted the regular staff at one of the eight daily or Sunday Masses, or the twelve Masses on holy days.[16]

Sometimes volunteers were asked to rearrange their personal schedules on short notice when help was needed, and with remarkable dependability they responded regularly. Often they were called for assistance at funerals of well-known

Chris Sheridan

The current Director of Volunteers is Roberta Shea. This marvelous picture catching her in the reflection of the cathedral on the building across from it speaks eloquently both of the Cathedral's concern for the community and the role of the laity in its mission.

figures when a large attendance was expected. At the 1985 funeral of Roger Maris, who had set the all-time record for Major League Baseball home runs in a single season, sports personalities were in abundance in the Cathedral.[17] The next year funeral Masses were offered for Harry Van Arsdale, the labor leader, and Congressman Joseph Addabo.[18] Four thousand fire and police officers came to honor police officer Francis J. La Sala who died of injuries sustained in a heroic effort rescuing people from a burning building.[19] In 1987, Prince Michael of Greece attended a memorial Mass for Andy Warhol, the artist.[20] Later

that year, former President Richard Nixon attended the funeral Mass of Clare Boothe Luce.[21] Cardinal O'Connor regularly was the principal celebrant at all these special liturgies, as he was on many other occasions which attracted large crowds, such as a Mass at the opening of the Marian Year;[22] a Mass in celebration of the six hundredth anniversary of Lithuanian Christianity; and a Mass of welcome for President Oscar Arias-Sanchez of Costa Rica, recipient of the Nobel Peace Prize.[23]

The Cathedral stayed in tune with the traditions of the nation and was a popular place to celebrate them.

A year earlier, to mark the centenary of the Statue of Liberty, a bell-ringing ceremony on the Cathedral steps (*right*) brought together an illustrious group of religious, political and entertainment industry figures: Cardinal William Baum from Rome; Archbishop Pio Laghi, the Apostolic Delegate to the United States; former Chief Justice of the Supreme Court Warren Burger; United States Senators Alfonse D'Amato and Daniel Patrick Moynihan; United Nations Ambassador Vernon Walter; Mayor Edward Koch; Chrysler Corporation President and Liberty Weekend Chairman Lee Iacocca; and entertainment figures Bob Hope, Helen Hayes, Frank Patterson and Robert Merrill.

Chris Sheridan

After the Marian Year Mass, a replica of the Lady Chapel statue, Our Lady of New York, was carried from the Cathedral to begin a year-long journey through the Archdiocese, as a pilgrim statue for the parishes. Each year during Holy Week, Cardinal O'Connor conducted all the major services and gave the Good Friday *Three Hours Reflections* on the passion and death of Christ, as Archbishop Sheen had done through several decades. All afternoon, thousands passed in and out to hear portions of the service, and some stayed all day in a spirit of prayer and penance on the most solemn day of the Church year. Holy Week culminated in glorious Easter morning rejoicing at the Cardinal's solemn pontifical Mass whose joy equaled or surpassed that of the traditional Christmas midnight Mass.[24]

On the most festive occasions, magnificent floral arrangements were created by Frank Simeola of New Rochelle, New York, a work of loving care since 1949. After his death, the Roehrs Company carried on the tradition of design excellence.[25] One very special occasion was the June 1985 ceremony of profession of vows of the Missionaries of Charity, the order founded by Mother Teresa of Calcutta, who delighted those in the Cathedral when she attended the ceremony. Noone more happily caught the attention of visitors than Mother Teresa whose deep reverence and prayerfulness was evident to those fortunate enough to be in the Cathedral on that occasion, or in October the same year when Cardinal O'Connor invited her to address the congregation during a solemn pontifical Mass.[26]

Chris Sheridan

Unknown to many, the Cardinal founded a diocesan congregation of religious himself. It is called the Sisters of Life and is flourishing today.

Security at the Cathedral had to be strengthened when the same problems the rest of the City, indeed the country, was experiencing began to affect St. Patrick's with troubling frequency. In April 1985, before the beginning of a scheduled concert, an unemployed man entered the sanctuary and announced to those gathered for the program that he held a bomb in a plastic bag he was carrying. After he was removed, the bag was found to contain no explosives and he was committed to Bellevue Hospital for psychiatric evaluation. In November, armed robbers forced ushers to empty the Church safe of $7000. They were arrested two weeks later. The following winter, two burglars fled from the Archbishop's residence when confronted by the Vicar General and a housekeeper.[27] Because they affected the sacred liturgy, the most troubling problems were those by members of the homosexual organization *Dignity*, which wanted Catholic teaching changed to reflect their position that homosexual behavior was not immoral. Before 1987, their protests were held outside the Cathedral during the annual Gay Pride Parade in June. But, beginning in 1987, members began appearing inside the Cathedral during Cardinal O'Connor's Sunday Mass, standing during his homilies, and turning their backs to him while he addressed the congregation. When the protests became a regular occurrence on the first Sunday of each month, a court injunction was issued against further interference with the sacred liturgy.

Eventually, police officers were summoned to remove those who refused to desist from their behavior during the Mass.[28]

A sad announcement was made in the summer of 1987 that, upon advice of his physician, Msgr. Rigney had requested a leave of absence from his office, as his progressively more burdensome sickness showed no signs of improving. Cardinal O'Connor granted the leave and appointed Rev. Anthony Dalla Villa, an assistant at the Cathedral, as temporary administrator, beginning in September 1987.[29]

Early in 1988, Monsignor Rigney informed Cardinal O'Connor that he had been advised by his physicians not to return to work, and had decided, therefore, to retire. At the conclusion of the Mass of Chrism during Holy Week in March, the Cardinal announced the appointment of Father Anthony Dalla Villa as the fifth Rector of St. Patrick's.[30]

Anthony Dalla Villa was born in New York City in April 1938, the son of immigrants from Colombaro in Brescia, northern Italy. His early education took place in the Bronx, and after a year of high school, he attended Cathedral Preparatory Seminary. He entered St. Joseph's Seminary in 1958 and was ordained a priest in May 1964. His first assignment was as a curate in St. Dominic's parish in the Bronx, after which he served at Our Lady Queen of Peace parish on Staten Island. Meanwhile, he continued his education specializing in family therapy. He received a master's degree in clinical social work and was licensed in New York as a social worker. He was assigned to St. Patrick's Cathedral as an assistant in 1980.

The Cathedral was not strange territory for him, since he had often been an altar server when he was young. Beginning in 1982, while still performing his duties at the Cathedral, he was Director of the Italian Apostolate of the Archdiocese. When appointed Rector, he was moved to comment that he felt deeply privileged to lead a community of strong faith, evidenced by the high occupancy of the pews on Sundays and holy days and especially during Holy Week each year, and by the long lines at the confessionals.[31]

During his first year in charge, Father Dalla Villa continued the improvements begun by his predecessor. He found that, after fifty years of heavy traffic and because of damage from water seepage, the Fifth Avenue steps needed extensive repair. During a program lasting several months, each section of granite was removed and carefully reset. A more serious problem was a leaking roof; repairs were required over the chapels and the nave, and the entire triforia roof areas had to be replaced. The frequent presence of television cameras in the Cathedral for the daily morning Mass offered for the homebound by Cardinal O'Connor, for the Cardinal's Sunday solemn pontifical Mass and for special liturgies such as Christmas midnight Mass required improved lighting. An extensive system of high power lamps which could be moved automatically on tracks from the triforia into the nave, and other non-movable lamps in the triforia directing light toward the high altar were the centerpiece of a general illumination improvement throughout the building. New accent lighting was also installed at altars and several other areas such as the Pieta statue. But the extremely hot temperatures produced by the new dimmers needed for the lighting caused concern about fire breaking out in the triforia. Over the next two years, modifications were made and the dimmers were moved into the towers where masonry walls reduced the danger.[32]

The presence of television camera crews, sometimes several at the same time, often caused obstruction of the view of worshippers by electronic equipment. Cardinal O'Connor wanted to provide the media an open view, but wished also to eliminate distractions. Thus, several pews were removed from a section in the south transept where a media platform was built, equipped with power lines for cameras and lights, close to the sanctuary but behind the pews of the congregation. Another improvement was a new speaker system controlled from a sound booth in the north ambulatory near the console of the chancel organ. A technician in attendance at all special liturgies controlled the system, which had a wireless sound feature and zone volume control.[33]

The Rector also appointed a volunteer who for several years had conducted research of the Cathedral's history to organize a small archives consolidating files scattered about the buildings. Two years later, a small room was renovated to house the archives, which began to acquire important historical records from a variety of sources and to preserve current records. Among the acquisitions were many Renwick drawings previously believed lost.[34]

In June 1988, Cardinal O'Connor blessed small statues of two saints new to the Cathedral. Herbert Gunther designed ivory statuettes of St. Benilde Remancon and St. Miguel Cordero for the altar of St. John Baptiste de la Salle, founder of the order of Christian Brothers. Both saints were members of the order and had been canonized in recent years.

St. Benilde was a teacher in France in the nineteenth century and St. Miguel served in Ecuador in both the nineteenth and twentieth centuries. James O'Donnell, a benefactor of the Christian Brothers, paid for the statues.[35]

St. Frances Cabrini, who had worked among the poor in New York, did not yet have a shrine or statue in St. Patrick's, although a statuette was on the exterior doors. Father Dalla Villa was eager that a memorial in her honor join those of other New York saints inside the building. He decided against replacing existing altars or shrines to construct one for St. Frances. Instead, he commissioned Elizabeth Gordon Chandler, a sculptress from Old Lyme, Connecticut, to create a relief sculpture which could be affixed to the west wall near the north tower entrance. Ms. Chandler wrote that her goal was to capture in the high relief figure of the saint her love and compassion, and in the bas relief representing Italian immigrants their determination to overcome the hardship and uncertainty of a new life in America. The

Perhaps Father Dalla Villa was impressed with this amazing Sister who founded sixty-seven schools, hospitals, orphanages, and missions — one for every year in her life — spread over eight States, four Latin American and four European countries.

sculpture was erected before Christmas 1989 in memory of Bette Friedheim, and was a gift of her husband, Eric. Ms. Chandler's work is found in many public buildings in the United States, and has won her dozens of awards. Her artistic talents extend beyond sculpture to the field of music: she was a concert harpist earlier in her life.[36]

Fr. Dalla Villa continued to beautify the Cathedral in several ways during 1990, the year he was honored by the Holy Father by receiving the title *monsignor*.[37] He replaced concrete walks with bluestone on the Fiftieth Street terrace and had new shrubs and ground cover planted on both north and south terraces.[38] During warm months, flower beds provided colorful blossoms. Inside, beautiful floral arrangements began to appear regularly on the high altar, in the Lady Chapel, at the Blessed Sacrament altar and often at other altars. The flowers were donated by Florence D'Urso who had worshipped at the Cathedral for many years. On one occasion, someone had given her a bouquet of roses as a gesture of thanks for her generosity to Calvary Hospital. She placed the flowers in the Lady Chapel, afterwards deciding she would continue her floral donations on a weekly basis. She spent long hours personally arranging floral creations each week, not only in the Lady Chapel, but at the high altar and other altars; in time, visitors found her designs rarely missing. Monsignor Dalla Villa also engaged the Patrick Baker Company of Southington, Connecticut to execute a restoration of the stations of the cross. Damaged marble was repaired and the figures were cleaned to a high lustre.[39]

Near the end of the year, Cardinal O'Connor made two important decisions affecting St. Patrick's. Troubled that a large number of tourists often passed the Blessed Sacrament altar in front of those praying in pews, he directed that the tabernacle where the Holy Sacrament reposed be moved to the Lady Chapel altar; there visitors would pass *behind* those at prayer. The move was made in November and, as a temporary measure, a bible was set on the empty pillar where the tabernacle had been. In December, the remains of Pierre Toussaint, the saintly former slave who had been buried in the graveyard of Old St. Patrick's Cathedral, were reinterred in the crypt under the high altar. He was the first layman whose remains were placed in the crypt. Many New Yorkers maintain a devotion to Pierre Toussaint, hoping for his canonization as a saint. Cardinal O'Connor hoped that, with the saintly man's remains in the Cathedral crypt, devotion to him would spread.[40]

It was becoming evident by 1990 that extensive repairs and restoration work required new sources of capital.[41] For example, the organs had endured decades of stop-gap repairs, but a complete restoration or replacement was overdue; a sprinkler system was decidedly the only dependable safe measure against the danger of fire; the original window frames in the rectory and Archbishop's residence were decaying; the striking mechanisms for the bells were barely functional; and the air conditioning system was considered unrestorable. The largest fund-raising campaign in the Cathedral's history was launched with a goal of raising almost ten million dollars over several years. Msgr. Dalla Villa expanded the space in the gift shop and increased the hours it was open while widening the variety of materials for sale. Almost immediately revenue increased, thus alleviating some of the problems of funding necessary repairs.[42]

Impetus for a successful drive was provided by a pledge of one million dollars by Florence D'Urso. After other pledges brought the total to over two million dollars, preparations began to restore the organs. Even though under John Grady there had been a rebuilding and revoicing of sections of five of the seven main organ divisions, those measures could delay, but not remedy, the failing condition of the instrument. The organs were six decades old and during their lifetime had been subjected to usage unparalleled in other churches in the City; indeed, some consultants were convinced they ought to be retired and new instruments built. So, John-Michael Caprio, Grady's successor, wanted a professional evaluation. He urged the Board of Trustees to appoint Nelson Bardon of Bardon Associates to complete a study. The Bardon consultants were curators of the Boston University symphonic organ. They had restored hundreds of instruments in this country including the historic Old South Church organ in Boston and organs in the Cathedrals of Buffalo and Philadelphia. Bardon's report found the gallery organ was "built like a battleship," and was "perfectly placed in a magnificent building"; he believed that with attentive maintenance and periodic restoration it would last through the next century and even beyond. He called it "an American-made Packard touring car," and said its case was considered by organ authorities to be the most beautiful in any Roman Catholic church in America, and one of the finest in the world. He recommended that new twin consoles be built linking the gallery and chancel organs so that both could be played simultaneously from either console. He suggested that they be rebuilt entirely and that the facades be restored to their original luster. The Board agreed. Robert M. Turner of West Covina, California was awarded the contract for the new consoles and the Peragallo Pipe Organ Company of New Jersey won the contract to restore the facade and all the pipes.[43]

The consoles arrived in October 1993 and were in full use by the end of January. Before work began on the chancel console, it was brought into the narthex where it was displayed for several weeks allowing visitors a close inspection of the imposing five manuals, pedals and stops. By the end of February 1994, the gallery facade was unveiled, fully cleaned and restored by Warwick Refinishers. Its magnificence was highlighted by special lighting. Meanwhile, in the chambers behind it, setting the summer of 1996 as a target date for completion, the Peragallo Company slowly restored pipe after pipe, division after division.[44]

The caprices inherent in old age afflicted more than just the organs. More than just occasionally the north tower elevator stranded choir members midway between floor and gallery during 1991. A new elevator which lowered the singers achieved the same result for their blood pressure. At the opposite end of the building, the Lady Chapel's marble mosaic floor was in extremely poor condition. Decades earlier, about one-third of the mosaic had been replaced with Tennessee marble, but the remaining floor was cracked and parts of the mosaics were missing. In 1990, the worst section, the east end near the altar, was replaced. Plans to restore the entire surface with marble identical to the original mosaic had to be abandoned in 1993 in favor of the more demanding needs of the organ and fire prevention. Attention to the bells in the north tower above the office of the Director of Music could not be postponed. Msgr. Dalla villa was informed by an inspector that the music office might be threatened with unwelcome visitors from above unless immediate work begin to recondition them. Ladders and platforms located at internals were removed and steel replacements were built. New strikers were installed for the bells by the Schulmerich Carillon Company. Months of silence were broken in February 1992 when the bells rang out a Westminster chime every hour until 8 p.m. At noon and at 6 p.m. the Angelus was sounded, each time followed by the playing of several hymns. A series of hymns was played also every Sunday morning before the solemn pontifical Mass.[45]

Just before Christmas 1991, Cardinal Ernesto Corripio, Archbishop of Mexico City and Primate of Mexico, presented Cardinal O'Connor with an eighteenth century painting of Our lady of Guadalupe, patroness of Mexico. The anonymous artist was probably a disciple of Miguel Cabrera, and the painting was a gift of the faithful of the Archdiocese of Mexico to St. Patrick's. A Mexican peasant, Juan Diego, saw an apparition of the Virgin Mary in 1531 after which her image appeared miraculously on his cactus cloak. The cloak today is enshrined in a Mexico City basilica where millions of pilgrims gather each year to pray. After several attempts to settle upon a location in St. Patrick's suitable for the painting, it was lifted over the pillar in front of the Sacred Heart altar and

suspended from the magnificent canopy above it (*above*) New York's Mexican-American community find it a favorite place of devotion to their patron.[46]

The baldachin over the high altar reached its fiftieth birthday in 1992. It had last been refinished in 1970, but by the 1990s had become dull. Florence D'Urso donated costs of cleaning and polishing it early in 1993, after which it was sealed by a protective coating. The cost was $35,000. Matching its new brilliance were the consecration crosses and candle holders mounted at various locations of the Cathedral walls and the candlesticks and crucifixes on all the altars in the chapels which also were refinished.[47]

The Shanley and Sturges survey of 1963 had suggested that television monitors be placed in locations in the Cathedral where there was no open view of the sanctuary, such as sections of the chapel aisles where pillars rose between the pews and the high altar. Electronic Media Tech of Long Island, New York, the company which had installed the sound system in 1989 and whose technicians controlled it from the sound booth during special events, were engaged to affix platforms to pillars and set television monitors on them during the summer of 1994. By September the monitors were in use each Sunday during the solemn pontifical Mass celebrated by Cardinal O'Connor and whenever large numbers of congregants filled the chapel aisles. Cameras for the closed-circuit system were set unobtrusively high on pillars and the sound booth technicians controlled their movements and recorded the liturgies on video tape. Aesthetics suggested that the audio-video sound booth, adjacent to the chancel organ console, should be enclosed with the console by a screen which duplicated the Robert Reiley carvings of the sanctuary screen. Patrick Baker and Sons received the commission. Under their direction, Hans Kraenzlein, a German wood-carver, executed the English oak screen, working for six months to complete it in time for Easter 1995. The screen was built in sections which could be opened to allow the organ console to be moved on a sled-like platform upon which it rested for routine maintenance, as well as for facile access to components of the sound system. Plans were drawn by the James E. Mitchell Company, and the finished ensemble blended perfectly with the sanctuary screen abutting it.[48]

One hundred sixteen years after the Cathedral opened, what had preoccupied architects, rectors, trustees and archbishops almost from the beginning — the danger of fire — was reduced somewhat when the first elements of a fire suppression system were adopted by the Board of Trustees. Earlier fears that plaster loosened by water from sprinklers might prove a greater danger than fire were allayed by advances in technology. Modern dry pipe or mist automatic sprinklers were available in the 1990s, as was technology for early warning systems facilitating rapid evacuation before injury to people could occur. When this information was presented to the trustees in June 1991, preliminary studies were ordered. The architectural firm Beyer, Blinder and Belle prepared drawings for the first phase – the basement and cellar – and the installation was completed during 1995. Planned for phase two was the protection of the ceiling and triforia of the Cathedral.[49]

Pope John Paul II was expected to visit St. Patrick's for a second time as Pope in 1994. The entire exterior facade had been cleaned before the last visit; this time a more modest program of brightening the stone was deemed sufficient. Steam and water was applied as high as the balustrade on the Fifth Avenue front and as high as the chapel roofs on the north and south sides. To reduce costs, the Cathedral maintenance staff did the work rather than a professional company. It was critical to keep costs moderate because in just one year — 1994 — operating expenses had increased by 16% due to the addition of personnel and the need to "catch up" with projects not addressed for a long time. After the cleaning was done, the marble had an even color shade. Inside the building, most of the sixty-seven-year-old pews were stained in preparation for the papal visit.[50]

The new personnel at the Cathedral included, for the first time, a permanent deacon assigned a few days each week. For several years, deacons had assisted only at the midday Masses and at the solemn Mass on Sundays. By 1995, two deacons were at the Cathedral four days each week. Before their arrival, a full-time social worker had been employed to assist the clergy with non-spiritual counseling, working especially with the homeless and the elderly. In the parish house, to prepare meals, care for laundry and keep the residence in good order, three religious sisters, members of the Congregation of the Oblates of the Blessed Trinity, were assigned. The sisters were the first Eucharistic ministers at St. Patrick's, beginning their ministry in 1994. It was also necessary to hire additional ushers who were provided with Cathedral uniform ties and jackets to make identification easier for visitors. Their very presence precluded many security problems. Possibly the most familiar of all employees to generations of parishioners, the sacristan of over fifty-seven years, Bernard Carroll (*right*), retired in 1994 after

Maria R. Bastone

Only one person served longer, Msgr. Lavelle.

an extended sick leave. Michael Weekes, his assistant since 1986, was appointed to succeed him in March 1994. Other familiar faces belonged to many of the volunteers who had joined the program at its inception two decades earlier. In the early 1990s, volunteers in the information service were donating almost three hundred hours each month; over fifty men and women continued helping the *Our Neighbors* program; the young adults increased their social activities and expanded their popular lecture series; and many others helped with a wide range of Cathedral activities. Easily recognized names of trustees during the final decade of the century included Florence D'Urso; Wellington Mara, owner of the National Football League's New York Giants; and Malcolm Wilson, former Governor of New York.[51]

Some members of the homosexual community in New York grew progressively more strident in their opposition to Cardinal O'Connor's defense of Catholic teaching condemning homosexual behavior. Despite his repeated affirmation that the Church did not condemn homosexual inclination, and his counsel to Catholics to love all persons "made in the image and likeness of Almighty God," members of *Dignity* and others supporting them continued to resist his teaching. In July 1987, after President Ronald Reagan selected the Cardinal to serve on a national commission on AIDS, possibly in recognition of the care given by the Archdiocese of New York to those suffering from that disease, three hundred demonstrators rallied in front of the Cathedral. In December, eleven members of *Dignity* were arrested for interrupting a Mass in the Cathedral in defiance of a court order. Two months later, twenty-three demonstrators were arrested for blocking a sidewalk during a protest. Demonstrations and arrests continued in 1988. After a restraining order was issued by a New York State court, protestors met at side altars in the Cathedral on the first Sunday of each month before the solemn pontifical Mass. They recited prayers and left before the Mass began. In December 1989, members of *Act-Up*, an organization advocating homosexual rights, disrupted a Mass, blowing whistles, shouting obscenities, hurling condoms into the aisles and chaining themselves to pews. One hundred eleven persons were arrested, even as Cardinal O'Connor continued to offer the Mass over the din. With deep sorrow many of the faithful witnessed the desecration of the Blessed Sacrament, as some protestors received Holy Communion only to spit out the sacred hosts on the floor. Thousands outside supported disrupters inside. Former Mayor Edward Koch attended the Mass in support of the Church's right to worship without interference. Six of those arrested were convicted of disrupting a religious service. Cardinal O'Connor vowed that the Mass would not be stopped, no matter what action might follow. Periodic protests erupted on the street during subsequent years, notably during the Gay Pride parades each June, but services inside were not disrupted.[52]

In September 1988, another incident, unrelated to the other protests but no less deplorable, shocked New Yorkers. For some time before, a disturbed man often had entered the Cathedral acting in an agitated manner. Routinely, he was asked to leave by security personnel whenever his behavior became disruptive or threatening. On one occasion, he removed a crucifix from the Lady Chapel altar; on another, he toppled a heavy marble holy water font. On a September afternoon, he removed all his clothes on the street and entered the Cathedral, sending those at prayer scurrying from the pews. With a display of great strength, he dislodged a metal prayer plaque affixed to the floor and used it to strike an

Chris Sheridan

But while the world sought out the Cathedral, Cardinal O'Connor came alive at moments when he could bring the Cathedral, so to speak, to the world. Whether it was the Easter parade (top), the Pulaski parade (middle), the Columbus Day parade (bottom, with Msgr. Dalla Villa), the Steuben Day or St. Patrick's Day parades (at both of which he was Grand Marshal), or holding Benediction on the Cathedral steps, there was always that reach outward.

elderly usher who was attempting to calm him. John Winters was killed instantly. A police officer was knocked unconscious when he attempted to intervene. Another officer, called to the scene, shot and killed the man with a single bullet. The tragic deaths of a gentle usher and that of a mentally disturbed man, and the disabling of the dedicated officer who was struck moved the City to reassess its policies towards the mentally ill homeless, and gradually fewer of them were evident in the streets. At the Cathedral, social workers worked with them, hoping to convince them to seek out medical and other available aid.[53]

The unfortunate incidents did not dampen the eagerness of throngs of tourists to come to St. Patrick's. Heavy crowds made their way into the building, especially in the weeks before and just after Christmas and during Lent, the Easter season and the summer vacation months. So also grew the list of prominent figures who were visitors, among them Prince Philippe of Belgium; United States Interior Secretary Manuel Luhan; Italian Prime Minister Giulio Andreotti; New York Mayor David Dinkins; Illinois Senator Paul Simon, a frequent visitor; Supreme Court Justice Antonin Scalia; United States Attorney General Janet Reno; F. B. I. Director Louis Freeh; Maltese President Censu Tabone; Senator Edward Kennedy of Massachusetts; Governor Robert Casey of Pennsylvania; Chancellor Helmut Kohl of Germany on two occasions; Governor Mario Cuomo of New York; Prime Minister Albert Reynolds of Ireland on two occasion; President-elect Sixto Duran of Ecuador; Prime Minister Edward Fenech-Adami of Malta; Prime Minister Jim Bolger of New Zealand; United Nations President Ganev; President Bill Clinton, whose impromptu visit caught the staff by surprise; the Presidents of Zimbabwe, the Philippines and Nicaragua; United States Secretary of Health and Human Services Donna Shalala; the President of the Slovak Republic; United States Ambassador to the Vatican Raymond Flynn; Senator Alfonse D'Amato of New York; Mayor Rudolph Giuliani of New York on many occasions; Prime Minister Leon Kengo Wa Dondo of Zaire; and Governor George Pataki of New York. High Church officials were often concelebrants when they visited and included Cardinal Glemp of Poland; Cardinals Gagnon and Willebrands from Rome; Cardinal Corripio-Ahumada of Mexico; Cardinals Angelini and Cassidy from Rome; Cardinal Bevilacqua of Philadelphia; Cardinal Law of Boston; Cardinal Lustiger of Paris; Cardinal Daly of Ireland; Cardinal Lopez-Rodrigues of the Dominican Republic; and Cardinals Laghi, Sanchez, Stickler and Lopez-Trujillo from Rome. Cardinal William Baum, a high Vatican prelate and friend of Cardinal O'Connor, visited so frequently that he became readily recognized by many churchgoers. Mother Teresa of Calcutta repeated her earlier visits, and Terry Anderson, the American hostage in the Middle East, attended Christmas midnight Mass in 1991 shortly after his release from captivity. From the sports and entertainment industries came former New York Yankee Joe DiMaggio, actress Sophia Loren, Los Angeles Dodgers manager Tommy Lasorda, Dolores Hope, actor James Darren and many television personalities associated with the National Broadcasting Company whose studios were in Rockefeller Center. Often, sometimes regularly,

figures known widely in the business, entertainment and political worlds slipped quietly into secluded corners of the Cathedral for silent prayer or meditation.[54]

Every autumn after Labor Day, John Grady, the Cathedral's Director of Music and organist (*right*) for twenty years, held auditions for new choir members and began rehearsals for the music program of the coming year. In September 1990, in the midst of this work, he suffered a heart attack and died in his sleep.[55] A Mass of Christian Burial for his soul was offered on October 3rd by Cardinal O'Connor accompanied by auxiliary bishops and fifty other members of the clergy. Friends from the City and from throughout the country, including masters from the music world, joined in paying tribute to him as his choir beautified the service with some of the music he most cherished, works by Brahms, Mozart and Fauré. His long-time assistant, Donald Dumler, presided at the organ.[56]

John-Michael Caprio, Director of the Commission on Church Music of the New York Archdiocese, was asked to serve as interim music director while continuing at his Archdiocesan post. His first important task, besides preparing music for the Sunday liturgies, was to ready the choir for the televised midnight Mass at Christmas. Earlier music directors had directed the choir while simultaneously playing the organ. Mr. Caprio decided to separate the positions of organist and conductor, assigning Donald Dumler to accompany the choir which Mr. Caprio himself conducted. For the midnight Christmas

Mass, he invited a soloist from the Metropolitan Opera Company, soprano Diana Soviero, to sing the *Cantique de Noel*, continuing the tradition begun by Mr. Grady. At previous Christmas Masses, the moving strains of that hymn had been carried through the nave by Jessye Norman, Marilyn Horne, David Rendall, Tatiana Toyanos and Carol Vaness. In June 1991, Mr. Caprio was appointed Director of Music.[57]

John-Michael Caprio completed his undergraduate study at the Manhattan School of Music and at Rutgers University, and continued study at the Juilliard School and Notre Dame University. He taught in Clifton, New Jersey, and at Rutgers University while directing music programs in various New Jersey churches. He became Director of Liturgical Music of the Diocese of Paterson, New Jersey in 1973, and from 1979 until his appointment at St. Patrick's, he was music director at churches in Rye, New York and Lambertville, New Jersey. He became head of the church music office of the New York Archdiocese in 1983, holding that post even while taking the baton as Director of Music at the Cathedral. He continued, also, to direct the Riverside Symphonia, a chamber orchestra. He frequently was a guest conductor both in this country and abroad.[58]

When Mr. Caprio received his appointment at St. Patrick's, Donald Dumler was made principal organist and Alan Davis began his assignment as associate organist.[59] Mr. Davis studied in North Carolina and at the National Conservatory of Rueil-Malmaison, France, before earning a master's degree at the Manhattan School of Music. He gained experience at churches in Winston-Salem, North Carolina, and at the American Cathedral in Paris.[60] Lorenz Maycher, who had earned his undergraduate and master's degrees at Rice University in Houston, Texas assisted as part-time organist. Outside the Cathedral, he performed in recitals in New York, recorded major works on organ, and regularly played in several Manhattan churches.[61] Mr. Caprio employed several soloists with wide experience and training, including Arn Prince, Cori Ellison and Charlene Verkowitz, to lead the congregation in hymns. Other professionals, including John West, sang with the volunteer choir.

One of Mr. Caprio's innovations was the revival of vespers services at the Cathedral. Several times each year, musical selections of great beauty accompanied evening prayer during the vespers service. Mr. Caprio also re-introduced a Good Friday morning *tenebrae* service. He formed the St. Patrick's Cathedral Orchestra to present orchestral selections or accompany the choir during several concerts of sacred music held each year. These included Mozart's *Requiem* and Ralph Vaughan Williams' *Hodie,* besides the annual Christmas and St. Patrick's Day programs. Guest choral groups from Europe were often in special presentations, in addition to the weekly Sunday afternoon concert or recital programs. Guest soloists at the Christmas midnight Masses in the early 1990s were Metropolitan Opera Company singers Jerry Hadley, Aprile Millo, Benita Valente and Renee Fleming.[62]

The choir was heard most often at the Sunday morning solemn pontifical Masses celebrated by Cardinal O'Connor with many concelebrants. All the pageantry of the Roman liturgy was evident at these services in which well-trained and polished servers carried incense, crosses and candles, and His Eminence intoned the *Asperges* rite of sprinkling the congregation with holy water. He walked the full length of the central nave, often taxing the athletic prowess of far younger deacons accompanying him and struggling to maintain his quick pace. Besides the priests, bishops and occasional archbishops and cardinals in the sanctuary on these occasions, one Sunday each month the seminarians of St. Joseph's Seminary filled the sanctuary seats. Cardinal O'Connor was hopeful that their presence might inspire other men attending the Mass to join their ranks in dedication to God. Most often, all the pews in the church were filled and aisles were crowded with standees. Attendance totals varied at the Sunday Masses from under five thousand in January and February to almost twelve thousand on Palm Sunday and thousands more on Easter Sunday.[63]

Cardinal O'Connor was also the principal concelebrant at most special liturgies, especially funerals of well-known figures. The Cardinal eulogized Clare Boothe Luce at her funeral in the Cathedral in October 1987.[64] The next year His Eminence marked the millennium of Ukranian Christianity with a Mass in May.[65] In January 1989, labor union representatives filled the pews at rites for John Lawe, International President of the Transport Workers Union.[66] The funeral of baseball celebrity Billy Martin in December filled the Cathedral with mourners including baseball figures Whitey Ford, Willie Randolph, Mickey Mantle and George Steinbrenner.[67] The following May, there was a funeral for Rocky Graziano, the former boxer.[68] Family friend Cardinal William Baum offered the liturgy after the death of former mayor Robert Wagner early in 1991. Great sorrow afflicted members of the Wagner family who returned within a few years for the funeral of son Robert Wagner, Jr., a high office holder in New York.[69] In the spring of 1991, St. Patrick's mourned the death of Edward Rivetti, Chancel Organist from 1933 to 1973. His funeral Mass was in the Cathedral.[70] The quincentennial year of the discovery of America was opened at the Cathedral with a Mass on September 14, 1991. In May 1993, the first Tridentine Latin Mass held in twenty-five years in the Cathedral was offered. The Tridentine liturgy had been the standard liturgy for hundreds of years before the vernacular Mass was introduced by the Second Vatican Council.[71] During the 1994 funeral of New York Fire Department Captain John Drennan, Fifth Avenue was closed to all traffic so that, after all seats were filled inside the Cathedral, thousands of firefighters might assemble in formation outside in tribute to a fallen hero.[72] That same year, although not for a religious service, one thousand choir members from the metropolitan area gathered in St. Patrick's to record and videotape a program called "Songs of Praise," produced by the British Broadcasting Company for viewing in Europe and Australia.[73]

To encourage deeper devotion to and reverence for the Blessed Sacrament, Cardinal O'Connor in 1988 instituted the nocturnal adoration devotion held in the Lady Chapel on the first Friday of each month. One door of the church was left unlocked throughout the night to permit visitors into the chapel where the Blessed Sacrament was exposed all night. Catholics spent a few minutes, a few hours or the entire night in prayer. In 1995, the hours of exposition were extended to every day from 9 a.m. until 6 p.m. in addition to the monthly all-night hours.[74]

On the Cardinal's seventy-fifth birthday in January 1995, in accord with the Code of Canon Law promulgated after the Vatican Council, he sent his resignation as Archbishop of New York to Rome. On the same day, the *New York Times* carried an article entitled: "The Task of Choosing a Successor," prematurely, as it happened, since Cardinal O'Connor announced two months later that Pope John Paul II had urged him to continue in his post for an indefinite period. Nobody was surprised by the revelation; news stories had been suggesting an extension since January, and the Holy Father's esteem for the Cardinal and his work was well-known. Among observers of the event there was general agreement that "as long as he continues healthy and mentally alert for another five years, until he is eighty," he likely would remain Archbishop of New York.[75]

Meanwhile, the Cardinal maintained his exhausting pace of activity. In February, he was installed as the Grand Marshal of the 1995 St. Patrick's Day Parade, becoming the first Archbishop of New York to accept the honor. As a remembrance of the occasion, he was presented with a Waterford crystal monstrance handcrafted and engraved by the company's senior artisan. Two weeks later, news arrived from Rome that Pope John Paul II had re-scheduled his canceled 1994 trip to New York and other American cities for October 1995.[76] But, in March, the more distant papal visit was overshadowed by the immediate excitement of the St. Patrick's Day parade. On March 17th, a solemn and festive Mass was celebrated by his Eminence in the Cathedral. Before he accepted the honor of leading the parade as Grand Marshal, he had stipulated that the Mass would not be eclipsed in impor-tance by the parade. When the march stepped off, an ebullient reception greeted him and followed him for the entire forty-two blocks he walked to the end. He was then trans-ported back to the Cathedral to review the rest of the parade from his traditional place on the steps; this time, however, the reviewer himself was the star of the day.[77]

The year 1995 marked the fiftieth anniversary of the founding of the United Nations, an event which attracted world leaders to its headquarters in New York for the October celebration. About one hundred seventy-five heads of state or government participated in ceremonies during the month, bringing together in one place a large portion of the rulers of the earth. Heading the impressive host was His Holiness Pope John Paul II who sched-uled an address to members on October 5th. The New York visit was one stop on an itiner-ary to several locations in America. Preparations were made for six events in the metropoli-tan area — three outdoor Masses, a service in the Cathedral of Newark, New Jersey, a visit to the Archdiocesan seminary and a rosary service at St. Patrick's Cathedral. The most extensive security arrangements in the history of New York City began to take shape months before the events, as officers of the United States Secret Service and other federal agencies collaborated with New York City police and other officials. The Cathedral maintenance staff worked feverishly to bring a gleam to the building inside and outside. The organ restoration, due to be completed in January 1996, was accelerated and, except for the antiphonal division, was finished a week before the Pope's arrival.[78]

A crescendo of excitement in the months before the visit was diminished by the deaths and funerals of two members of the clergy close to St. Patrick's. Rev. Eugene Connolly, the master of ceremonies for almost ten years, known for the reverence he brought to the elaborate ceremonies he supervised, died in September. His body lay in state in the Lady Chapel on the day before his funeral Mass offered by Cardinal O'Connor. A week later, the funeral of Bishop Emerson Moore, an auxiliary bishop, was held in the presence of two cardinals, thirty-six archbishops and bishops, about two hundred priests and a very large congregation. Bishop Moore had been the country's first African-American monsignor, New York State's first African-American bishop and one of the first African-American bish-ops in America.[79]

As the day of the Pope's arrival approached, an air of excitement seemed to reappear throughout the entire City. On October 4th, His Holiness' plane touched down at Newark Airport where President Bill Clinton welcomed him to America. Pope John Paul conducted a service at Newark's Sacred Heart Cathedral before crossing the Hudson River to New York and visiting the Vatican Mission to the United Nations. The following day he addressed the General Assembly of that body, and later celebrated a Mass before a rain-drenched crowd in Giants Stadium in the New Jersey Meadowlands. Virtually the entire assemblage remained throughout the storm, seemingly oblivious to their own discomfort. On the next day, there was a Mass for Catholics of the Diocese of Brooklyn at Aqueduct Race Track in Queens County, followed by a service at St. Joseph's Seminary in Yonkers.

The largest crowds of the visit assembled in Central Park on the Feast of Our Lady of the Rosary, October 7th, when the Pontiff celebrated a Mass for the people of the Archdiocese of New York. The Cathedral event was held on the same day at 3:30 p.m. With the tightest security in memory, the entire grid of blocks from 48th to 52nd Streets was sealed, and only those with tickets for the Cathedral service were permitted to enter the area. Even the thousands assembled outside to watch the service on huge television screens were issued tickets. Inside, representatives of all the religious orders in the Archdiocese, members of families from every parish and ecclesiastical and government officials including New York Governor George Pataki, United States Senator Alfonse D'Amato, FBI Director Louis Freeh, New York Mayor Rudolph Giuliani and former Mayor Edward Koch filled all the pews and every foot of standing room. Deafening applause signaled the Pope's entrance through the great doors at

Arturo Mari, L'Osservatore Romano

In his speech to the UN, John Paul issued a ringing affirmation of both individual freedom and cultural pluralism, but stressed that freedom depends for its life on human solidarity and international cooperation.

Fifth Avenue, and an almost equivalent response met Cardinal O'Connor's words of greeting: "No one can welcome you with greater love than you find here today at St. Patrick's Cathedral." The Pope spoke words of encouragement to the religious priests, sisters and brothers to persevere in their vocations in the face of severe demands of modern times; to parents he stressed the importance of family prayer and the religious education of their children, aware of the difficulties they encounter from "false teachers and dissenting voices from within the Church" and from "a self-indulgent culture" severely undermining family life.

After the recitation of the Rosary, when the Pope was expected to exit from the Lady Chapel into the Archbishop's residence, instead he made his way back into the body of the Cathedral, blessing those in wheelchairs at the front, and wading through the sea of well-wishers in the center of the nave. When the bronze doors were thrown open, he descended into the midst of the throng on Fifth Avenue, proceeding slowly to Fiftieth Street with

Cardinal O'Connor at his side, blessing and shaking the hands of those he passed. Despite, or perhaps because of the crowd's excited, even ecstatic welcome, police and Secret Service agents appeared alternately startled or worried. But, the Pope's warmth radiated from him, and his joy was apparent as he mingled closely with his people for the first time since his visit began. The next morning, His Holiness departed for Baltimore, the final stop before returning to Rome.

No other pope since the foundation of the Church had ever traveled over the whole world. Now journalists wondered if this might be Pope John Paul's last trip to America; some suggested that travels by future popes might be rare events. For St. Patrick's, however, whatever was to transpire in the next millennium, the memory of three papal visits in thirty years was a source of great love and pride. Perhaps Pope John Paul's own words suggest why this great Cathedral was so often favored: he called St. Patrick's "a kind of spiritual landmark for all New Yorkers; in a sense, for all Catholics in the United States." [80]

The exhilaration Catholics felt in the heady days of October had hardly subsided when preparations began for three days of religious celebration of the golden anniversary of Cardinal O'Connor's ordination. At the principal liturgy on December 15th, the Cardinal concelebrated a special Mass with seven other cardinals, the Apostolic Pro-nuntio to the United States, almost ninety archbishops and bishops and about five hundred priests including abbots and heads of religious communities. Fifteen members of the Cardinal's ordination class of 1945 joined him at the altar, while family, friends and civic leaders were in the pews. The next day, the ecumenical clergy of the City attended a Mass for people from all the parishes of the Archdiocese. And the following evening a special musical concert was presented. [81]

The last Tridentine Mass prior to implementation of changes in the liturgy decreed after the Second Vatican Council was offered in the Archdiocese on November 29, 1969. Although a private Tridentine wedding Mass had been celebrated at the Cathedral since that date, the first public celebration of a Tridentine Mass at St. Patrick's since 1969 was in

May 1996, offered by Cardinal Alfons Maria Stickler, a retired Vatican prelate, with pageantry almost never seen by many younger Catholics. Two months earlier, Cardinal O'Connor had offered a Latin Mass at the Cathedral, but using the *novus ordo,* or new rite, adopted after Vatican Council II. That Mass was the ritual familiar to contemporary Catholics, but the language used was Latin. The new rite Latin Mass is regularly used in Rome and in Cathedrals worldwide.[82]

During the summer that year, the American Guild of Organists, in New York for their national convention, attended a service at the Cathedral and heard the glorious sounds of the refurbished organs. Another special liturgy that year was held for Mel Allen, the New York sportscaster known as the "voice of the Yankees," shortly after his death. And in December, Dr. Bernard Nathanson, formerly one of the foremost leaders of the abortion movement in the United States, was baptized and confirmed by Cardinal O'Connor in the Cathedral sacristy chapel. He also received his first Holy Communion from the hands of the Cardinal. Dr. Nathanson, who had personally presided over 75,000 abortions during his lifetime, became a dedicated proponent of the cause of life. A few weeks later, the Cardinal celebrated *two* midnight Masses for Christmas. The first was televised live to Ireland at 6 p.m. in New York when it was midnight in Ireland; the second was televised in this country at midnight in New York.[83]

In 1997, in preparation for a renewal of evangelization in the Church as a new millennium approached, Corpus Christi processions moved through the streets surrounding St. Patrick's. This annual event attracted large crowds both inside and outside the building. Another annual service was the Mass the Cardinal offered for young people with special needs at which he confirmed them. This was one of Cardinal O'Connor's favorite liturgies. Recalling his first priestly assignment half-a-century earlier when he worked with disabled children, he remarked: "I get to be a real parish priest ... with people that I love in a very special way ...." Following the death of Mother Teresa of Calcutta, a memorial Mass was offered in September by her friend Cardinal O'Connor. The following month he conducted the liturgy for the 175th anniversary of the Society for the Propagation of the Faith, and shortly afterwards the funeral Mass for Nancy Dickerson, the first woman correspondent of CBS News.[84]

World problems near the end of the second millennium loomed as large as they had for centuries. In February 1998 the Cardinal made a public appeal to Secretary General of the United Nations Kofi Annan, seated in the Cathedral, to visit Iraq to attempt to prevent the outbreak of war. The United Nations leader did just that. There followed that year an interfaith service for the poor, the homeless and the hungry, and a Mass for victims of Swissair Flight 111 lost in a crash at sea. In 1999 a liturgy for healing racial disharmony in the City was held, and a memorial Mass was offered for recently deceased Joe DiMaggio, the "Yankee Clipper." Towards the end of the year, enormous numbers of the faithful flooded the Cathedral to pray before the relics of St. Teresa of Lisieux during a national tour. And in the last years of the century, exceptionally large crowds — estimated at about 40,000 each year — entered the Cathedral to receive ashes at the beginning of Lent.[85]

Well-known visitors continued to arrive at the Cathedral during the final years of the century, indeed in increasing numbers. Church leaders who were visitors previously often returned, including Cardinal William Baum from Rome, Archbishop Couve de Murville of Birmingham, England and Archbishop Renato Martino, the Vatican representative at the United Nations. Other high churchmen included all the American cardinals; Cardinal Angelo Sodano, Vatican Secretary of State; Cardinal Pio Laghi (Rome); Cardinal Ignatius Gong (Shanghai); Cardinal Nicolo Lopez-Rodriguez (Santo Domingo); Cardinal Achille Silvestrini (Rome); Cardinal José Moreira-Neves (Salvador, Brazil); Cardinal Adrian Simonis (Utrecht); Cardinal Joachim Meisner (Cologne); Cardinal Paul Shan Kuo-hsi (Taiwan); Cardinal Jaime Ortega y Alamino (Havana); Cardinal Vargas Alzamora (Lima); Cardinal Cahal Daly (retired Primate of All Ireland); and Cardinal Lopez-Trujillo (Rome). Perhaps best-known of all was Mother Teresa of Calcutta who returned once more before her death.

In addition to many local state and city leaders and some national government and United Nations figures often at St. Patrick's, other world leaders included former Prime Minister of Ireland Albert Reynolds; Irish Republican Army Sinn Fein leader Gerry Adams; former Polish President Lech Walesa; Prime Minister Antonio Guterres of Portugal; Yasir Arafat, President of the Palestinian Liberation Organization; King Hussein of Jordan; President Duran-ballen of Ecuador; Princess Maria Teresa of Luxembourg; and Princess Asrid and Archduke Lawrence of Belgium. Some notable sports and entertainment world figures were opera diva Renata Tebaldi; baseball figures Joe Dimaggio, Stan Musiel, Yogi Berra, Phil Rizzuto, Joe Pepitone, Bernie Williams, Orlando Hernandez, Sammy Sosa, George Steinbrenner, Curt Gowdy and Marty Glickman; former Notre Dame football coach Lou Holtz; Olympic skater Tara Lipinski; tenor Frank Patterson; television notables Mike Nichols and Diane Sawyer; and singers Rosemary Clooney and Dolores Hope.[86]

Helping accommodate these and the millions of visitors each year were the ever-faithful volunteers. At the end of the century the volunteer program had been in existence for twenty-five years, and some of the original volunteers were still members of the program. There was a steady supply of new volunteers each year. In 1998 volunteers logged more than 25,000 hours of service including those who guided visitors through the new "walk-in" tours held on Tuesday and Thursday afternoons when no appointment was required. Roberta Shea was the Director of Volunteers who initiated this and other programs. Cardinal O'Connor each year recognized the volunteers' work by presenting them service awards at an annual Mass.[87]

Meanwhile, the music program under John-Michael Caprio expanded its scope. There was no longer a single choir, but four ensembles each with a specific assignment of musical duties. The Principal Choir provided music for the solemn pontifical Mass each Sunday and for liturgies on major feast days of the year, especially Easter and Christmas. The Choir Singers, consisting primarily of Principal Choir members, but joined by others forming a much larger group, performed major choral works each year accompanied by a professional orchestra. Presentations included works by Vivaldi, Poulenc, Mozart, Rutter, Vaughan-Williams, Rossini and Puccini. The Chapel Choir presented two concerts of chamber music in the Lady Chapel each year. And The Schola, a group of twenty-one voices, sang at Sunday Vespers and at Tenebrae services on Good Fridays. There also were special concerts such as the Famine Remembrance Concert held in March 1997 in observance of the 150th anniversary of the Irish Famine. A new assistant organist, Stanley H. Cox, trained at Juilliard School, joined the staff at the end of 1996.[88]

In a steady stream, guest choirs continued to perform at the Cathedral, including the Cantate Domino Choir of Belgium and the Zurich Boys Choir. A rare treat for worshipers — possibly the only time such an event had occurred at the Cathedral — was in September 1996 when Cardinal Adrian Simonis of Utrecht, the Netherlands, an accomplished organist, took command of the organ and produced stirring music for thirty minutes after concelebrating Mass with Cardinal O'Connor.. The mighty roar of the instrument caused visitors exiting the Mass to halt in their tracks while marveling at the glorious sounds.[89]

The organ, or more correctly the organs, the Cardinal was playing (since the gallery and chancel organs were now electronically connected so that they could be played simultaneously from either console) were almost completely restored at the time of his visit. The last of the restoration was completed in the summer of 1997 when the echo organ, renamed the nave organ, was renewed with many ranks and pipes added.[90]

That welcome news was darkened by the report in July that John-Michael Caprio was suffering from cancer. Despite surgery and subsequent chemotherapy treatments, Mr. Caprio continued a full work schedule after the summer, conducting the choirs, rehearsing for concerts and liturgies, and carrying out his duties at Archdiocesan headquarters. With courageous dedication he conducted the Chamber Singers at a Christmas concert on December 11th, and appeared for choir rehearsal prior to the Sunday pontifical Mass on December 14th. Too ill to continue that morning, he was taken home and later to a local hospital where he suffered a seizure and slipped into a coma. He died at 3:15 a.m. shortly after the end of Christmas midnight Mass at which Cardinal O'Connor asked the congregation and those viewing by television for prayers on his behalf. Many bishops and over thirty priests concelebrated his funeral Mass with Cardinal O'Connor leading the liturgy.

John C. West, a professional singer and member of the Principal Choir, conducted the music of the midnight Mass at which Metropolitan Opera tenor Marcello Giordani was soloist. The next month he was appointed interim music director until a new permanent director could be engaged. He had occasionally substituted as conductor in earlier years. He had graduated from the Curtis Institute of Music in Philadelphia and the Eastman School of Music in Rochester, New York. He had performed with the New York City Opera, appearing in twelve productions including five premieres. He also had appeared in Germany, Italy, Mexico, Venezuela, Canada and the Netherlands. For eleven years he taught at the Juilliard School of Music.

After an extensive search, a new Director of Music, Robert J. Long, was appointed in the summer of 1999. Holder of two degrees in music, he was a candidate for a doctoral degree in liturgical music at the Catholic University of America at the time he took the post. Moving to New York with his wife and three children, Mr. Long arrived from Altoona, Pennsylvania where he had been Director of Music Ministries and Principal Organist at the Cathedral of the Blessed Sacrament. Even after he assumed his new position in New York he continued as music director of the Academy of Sacred Music in Altoona. His experience included concert tours with his Cathedral Festival Choir through twelve European countries and an appearance at the National Shrine of the Immaculate Conception in Washington, D. C. [91]

Large everyday expenses coupled with major outlays for repairs and renovations continued to rise in the late 1990s. But Msgr. Dalla Villa's success in increasing revenues, principally through the expansion of space and items for sale in the gift shop, began to yield small surpluses which could be used for planned projects such as replacement of the Lady Chapel floor, completion of the fire suppression system, replacement of parish house windows and other needed work. In 1997 he arranged to open a second, much larger gift shop in rented space on 51st Street opposite the north side of the Cathedral. Architect Peter Marino donated his services producing an attractive, roomy sales area, and as soon as the doors opened after Cardinal O'Connor blessed the shop late in November, its popularity was evident. Revenues increased significantly, finally giving hope to the Rector that planned projects could be carried to completion. Behind the gift shop, a small display area was opened where sacred vessels and other artistic treasures of St. Patrick's were displayed. Into that area were moved from the Cathedral the sculptures of Popes Pius XII and Paul VI. One floor above the store, a large area was provided for housing a new Archives.

Some of the new revenue was used for such devotional purposes as a new statue of St. Joseph placed above his altar. Staff and volunteers also contributed generously towards the cost, a gift in honor of Cardinal O'Connor's 50th jubilee as a priest. He blessed the sculpture during a ceremony on December 15, 1996, his 51st anniversary of ordination. The Dolfi Simoncini Company of Rome carved the Carrara marble statue. Another addition, the figure of a camel, was added to the Christmas creche group that year. It was made by the Italian firm Demetz which had designed the other creche figures. And in May 1998, to mark one hundred years of service by the Salesians in the United States, a bronze relief sculpture of their founder, St. John Bosco, was mounted on the northwest tower wall in symmetrical balance with the sculpture of St. Frances Cabrini on the southwest tower wall. Cardinal O'Connor blessed this work of Elizabeth Chandler on May 3rd.[92]

Few, if anyone, expected that Cardinal O'Connor's active pace would decelerate after his seventy-fifth birthday, and indeed, the intensity of his activities in his last years as Archbishop of New York was hardly distinguishable from that of his earlier ones. In 1996 he was grand marshal of the German-American Steuben Day parade, the second time he was chosen to lead a major New York march. In May 1999 he accepted the Pierre Toussaint Award on the occasion of its twenty-fifth anniversary, so esteemed was he by black Catholics of the Archdiocese for his work on their behalf.

Beginning in 1995, he devoted over a year to explaining and commenting on the Catechism of the Catholic Church during his Sunday homilies. Another long-term series dealt with teachings of the Church relating to marriage. In 1997 he announced from the Cathedral pulpit that he was initiating steps towards the canonization of Dorothy Day, the New York advocate for social justice and co-founder of the Catholic Worker Movement. The following year, he forthrightly criticized President Clinton, a non-Catholic, for receiving Holy Communion at a Catholic Mass in South Africa in violation of Catholic tradition. This he did, he explained, in response to a "flood" of letters he had received from Catholics perplexed by the President's action, when they themselves had been denied Holy Communion following their divorce and remarriage unsanctioned by the Church. He used the pulpit that year to condemn a New York City proposal to make unmarried domestic partners the legal equals of married couples in violation of natural law. He commented that the President's behavior leading to his impeachment was "unspeakable," while soundly condemning actions of members of Congress who supported partial-birth abor-

tion as they expressed their abhorrence of the President's behavior. He did not hesitate to read to the congregation a "shockingly graphic description of a partial-birth abortion" to illustrate the depths to which public acceptance of "the culture of death" had fallen. After a videotape of Dr. Jack Kevorkian assisting a man with Lou Gehrig's disease to commit suicide was televised, he denounced the physician's "macabre crusade." And he begged various factions in the City to enter a dialogue for rebuilding trust after "an emotional and political storm" arose following the killing of a citizen.

The Cardinal's unflinching statements from the pulpit were not merely occasional comments, as he consistently spoke out upholding Catholic teaching, not only at the Cathedral Masses, but in his weekly newspaper column and in other public announcements. But it was at St. Patrick's where he was most visible, and there he most often left congregants with a message of hope, rather than discouragement, at declining public moral standards. His sense of humor and his ready wit were a staple treat for visitors. For example, when a visiting prelate addressed the congregation to thank the Cardinal and the people of *Hartford* for their generosity of donations for disaster relief in his diocese, Cardinal O'Connor replied to the de-

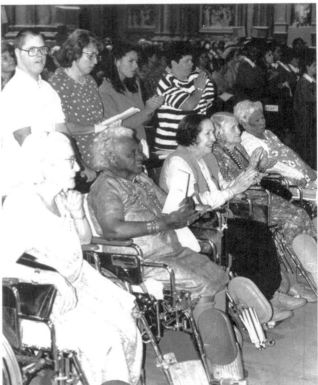

The top picture was the Cardinal's favorite. Like his predecessors, he remembered the original inspiration of St. Patrick's Cathedral — to hold out a deeper kind of promise to the City's tired, hungry and poor.

light of listeners: "First of all, you didn't get a nickel yet. And second, if you ever again refer to the Archdiocese of New York as Hartford, you never will." On another occasion he mentioned that some priests observed that his "running up and down the Cathedral altar steps" would cause him to "fall flat" on his face, or to "trip and go soaring out over the congregation." He acknowledged that, considering he was seventy-eight years old, they were "probably right."

In fact, the Cardinal mentioned that his time as Archbishop was drawing to a close. Late in 1998 he told the Archdiocesan Pastoral Council, that "come the year 2000, if I'm alive, that has to be the end [of my episcopal term]." The following March, he wrote to the priests of the Archdiocese that "this may well be my final Chrism Mass as Archbishop of New York." At the end of August, 1999, after suffering weakness, the Cardinal entered Memorial Sloan-Kettering Cancer Center for tests. A small tumor was removed from his brain and after returning home he began radiation treatments. By October 10th the treatments had so weakened him that he returned briefly to the hospital and afterwards was unable to celebrate Mass publicly for several weeks. In mid-November at the Cathedral he stumbled and fell while descending from the *cathedra*. Clearly near exhaustion, he once again stumbled at the end of November during a Mass at which he was compelled to remain seated for his short homily. He did not appear in public again until December 19th when he celebrated Mass from the high altar where a chair had been placed for his use, in order not to drain his strength from ascending the stairs to the *cathedra*. He used the same arrangement at Christmas midnight Mass and on the following Sundays, appearing stronger at each appearance.

Despite his improvement, media accounts grew more and more speculative about his retirement and a possible successor. Most frequently cited as a possible future Archbishop of New York were Archbishop Justin F. Rigale of St. Louis, Archbishop Theodore E. McCarrick of Newark, Archbishop Edwin F. O'Brien of the Military Archdiocese, Bishop Henry Mansell of Buffalo, Bishop Sean O'Malley of Fall River, Massachusetts, and Bishop Edward Egan of Bridgeport, Connecticut. [93]

Throughout January 2000, His Eminence maintained a curtailed schedule, but regularly celebrated the solemn pontifical Mass on Sundays. He happily took part in a special dinner arranged for his eightieth birthday and continued to write his weekly column for Catholic New York. Early in February he announced he would visit Rome "to say thanks and good-bye" to the Holy Father and other Vatican officials. But in the following weeks weakness prevented him from further public appearances, although he met privately with visitors such as New York Mayor Rudolph Giuliani and United States Congress Representatives who informed him that the Congress had voted to award him the Congressional Gold Medal, its highest civilian honor, in recognition of his outstanding lifetime work on behalf of his fellow-Americans. But by April he was unable to officiate at Holy Week or Easter liturgies. Then, during the night of May 2nd, his health declined rapidly and, with his family and close friends on hand, including Cardinals William Baum and Bernard Law, he peacefully died at 8:05 p.m. on May 3, 2000. [94]

Two days later, the Cardinal's body was received in a solemn ceremony at the Cathedral, the first of many liturgies filling the following days. Tens of thousands filed past the coffin placed just inside the altar rail near the *cathedra,* while thousands of others attended special Masses and other services. A "solemn and majestic" funeral Mass was celebrated on Monday, May 8th attended by thousands including President and Mrs. William Clinton, former President George Bush, Governor George Pataki, Mayor Rudolph Giuliani, Presidential candidates George Bush, Jr and Al Gore, United States Senators and Representatives and hundreds of well-known figures from many areas of American public life. Fifteen cardinals led by Pope John Paul II's personal representative, Vatican Secretary of State

Cardinal Angelo Sodano, were joined in concelebrating with about one thousand archbishops, bishops and priests. Throughout New York State, flags flew at half-staff upon orders of the Governor, and the Empire State Building was flooded in red and white light, the cardinal's colors. Before each New York Yankee baseball game during the funeral weekend, a moment of silence was observed in his memory at Yankee Stadium. The funeral Mass was televised by all major networks. During Cardinal Law's homily, his mention of Cardinal O'Connor's deep commitment to pro-life issues evoked "thunderous applause that grew into a standing ovation [which] rocked St. Patrick's Cathedral ...." The ovation lasted almost two minutes. With a smile, Cardinal Law remarked: "I see he hasn't left the pulpit."

Indeed, his legacy of unflinching support of Church teaching seemed written in that very pulpit. One of the most remarkable terms in the history of the Church of New York ended as the Cardinal's remains were interred in the crypt under the high altar of St. Patrick's.[95]

1. *New York Times*, April 25, 1985; *Curriculum Vitae* of Archbishop John O'Connor, Office of Communications, Archdiocese of New York, March 1984.

2. *Ibid.;* Kelly, *In My Father's House*, pp. 341-346, *passim.*

3. *Curriculum Vitae* of Archbishop John O'Connor, March 1984; file: Installation of Archbishop O'Connor, March 1984, ASPC; *New York Post*, special edition, April 1984.

4. *Curriculum Vitae* of Archbishop John O'Connor, March 1984; *Alive and Well* magazine, August 1984.

5. *New York Post*, March 17, 1984.

6. *New York Post*, August 7, 1984.

7. program of installation, Archbishop Joseph Ryan, April 30, 1985, ASPC.

8. *New York Times*, April 25, 1985; *New York Daily News*, June 1, 1985.

9. *New York Times*, April 25, May 26, 1985; *New York Daily News*, May 8, 1985.

10. *Alive and Well* magazine, February, September 1986; file: Proposed Relocation of High Altar, 1980, 1984, ASPC; Move of Holy Family Altar, 1985, 1986, ASPC. The altar was moved and set by the Lorenzoni Marble Company under the direction of the Mitchell Company.

11. *Alive and Well* magazine, August 1986; file: Repairs and Renovations of Archbishop's Residence, 1984-1985, ASPC. The restoration of the transept doors was carried out by Cono Frabosilio.

12. file: Statue of St. Jude, 1984, ASPC. The donors owned the Holloway Corporation in Ardmore, Pennsylvania.

13. file: Creche, 1985, ASPC. The price of the original figures was approximately $20,000. Additional figures were added in subsequent years.

14. *Alive and Well* magazine, May-June 1989; Valuation Report: Tiffany Monstrance, 1986,

ASPC. The exhibition was entitled: "Marks of Achievement: Four Centuries of American Presentation Silver."

15. *Alive and Well* magazine, December 1986; *Catholic New York*, April 3, 1986

16. Report: "St. Patrick's Cathedral Volunteers," November 19, 1984, ASPC; *Alive and Well* magazine, February 1987.

17. program: Funeral of Roger Maris, December 23, 1985, ASPC. At the funeral Mass on December 23, 1985, Phil Rizzuto read the *Prayer of the Faithful,* Howard Cosell delivered a tribute and Robert Merrill of the Metropolitan Opera Company sang.

18. *New York Times*, February 21, 1986, April 16, 1986. Three buses transported Members of Congress and Capitol Hill staff members to the Cathedral for Congressman Addabbo's funeral.

19. *New York Times*, January 14, 1987

20. *New York Times*, April 2, 1987. The funeral was on April 1st.

21. *New York Times*, October 14, 1987; program: Funeral of Clare Boothe Luce, October 13, 1987, ASPC. Attending the rites was former American Ambassador to the United Nations Vernon Walters.

22. A concert for the Marian Year was held in the Cathedral on December 6, 1987. John Grady directed the St. Patrick's Cathedral Choir accompanied by members of the Metropolitan Opera Orchestra.

23. The Mass was on December 7th.

24. file: Bellringing Ceremony, Centenary of Statue of Liberty, July 3, 1986; programs: Reception for President Oscar Arias-Sanchez, 600th Anniversary of Lithuanian Christianity, 1987, ASPC; *Alive and well* magazine, July 1987. The sculptor Mario Noto made the reproduction of the statue of Our Lady of New York.

25. Carthy, *Magnificence,* p. 131.

26. *New York Times*, June 13, 1985; Rigney to Anne Dini, December 10, 1985, ASPC. Mother Teresa attended the profession of vows on June 12th and spoke to the congregation on October 27th.

27. At the April concert, police cleared the Cathedral as a precaution. During the November incident, four ushers were handcuffed by the armed intruders who wore ski masks.

28. file: Demonstrations, 1988, ASPC.

29. Cardinal John O'Connor to Rev. Anthony Dalla Villa, August 5, 1987, ASPC.

30. *Catholic New York*, April 7, 1988. The announcement was made on March 29th.

31. *Curriculum Vitae* of Msgr. Anthony Dalla Villa, July 5, 1994, ASPC; *Alive and Well* magazine, June 1988. Father Dalla Villa attended Our Lady of Mt. Carmel Elementary School and St. Agnes High School. On December 27, 1987, the Acting Rector was awarded the honor *Cavaliere Della Republica* by the Italian government. The ceremony took place at the Consulate of Italy in New York on March 8, 1988, a few weeks before his appointment as Rector.

32. Minutes of the Board of Trustees, February 1988, April, 1991, June 1991; *Catholic New York*, March 31, 1988; file: Sound System, 1987, ASPC; file: Electricity and Lighting, 1988, Rector's File, St. Patrick's Cathedral.

33. Report of Building Manager, June 1990, ASPC.

34. Information supplied by author.

35. file: Statues of St. Benilde Ramancon and St. Miguel Cordero, 1984, 1988, ASPC; *Catholic New York*, July 7, 1988. There was unusual treatment by the sculptor in his use of black ivory rather than the white marble used for the other statuary at the altar. The dedication was on June 22nd. The cost was about $15,000.

36. Chandler to Young, June 12, 1990, ASPC; file: sculpture of St. Frances Cabrini, 1989, Rector's file, St. Patrick's Cathedral. The cost of the group was $28,500.

37. Father Dalla Villa was informed of the honor in August 1990 and was invested on Septem-

ber 18th. *See:* program of investiture, 1990, ASPC.

38. Report of Building Manager, June 1990, ASPC.

39. *Alive and Well* magazine, July-August 1990; Patrick Baker to Dalla Villa, July 30, 1990, Rector's file, St. Patrick's Cathedral.

40. *Catholic New York*, December 6, 1991; *Alive and Well* magazine, February 1991. Before the renovations of 1972-73, the Blessed Sacrament had reposed in the tabernacle in the Lady Chapel to which location it was returned.

The Pierre Toussaint interment was on December 4, 1990.

41. Expenditures for such basic requirements as adequate lighting, roof replacement over the triforia, other roof repairs, repair to the Fifth Avenue steps and similar needs was estimated at over three million dollars in 1988. *See:* Board of Trustees budget authorization, Rector's file, February 1988, St. Patrick's Cathedral.

Father Dalla Villa eventually put into effect a plan to reduce expenses by using Cathedral maintenance staff for projects formerly assigned to contractors. Frank Boyle, the building manager in charge of maintenance, hired some specialists with skills in carpentry, decorating and construction. Fully equipped work shops were built in basement areas after which such jobs as painting, repair of pews, steam cleaning, plumbing and electrical repair were assumed by the regular maintenance staff. Further savings were effected by the installation of surveillance cameras to reduce theft from donation boxes, an innovation which also enhanced security. The use of two-way radios by ushers and maintenance personnel also contributed to improvement in security. *See:* Building Manager's Reports, 1900-1995, ASPC.

42. *Catholic New York*, June 6, 1991; Report of Gift Shop Manager, June 1994, ASPC.

43. Proposal of J. H. Steinkampf and related correspondence, July 7, July 17, 1974, ASPC; Minutes of Board of Trustees, April 1991-April 1994; Report of Nelson Bardon on the 1930 Kilgen Organ, April 1992, ASPC; file: Organ Restoration, 1991-1995, ASPC. The Turner contract for the consoles was for almost $450,000. It was awarded in February 1993.

44. Minutes of the Board of Trustees, November, 1993, February, April, November 1994. The organ consoles were "twins," i.e., identical both in appearance and in capability.

45. Minutes of the Board of Trustees, June 1985, November 1991, January 1993; file: bell restoration, 1991-1992, Rector's file, St. Patrick's Cathedral; Dalla Villa to O'Connor, February 14, 1992; Curran to New York Elevator Company, October 23, 1991, Rector's file, St. Patrick's Cathedral; proposal of Beyer, Blinder and Belle: Floor of Lady Chapel, December 11, 1991, Rector's file, St. Patrick's Cathedral. The ladders in the bell tower were installed by Artistic Metal Work Company, the strikers were installed by the Schulmerich Carillon Company and MJC Electric Company completed the wiring.

Work on the east end of the Lady Chapel floor was finished by the Malcolm-Cohen and Miller-Druck Companies in September 1990. In January 1993, Msgr. Dalla Villa requested that the Board of Trustees postpone further work on the floor in favor of the organ and fire suppression system work.

46. file: Painting of Our Lady of Guadalupe, 1991, ASPC. The presentation ceremony was held on December 8, 1991 and was attended by Manuel Alonso, Consul General of Mexico.

47. Report of Building Manager, June 1993, ASPC. The baldachin was refinished in January.

48. Survey of St. Patrick's Cathedral, Shanley and Sturges, 1963, ASPC; *New York Times*, September 11, November 17, 1994; *America* magazine, November 5, 1994; John P. Knetge of Electronic Media Tech to author, August 1994; Brian Baker of Patrick Baker and Sons to author, July 1995. At first, the Board of Trustees approved the inclusion of a ramp for the handicapped in the organ console-sound booth project, since two sets of steps were located nearby. The final plan eliminated the ramp. Instead two portable ramps were used. *See:* Minutes of the Board of Trustees, April, November 1991.

49. Minutes of the Board of Trustees, June 1991-April 1995, *passim.* The architectural firm Beyer, Blinder and Belle was prominent in New York restoration work. One of their most visible commissions was Grand Central Terminal at Forty-Second Street. The sprinkler installation was accomplished by Active Fire Sprinkler Corporation and the electrical work was by MJC Electric Company.

50. Minutes of the Board of Trustees, April, 1995; Report of Building Manager, June 1995, ASPC.

51. *Catholic New York*, February 3, 1994; Report of Social Worker, February 9, 1994, ASPC; Report of *Our Neighbors* program director, June 1994, ASPC; Records of Trustees, ASPC. Information was made available through the information service in six languages: English, Spanish, German, French, Italian, and Japanese.

The *Our Neighbors* program director instituted a monthly newsletter which was mailed to all members and volunteers. Several bus trips also became annual events.

52. *New York Times*, July 27, 1987, January 27, February 8, October 4, December 5, 1988; most major New York newspapers, December 11, 12, 14, 1989; *New York Times*, September 24, November 11, 1990, January 8, 1991; *Catholic New York*, July 3, 1987, January 16, 1991, June 30, 1994.

53. Major New York newspapers, September 22, 1988. As at other locations in New York which were readily recognized by a large percentage of people, St. Patrick's was frequently the site of demonstrations by a variety of organizations which found media publicity for their causes almost assured. Usually the groups assembled on Fifth Avenue opposite the west front. Often, their messages were unrelated to teachings or policies of the Catholic Church or the Cathedral. But, sometimes even Catholic groups held protests such as those of some Catholic school teachers dissatisfied with contract negotiations with the Archdiocese of New York. Cardinal O'Connor voiced his disapproval of the group's choice of time for a demonstration — during a Mass. He felt the noisy protest was not appropriate during the sacred liturgy, although he supported the right of demonstrators to voice their views. *See: Catholic New York*, September 14, 1995.

54. file: Visitors to St. Patrick's Cathedral, 1990-1995, ASPC. Tenor Placido Domingo sang during a Mass celebrated by Cardinal Ernesto Corripio-Ahumada on October 7, 1992.

55. Mr. Grady died on September 27th.

56. *New York Times*, September 30, 1990; Tribute to John Grady, Conference of Roman Catholic Cathedral Musicians, National Shrine of the Immaculate Conception, Washington D. C., November 9, 1990.

57. programs of Christmas midnight Mass, 1990-1995, ASPC.

58. *Curriculum Vitae* of John-Michael Caprio, 1990, ASPC.

59. Dalla Villa to Staff, June 27, 1991, ASPC.

60. *Curriculum Vitae* of Alan Davis, 1991, ASPC.

61. *Curriculum Vitae* of Lorenz Maycher, 1992, ASPC.

62. programs of services, 1990-1995, ASPC.

63. Mass attendance counts, 1994, ASPC.

64. *Catholic New York*, October 15, 1987. Mrs. Luce, former Member of Congress and Ambassador to Italy, died in Washington D. C. on October 9th. Her funeral service was on October 13th.

65. The Mass was on May 28, 1988.

66. *Catholic New York*, January 12, 1989. The Mass was on January 9, 1989.

67. The Mass was on December 29, 1989.

68. *New York Times*, May 26, 1990. The Mass was on May 25, 1990.

69. *Catholic New York*, February 14, 1991; *New York Newsday*, February 17, 1991. Robert Wagner, Sr. had been Mayor of New York for twelve years. After he left office, he was the American

President's personal representative to the Holy See. Robert Merrill, retired from the Metropolitan Opera Company, sang at the funeral.

70. *Catholic New York*, May 16, 1991. Mr. Rivetti died at the age of 83 on May 6, 1991. The Mass was offered on May 10th.

71. *The Latin Mass,* special edition, March-April 1994, p. 19. The Mass was a nuptial (wedding) on May 8, 1993.

72. *New York Times*, May 12, 1994.

73. *Catholic New York*, February 24, March 17, 1994. Although their funeral services were not held in the Cathedral, in 1992 St. Patrick's lost the talents of two individuals who had contributed much to its heritage. W. Knight Sturges, the consulting architect from 1967 until 1984, died in Bedford, Massachusetts on May 14, 1992. Sister Margaret Carthy, author of a history of the Cathedral parish entitled *A Cathedral of Suitable Magnificence,* died on June 21, 1992. *See:* The Enterprise, May 22, 1992; *Catholic New York*, June 25, 1992.

74. Dalla Villa to Priests Staff, January 20, 1995, ASPC; file: Nocturnal Adoration Devotion, 1989, ASPC.

75. *Catholic New York*, January 12, March 23, 1995; *New York Times*, January 15, 1995; *New York Daily News*, January 16, 1995.

76. Pope John Paul had suffered a fall from which he sustained injuries to his leg and hip, necessitating a rescheduling of the trip to the United States. *See: Catholic New York*, September 29, 1994; *New York Times*, October 5, 1994.

77. *Catholic New York*, February 16, March 9, March 23, 1995; *New York Times*, March 3, March 18, 1995.

78. file: Visit of Pope John Paul II, 1995, ASPC.

79. programs: Funerals of Rev. Eugene Connolly, Most Rev. Emerson Moore, 1995, ASPC; *Catholic New York*, September 14, September 21, 1995.

80. file: Visit of Pope John Paul II, 1995, ASPC; *Catholic New York*, September 28, October 5, October 12, 1995. Secret service agents played a major role in security arrangements at St. Patrick's. They required that every person entering the building pass through a metal detection scanning device. All employees and others participating in the event wore special identification badges. For the first time in history, no Masses were scheduled at St. Patrick's, except for Good Fridays when no Mass is ever permitted. In honor of the Pope's native land, a painting of Our Lady of Czestochowa was suspended over the baptistry. A very special tribute was a commemorative stained glass window which was on display near the Sacred Heart altar. It was made by Mr. Patrick Clark and his assistants who donated their skills. The Cathedral paid the cost of the materials. The window was later suspended above the statue of St. Stanislaus Kostka, the Polish saint. Mr. Clark restored windows in about one hundred churches in New York, including the windows of St. Jean Baptiste Church which were made by Nicholas Lorin, who made many of the original windows of St. Patrick's. *See: Catholic New York*, September 18, 1997; *The Stained Glass 1995 Papal Visit Commemorative Window at St. Patrick's Cathedral,* a description written by Patrick Clark, 1995, ASPC.

81. *Catholic New York*, December 14, December 21, 1999.

82. Sr. Marguerita Smith to Thomas Young, April 24, 1996, ASPC, correspondence file; file: Tridentine Mass, ASPC, 1996 #5; *New York Times*, May 12, 1996; *Catholic New York*, February 1, March 21, May 6, 1996.

83. file: programs, ASPC, 1996 #6; *Catholic World Report*, April 1997; *Catholic New York*, December 19, 1996, September 11, October 23, October 30, 1997.

84. *Catholic New York*, May 22, June 5, 1997, June 18, September 10, October 15, 1998, June 10, 1999.

85. *Catholic New York*, February 19, June 4, 1998, April 22, April 29, October 21, 1999; *New York Times*, April 21, April 24, 1999.

86. file: Visitors, ASPC, 1995 #8, 1996 #7, 1997 #2; *Catholic New York*, September 11, October 23, 1997, March 19, 1998, November 11, 1999; *New York Times*, April 24, 1999; Cathedral announcements, *passim*.

87. Roberta Shea verbally to Thomas Young, October 1999; *Catholic New York*, July 16, 1998, April 15, 1999; *Alive and Well*, September 1998.

88. *Alive and Well*, June, 1997; *Catholic New York*, March 134, October 2, 1997; The Irish Echo, March 19-25, 1997; *curriculum vitae* of Stanley Cox, ASPC correspondence file, 1997.

89. witnessed by the writer, September 1996.

90. John-Michael Caprio verbally to Thomas Young, November 1997.

91. *Catholic New York*, December 18, 1997, January 1, January 29, 1998, September 9, 1999; *New York Times*, December 27, 1997; *Alive and Well*, October 1999; Donald Dumler verbally to Thomas Young, January , 1998.

92. Minutes of meetings of the Board of Trustees, April 19, 1995, June 23, 1997, June 30, 1998; *Catholic New York*, May 29, November 13, 1997, May 7, 1998; New York Magazine, November 14, 1997; Frank Boyle verbally to Thomas Young, November, 1997; Roberta Shea verbally to Thomas Young, November 1997, May 1998; Brian Baker verbally to Thomas Young, August 1996.

93. *Catholic New York*, weekly throughout 1995-1996 and September 3, 1996, October 13, 1997, January 15, April 9, May 28, September 17, October 8, November 26, 1998, March 25, September 9, 16, October 14, November 18, December 9, 16, 23, 1999; *New York Times*, October 10, 1997, May 25, 1998, March 9, 22, August 27, October 11, 1'8, 19, 21, 25, November 16, 17, December 6, 16, 17,20, 1999, January 3, 2000; accounts of author who attended many Cathedral liturgies.

94. *Catholic New York*, January 7, 13, 20, February 3, 10, 17, March 2, 9, 16, 23, April 20, 2000; *New York Times*, January 10, 17, 20, 22, February 2, 3, 10, 11, 14, 28, March 3, April.

22; May 4, 2000; *New York Post*, May 4, 2000; Newsday, May 4, 2000; *New York Daily News*, May 4, 2000.

95. *Catholic New York*, May 11, 2000; *New York Times*, May 6, 7, 8,9, 2000; *New York Daily News*, May 9, 2000.

EPILOGUE

One of the prelates in attendance at Cardinal O'Connor's funeral Mass was Bishop Edward M. Egan, Bishop of Bridgeport, Connecticut. His name had been mentioned as a possible successor to the Archbishop of New York on various occasions over several years; but with increasing frequency in the days before the funeral, media reports made it appear likely that he was the choice of Pope John Paul II to succeed Cardinal O'Connor. On May 11th, three days after the Cardinal's funeral Mass, the Vatican announced Bishop Egan's appointment to the See of New York. Upon learning of his appointment, the Archbishop-elect recalled that he said to himself: "Get down on your knees and beg the Lord to give you a hand, and don't get up too quickly."

Edward M. Egan was born on April 2, 1932 in Oak Park, Illinois. He was one of four children, the son of a businessman, Thomas J. and Genevieve Costello Egan. When he was ten years old, he suffered from polio. After his recovery he attended St. Giles School and later Quigley Preparatory Seminary in Chicago. He received his bachelor's degree in philosophy from St. Mary of the Lake Seminary in Mundelein, Illinois. His seminary studies were completed in Rome at the Pontifical North American College. He was ordained in the Holy City on December 15, 1957 and the following year received a Licentiate in Sacred Theology from the Pontifical Gregorian University. His first priestly assignment was to Holy Name Cathedral in Chicago and shortly afterwards he joined the Chancery Office assisting Cardinal Albert Meyer. Father Egan's work included serving on various ecumenical commissions. Returning to Rome, from 1960 until 1964 he earned a doctorate in canon law summa cum laude from the Pontifical Gregorian University and was assigned to be a repetitor, repeating in English the Latin lectures being delivered to students at the University. One time he mentioned that after his return to this country he sometimes groped for words in English because he thought in Latin. For the next seven years he was co-chancellor and secretary of Cardinal John Cody of Chicago. Once again assigned to the Vatican, he spent fourteen years there as a judge on the Sacred Roman Rota, an appeals tribunal dealing with church law, and taught canon law at the Pontifical Gregorian University. During that time he and other canon law experts took part in breakfast meetings with Pope John Paul II reviewing the revisions to the Code of Canon Law.

Named a bishop by Pope John Paul, he was consecrated in the Basilica of Saints John and Paul on May 22, 1985 by Bernardin Cardinal Gantin with John Cardinal O'Connor and Bishop John R. Keating of Arlington, Virginia as co-consecrators. He chose the words "In the Holiness of Truth" as his episcopal motto. The following month he became an auxiliary bishop and Vicar for Education in the Archdiocese of New York. On November 8, 1988, he was appointed by the Holy Father as Bishop of the Diocese of Bridgeport, Connecticut and was installed in that office on December 14, 1988.

Notable work in Bridgeport included his regionalization program of the diocesan elementary schools, the establishment of Hispanic and Haitian apostolates, the foundation of St. John Fisher Seminary Residence for those considering entering the priesthood, reorganization of healthcare facilities and initiation of the Inner-City Foundation for Charity and Education. He served on several boards of the National Conference of Catholic Bishops and received honorary doctorates from several colleges.

On January 21, 2001, Pope John Paul II announced that Cardinal Egan was to be elevated to the College of Cardinals. He was elevated in the Consistory of February 21, 2001. In New York, he works hard at the enormous task of realigning the Archdiocese's schools, churches and hospitals. He is known for setting its finances on a firmer setting. He is dedicated to promoting the spiritual growth of priests, religious and laity. He is an interesting preacher and is most gracious in attending the many anniversaries and other events going on in the Archdiocese. He meets the usual unforgiving deadline for his regular column in *Catholic New York*. He was also appointed by Pope John Paul II to numerous Vatican Institutions that spell even more work. For all that, Cardinal Egan is an expert pianist, is fluent in several languages and finds time to pursue his many interests which are as varied as quantum physics, cosmology and music.

Over the years, Cardinal Egan was well-served by the Cathedral Rectors. In 2001, Monsignor Dalla Villa (who plays a large role in Chapter 10 of this history) completed his second six-year term as Rector of St. Patrick's and was named pastor of the Church of St. Agnes on East 43rd Street. He replaced there Monsignor Eugene V. Clark, who became his successor as Rector of the Cathedral. Both held the high honor of being named *prothonotary apostolic* by Pope John Paul II. Rev. John Ferry was appointed Associate Rector to Monsignor Clark and was honored by Pope John Paul II with the title *monsignor*.

Monsignor Clark was educated at Cathedral Preparatory School and Cathedral College before he entered St. Joseph's Seminary where he was awarded his B. A. and M. A. degrees in Theology. He received a second master's degree in European history from Fordham University, a Ph. D. in European history from the University of Notre Dame and an honorary Doctorate in Humane Letters from St. John's University. His first assignment after ordination in 1951 was as a curate at the Church of St. Francis of Assisi in Mount Kisco, New York. He taught at Dubois High School, Fordham University, Notre Dame College in New York, St. Joseph's Seminary and Cardinal Spellman High School. He also served as advocate before the Archdiocesan Tribunal and later was a judge of the Metropolitan Tribunal. He was Editor of the United States Catholic Historical Society for eight years and served as Personal Secretary to both Cardinal Spellman and Cardinal Cooke. For nine years he was Director of Communications of the Archdiocese until his appointment as Pastor of Annunciation Parish in Crestwood, New York. In 1986 he became Pastor of St. Agnes Parish. He is well-known for his earlier years when he conducted a weekly discussion program on CBS Radio and was a columnist for the *Catholic News*. He held many positions relative to assisting the Vatican Museums, and was associated with the American Irish Historical Society, Saint John's University, Alternatives to Abortion

International, the Order of the Holy Sepulchre, the Order of Malta, the Homeland Foundation and the Wethersfield Institute.

One his first duties as Rector was arranging funeral services at the Cathedral for many of the victims of the September 11, 2001 attack on New York's World Trade Center, services which were held for many months after the tragedy. Later, he arranged for the complete restoration of the Lady Chapel interior which boasts a new marble floor, a complete cleaning and restoration of its pews and priceless windows. He began other improvements throughout the Cathedral as well.

On Feb. 8, 2006, Cardinal Egan appointed Rev. Robert T. Ritchie the seventh Rector of St. Patrick's Cathedral. Within a few weeks of his appointment. Father Ritchie was named Chaplain to His Holiness, Pope Benedict XVI, a honor bearing the title *monsignor.*

Robert T. Ritchie was born in Washington Heights, New York, on March 26,1945, the oldest of three brothers, children of David and Eugenia Ritchie. He was educated in St. Elizabeth's School, Washington Heights and Sacred Heart School, the Bronx. After attending Regis High School and graduating from Cardinal Hayes High School, he attended Cathedral College followed by his entrance to St. Joseph's Seminary, Yonkers, New York. After ordination by Cardinal Cooke on May 29,1971, he completed studies of the Spanish language begun during his seminary years including work in Puerto Rico and the Dominican Republic, and his first pastoral assignment was in the Diocese of Buga, Colombia, South America. After his return to the United States, he was assigned as Assistant Pastor of St. Catherine of Genoa Parish in Washington Heights where he served as a member and later as chairman of Community Board 9 and also as secretary of the Priest Senate of the Archdiocese of New York.

He became Director of Youth Ministry in the Catholic Youth Organization in 1975 and subsequently Executive Director of the Catholic Youth Organization for the Archdiocese. He was appointed Pastor of St. Catherine of Genoa Parish in 1983 where he served until 1999 when he became Pastor of Our Lady of Angels Parish in the Bronx. During that period he served on the Interparish Finance Commission and the board of the Association of Catholic Schools. Cardinal Egan appointed him Regional Vicar of the Northwest Bronx in 2002, an office he held until his appointment as Rector of St. Patrick's Cathedral on February 13, 2006.

This short summary of Cardinal Egan's association with the Cathedral hardly does justice to the historical record of his work and that of many members of the clergy, the staff and volunteers of the Cathedral. Imagine any account that would not give special place, say, to the celebration of the 125th anniversary of the opening of the Cathedral which took place on Cardinal Egan's watch — a gala dinner held at the Plaza Hotel and Cardinal Egan, joined by many cardinals, bishops and priests, celebrating the Mass in the Cathedral. Perhaps a new edition of this history, or another history, will present a properly detailed portrait of these past years and the future years of Cardinal Egan's part in the drama of St. Patrick's Cathedral. Meanwhile, as it enters the second quarter of its second century as the center of Catholic life in New York, the ever-changing and ever-the-same beloved St. Patrick's Cathedral continues to welcome another generation of visitors from all parts of the world.

INDEX

A

Abarno, Frank, 98
Academy of Music, 20
Adams, Gerry, 223
Adams, John Quincy, 16
Addabo, Joseph (Congressman), 206
Agricola, 6
air conditioning, 174, 175
Albany Diocese, 15, 32
Alexander Pelli Co., 114, 126, 133
Alive and Well and Living in New York City, 181
Alive and Well at St. Patrick's Cathedral, 109
Allen, Mel, 222
Allen, "Wes," 38
altar railing 117
altars, 60
altars: Blessed Sacrament, 175, 176, 210
altars: high altar, 39, 115, 133-35, 163, 175
altars: Holy Family, 40, 61
altars: Lady Chapel, 81, 115, 132-133
altars: liturgical altar, 202, 204
altars: location, 51
altars: Sacred Heart, 40, 94, 175-176
altars: St. Andrew, 110
altars: St. Anthony, 61, 142
altars: St. Augustine, 61, 179
altars: St. Bernard and St. Brigid, 86, 97
altars: St. Elizabeth, 83
altars: St. John Baptiste de la Salle, 61, 142, 192
altars: St. John the Evangelist, 60
altars: St. Joseph, 40, 110
altars: St. Michael and St. Louis, 83
altars: St. Rose of Lima, 87
altars: St. Stanislaus Kostka, 61, 178
altars: St. Therese of Lisieux, 113-114
altars: St. Veronica (Holy Face), 60
Alzamora, Vargas (Card.), 223
American Architect and Building News, 64
American Expeditionary Forces, 108
American Symphony Orchestra, 189
Anderson, Mary, 44, 104
Anderson, Terry, 216
Andreotti, Giulio (P. M.), 215
Andrew, John (Rev.), 182

Angel, John, 135, 143
Angelini, Fiorenzo (Card.), 216
Annan, Kofi (Sec. Gen.), 222
anniversary of SPC, 110, 195, 236
anti-Catholicism in N. Y., 11
Apostolic Administrator of Military Vicariate, 202
Arafat, Yasir, 223
Archdiocese of N. Y., 74
Archduke Lawrence, 223
architecture of SPC, 24, 34, 36, 43
archives, 209
Arias Sanchez, Oscar (Pres.), 206
Armand Calliat Studios, 63
Arndi-Condo, Enrico, 190
Arnold, William (Bish.), 148
Arthur, Chester (Pres.), 35
Arts and Crafts Movement, 82, 100
Aspinwall, Anna Lloyd, 28
Atkins, Albert, 117, 127
Atkins, George A., 98
Atlantic Cable, 23
Auriesville, N. Y., 1

B

Bacon, Henry, 94
baldachin, 39, 115, 135, 163, 175, 212
Baltimore Diocese, 4, 7
baptistry (baptismal font), 40, 47, 118, 180, 204
Barclay Street, 2
Bardstown, Ky., 5
Bardon, Nelson, 210
barge canal, 10
Basilica of the Incarnation (Nazareth), 179
Baum, William (Card.), 206, 216, 222
bells, 64, 76, 77, 87, 211
Belmont, August, 35
Bennett, Fred, 101
Bennett, James Gordon, 15, 16
Benziger Company, 127
Benziger, Mr. and Mrs. Bruno, 118
Bernstein, Leonard, 173
Berra, Yogi, 223
Berres, Battle (Pres.), 156

Best and Company, 140
Bicentennial of U. S. A., 183
Beverly Minster Cathedral, 26
Bevilacqua, Anthony (Card.), 216
Beyer, Blinder and Belle, 213
"Big Red Scare," 110
Board of Trustees, 59
Boland Trade School, 69, 74
Bolivar, Simon, 120
Bolger, James (P. M.), 215
Bonzano, John (Card.), 97, 99, 106, 111
Borden Family, 175
Borgia Company, 62
Borgognini-Duca, Francesco (Arch.), 129
Boston, Mass., 5
Boston University, 136
boundaries of SPC parish, 44
Bouvier Family, 63
Bouvier, Louise Vernoa, 83
Bouvier, Michael C., 83
Bowes, Edward (Maj.), 131, 132, 138, 141,
    143, 148
Boy Scouts of America, 120
Boyle, Frank, 230
boys choir, 59
boys club, 66, 109
Brady, Genevieve, 113
Brady, Mr. and Mrs. Nicholas, 123
Breckinridge, John (Rev.), 14
Brevoort Family, 17
Broderick, Edwin, (Bish.), 145
Brooklyn Bridge, 54
Brooklyn Diocese, 70
Brooklyn, N. Y., 69
Brother Roger of Taize, 193
Broun, Heywood, 120
Brown, Andrew, 100
Buba, Joy, 192
Buchanan, James (Pres.), 23
Buckingham Palace, 63
Budenz, Louis, 148
Buffalo Diocese, 15
Bundschuh, John, 178
Burger, Warren (Chief Justice), 206
Burton, Katherine, 158
Bush, George H. W. (Pres.), 227
Bush, George W. (Pres.), 227

C
Cabaret, Paul, 88
Cahill, Kevin (Dr.), 195
Calhoun, John C. (V.P.), 16
Calvary Cemetery, 18, 57, 109
canteen of SPC, 138
Canterbury Cathedral, 63
Canterbury School (Ct.), 82
Capital of U. S. A., first, 4
Capitol Building, U. S., 34
Caprio, John-Michael, 210, 216, 223-224
Carbone, Carmine, 98
Cardinal Cooke Guild, 203
Cardinal's Special Gift Committee, 119
Carey, Hugh (Gov.), 184
Carimini, 39
Carnegie Hall, 54, 92, 112
Carreras, Jose, 194
Carroll Bernard, 122, 213
Carroll, Charles (of Carrollton), 11
Carroll, John (Arch.), 4, 7, 8
Carthy, Sr. Margaret, 232
Caruso, Enrico, 112, 125
Casey, Robert (Gov.), 215
Cassidy, Edward (Card.), 216
Cassidy, Richard, 190
cathedra, 39, 116
Cathedral bulletin, 109
Cathedral Club, 59
Cathedral; College, 89, 106, 174
Cathedral College (Douglaston, N. Y.), 174
Cathedral elementary school, 132
Cathedral Free Circulating Library, 59, 66
Cathedral High School, 89
Cathedral Literary Society, 59
Cathedral Sanctuary Society, 63
Catholic Charities, 106
Catholic Club, 66, 92
Catholic Library Association, 59
Catholic Summer School of America, 59, 69
Catholic Theater Movement, 109
Catholic University of America, 71, 90, 106,
    111-112, 171
Catholic Youth Organization, 171
Catholics of N. Y., 1-2, 5, 7, 10-11, 16, 33,
    47-48, 89, 149-150, 172, 182
ceiling, 24, 35-36, 50, 51, 59, 176
cemetery in N. Y., Catholic, 8

cemetery on site of SPC, 18
Centenary of Diocese of N. Y., 92
Centenary of SPC, 184-185
Central Park Apartments, 44
chair used at blessing of cornerstone, 156
Champ, H. C., 65
Chandler, Elizabeth Gordon, 209
Chapel of St. Elizabeth, 178
Chapel of Sts. Faith, Hope and Charity, 153, 191, 205
Chapel of St. Michael and St. Louis, 178
Charles II, 1
Cheverus, John (Bish.), 9
Chicago, 17
Chicago World's Fair of 1893, 63
chimes, 60
Chippendale chair, 192, 199
Christian Brothers (Brothers of the Christian Schools), 15, 47, 61
Christmas Midnight Mass, 132, 146, 156
Churchill, Winston (P.M.), 149
civic events and ceremonies, 91-92
Civil War (U.S.), 26, 33
Clark, Eugene (Msgr.), 235
Clark, Patrick, 232
Clay, Henry, 16
Clemente, Roberto, 182
Clinton, DeWitt (Gov.), 10
Clinton, Hillary (Sen.), 227
Clinton, William (Pres.), 215, 227
Clonmacnoise Monastery, 86
Clooney, Rosemary, 223
Coadjutor Bishop of N. Y. , 11
Cochran, W. Bourke (Congr.), 79, 86
Cody, John (Card.), 172
Coleman Family, 63
Coleman, George B., 66
Coleman, J., 74, 86, 93
Coleman, John A. 157, 179, 191-192
Coleman, Michael S., 66
college (first Catholic) in N. Y., 9
Collegio Angelico, 112
Cologne Cathedral, 18, 63,185
Colton, Stockton B., 71
Columbia College, 17, 46
Columbian Centennial of 1892, 66, 67
Columbian Marble Quarrying Co., 73
communion breakfasts, 70

Como, Perry, 156
Concanen, Richard Luke (Bish.), 7
concerts, 189-190, 199
confessionals, 40
Congress, U. S. (under Articles of Confed.), 2
Connick, Charles J.,135, 141
Connolly, Eugene (Rev.), 219
Connolly, John (Bish.), 9-10
Connolly, Joseph (architect), 71
Connolly, Joseph (usher), 192
Consecration of SPC, 92
Considine, Bob, 183
construction of SPC, 34-36
contract for construction of SPC, 25
Cook, Leland, 177
Cook, Clarence, 42
Cooke, Terence (Card.), 7, 11, 171, 173, 185, 194-195, 203
Cooper-Hewitt Museum, 100
Corcoran Gallery, 17
cornerstone, 21-23
Corpus Christi Cemetery (Pa.), 27
Corpus Christi Church, 171
Corrigan, Michael (Arch.), 47, 54, 58-60, 68, 73, 79
Corripio-Ahumada, Ernesto (Card.), 211, 216
cost of construction, 25, 56
cost of renovation, 116
County Meath, 9
Courboin, Charles, 142, 145-146, 156, 167
Court of General Session, 9
Coveney, John, 57
Cox, Stanley, 223
Cram and Wentworth, 71
Cram, Ralph Adams, 136
creche, 204
Crimmins, John D., 66, 74, 83, 89-90, 93, 104
Crimmins, Lily Louise Lalor, 83
Cronkite, Walter, 183-184
Croton Distributing Reservoir, 17
Croton reservoir system, 88
crypt, 47, 173, 196, 210
Cuomo, Mario (Gov.), 195, 215
Cusack, Thomas F. (Bish.), 87, 106
Cushing, Richard (Card.), 172
Cuypers, Peter J. H., 63, 76

D

Dalai Lama, 186

Dalla Villa, Anthony (Msgr.), 208-209, 219, 235

Daly, Augustine, 61, 66, 75

Daly, Cahal (Card.), 216

Daly, Daniel, 60

Daly, William J. (Rev.), 60, 135

D'Amato, Alfonse (Sen.), 206, 215, 220

Danner, Harry, 194

Dargin, Edward V. (Bish.), 112

Darren, James, 216

Daughters of Mary, Help of the Sick, 133

Davis, Alan, 217

Day, Dorothy, 225

Deacy, Michael (Rev.), 145

de Bouche, Carl, 82, 101

de Brebeuf, St. Jean, 1, 139

Dedication of SPC, 42

dell'Acqua, Agnelo (Card.), 172

Delmonico's Restaurant, 33, 57

de Murville, Couve (Arch.), 222

del Sarto, Andrea, 88

de Macchi, Clement, 90

de Moya, Pedro, 88

Dempsey, Jack, 183

de Navarro, Alfonse; Antonio; Ellen Dykers, 94, 104

de Navarro, Jose F., 44, 50

de Paul, Vincent (Rev.), 29

Desmoulins, Camille, 11

de Valera, Eamon, 108

Dewey, Thomas (Gov.), 140, 148

Dickerson, Nancy, 222

Di Maggio, Joe, 216, 222, 223

dimensions of SPC, 23-24,39,86,102

dimensions of SPC in St. Peter's Basilica, 145

Dinkins, David (Mayor), 215

Diocese of N. Y. centenary, 92

Dix, John (Gov.), 97

Dix Island granite, 26

Dom Augustine, 18, 29

Domingo, Placido, 194

Dominican Order (Order of Preachers), 7

Donahue, Stephen (Bish.), 121, 129-130

Dongan, Thomas (Gov.), 2

Donnellan, Thomas (Arch.), 145

Donohoe, Joseph, 61

Donohoe, Mrs. Joseph, 61

Dona Pilar, 195

doors, 39, 88, 141-142, 204

Dougherty, Andrew, 110

Dougherty, Dennis (Card.), 132

Douglas, Stephen A. (Sen.), 16

Draddy Brothers, 48, 62, 86

Draddy, John, 60, 62, 76

draft riots (N. Y.), 27

Drennan, John (Capt.), 218

Drexel, Mrs. Joseph, 62

Drew, John, 61

DuBois, John (Bish.), 11, 14-15, 32

Duffy, Francis (Rev.), 108, 120, 124

Duffy Square, 108, 120

Duke of Verague, 67

Duke of Windsor, 149

Dumler, Donald, 188, 216-217

Dunn, John (Bish.), 121

Dunne, Thomas, 107

Duran-ballen, Sixto (Pres.), 215, 223

Durer, Albrecht, 86

D'Urso, Florence, 210, 212, 214

Duval, George F., 94

Dyer, Thomas, 26

E

Eastchester quarry, 25

economic conditions in N. Y., 54

ecumenism, 182, 193

Egan, Edward (Card.), 228, 234-236

Eggers and Higgins Co., 142

E. Howard Clock Co., 64

elevator, 151, 211

Elgin Gardens, 9, 18

Ellis Island, 54

Ellison, Cori, 217

Ely, Henry, 41, 51, 52

Ely, Smith (Mayor), 37

Empire State Building, 34, 148

Equitable Life Assurance Co., 44

explosion, 97

F

fair, 36, 37

Falconio, Diomede (Card.), 81, 90, 99

Farley, John (Card.), 44, 52, 68, 80-81, 86-87, 90, 92, 94, 96, 99, 106

Farley, James A., 121, 147, 183, 191-192, 199
Farmer, Ferdinand (Rev.), 2
Fathers of Mercy, 15
Feeney, Leonard (Rev.), 121
Fellowes, Mrs. Maren, 151
Fenech-Adami, Edward (P.M.), 215
Ferrante, Gerard (Rev.), 66
Ferrer, Francisco, 97
Ferro Studios, 118
Ferry, John (Msgr.), 235
Field, Cyrus W., 23, 38
fife and drum corps, 66
Fifth Avenue, 1
Fifth Avenue Coach Co., 89
Figlio, Vincenzo Demetz, 204
finances, 66, 71, 73, 89-90, 92, 109, 118-119,
    138, 150, 158, 190, 192, 210, 224-225,
    230
financing construction of SPC, 20-21, 26, 33-
    34, 36, 49, 81
Finney, Mrs. C., 62
fire danger; precautions, 59, 70, 107, 158,
    175, 212-213
first resident priest in N. Y., 2
Five Points section of N.Y., 106
Flannelly, Joseph (Bish.), 132, 134, 141, 148,
    173,   182-183, 197
Flannery, Michael, 194-195
flags, 143-144
Flatiron Building, 88
Fleming, Renee, 217
floor, 39, 51, 115, 142, 211
flying buttresses, 59
Flynn, Raymond (Ambass.), 215
Foch, Ferdinand (Mar.), 111
Foley, John Philip, 97, 110
Ford, Whitey, 218
Fordham University, 15, 129, 134, 171
Fox, Edward, 66
Fox, James Edward, 66
Franciscans, 62
Franz Joseph (Emp.), 99
Franz Meyer Co., 82, 101
Freeh, Louis, 215, 220
French, Daniel Chester, 94
Friendly Sons of St. Patrick, 92
Furlong, Philip (Bish.), 126, 145
furnishings, 35

G

Gagnon, Edouard (Card.), 216
galero, 35, 49, 90, 161, 177, 195
Ganev, Stoyan (Pres.), 215
Gannon, Robert (Rev.), 161, 173
Garden State Art Center, 176
Garfulla's Band, 37
gargoyles, 140
Gasparri, Pietro (Card.), 114
Gasparri Studios, 178
Gau, F. -C., 17
General Bronze Co., 134
George, Henry, 54
George Fuller Co., 140
George Kilgen Co., 116
George Mann Co., 56
Georgia Marble Co., 141
Georgetown Academy (University), 3
Giaquinto, Paolo, 122
Gibbons, James (Card.), 74, 90, 92
gift shop, 225
Gill, Patrick, 138
Gillespie, George J., 133
Gillis and Geoghegan, 51
Gilmore's Band, 37
Gilsoul, Benoit, 192-193
Giordani, Marcello, 224
Giuliani, Rudolph (Mayor), 215-216, 220,
    227
Glemp, Jozef (Card.), 216
Glennon, John (Card.), 90
Glickman, Marty, 223
Goldberg, Arthur (Ambass.), 172
Gong, Ignatius (Card.), 223
Gore, Al (V. P.), 227
Gothic architecture, 17
Gould, Jay, 45
Gousset of Rheims, 71
Gowdy, Curt, 223
Grace Church, 17
Grace, William Russell, 44, 74, 79, 93, 104
Grady, John F., 188, 193-194, 216
Grand Central Palace, 66
Grand Central Station, 88
Grand Duchess Charlotte, 149
Grant, Hugh, 74, 93
Grant, Julia, 133, 135, 138

Grant Memorial (Wash., D. C.), 178
Graziano, Rocky, 218
Great Depression, 115, 118, 130
Greeley, Horace, 16, 21, 47
Greene, William (Rev.), 146
Greenwood Cemetery, 76
Griffiths, James (Bish.), 145
Groeschel, Benedict (Rev.), 203
Gronchi, Giovanni (Pres.), 156
Guard, S., 144
Guibe, Paul, 39, 41
Guilfoyle, George (Bish.), 145
Gunella, Paul, 83, 101
Gunther, Herbert, 179-180
Guterres, Antonio, (P. M.), 223

H
Hadley, Jerry, 217
Haight, C. C., 71
Halback Co., 143
Hall and Joyce Co., 25
Hall, James, 25-27, 33
Hamilton, Peter, 56
Hammarskjold, Dag (Sec. Gen.), 156
Hammer, Henry, Rev. 109
Hardin, Adlai S., 193, 204
Harlem Railroad, 34
Harriman, Averell (Gov.), 156
Hart, William T. A., 58
Hartford Cathedral, 62
Hayasaka, Januarius (Bish.), 111
Hayes, Patrick (Card.), 97-98, 106-107, 109-
    111, 114, 117-118, 120, 123
Hayes, Helen, 183, 206
Hearst. William Randolph, 183
heating, 39, 87, 115, 136-137
Heeney, Cornelius, 6
Heins and LaFarge, 71
Helmsley Palace Hotel, 191
Henry, Charles, 150
Henry, Patrick, 11
heraldic arms, 177
Hernandez, Orlando, 223
Hildreth, Amelia Dougherty, 110
Hildreth Family, 63
Hitler, Adolf, 130
Holloway, Mr. and Mrs. Caswell F., 204
Holtz, Lou, 223

Holy Cross Church, 108
Holy Family Church, 188
Holy Name Society, 59, 66
Holy Trinity Church, 72
holy water fonts, 63
holy water well, 62, 117
home of Archbishop Hughes, 20, 26
honorary ushers, 70
Hope, Dolores, 216, 223
Hope, Bob, 183, 206
Horne, Marilyn, 216
horse and carriage of Card. McCloskey, 50
House of Representatives (U. S.), 16
Howard, William, 38
Hubbard, Elbert, 101
Hudson-Fulton Festival, 91
Hudson River, 10
Hughes, Barnard, 194
Hughes, John (Arch.), 1, 11, 26, 31, 47
Humphrey, Hubert (V. P.), 161, 172
Hurons, 1

I
Iacocca, Lee, 206
Iakavos, Archbishop, 182
I. J. Verdin Co., 151
immigrants, 110
immigrants, Irish, 3
immigrants, Italian, 109
information center of SPC, 152
Ingersoll-Rand Co., 44
interment of remains of Arch. Hughes, 47
Ioli, Georgiana, 193
Irving and Casson, 117

J
Jackson, Andrew (Pres.), 11
Jadot, Jean (Arch.), 185
James E. Mitchell Co., 178
James II, 1
Jardine, George, 41
Javore, James, 194
Javits, Jacob (Sen.), 161
Jesuits (Society of Jesus), 1, 15
Jogues, St. Isaac, 1
John Hardman Co., 82
Johnson, Lyndon (Pres.), 161, 172

Journal of the Fair, 28
Joyce William, 25-27, 33, 49

K

Kelleher, Michael, 144
Kellenberg, Walter (Bish.), 120
Kellner, John (Rev.), 59, 67
Kelly, Eugene, 44, 50, 53, 60, 71, 74, 78
Kelly, Eugene, Jr., 73, 81, 82
Kelly, Margaret, 71
Kelly, Thomas, 66, 73, 82, 121, 163
Kendall, Edward, 72
Kennedy, Edward (Sen.), 215
Kennedy, John F. (Pres.), 83, 130
Kennedy, Joseph P., 129
Kennedy, Robert (Sen.), 161, 172, 196
Kennedy, Thomas (Arch.), 90, 99
Keyes, Eleanora, 66
Kilbegnet, Ireland, 7
Kilmer, Joyce, 98
King Hussein, 223
King, John A. (Gov.), 23
King Louis XV, 11
King, Martin Luther (Dr.), 172
King Victor Emmanuel III, 112
Knights of Columbus, 99
Know-Nothing Party, 16
Koch, Edward (Mayor), 180, 184, 203, 206, 220
Kohl, Helmut (Chan.), 215
Kohlmann, Anthony (Rev.), 7-9, 13, 18
Koop, John and Mary, 66
Korbel, Mario, 114, 126
Korean War, 149
Kraft, Adam, 39
Krol, John (Card.), 172
Kuhn, Bowie, 182-183
Ku Klux Klan, 110

L

Lady Chapel, 40, 56, 59-60, 71, 78, 81, 100, 235
Laetare Medal, 61
La Farge, John, 53
Lafayette, Marquis de, 11
Laghi, Pio (Card.), 207, 223
Lake Champlain, 10
Lake Huron, 1

Lammell, Anthony (Rev.), 44, 59
landmark, 158, 190-191
La Sala, Francis J., 206
La Salle Academy, 57, 106
Lasorda, Tommy, 216
Lateran Basilica, 7
Lateran Treaty, 111
La Trappe (Tracadie), 29
Lauria, Charles, 146
Lavelle, Michael (Msgr.), 23, 43, 57-58, 60, 65, 67- 68, 80-82, 87, 89, 92, 99, 108-109, 114, 117-118, 128, 130, 133, 162
law banishing Catholics, 2
Law, Bernard (Card.), 201, 228
Lawe, John, 218
League of the Sacred Heart, 59, 63
Leary, Anne, 96
Leary, George, 96
LeBrun, Napoleon, 71
Lee Marble Works, 34
Le Febvre, Philippe, 190
Leghorn (Livorno), Italy, 7
Lehman, Herbert (Gov.), 147
Leipzig Conservatory of Music, 44
Letters From An American Farmer, 6
library: *See:* Cathedral Free Circulating Library; New York Public Library
lighting, 39, 67, 87, 100, 117, 208
Likar-Waltersdorff, Maria, 178
Lipinski, Tara, 223
Lincoln Center for the Performing Arts, 179
Lincoln Memorial (Washington, D. C.), 94
Lincoln, Abraham (Pres.), 26
Lindbergh, Charles, 111
Lindsay, Antoinette, 152
Lindsay, John (Mayor), 161, 172
Liszt, Franz, 113
Little and O'Connor, 71, 81
Lockwood-Mathews Mansion Museum, 72
Lodge, Henry Cabot (Ambas.), 156
Logue, Michael (Card.), 92
Lombardi, Vince, 182, 197
Lord Halifax, 147
Long, Robert J., 224
Lopez-Rodriguez, Nicolo (Card.), 216, 223
Lopez-Trujillo, Alfonso (Card.), 216
Loren, Sophia, 216
Lorin, Nicholas, 41, 52

Louis Le Grand, College of, 11
Louvain, Belgium, 7
Louvain University, 112
Luce, Clare Boothe, 148, 206, 218
Luhan, Manuel (Sec.), 215
Lusitania, 97
Lustiger, Jean-Marie (Card.), 216
Lylburn, Robert, 18, 21, 46
Lynch, Dominick, 3, 10
Lynch, John (P. M.), 172
Lynch, Kenneth, 180

M

MacArthur, Douglas (Gen.), 156
MacDonald, George (Marquise), 153
Mack, John, 34
MacSwiney, Terence (Mayor), 108
Maginnis and Walsh, 114-117, 140
Maginnis, Charles, 115, 126, 132-133, 141-142
Maguire, John (Arch.), 171
Mahoney, James (Bish.), 187
Maldarelli, Oronzio, 133
Mangin, Joseph, 8
Manhattan Bridge, 88
Manhattan College, 57, 106, 174
Manhattanville, 20
Manning, John B., 66, 70, 74
Mansell, Henry (Bish.), 227
Mantle, Mickey, 218
Mara, Wellington, 214
marble of SPC, 24-25, 30, 34, 50, 56, 73, 107, 119, 140, 164, 165, 177, 179-180
Marechal, Ambrose (Arch.), 11
Maris, Roger, 205
Marquise de San Marzano, 63, 66
Marshall, Alton, 184
Marshall, Mrs. J. L., 113
Martin, Billy, 218
Martinelli, Giovanni, 122, 145
Martino, Renato (Arch.), 223
Mass, first in N. Y., 2
Mathews, Charles T., 71-72, 78, 81-83, 86-87, 121
Maycher, Lorenz, 217
McAleenan, Henry, 66
McCall, Cormack, 23
McCarrick, Theodore (Card.), 227

McCormack, John, 111, 148
McCormick, Owen, 107, 147
McCloskey, John (Card.), 15, 27, 80
McCloskey, Thomas (Rev.), 58
McDonnell, Charles (Bish.), 44, 52
McDonnell, Thomas (Bish.), 134
McEntegart, Bryan J. (Bish.), 112
McGlynn, Edward (Rev.), 52, 55, 102, 106
McGovern, Mrs. Patrick, 136
McIntyre, James (Card.), 134, 137, 172
McMahon, Joseph (Rev.), 59, 73
McManus, Charles (Rev.), 152
McKim, Mead and White, 46, 94
McMackin, Daniel (Rev.), 86
McMillan, Marion, 117
McNally, Augustine, 121
Medeiros, Humberto (Card.), 186
Medici, Paolo, 81, 83
meeting rooms, 178
Mehta, Zubin, 189
Meiere, Hildreth, 133
Meisner, Joachim (Card.), 223
Melba, Nellie (Dame), 68, 77
Mellifont Monastery (Ireland), 86
Mercier, Desire (Card.), 107-108
Merle, Vincent (Rev.), 29
Merrill, Robert, 206
Metropolitan Elevated Railway system, 44
Metropolitan Museum of Art, 26
Metropolitan Opera Company, 188
Metropolitan Opera House, 90
Metropolitan Opera Orchestra, 189
Middle Road, 1
Military Archdiocese of U. S., 203
Military Diocese of U. S., 106
Military Vicar of the Armed Forces, 137
Millo, Aprile, 217
Mills Family, 63
Mills, Maria A., 66
Mindszenty, Joseph (Card.), 183, 198
Minervini, Anthony, 176, 179
Miniter, Aloysia, 66
Miracle In The Rain, 157
Mitchell Co., 176
Mitchell, Philip, 151, 175, 204
Mitty, John (Arch.), 131
Monaco stamp, 185
Monroe, James (Pres.), 11

Montes de Oca y Obregon, Jose Ignacio (Arch.), 109
Moore, Emerson (Bish.), 219
Moore, Mary Young, 138, 143, 167
Moreira-Neves, Lucas (Card.), 223
Morgan Brothers, 40
Morgan, J. Pierpont, 54
Morris, Andrew, 5
Morris, William, 100
Morron, Isabelle G. (Marquesa), 152
Morron, John R., 152
Moscona, Nicola, 122
Mother Teresa of Calcutta, 207, 216, 222-223
Mott Street, N. Y., 8
Mt. St. Mary's College and Seminary, 14, 32, 54
Mt. St. Vincent College, 112, 174
Moynihan, Daniel Patrick (Sen.), 206
Mundelein, George (Card.), 123
Municipal Art Society, 180
Municipal Building, 88
music program, 44, 68, 90-91, 110-111, 113, 122, 146, 156-157, 188-190, 193-194, 217, 223-224
musical and dramatic society, 66
Musiel, Stan, 223

N
Naples, Italy, 7
Napoleonic wars, 7
Nathanson, Bernard (Dr.), 222
National Academy of Sciences, 133
National Catholic War Council, 106
National Shrine of the Immaculate Conception, 115
nativists in N. Y., 11, 15-16
NBC Symphony Orchestra, 112
Nebraska State Capitol, 133
neighborhood, 35, 45-46, 89, 93, 150
New Amsterdam, 1
New York Archdiocese, 16, 48
New York Association for the Care of Troops, 109
New York City growth, 69, 88, 93
New York City problems, 172
New York Diocese, 7
New York Herald, 15

New York Literary Institution, 9, 18
New York Mutual Company, 51
New York population, 5, 7, 10, 130, 172
New York Public Library, 17, 59, 88
New York subway system, 88
New York transportation, 199
New York Tribune, 16
Nichols, Mike, 223
Nicholson and Galloway Co., 179
Nielson, Thomas (Msgr.), 188, 198
Nixon, Richard (Pres.), 206
nocturnal adoration, 218
Norman, Jessye, 216
North American College (Rome), 54, 86, 129, 174
Notre Dame Cathedral (Paris), 17
Nugent, Andrew (Rev.), 3
Nuremberg Cathedral, 39

O
Oblates of the Blessed Trinity, 213
O'Boyle, Patrick (Card.), 172
O'Brien, Edwin F. (Arch.), 187, 227
O'Brien, William (Rev.), 4, 7
O'Connor Family, 63
O'Connor, John (Card.), 201, 203, 217, 218, 211, 225-228
O'Connor, John, 110
O'Donnell, James, 209
O'Donohue, Thomas (Col.), 70
O'Donohue Family, 63
O'Donohue, Joseph J, 66, 110
O'Dwyer, William (Mayor), 140
O'Farrell, Michael C. (Rev.), 57
O'Farrell Michael J. (Bish.), 47
O'Keefe, Joseph, (Bish.), 201
O'Malley, Sean (Bish.), 227
Onassis, Jacqueline Bouvier Kennedy, 83, 180
O'Reilly Family, 63
organs, 210, 224
organs: chancel, 44, 116
organs: gallery, 41, 115-117, 188
orphanages, 9, 18, 38, 46, 53, 56, 69
Ortega y Alamino, Jaime (Card.), 223
Our Lady of Einsiedeln, 118
Our Lady of Guadalupe painting, 211-212
Our Lady of Lourdes Church, 73, 79
Our Lady of the Rosary Church, 132

Our Neighbors program, 181, 193
Oursler, Fulton, 157

P

Paccard Co., 77
Paccard, Georges and Francisque, 64
Pacelli, Eugenio (Card.) (Pope Pius XII), 122, 123, 129
Paderewski, Ignace Jan, 147
Page, J. August (Col), 46
paintings, 88, 143, 211-212
pallium, 16, 55, 106, 132, 202
papal visits to SPC, 159-160, 186, 219-221, 232
parades, 66, 92, 103, 104, 124, 219, 225
Paris International Exposition, 17
parish house (rectory), 44, 46, 53, 132, 178, 193
Parish Visitors, 133
parishioners of SPC, 58
Park Avenue, 46
Partridge, William Ordway, 94
paschal candle holder, 110
Pastore, Joseph, 157
Pataki, George (Gov.), 216, 220, 227
Patrick Baker and Sons, 210, 212
Patterson, Frank, 194, 206, 223
Paulists, 15
Pavarotti, Luciano, 194
Pax Romana, 121
Peabody Conservatory of Music, 146
Pecher, William, 42, 44, 52, 64, 67-68, 90
Pelligrini, Ernest, 139
Pennsylvania Academy of Fine Arts, 135
Pennsylvania Station, 88
Pepitone, Joe, 223
Peragallo Pipe Organ Co., 211
Perez, Raymond B., 93
Perez, Juan (Rev.), 93
persecution of Catholics in N. Y., 2
Pershing, John J. (Gen.), 108
pewholders, 192
pews, 39, 44, 66, 117, 177, 192
Philadelphia, Pa., 5
Philadelphia Centenary Exposition of 1876, 41
Philadelphia City Hall, 56
Philadelphia Diocese, 14

Philharmonic Society Orchestra, 68
Phillips, Etta, 110, 124, 125
Piccirilli Brothers, 81, 83, 101, 133
Piccirilli, Joseph, 153
Pieta, 94, 151
pigeons, 144
Pitti Chapel of the Princes, 153
plague (yellow fever), 4
Polk, James K (Pres.), 16
Poole, Thomas, 88
Pope Clement X, 113
Pope John XXIII, 156-157
Pope John Paul II, 186-187
Pope Leo XIII, 42, 96, 103
Pope Paul VI, 159-160, 183
Pope Pius VII, 7, 8
Pope Pius IX, 16, 23, 32, 40
Pope Pius X, 90, 92
Pope Pius XI, 121, 129
Pope Pius XII, 114, 122, 129
population of New York, 5, 7, 10, 130, 172
Portland Cement Co., 44
Post, George B., 71
Pottier and Stymus Co., 62
Powderly, Terence, 54
Power Brothers Co., 35-36
Power, John (Rev.), 11
Prefect Apostolic of the United States, 4
Prince, Arn, 217
Prince Philippe, 217
Prince Street, 8
Princess Asrid, 223
Princess Eulalie, 67, 77
Princess Maria Teresa, 223
Princeton University, 136
protests, 160, 190, 194, 207, 214, 231
Prothonotary Apostolic, 80, 171
pulpit, 48, 53, 135
Purcell, John (Arch.), 52

Q

Quebec, 1
Queen Wilhelmena, 111
Queensboro Bridge, 88, 90
Quinn, John (Rev.), 109
Quinn, William (Msgr.), 43, 52, 57

R

Rachmaninoff, Sergei, 146
Raimondi, Luigi (Arch.), 151, 158
Rambusch Co., 175
ramp, 176
Randolph, Willie, 218
Raphael, 88
Reagan, Ronald (Pres.), 195
Redemptorists, 15, 62
Reh, Francis (Bish.), 145
Rehan, Ada, 61
Reid, Whitelaw, 52
Reign of Terror, 11
Reiley, Robert J, 115-118, 126, 133
relics, 149, 222
Rendall, David, 216
Reno, Janet (Atty. Gen.), 215
renovations of SPC, 114-118
Renwick and Aspinwall, 71
Renwick, Aspinwall and Owen, 76
Renwick, Aspinwall and Russell, 75
Renwick, James Jr., 17, 20, 28, 33, 59, 76,
    102, 144, 191
residence of Archbishop, 44, 46, 142, 204
restoration of exterior of SPC, 179-180
restoration of interior of SPC, 176-177
reviewing stand, 92
Revolutionary War, 2
Reynolds, Albert (P. M.), 215, 223
Rhind, John Massey, 62
Richards, Maria Louisa Fernandez Criada, 153
Rigale, Justin, (Arch.), 227
Rigney, James F. (Msgr.), 174, 181, 185, 196,
    208
Rigney, P. (Rev.), 61
Ritchie, Robert (Msgr.), 235
Rivetti, Edward, 122, 145-146, 156, 218
Rizzuto, Phil, 223
Robespierre Maximilien, 11
Rockefeller Center, 18, 175
Rockefeller, Nelson, (V. P.), 151, 161, 172
Rockwood Alabama Stone Co., 141
Rodrigue, William, 20, 34
Roehrs Co., 207
Roman Catholic Orphan Asylum, 110
Romanesque architecture, 17
Romulo, Carlos (Gen.), 183
roof, 51, 141, 208

Roosevelt, Eleanor, 148
Roosevelt, Franklin Delano (Pres.), 106, 116,
    118, 130, 148
Roosevelt, Theodore (Pres.), 74, 92
Rostagno, Joseph (Msgr.), 113, 125
Roth, Mr. and Mrs. Arthur, 175
Royal Academy (London), 135
Royal Conservatory (Milan), 112
Rummel, Joseph (Arch.), 123
Ruppert, Jacob, 121
Rusk, Dean (Secy.), 172
Ruth, Babe, 148
Rutledge, Joseph, 62, 87
Ryan, Clendenin, 142
Ryan, Joseph (Arch.), 203
Ryan, Mrs. Thomas F., 66
Ryan, Patrick, (Bish.), 42
Ryan, Penelope, 181
Ryan, Thomas Fortune, 45

S

Sacred Heart Church, 174
Sacred Heart Sisters, 15
sacred vessels, 135, 152
sacred vessels: chalice of Archbishop Sheen,
    187
sacred vessels: chalice from Pope Leo XIII, 48
sacred vessels: monstrance (ostensorium) of
    1893, 63
sacred vessels: Tiffany monstrance, 204, 205
sacristy, 40, 56, 59, 81, 87, 96
St. Ann's Academy, 146
St. Aloysius Church, 174
St. Alphonsus Church, 97
St. Andrew's Church, 106
St. Brieuc (France), 40
St. Cecilia's Academy (Rome), 112
St. Charles Borromeo Seminary, 201
St. Francis Xavier Church, 112
St. Francis Xavier Church (St. Louis), 62
St. Francis Xavier College, 44
St. Gabriel's Church, 80, 106
Saint-Gaudens, Augustus, 94
St. Gudule Cathedral, 26
St. Isaac Jogues, 1, 120
St. Jean de Brebeuf, 1
St. John Bosco, 120
St. John de Crevecoeur, Hector, 3, 6

St. John the Divine Cathedral, 54, 135, 136
St. John the Evangelist Church, 18, 21, 29, 41, 46
St. John the Evangelist Church (Philadelphia), 20
St. John's College (Fordham University), 20, 32, 80
St. Joseph's Church, 11, 32
St. Joseph's Institute for the Deaf, 38
St. Joseph's Seminary (Troy, N. Y.), 57
St. Joseph's Seminary (Yonkers, N. Y.), 62, 70, 94, 110, 171
St. Lawrence River, 1
St. Louis Exposition of 1904, 62
St. Luke's Hospital, 59
St. Mary's Church, 11
St. Ouen Cathedral (Rouen), 26
St. Patrick's Day, 92
St. Patrick's Day Parade, 108
St. Patrick's Old Cathedral, 8, 10-11, 14, 16, 32-33, 57, 96
St. Paul's Cathedral (Pittsburgh), 62
St. Paul's Church (Brooklyn, N. Y.), 6
St. Peter's Basilica (Rome), 83
St. Peter's Church, 3-4, 7-8, 32
St. Peter's Church, (Staten Island), 80
St. Peter's School, 5
St. Stephen's Cathedral (Vienna), 179
St. Stephen's Church, 102, 106
St. Thomas Church, 202
St. Thomas Episcopal Church, 45, 87
Ste. Clotilde Church (Paris), 17
San Domenigo Maggiore Church (Naples), 7
Sanchez, Jose (Card.), 216
sanctuary, 39, 115-116
Santo Domingo, 20
Sawyer, Diane, 223
Scalia, Antonin (Justice), 215
Schickel, William, 71
Schmieg, Karl, 192
school of SPC, 47
Schulmerich Carillon Co., 211
Scorzelli, Lello, 192
Scotto, Renata, 193
Scully, William (Bish.), 134, 145
seal of confessional, 9
Second Bank of the U. S., 20

security problems; precautions, 66, 158, 190, 207, 214
sedelia, 39, 116
seminary, 19
seminary (Nyack, N. Y.), 11
seminary on site of SPC, 29
September 11, 2001, 235
services, 58, 68, 91, 97-99,119, 138, 147-148, 150, 154-155, 157-158, 182-183, 205-208, 213, 217-218, 221-222, 235
Seton Hall Seminary, 55
Seton, St. Elizabeth Ann Bayley, 5, 11, 14
Seward, William H. (Secy.), 16, 26
Shalala, Donna (Secy.), 215
Shan Kuo-hsi, Paul (Card.), 223
Shanley and Sturges, 175
Shea, John Gilmary, 6
Shea, Roberta, 223
Sheen, Fulton J. (Arch.), 111, 119-120, 123, 146, 148, 155, 158, 183, 185, 187, 198
Shrady, Frederick Charles, 178-179
shrine of St. Elizabeth Ann Seton, 178-179
shrine of St. John Neumann, 179
shrine of St. Stanislaus Kostka, 181
Sibbel, Joseph, 62, 70
Silva, Jose Roiz, 3
Silvestrini, Achille (Card.), 223
Simeola, Frank, 207
Simon, Paul (Sen.), 215
Simonis, Adrian (Card.), 224
Sisters of Charity, 5, 10, 15, 18, 47, 91
Sisters of Mercy, 15
site of SPC, 1, 18, 19, 28, 29-30, 43, 46,109, 137, 150, 163
Sixty-ninth Regiment (Army), 91, 98
Skinner, Orin, 141, 152
Slade School of Art, 82
Smith and Crane Co., 39
Smith, Alfred (Gov.), 111, 119, 147
Smith, Peter, 87, 107
Smith, Thomas, 45
Smithsonian Institution, 17
Sobel, Ronald (Rabbi), 183
Society of American Sculptors, 95
Sodano, Angelo (Card.), 223, 227
Soldiers and Sailors Club, 109
Sosa Molina (Gen.), 144
Sosa, Sammy, 223

Soviero, Diana, 216
speaker system, 209
Spellman, Francis (Card.), 123, 129-130, 137, 139, 149, 154-155, 157, 160, 161, 164
spires, 56, 74, 75
Stanley, Dean, 38
Starrs, William (Msgr.), 26
stations of the cross, 63, 76, 210
Statue of Liberty, 54
statues: bronze doors, 143
statues: Doctors of the Church, 62
statues: Holy Child of Earth and Heaven, 139
statues: Immaculate Conception, 62
statues: Our Lady of Lujan, 144
statues: Our Lady of New York, 133
statues: pilgrim statue of Our Lady of Fatima, 149
statues: Pope John Paul II, 192
statues: Pope Paul VI, 170, 192
statues: Pope Pius XII (Cardinal Eugenio Pacelli), 153
statues: Sacred Heart, 70
statues: St. Alphonsus Liguori, 62, 76
statues: St. Ambrose, 62
statues: St. Anne, 61
statues: St. Anselm, 62
statues: St. Anthony, 180
statues: St. Athanasius, 62
statues: St. Augustine, 110
statues: St. Basil the Great, 62
statues: St. Benilde Remancon and St. Miguel Cordero, 209
statues: St. Bernard, 62
statues: St. Bonaventure, 62
statues: St. Catherine of Alexandria, 87
statues: St. Dominic, 62
statues: St. Frances Cabrini (relief), 209
statues: St. Francis de Sales, 62
statues: St. Francis of Assisi, 113
statues: St. Gregory Nanzianzen, 62
statues: St. Gregory the Great, 62
statues: St. Jerome, 62
statues: St. John Bosco (relief), 225
statues: St. John Crysostom, 62
statues: St. Joseph, 62, 225
statues: St. Jude, 204
statues, St. Margaret, 87
statues: St. Monica, 61, 110
statues: Our Lord, 39
statues: St. Patrick, 70, 134-135
statues: St. Peter Canisius, 168-169
statues: St. Peter and St. Paul, 39-40, 134, 193
statues: St. Pius X, 152-153
statues: St. Rose of Lima, 75
statues: St. Thomas Aquinas, 62
statues: Virgin Mary, 179
Steinbrenner, George, 218, 223
Stengel, Casey, 183, 198
steps, 208
Stewart, John, 46
Stickler, Alfons Maria (Card.), 216, 221
Stokowski, Leopold, 189
Stoltzenberg Co., 62-63, 76
Stonyhurst (England), 82
Stoughton, Thomas, 3
Strickland, William, 20
Sturges, W. Knight, 151, 158-159, 176, 180, 204, 232
Sullivan, Ed, 154, 183, 197
surveys, 181
Swanke, Hayden and Connell, 204

T
tabernacle, 210
Tabone, Censu (Pres.), 215
Taft, William (Pres.), 97
Taofinu'u, Pio (Card.), 183
Taylor, William (Rev.), 11
Tebaldi, Renata, 223
television, 208-209, 212
terrace, 94, 209
terrace passage, 166
The Awful Disclosures of Maria Monk, 11
The Challenge of Peace ..., 202
Theis, Peter, 61
The Triumph of St. Patrick, 122
Theta Pi Alpha, 109
Third Plenary Council of Baltimore, 80
Thorne, Inspector, 38
Tiemann, Daniel F. (Mayor), 23
Tiffany and Company, 139
Tiffany Co., 83
Toscanini, Arturo, 112. 155
Toulmin, Montell, 87, 150
Toussaint, Pierre, 4, 210
Toyanos, Tatiana, 216

Transfiguration Church, 106
Trappist monks, 9-10, 18, 29
Trappist nuns, 10
Treasury Building (U. S.), 26
trees, 131-132, 151
Trinity Church, 62
Truman, Harry (Pres.), 156
trusteeism, 4, 10-11, 15
Trustees of St. Patrick's Cathedral, 19, 93
Trustees of St. Peter's Church, 19
Tucker, Richard, 173
Turner, Robert M., 211

U

Ungerer, James (Jacques), 59, 68, 77, 90, 97,
    110, 125
Union Club, 108
United Nations, 219
U. S. Air Force Academy, 156
U. S. Capitol Building, 56
U. S. Customs House, 2
U. S. House of Representatives, 131
U. S. Military Academy, 146, 156
U. S. Naval Academy, 156
USS New York, 143
University of Chicago, 171
Ursuline nuns, 9-10, 13, 15
Ury, John, 6
ushers, 213
U Thant (Secy. Gen.), 172

V

Valenti, Benita, 217
Van Arsdale, Harry, 206
van Bommel, John, 111
vandalism, 138
Vanderbilt homes, 45
Vaness, Carol, 216
Vassar College, 17, 33
Vatican Council II, 157
Vatican museums, 179
V-E Day, 138
Verdier, Jean (Card.), 122
ventilation, 66, 102
verger, 103
Verkowitz, Charlene, 217
Victorian Society in America, 180
Vietnam War, 157, 160

Villard, Henry, 46
Villard Houses, 46, 144, 173, 191
visitors, 181, 215
V-J Day, 138
volunteer program, 181-182, 205, 214, 223
von Hindenburg, Paul (Pres.), 120
von Preysing, Conrad (Card.), 140

W

WaDondo, Leon Kengo (P. M.), 216
Wagner, Robert F. (Mayor), 156, 218
Waldorf-Astoria Hotel, 109
Walesa, Lech (Pres.), 223
Walker, James (Mayor), 148
Walter, Vernon (Ambas.), 206
Wanamaker Co., 146
War of 1812, 10
Ware, William R, 71-72
Warhol, Andy, 206
Warren, Earl (Chief Justice), 172
Washington, D. C., 17
Washington, George (Pres.), 4
Washington, George (birth bicentennial), 120
Washington Monument, 34, 56
Weekes, Michael, 213
West, John C., 218, 224
Whall, Christopher, 82
Whelan, Charles (Rev.), 2
Whalen, John. 117
Whitcombe, Sergeant, 38
White, James, 42
Wickham, William (Mayor), 35
Willebrands, Johannes (Card.), 183, 216
William Bradley Co., 134
William II, 63
Williams, Bernie, 223
Williams, John, 81
Wills, Charles T., 72, 78, 81
Wilson, Malcolm (Gov.), 214
Wilson, Robert Burns, 94
Wilson, Woodrow (Pres.), 92, 97
windows, 40-41, 50, 87, 177
windows: apsidal, 135-136
windows: Lady Chapel, 81-82, 115, 142
windows: nave clerestory, 152
windows: Rose Window, 40, 52, 141, 165,
    166
windows: St. Henry, 41

windows: Three Baptisms, 177
windows: transept, 136
Winters, John, 214
Wlonski, Pio, 95
Wojtyla, Karol (Card.) (Pope John Paul II),
173, 183
Wolff, Alfred R., 87
Woodroffe, Paul Vincent, 82, 115
Woolworth Building, 88
WOR radio station, 132
World Eucharistic Congress, 111
World War I, 82, 97, 105
World War II, 130, 134, 137-138
World's Fair of 1939-1940, 130
Wylie, General Daniel, 38
Wynn, Henry G., 71, 86

Y
Yardumian, Richard, 189
Yellin, Samuel A., 114, 126
Yon, Constantino, 125
Yon, Pietro, 112-113, 116-117, 122, 125, 145
York Minster Cathedral, 26
Young-at-Heart Club, 181
Young, John (Rev.), 112, 125

Z
Zentmaier, Ludwig, 126

GLOSSARY

Aisles The sections of the Cathedral along the sides parallel to and divided from the nave by piers.

Alto Relievo See **High Relief.**

Ambulatory The aisle enclosing the apse and sanctuary of the Cathedral.

Apse A semicircle of vaults forming the end of the chancel, just beyond the high altar.

Baldachin (Baldachino) The canopy over the high altar.

Bas-Relief Sculpture in which figures project only slightly from the surface.

Bay A vertical section of the Cathedral between buttresses, piers, etc.

Buttress A massive masonry structure built against a wall for strength and support.

Canonization Official declaration of sainthood by the Church.

Catafalque A structure for supporting the body of a deceased person lying in state.

Chancel The east end of the Cathedral where the main altar is placed; the area east of the transept.

Clerestory The upper section of the main wall containing windows.

Crocket Decoration in the shape of a leaf projecting from pinnacles, spires, etc.

Crosssing See **Transept.**

Cusp An ornamented projecting point in the tracery of the windows.

Decorated Style Gothic style common from late 13th to late 14* centuries, often with geometric window tracery.

Doctor of the Church An eminent and learned expounder of the doctrine of the Church.

Finial A decoration at the top of pinnacles, spires, etc., often in the shape of a foliated fleur-de-lis.

Foliated Ornamented with leaf carvings.

Flying Buttress A masonry vault rising from an outer buttress to the upper part of a wall or roof to support its weight.

Gallery The platform above the west doors of the Cathedral housing the main organ and over-looking the body of the Church.

Gargoyle A water spout carved in the form of a grotesque figure.

Gothic Architecture A style characterized by pointed arches and vaulting, slender vertical piers and heavy buttresses.

Gregorian Chant Ancient music used by the Church from the time of Pope Gregory I (c. 600 A. D.), characterized by free rhythm.

High Mass Term used before the Second Vatican Council for a Mass with parts sung by the celebrant and the choir.

High Relief (Alto Relievo) Sculpture in which at least one-half the circumference of the figures project from the surface.

Lanterns The windowed polygonal turrets supporting the spires on the West Front of the Cathedral.

Lavabo Sacristy basin fastened to a wall for cleansing sacred objects used for liturgical services.

Monstrance (Ostensorium) A sacred vessel in which the consecrated Host is exposed for adoration.

Mullion A vertical masonry post dividing the windows into lights (sections of glass).

Narthex The area just inside the west doors of the Cathedral below the choir gallery.

Ostensorium See **Monstrance.**

Pallium A woolen band worn over vestments by a pope or archbishop signifying his authority.

Pier A vertical support for an arch, resembling a high slender pillar.

Pinnacle The highest termination of a turret, buttress or spire, usually ornamented.

Reredos A decorated stone screen rising behind an altar.

Romanesque Architecture A style characterized by rounded arches and vaults, and decorative ornaments.

Rose Window The circular window filled with tracery over the west doors of the Cathedral.

Sacrarium A place in the sacristy for housing sacred objects.

Sacristan (Sexton) Person in charge of sacred objects, vestments and other equipment for use in liturgies.

Synod An ecclesiastical meeting or assembly.

Tracery Ornamental stone work in the upper part of the windows forming designs. When it is applied to the surface of walls without allowing light to pass through window glass, it is called 'blind' or 'blank' tracery.

Transept (Crossing) The crossing arms of the Cathedral between the nave and the chancel.

Triforium A passage in the wall above the arcades (range of arches) and below the clerestory windows. Its arches open into the nave.

Vault An arched masonry ceiling

Verger An attendant in charge of seating and keeping order during services; an usher.